AN
EXTRAVAGANT
LIFE

BOOKS BY STUART WOODS

FICTION

A Safe House*

Criminal Mischief*

Foul Play*

Class Act*

Double Jeopardy*

Hush-Hush*

Shakeup*

Choppy Water*

Hit List*

Treason*

Stealth*

Contraband*

Wild Card*

A Delicate Touch*

Desperate Measures*

Turbulence*

Shoot First*

Unbound*

Quick & Dirty*

Indecent Exposure*

Fast & Loose*

Below the Belt*

Sex, Lies & Serious Money*

Dishonorable Intentions*

Family Jewels*

Scandalous Behavior*

Foreign Affairs*

Naked Greed*

Hot Pursuit*

Insatiable Appetites*

Paris Match*

Cut and Thrust*

Carnal Curiosity*

Standup Guy*

Doing Hard Time*

Unintended Consequences*

Collateral Damage*

Severe Clear*

Unnatural Acts*

D.C. Dead*

Son of Stone*

Bel-Air Dead*

Strategic Moves*

Santa Fe Edge†

Lucid Intervals*

Kisser*

Hothouse Orchid‡

Loitering with Intent*

Mounting Fears§

Hot Mahogany*

Santa Fe Dead†

Beverly Hills Dead

Shoot Him If He Runs*

Fresh Disasters*

Short Straw†

Dark Harbor*

Iron Orchid‡

Two Dollar Bill*

The Prince of Beverly Hills

Reckless Abandon*

Capital Crimes§

Dirty Work*

Blood Orchid‡

The Short Forever*

Orchid Blues‡

Cold Paradise*

L.A. Dead*

The Run§

Worst Fears Realized*

Orchid Beach‡

Swimming to Catalina*

Dead in the Water*

Dirt*

Choke

Imperfect Strangers

Heat

Dead Eyes

L.A. Times

Santa Fe Rules†

New York Dead*

Palindrome

Grass Roots§

White Cargo

Deep Lie§

Under the Lake

Run Before the Wind§

Chiefs§

COAUTHORED BOOKS

Bombshell** (with Parnell Hall)

Skin Game** (with Parnell Hall)

The Money Shot** (with Parnell Hall)

Barely Legal†† (with Parnell Hall)

Smooth Operator** (with Parnell Hall)

AUTOBIOGRAPHY

An Extravagant Life

TRAVEL

A Romantic's Guide to the Country Inns
of Britain and Ireland (1979)

MEMOIR

Blue Water, Green Skipper

*A Stone Barrington Novel

†An Ed Eagle Novel

‡A Holly Barker Novel

§A Will Lee Novel

**A Teddy Fay Novel

††A Herbie Fisher Novel

AN EXTRAVAGANT LIFE

AN AUTOBIOGRAPHY INCORPORATING
BLUE WATER, GREEN SKIPPER

Stuart Woods

G. P. PUTNAM'S SONS

NEW YORK

PUTNAM
— EST. 1838 —

G. P. PUTNAM'S SONS
Publishers Since 1838
An imprint of Penguin Random House LLC
penguinrandomhouse.com

This work contains, in its entirety, *Blue Water, Green Skipper* by Stuart Woods,
originally published by W. W. Norton & Company in 1977.
Copyright © 2022 by Stuart Woods

Hardcover ISBN: 9780593188514
Ebook ISBN: 9780593190340

Printed in the United States of America
1st Printing

Book design by Elke Sigal

Penguin Random House is committed to publishing works of quality and integrity. In that spirit, we are proud to offer this book to our readers; however, the story, the experiences, and the words are the author's alone.

In loving memory of my mother, Dot,
who gave me not just my life, but my life as a writer.

I miss her every day.

AN
EXTRAVAGANT
LIFE

THE LAUNDERING
OF SLIGHTLY
SOILED LINENS

1

In the late 1920s, in Detroit, Michigan, a nineteen-year-old youth stood in court and, having been convicted of the crime of stealing sixteen cars, faced a judge for sentencing.

His name was Stuart Franklin Lee, and he had been in trouble for several years. He was born in Atlanta, Georgia, in 1907, to one Arthur Lee, son of a prosperous builder, and Annie Lee Jones, who had led a hard life.

Arthur Lee had served as his illiterate father's bookkeeper, secretary, and assistant in his successful construction business, but when his father died, Arthur Lee was unable to hold the company together. He moved his family north, to Detroit, where he found work as a circulation manager for a large newspaper—a somewhat inflated title, since it meant that he was in charge of filling and collecting coins from a string of newspaper vending machines. Arthur began to drink.

Annie Lee Jones, a farmer's daughter, had been orphaned at the age of six and, with her younger brother, Willie, sent to a children's home where little Willie later died in her arms, apparently of institutional neglect. Annie Lee's fortunes took a turn for the better when she was adopted by a St. Louis family named Chevalier. (Their Missouri neighbors had apparently been unable to handle the French pronunciation of their name, so they pronounced it Chev-a-LEER.) The adoption was not an entirely altruistic one. Annie Lee was put to work in the Chevalier household and, although she was treated kindly, especially by her adopted older brother, Stuart, she was little more than a servant.

Annie Lee and Arthur had three sons, Ohree, Stuart, and Brown, and a daughter, Palestine, called Pal. Although raised in a strict Baptist household by their mother, their father was not much of an example, and the boys became wild in their teens. They got away with vandalism, but soon they turned to joyriding in stolen cars. As a result, Stuart spent some time in a reformatory, where he managed to get himself charged with assault with intent to kill, for hitting a guard who called him "a filthy name." The charges were later dropped. After his release he turned to car theft and, eventually, tried to pull off an armed robbery. Finally, Stuart was arrested, charged, and jailed. While awaiting trial he escaped from custody and was recaptured.

The family rallied around him, concocting an alibi that he had been at home on the evening of the crime, playing pinochle. The defense called his parents, brothers, and sister to the stand, and each of them related the alibi. Then, when the prosecutor confronted Stuart with evidence that they had lied and threatened to charge the whole family with perjury, Stuart changed his plea to guilty.

At his trial, when asked by the judge if he had anything to say for himself, Stuart replied, "A man's got to have a car."

Not amused, the judge sentenced him to fifteen years in the Michigan state penitentiary.

His uncle, Stuart Chevalier, meanwhile, had become a prominent attorney in New York and Washington, specializing in tax law. Stricken with polio at the age of four, he walked on crutches, and as a young man he was told by his physicians that he had only a short time to live. His reaction was to write a reflective book, *A Window on Broadway*, offering advice to young men on living a responsible life, advice his nephews did not follow. He wrote much of the early federal income tax code and taught law at Washington and Lee University.

When his friend and fellow polio victim, Franklin Roosevelt, started a polio treatment center in Warm Springs, Georgia, and built a house there, Chevalier built a house next door and was treated in the waters from the hot springs. He married a beautiful and capable young woman named Elizabeth Pickett, a novelist and screenwriter who wrote the screenplay for the first full-length, Technicolor motion picture, *Redskin*, starring Richard Dix, and whose novel, *Drivin' Woman*, a Southern saga in the mold of *Gone With the Wind*, was #3 on the first-ever *New York Times* best-seller list in 1942 and achieved a higher price from the movies than had Miss Mitchell's book. The film was shelved because of the advent of World War II and was never made.

The law firm that Chevalier cofounded in Washington, D.C., Miller, Chevalier, Peeler & Wilson, survives today as Miller & Chevalier.

WITH HER SON IN PRISON, Annie Lee sought the help of her adopted brother, and Chevalier, in one way or another, managed to get the boy released after serving seven years. Since he had not impressed the Michigan authorities with his respect for the law, a condition of his release was that he take up residence in another state.

Stuart's sister, Pal, married a Detroit policeman, Garrell Noah, and settled down to raise a family in that city, but Stuart Chevalier, mindful that his namesake was persona non grata in

Michigan, moved the Lee family to Warm Springs, where he bought them a small farm. Since none of the Lees were farmers by experience or inclination, this was not a happy time for the family, but Stuart got a job at Roosevelt's polio treatment center, later called the Georgia Warm Springs Foundation. He worked as a pushboy, a position unique to that institution; a pushboy's duties consisted entirely of pushing patients in their wheelchairs or on tables to their surgeries, treatments, and meals. It wasn't much, but Stuart Lee was a free man.

Whether his prison experience had changed him is hard to say, but it cannot have been easy for him. These were rough years in the penal system, and the Michigan authorities were not noted for being leaders in prison reform. Still, Stuart's reputation among his youthful peers in his new town was one of being handsome, charming, and an all-round good fellow, who boxed as an amateur in local bouts.

Soon he met a young woman from nearby Manchester who, a gifted pianist, was often asked to play as entertainment for the Warm Springs patients, and they fell in love. Her name was Dorothy Callaway, called Dot by all who knew her.

2

The Callaways were an old pioneer family in Meriwether County. The first of their ancestors in America, one Sir Thomas Callaway, a Cornishman, had received a king's grant of land in Kentucky and had arrived in the New World in 1688. His son, Colonel Richard Callaway, was a friend of Daniel Boone, who rescued Callaway's kidnapped daughters from the Indians, as related in the novel *The Last of the Mohicans* by James Fenimore Cooper.

Some of the family radiated south, one branch to Meriwether County, another to LaGrange, in Troup County, where Fuller Callaway founded Callaway Mills. In 1909, Fuller Callaway founded a new town in Meriwether County at the spot where Georgia's Highway 41 crossed the Birmingham Southern Railroad. The railroad would site the repair shops for their engines in the new town, becoming an important employer. But Callaway would build a cotton mill, which would become the town's major employer for more than half a century. He called his new town Manchester, after the English textile center. (Incidentally, there is a Manchester in each of the contiguous forty-eight states, except

Rhode Island. This is the sort of thing one learned in the Manchester public schools.) Callaway bought some of the land, where the mill and the workers' houses would be built, from William Henry Callaway, a distant cousin, who was a farmer, landowner, and a lay Baptist preacher in the county.

W. H. Callaway had two sons, W.H., Jr., called Will Henry, and Tom. With the money from the sale of land to his kinsman, W.H. created farms for his two sons and built a comfortable house on each. The brothers settled down, married sisters, Carrie and Lesta Fowler (thereby making their respective children double first cousins), and farmed cotton. In the late nineteen-teens, the boll weevil swept through the county, ruining most of the cotton farmers. Tom, regarded as the less responsible of the brothers, got a job on the railroad and managed to hold on to his property, though he never seriously farmed it again. Ironically, Will Henry, who was regarded as hardworking, upright, and the better farmer, lost everything. He took himself to town and called on James S. Peters, the president of the Bank of Manchester, a member of the city council, and the major political power in the town.

JIM PETERS AS A YOUNG man had been a schoolteacher, then had worked as cashier of the bank at Woodbury in the northern part of Meriwether County. One Saturday afternoon in 1908, along with a few dozen other local citizens, he boarded a train for the ten-mile trip to Warm Springs, for a church picnic. Halfway there the train broke down where the tracks ran through a pine forest, and the conductor told his passengers that they could get off and stretch their legs while repairs were made; the engineer would blow the whistle when they were ready to proceed again.

Peters wandered off into the woods and came into a clearing, where he found three men poring over a set of plans spread out on the hood of a car. The three men were: the president of the

Birmingham Southern Railroad; a Norwegian gentleman, who was an architect and town planner; and Fuller Callaway. Introductions were made and Callaway, who had heard good things about Jim Peters, explained about the new town they were planning. It would need a bank, he said, and the bank's first customers would be the railroad and the mill. How would he like to run the bank? Jim Peters said he would like that just fine. The whistle blew, and Peters returned to his train. His life had suddenly taken a major turn. And so, unbeknownst to him, had that of Will Henry Callaway. Of such material history is made.

Soon after that a barbecue was held on the still-empty site of the new town. Plans of the town were displayed, and a lottery was held for the purpose of distributing lots. The participants paid a hundred dollars a lot, then drew for location. Jim Peters bought two lots. One of the two he drew, oddly enough, was at the corner of what would become Main and Broad, dead center of the proposed business district, and a perfect site for a bank. The other was for a residential lot on what would become the town's best block.

TEN YEARS AFTER THE FOUNDING of the town in 1909, Manchester was ready for its first chief of police. The job was in the gift of James S. Peters, president of the bank and chairman of the town council. Will Henry Callaway, being out of work because of his farm's failure, applied for the job. Peters recommended him unreservedly to the city council, who voted to hire him. Fatefully, the banker insisted that the new chief's pay include an insurance policy for ten thousand dollars, since he might be putting himself in harm's way. The council agreed, and Will Henry, so recently a cotton farmer, became a policeman.

Peters found the family a comfortable house, owned by the bank because of the failure of the mortgagee's feed and grain business, on Third Street, a block from his own, and Will Henry, along with his wife, Carrie, his son, Herman, and his daughter, Dorothy, moved in, settled down, and began a new life together.

Eight years later, in 1927, when Herman was at military school in Barnesville and Dorothy was a music student at Bessie Tift College, in Forsyth, Will Henry arrested a Black teenager for petty theft. The boy was sentenced to ten days in jail, during which time he would work on the city's streets. As the chief was about to go home that night the boy began to cry. He was afraid to spend the night alone in the jailhouse, and he begged to go home. Will Henry knew his parents and told the boy that he would allow him to go home every night, if he would promise to be at work on time each morning. The boy gave his promise and was allowed to go home. The following morning, he did not turn up for his assigned duties.

Will Henry got into his car and drove out to the family's house. He got out of the car and called for the boy to come out, so he could take him to work. Suddenly, the boy's father burst through the front door with a shotgun in his hands and fired at the chief of police. Will Henry, struck in the chest, fell to the ground, mortally wounded. The boy's father, it turned out, was in a malarial delirium and had mistaken the chief for someone else. He threw down the shotgun and ran.

Will Henry was taken to the local doctor's office where, an hour so later, he died in Carrie's arms.

If this story sounds familiar, then you have probably read the author's novel *Chiefs*, or seen the television miniseries based on the book.

The malarial shotgunner was captured after a manhunt and had three trials. At each, Carrie Callaway pleaded for his life, saying that he was not responsible for his actions. Eventually, though, he died in the electric chair. His body was shipped back to Manchester, but his family had left town and could not be found, so the stationmaster at the depot finally shipped the casket to the University of Georgia Medical School, in Augusta, where the cadaver was assigned to a medical student for his study of anatomy. The student was James S. Peters, Jr., son of the Manchester banker.

Carrie Callaway and her children were saved from poverty by the ten-thousand-dollar insurance policy, so presciently insisted upon by Jim Peters. Carrie opened a small ladies' shop, and her two children cut short their educations and returned home to help their mother.

THEN, IN 1928, A NEW merchant came to town. Henry Washington Denham had been born to a struggling farmer and his wife in nearby Upson County, near Thomaston. One of a large family, Henry was sent as a teenager to the Berry School, in Rome, Georgia. It was an institution founded by an heiress, Martha Berry, for the education and agricultural training of poor farm children. The students worked after school on the school's extensive farms, earning a few cents an hour. Henry Denham had, by the time of his graduation from high school, managed to save from his wages the amazing sum of one hundred dollars.

The boy found a job with a storekeeper in Zebulon, near his home, and worked industriously for the man. When the owner retired, Denham bought the business from him and made it more prosperous. Eventually, he sold that business in order to take up a new opportunity, a butcher's shop in a south Georgia town. In the following years he married twice and lost both young wives to illnesses which, today, would be routinely cured by antibiotics.

Then, told by his doctor that his work in the cold storage room of his butcher's business was affecting his lungs badly, he sold out to his partner and went to the new town, Manchester, where he opened a men's and ladies' clothing store. There, he met the widow Callaway, and in 1935 they were married. Carrie closed her shop and Herman and his sister, Dot, went to work for Mr. Denham.

Henry Denham was a small man—kind, generous, and gregarious in his way, but serious about his business and his church. His index fingers were missing the first joint, a genetic characteristic that appeared every other generation in the males of his family, and one that got him discharged from the Army during World War I, because his firing finger could not reach the trigger on his rifle.

Everyone, including his wife, called him Mr. Denham or Mr. D., and for the remainder of his long life, no one was ever heard to address him by his first name.

Shortly after their marriage, Mr. and Mrs. Denham built a comfortable brick house on Third Street, across the street from where the Callaway family had lived. Carrie planted an extensive garden, and the family prospered. Herman married Jewel Stevens, whose family lived in the next block, and Dot, a talented pianist and organist, played every Sunday at the First Baptist Church.

Then Dot Callaway, playing piano at a social function at the Georgia Warm Springs Foundation, met the charming Stuart Lee.

3

Carrie Fowler Callaway Denham, though not entirely immune to Stuart Lee's charm, was not amused by her daughter's interest in an ex-convict. When Dot announced her intention of marrying him, a major family crisis ensued. Love won out, though, and, in 1936, the two young people were married.

Uncle Stuart Chevalier came through with a fine wedding present: a Sinclair filling station, well-located at the corner of Broad and Second Streets, on the main route from Atlanta, seventy miles north, to Columbus, thirty-five miles southwest. Thus, Stuart Lee was saved from the hardships of the farm and the ignominy of pushing wheelchairs for a living. The young couple's future was, it appeared, assured. They moved into a rented house immediately next door to the Denhams and began their married life.

They were happy. Stuart pumped gas, changed oil, and fixed flat tires; Dot played the new Hammond organ at the First Baptist Church. Stuart boxed in amateur matches at the Manchester Community Building, and they had an active social life with other young couples, particularly Harold and Marguerite Guy, who would always remember Stuart as a delightful friend who was well-liked by his peers and other members of the community. Stuart's wild streak, however, had not been entirely tamed. He liked a drink, which would have horrified the strictly Baptist Denhams, had they known, and he enjoyed a little poker with the boys. On one occasion, returning from such an evening, he drove his car off a railroad bridge into a deep ravine and onto the tracks, demolishing the car but miraculously surviving unhurt. An automobile was then, as now, an important possession to a young couple, and it was the fashion for them to pose for photographs with the car, sometimes in the style of Bonnie and Clyde, who were at the time conducting their extended excursion through Texas and Oklahoma.

Then on a clear, cold, and windy Sunday afternoon, January 9, 1938, Dot gave birth to a son, who was named Stuart Chevalier Lee, after his generous great-uncle. The following day, the new father's own birthday, his sister, Pal, gave birth to a son who was named Stuart after *his* uncle, her brother. This promised much confusion at family gatherings. Almost immediately, Dot's new son's life conformed to Victor Borge's old line: "I was born at home, but when my mother saw me, she was taken to the hospital."

Dot had developed a life-threatening infection. In the company of Dr. Paul Kirkland, who had delivered the child, they were taken by ambulance to an Atlanta hospital, where her life was saved by the new sulfa drugs, early antibiotics. Thus began the life of one of the most loved and coddled children of the twentieth century. He became the only child of not only his parents, but of his whole extended family in Georgia.

THE NEXT TWO YEARS PASSED uneventfully, but then Stuart Lee's previously evinced larcenous tendencies came once again to the fore. The country was still in a deep depression, gasoline sold for a few cents a gallon and yielded little profit, and pumping gas and fixing flats were pitched somewhat higher than his low threshold for boredom. He got together with his brothers, Ohree and Brown, and maybe even their father. Though there is still some dispute about whose idea it was, the three broke into Mr. J. W. Smith's Nehi bottling plant, catty-cornered from Stuart's filling station, and stole cash, many cartons of cigarettes, and, presumably, all the Royal Crown Cola they could drink.

But the Lee Brothers, like the Jameses and the Daltons before them, were bolder than they were smart, and quite soon, Brown, who had been delegated to dispose of the tobacco booty, was caught selling cartons of cigarettes out of the trunk of his car. Ohree, wisely, beat it out of town immediately, and the authorities, perhaps out of respect for the Callaways' and the Denhams' station in the community, suggested to Stuart that he might feel more comfortable in another state, if he was real quick about it. Brown, having taken the rap, did a few months in the county prison farm, and when his nephew, Stuart, had lunch with him in the garden of the Beverly Hills Hotel fifty-odd years later, he was still pissed off about it.

There was a tearful scene as Stuart said goodbye to his wife and two-year-old son, climbed into his car, and headed west, promising to send for them at the first opportunity. One can only wonder what Stuart's thoughts were as he drove the more than two thousand miles across the county on two-lane roads, often dirt, stopping only for gas and to sleep, perhaps in his car. Was he wracked with guilt at the humiliation he had caused his wife and her family, or was he simply excited at the thought of yet another fresh start in an enticing new place? A good guess is a bit of both.

Stuart Lee fetched up in Los Angeles, where Pal and her husband, Garrell, had settled after Garrell had received a medical discharge from the Detroit police department, having had his leg crushed by a wildly thrown hammer (a shot put swung at the end of a chain) at a police department track meet. Ohree and, later, Brown also welcomed their brother.

Stuart's son spent a few days in his company when he was twelve and, not yet having been told the story, asked his father why he had left Manchester and his family. His father told the boy to ask his mother.

4

Y ou will have no doubt guessed by now that Stuart Chevalier Lee is the author himself, so I will hereafter speak for him in the first person.

The country was now poised on one of history's great cusps, that brief period at the end of the Great Depression and just before the start of World War II. The depression was not over, exactly, but the country was on the move again, and there was reason for optimism; Franklin Roosevelt had not tired of telling us so. In our county, the president was the next best thing to a local boy. If his election had given the country a boost, it had made Meriwether County very nearly ecstatic. He came to Warm Springs often, to what was now called the Little White House, and he could be seen driving his Ford convertible along country roads, doing his best to lose his Secret Service tail. Sometimes he did.

Roosevelt formed the habit of pulling up in front of the City Drug Company in Manchester and honking his horn. A soda jerk would rush out with a chocolate ice cream soda for him and would then be dispatched across the street to the bank to fetch James S. Peters, known to all as Mr. Jim. The two would spend an hour in the president's car, chatting about the county and the country and waving to passers-by.

Just down Main Street, Mr. Denham's eponymous men's and ladies' store was doing well, providing a middle-class income to himself, Herman, and Dot, and affording me an indoor playground. I loved burrowing under the stacks of work clothes in the back of the store, popping up to fire my cap pistol at unsuspecting customers. The place smelled of oiled wood floors and new cotton, and on rainy days the schoolroom lamps that lighted the place barely kept up with the gloom. It was the best store in town, and everybody came there for better-quality goods. You had to go to Atlanta to do better.

Henry Washington Denham and Carrie Fowler Callaway were married in 1935; the Denhams' brick house on Third Street, which they built shortly after their marriage at a cost of ten thousand dollars, provided a comfortable base for the family. Dot and I had moved into the spare bedroom after Stuart Lee's departure, and Herman and Jewel came for Sunday dinners. The house consisted of a large, rather formal living room, used only when company came or on special occasions; a comfortable family den; a good-sized kitchen; two bedrooms; two baths; a breakfast room; a dining room that seated up to ten; and a one-car garage out back. The furniture was all good reproductions by Baker, bought from Carrie Denham's first cousin Calvin Fowler, who had a large furniture store in Chattanooga, Tennessee. In the dining room the china was Wedgwood, the crystal and the chandelier were Waterford, and there was a Buick in the garage; it was the very picture of middle-class respectability and growing prosperity at the beginning of the 1940s.

At the very center of the family lay the First Baptist Church, not only a house of worship but a meeting place and a social institution, centered on a small, handsome Greek Revival sanctuary, with Sunday school rooms in the basement. Mr. Denham was a deacon and an important financial supporter; Dot played the organ; Carrie taught Sunday school; and Herman sang in the choir. The family took its religion seriously, in the certain knowledge of heaven and hell, and Jesus Christ as the only path to the former. Christianity was not simply a Sunday-morning activity but a way of life, a regulator of personal conduct and a fortress against liquor, gambling, and other forms of sin too embarrassing to mention here.

We went to church often. On Sunday mornings there was Sunday school and the main service; on Sunday evenings the B.Y.P.U. (the Baptist Young People's Union, later to become the B.T.U., the Baptist Training Union) and a nighttime service. On Wednesday evenings there was Prayer Meeting. A couple of times a year there was a revival, which featured a charismatic preacher from some distant church, and services every night for a week. Many souls were saved, crowding around the pulpit for their Public Profession of Faith.

At church we sang. *The Broadman Hymnal* provided us with dozens of familiar hymns, which were performed with gusto. At Easter and Christmas the choir gave us Handel's *Messiah* or some other elaborate piece; and before each service Dot soothed us with organ preludes by Schubert or Bach. Her playing was always lovely and brought many compliments from the worshippers. It was the only live classical music that many of them would ever hear except, perhaps, on the radio.

At home, for entertainment, we played Parcheesi or checkers and watched the radio, which gave us *Fibber McGee and Molly, The Great Gildersleeve, Mr. District Attorney, The Edgar Bergen and Charlie McCarthy Show, The Bob Hope Show, The Bing Crosby Show, The Fred Allen Show*, and Gabriel Heatter and H. V. Kaltenborn with the news. My favorite was Fanny Brice, playing Baby Snooks; I was astonished to be told that she was actually a grown woman, just as I was startled to learn that Charlie McCarthy was not a real little boy. I envied his wardrobe.

On our block I played with Jackie Smith and Ralph Green and endured Scott Haney's bullying; we went barefoot in the summer and caught lightning bugs in jars; we played in the creek next to the telephone company and tiptoed up the storm sewer until we got scared of the dark. Once it snowed enough to stick—a historic event in Manchester—and I made a snowman, the last I would see until I was a teenager. Our parents sat on their front porches after supper and fanned themselves during the warm summer evenings, calling us home at bedtime.

I had a succession of Black ladies for nurses, who took care of me when everyone was at work. My grandmother's work was in her garden and incessant. Another Black lady named Lizzie was our cook, and when we wanted chicken for dinner (the noon meal) she would buy a live one and ring its neck in the backyard before plucking it. I would laugh aloud at the headless bird's acrobatics. Lizzie's husband, Jasper, was the iceman. On hot days we would climb into the back of his truck and, covered by an insulating tarpaulin, suck on slivers of ice as he made his way down the block from house to house, making deliveries. Jasper had only one eye and wore an eye patch, giving him a piratical visage. He had lost the eye in a knife fight, I was told by a friend, and sometimes he would frighten us by lifting his patch, revealing where the missing orb had been.

On one occasion my grandmother heard me call Lizzie a "Nigger." She took a stout switch from a peach tree and wore it out on my legs; when I had recovered myself she explained the evil nature of that word, and I never, ever used it again, except to tell this story. The proper word was "Negro," not "Nigra," as the rednecks pronounced it—and "Colored" was considered a polite term by both races. "Black" was pejorative and not used at all. There was a kind of racial peace at the time, at least from the point of view of White people. I was taught as a Christian that everybody was as good as everybody else, and that I was to treat them accordingly. I was to refer to elderly Black men as "Uncle," a term of respect. Uncle Otis cut our grass once a week, pushing the lawnmower slowly up and down the rows. Mr. Denham treated his Black customers respectfully and opened charge accounts for them, something not all the White merchants did, thus earning their loyalty.

My best friend among Black people was John Pustelle, who did odd jobs for us and our neighbors. He was charming and funny, and on one occasion, he got my mother's permission to take me with him in his one-mule wagon to Chalybeate Springs, down the road apiece. This was an all-day trip, since we stopped at nearly every so-called Colored house for a drink of water from the well or a slab of cornbread or so that John could flirt with the ladies, whose husbands were in the fields. It was nearly dark when I got home, sunburned and happy. I was astonished to learn later that Chalybeate Springs was only three miles away.

The town of Manchester was, by design, one mile square and divided by the railroad tracks into town and the Mill Village. The Mill Village contained the Callaway cotton mill and several hundred modest frame houses that the mill rented, and later sold, to its workers. Callaway also provided for its employees' families a grammar school and a community center with a gymnasium, pool, and playground. I had to be invited by a friend from that side of town to use the Callaway pool; it would be many years before the City of Manchester provided a place for us to swim.

My playground was our block—Third Street between Broad Street and Second Avenue, at first only our side of the street. Later, I was allowed to cross unaccompanied, and still later my playground was expanded to include downtown. I would walk to our family store, Denham's, and visit most of the other stores on the block; my favorite was Maddox Hardware, which smelled of steel and had an amazing assortment of pocketknives, none of which could I afford on my allowance of ten cents a week. This was enough to take me to the picture show at the President Theatre, which charged nine cents, with a penny left over for candy. I felt quite prosperous. I could cut through Maddox's back door to the alley beyond and my favorite place in the whole town: the livery stable, owned by Uncle Ben Winslow; Uncle Ben was not Colored, but everybody called him "Uncle" anyway. He lived across the street from us and he always owned horses and buggies, driving one to work. For a while he even owned a stagecoach, and he would hitch up the horses for parades. The livery stable catered mostly to farmers' mules, and there were mule auctions every Saturday morning. I liked watching the blacksmith, who worked in an open-sided shed, as he shaped the red-hot shoes, then plunged them into a barrel of water, making a loud hissing noise. Most of all I loved the hayloft, which allowed my friends and me to throw ourselves about with abandon without being hurt, and we could glean tiny raw peanuts from the peanut hay.

During these years from age two to six, any memories I had of my father faded. He simply became a distant and nearly mythical figure, referred to always as Stuart Lee, never as "your father." When I asked where he was, I was told he had run away to California; I was never told why. It still amazes me that, although the whole town knew what had happened, not one person—adult or child—ever spoke to me about the events surrounding his departure, until I finally brought it up.

Since the father figure in our house was Mr. Denham, I called him "Daddy." Since Dot called Carrie Denham "Mama," I did, too. And since both of my grandparents called my mother "Dot," so did I—and for the remainder of her life, which was a long one.

I have many memories of these years, but the first memory to which I can put a date occurred on a mild winter Sunday afternoon. We had been to church and had our Sunday dinner and were sitting out on the front porch—it is not unusual in Georgia to have a warm spell or two in the middle of winter—when Mrs.

Irby Cook, who lived next door, came to the screen door and told us to turn on the radio; something was happening.

The Japanese had attacked Pearl Harbor, and I had difficulty understanding why everyone was so upset. I was almost four years old, and it had to be explained to me what war was and that Herman, being of draft age and childless, would have to go into the Army. Everybody was very worried.

5

The war swiftly changed all our lives; the nation was galvanized into the war effort, and we with it. There were scrap metal and rubber drives, and during these, free admission to the movies was available to those who brought a bit of scrap. I filched a skillet from the kitchen and happily went to the movies, returning home to a stern lecture on the difficulty of replacing metal pans in wartime. "But it was for the war," I explained. There were shortages of all sorts, but the one that cut me most deeply was the scarcity of bubble gum. I had a lot of trouble understanding why the war effort needed Bazooka's product more than I did, and I accepted this shortage with ill grace. Every few months word would travel like wildfire that the A&P had gotten in a small supply, and my friends and I would line up to get our single, rationed piece, which didn't last long. Once, in extremis, I paid Morris Allen twenty-five cents for a piece of bubble gum that had been chewed for only fifteen minutes. Times were hard.

Herman enlisted in the Army Air Corps and was sent to basic training in Biloxi, Mississippi, a resort town on the Gulf of Mexico, where we visited him. It was in Biloxi that a seminal event in my life occurred. One afternoon, Dot, Mama, and I paid our money and took a fifteen-minute ride in a sailboat of about thirty-five feet. I was enchanted with the idea that we could move along, powered only by the wind, and I remain so.

Listening to the evening news now became not just a habit, but an imperative. Gabriel Heatter and H. V. Kaltenborn told us each night, in ponderous tones, how the war was going, and it wasn't going well. When the firehouse siren went off at night, we rigged for the blackout; it seemed perfectly reasonable to me that the Germans might wish to bomb a small Georgia town, and I thrilled to the danger. On Monday nights we sometimes went down to the firehouse and watched the newly formed Home Guard drilling on the vacant lot next door. I was amused to see grown men I knew from their shops and businesses marching up and down in their civilian clothes; later they got uniforms and rifles. Once, I was escorted down into a room in the basement of the community building, where an arsenal was maintained, and allowed to hold a Thompson submachine gun, a great honor. When Herman came home on leave from officers' candidate school he was invited to drill with the Home Guard, and I was very proud of him.

Everything about the war was thrilling to a small boy. We had the Nazis and the Japanese to hate, an emotion reinforced weekly by the movies we saw. One of the dirty enemy snipers had the temerity to kill John Wayne at the end of *Sands of Iwo Jima*, an event that shocked me to my core. Most exciting of all was the proximity of Fort Benning, the world's largest infantry training facility, thirty-five miles down the road at Columbus. Convoys of military equipment passed regularly through our town, on the way to the war. On one occasion I went on a shopping trip to Atlanta with Mama and Dot. When I returned I was appalled to learn that, in my absence, a tank had broken down at the corner of Third and Broad and that, while the soldiers were repairing it, the neighborhood boys were allowed to go inside it for a look. I was irked about this for days.

All the young men in the town were in the services, and their return home on leave was always exciting for me. Herman brought me a model B-24 and, rarity of rarities, some Roman candles. We had great fun shooting them off in the front yard. Hardy Pilkington, who lived three blocks down the street, came home and, in his Navy uniform, tossed a football with me in our front yard, exciting the envy of my neighborhood friends. Herman wore glasses and was in his early thirties, so he was ineligible to fly and became the adjutant of a large training command in Kansas, but other Manchester boys flew fighters and bombers. There was hardly any theater of the war in which a Manchester serviceman was not involved. It was all wonderful, like a giant, worldwide football game, which I never doubted the home team would win.

Then Hardy Pilkington came home in a metal casket, and I began to understand better what war was. Hardy lay in state, in his mother's living room, and I visited him, laying my hand on the cold, sealed box.

Manchester supported a USO for the entertainment of soldiers from Fort Benning, and Dot, being single, went down and danced and played cards with them. Once she took me along, and I was delighted to be among so many men in uniform. Occasionally, she brought home a serviceman date to meet the family; for a while, she was engaged to a soldier named Jack Jackson, from nearby LaGrange. These fellows were always good for a dime or a pack of gum, and I was always eager to meet them.

Then Dot began seeing a traveling lingerie salesman named A. D. Woods, who came to the store while making his rounds. Every time he came through Manchester they got together, and he came to Manchester a lot. One day, she took me into our bedroom, sat me down on the bed, and said, "Did you know that if I married A.D. he would be your daddy?" She could not have put it to me better, since I missed a father figure badly. Mr. Denham, although I loved him dearly, was in his fifties, which seemed terribly old at the time, and he was not much interested in ball games or going hunting; he was happier staying home reading the *Christian Index* or listening to Gabriel Heatter.

Dot and A.D. were married in December of 1944, and because of the wartime housing shortage, the three of us moved into two rooms of the Manchester Hotel. I loved having my own room for the first time, and I liked the hotel and its permanent residents, who, like us, were unable to find other housing. There was a continual parade of salesmen and other travelers passing through the little hotel, and we took our meals in the dining room, where the food, although not as good at Lizzie's back at my grandparents' house, wasn't bad. The dining room was ruled by a stern Black headwaiter named Will, who seemed to like me. There was another waiter, also named Will, who was younger and my particular favorite. He would eventually finish college and become a physician, which must have been rare for a Black man from Georgia in the 1940s.

All sorts of goods were in short supply during the war, but A.D., in his travels, seemed to be able to get nearly anything from one source or another. He was able to get percale sheets, I recall, and other goods for Mr. Denham to sell at the store. A.D. owned two cars, a Studebaker sedan, which he drove on his rounds, and a Ford station wagon, which he rarely drove. The station wagon counted as a truck, and with the combined gasoline rationing stamps from both cars, he was able to buy enough gas to travel his route. He was also able to get a tiny bicycle for me that first Christmas. It was not new, but it had been well reconditioned, and I was out of my mind with happiness.

In August of 1945, we were driving to A.D.'s mother's home in Durham, North Carolina, and he and Dot decided to stop in Charleston, South Carolina, for the night. It wasn't really on the way, but it was a beautiful town and had lots of antique shops, which my mother loved. Two atomic bombs had already been dropped on Japan, and we were sure that the end of the war was near, but who could tell about the fanatical Japanese? They might well fight to the last man. As we pulled up in front of our Charleston hotel the radio told us to stand by for an important announcement. We sat in the car and waited. Finally word came that the Japanese had surrendered; World War II was over.

The city was home to a large naval base, and suddenly, thousands of sailors learned simultaneously that they were not going to die. All hell broke loose in Charleston, South Carolina. Gangs of deliriously happy, wildly drunk sailors roamed the town, dancing in the streets and kissing any available girl. There was an orphanage next door to the hotel; A.D. got a roll of dimes from the hotel cashier and passed them out to the children lined up on their garden wall. As we stood in front of the hotel, watching the continuing celebration, a dog walked up to A.D. and peed on his leg. This presaged some of the opinions I would, in time, come to hold of my new stepfather.

6

School now loomed ahead. Having spent a year in kindergarten with my contemporaries, I was looking forward to it. Then a serious problem arose having to do with the date of my birth, which was January 9. A state law decreed that any child entering the first grade must be six years old by January 1; I was nine days short, and there was nothing to be done about it. I would have to repeat kindergarten and watch all my friends get promoted to the neverland of The First Grade.

This immutable fact annoyed my mother no end. Like any mother, she could not understand why an exception could not be made in *her* child's case. In a fit of pique, she borrowed some first-grade books from a schoolteacher friend and began to teach me to read. She taught me the old-fashioned way, phonetically, and we read together daily. I remember well the moment at which I learned to read for myself: she was reading me the classic *Lassie Come-Home*, and I was rapt. About halfway through, as the dog was dragging herself through a swamp with a broken leg, or something, my mother closed the book and handed it to me. "You finish it," she said, and she could not be moved to do it for me. I had to find out what happened to that dog. I struggled through the book, syllable by syllable, right to the end, and when I had finished, I was astonished to learn that I could read. I could read billboards, magazines, and the funnies! This is a teaching method I commend to all parents; *Lassie Come-Home* is still in print. I credit that book, along with my mother's teaching skills, for the career as a writer I have today.

In full possession of this new skill, I read voraciously. I was enrolled in the Junior Library Guild and sent a horse and/or dog story every month, which I devoured on the day it arrived. I looked forward to the arrival of these books as another child might look forward to Christmas. I was given other books—Mark Twain, Charles Dickens, and others—and I read them all. When short of something new I dipped into my mother's Book-of-the-Month Club volumes. Dot also taught me to add, subtract, multiply, and divide. And, given my lack of talent with numbers, that was about as far as I got in mathematics, no matter how far I got in school.

Finally, September rolled around again, and I was entered in the first grade. I was terribly excited about this, because I had been given to believe I would have new books to read. On the first day I demanded books and was told to be quiet and work on drawing the letter A. For two long weeks we labored over the alphabet, until finally the books were passed out: they were the same books I had been taught with a year before. A tantrum ensued.

Faced with a child who was demanding more education than they were providing, my teacher and principal huddled and decided that it would be a lot less trouble just to promote me to the second grade; after all, there was no state law against that. As it turned out, I could read a lot better than anyone else in the second grade, but that was as far as the school was going to go, although I was occasionally paraded before fourth- and fifth-grade classes to demonstrate my reading skills, presumably to shame the older students into doing better. I made all A's until about the fifth grade, when I discovered the considerable charms of laziness.

WITH THE END OF THE war, building materials became less scarce. A.D. and Dot bought two adjoining lots on Third Street, four blocks down from the Denhams, razed an old house on one of them, and began planning to build a new one. They engaged an architect from Columbus who designed a comfortable, spacious (thirty-six hundred square feet) three-bedroom ranch house with a carport, and Dot became the general contractor. She knew nothing about building, but she was smart and organized. She hired subcontractors, inspected their work, and paid them in cash weekly. While the house was being built, we moved into a rented house next door, but when the new house was not ready for occupancy at the end of our lease, we moved into a small apartment a few blocks away.

Finally, on August 8, 1948 (I know this because I wrote the date in wet concrete just outside the carport), we moved into our new home, which was not quite finished. I spent the first night there on the living room sofa, next to a table saw in the middle of the floor, the smell of wet plaster in the house. The house cost thirty thousand dollars to build, the interest on the twenty-year FHA mortgage was four percent, and the payments were a hundred and fifty dollars a month.

Soon, with the cooperation of Cousin Calvin from Chattanooga, the house was filled with Baker furniture, Wedgwood china, and all the other nice things that had occupied my grandmother's house. Dot wanted a grand piano, but that was stretching the budget. Instead, she found a new Chickering upright, which remains the best-sounding small piano I have ever heard.

Meanwhile, I had to learn to get along with my stepfather. Angier David Woods was born in Raleigh, North Carolina, in

1900, the son of a sawmill operator. He was eight years old when his father died, and after the eighth grade of school he left and went to work supporting his mother, augmenting her widow's pension from the Spanish-American War by selling newspapers, something he never let me forget. He later became a salesman of ladies' lingerie and hosiery and married a buyer for a Miami, Florida, department store who bore him two sons, Dave and Bill; the youngest, Bill, was a good twelve years older than I. A.D. was usually an affable man, if a bit pompous, but he had a temper, which was regularly unleashed on me. I never received any corporal punishment from A.D. or anyone else that I did not richly deserve, but A.D.'s anger was sudden and continuing. When I committed some infraction of life's rules, he couldn't let it go—he would rant about it for days, a personal quality that, ever since, I have detested in other people. Looking back over the time I knew him, I think his greatest accomplishment was to persuade two attractive and intelligent women to marry him, although I never understood how he did it. I don't think I actively hated A.D., but the best thing about him, as far as I was concerned, was that he traveled for half the year, leaving me in peace. I was glad to see him go when he left on a trip, and I dreaded his return.

A.D., possibly because of his father, had sawdust in his veins. He always had some sort of woodworking business on the side—a cabinet shop, a children's playpen factory (two employees)—and there were always serious power tools in the basement, though I never saw him actually make anything. I exhibited the same lack of skill at woodworking as I did with virtually everything else except reading, and my native sloth, which persists to this day, annoyed A.D., making our relationship even more difficult.

I went to grammar school in two handsome, purpose-built buildings that were well designed, airy, and featured a very fine auditorium. But they had been built forty years before and had not been particularly well maintained. Instead of being renovated, they would soon be condemned and replaced by a tacky contemporary building nearer to the high school and, for some years, war-surplus barrack buildings.

I suppose I learned a lot in grammar school, but my chief memory is of making a bet with Buddy McClain on the 1951 pennant race. Given my Southern heritage, I could not bring myself to support a team called the Yankees, so I bet on the Dodgers, who were doing great until Bobby Thomson knocked one out of the park and cost me two and a half weeks of allowance. This experience, though, had a salutary effect, putting me off gambling for life and, no doubt, saving me millions of dollars.

THEN, ONE AFTERNOON WHEN I was in the fourth grade, my mother appeared at a school assembly and, with no immediate explanation, took me home. I thought somebody had died. In the car I insisted on knowing what was going on.

"Stuart Lee is here," Dot said.

I was stunned. For the whole of my childhood, I had had visions of my distant father, whose only communication was to send me ten dollars with a card at Christmas. In my mind he was a romantic figure who would come to save me if I ever got into real trouble, and now he was here. I was nine years old.

Dot drove me to my grandmother's house and, sure enough, he was there. He had brought along a new wife, Sallie, and his parents, a grandmother and grandfather I never knew I had, Annie Lee Jones Lee and Arthur Lee. My father and I went outside and he talked quietly with me for perhaps half an hour, asking me questions about school and what sports I played. I had been eyeing a baseball glove in a local store window, and I sensed an opportunity to score enough serious adult bucks to buy it, so I started dropping hints. He came through, and I loved him for it, the first emotion I was ever to feel for my father. My impression was of a kindly man with a sense of humor, who looked just like the only photograph I had of him. The photo was never displayed, it was tucked away in a bureau drawer. But after that, I took it out and looked at it often.

All too soon, he was gone. I would meet him again only once.

7

When I was ten or eleven, I spent a couple of weeks in the summer at my grandmother's house, in Clayton, Alabama. At some point after I met her when I was nine, she had divorced the hapless Arthur Lee and returned to her hometown of Clayton. There, she was eventually remarried to a man named Jim Martin.

Uncle Jim, as I would come to call him, was a prosperous small-town figure who owned a number of businesses, including the local cotton gin. He had a large family—four sons and their progeny, so I had a number of by-marriage cousins in Clayton. It was a nice little town, not unlike Manchester, and it had a county judge named George Wallace, who later became governor and made an impassioned run for president and an ass of himself. He was stopped only by the bullet of an attempted assassin and spent the remainder of his life in a wheelchair.

As summer approached, when I was twelve, Nannie, as her grandchildren called her, called my mother to ask if she could take me to California, to meet my father's side of the family, and not incidentally, my father. My mother agreed, so in June of that year, 1950, five of us—Nannie, Uncle Jim, and two of his grandchildren, girls of fourteen and sixteen, and myself—set out from Clayton for Los Angeles in her 1949 Nash Ambassador. I was very excited.

We didn't exactly take a direct route: we went north to Chicago, which I saw as a passing scene, since Nannie rarely stopped, except for food, gas, or some overwhelming view of the country, then we were on our way again at sixty, often seventy miles an hour. Nannie had a heavy foot, and there were no interstates, so you can imagine. She drove every mile of it herself; she was seventy, and Uncle Jim was eighty-five, and the rest of us were too young to drive and too scared to complain.

From Chicago we drove into Canada, for reasons I never understood, and then west through provinces and towns with strange names, that looked like an alternative-reality United States. I remember, particularly, Moose Jaw, Saskatchewan, which I thought a very funny name. I sent home lots of postcards from there. On the long drives between towns, my two cousins, in whispers, explained to me the why, where, and how of sex, for which I was both amazed and grateful. There were, however, no demonstrations. Nannie didn't hear all that well, and Uncle Jim was deaf as a post without his hearing aid, and it was just as well.

We reentered the States in Washington and drove through Crater Lake National Park. It was July, and there were snowdrifts six feet high on the sides of the road, which I found enchanting; I had never seen more than four inches of snow before. We hung a left somewhere near the Pacific and, eventually, fetched up in Los Angeles, which then was a sprawling low-rise city. We were received at a family home in a neighborhood called, oddly, Manchester. I never quite understood whose house it was, but it was teeming with Lees and Noahs and lots of first cousins; Deanna, Ohree's daughter, who was about my age and very pretty, was my favorite. I slept in a sleeping bag on the living room sofa.

The day after we arrived, I was taken to Whittier, where my

father and his second wife, Sallie (whom I had met when he visited Manchester when I was nine), lived with their recently born daughter, Sharon, whom I would get to know better later in life.

He was not there when we arrived, and my cousin Stuart Noah and I were playing on the living room floor when in walked Stuart Lee himself. "Who's this?" he asked, laughing, as he walked up to me. He looked very tall from my perspective on the floor.

We spent a week in Los Angeles, and I saw a lot of him. He took me horseback riding at a stable near a movie studio, where they supplied livestock for filmmaking. He also took me to his business, a small bar and grill that featured steaks. The bartender made me a sweet drink with a cherry on top, and I sat on a stool while he did business. It was a dark place, open only in the evenings. There was a small bandstand and a dance floor, and I imagined what it would be like on weekends—packed with diners and dancers.

After a few nights on the sofa, we moved to the Noah residence in yet another neighborhood, where Stuart and I slept on cots in the garage, which had been turned into sort of a rec room. Stuart and I got along very well, and he and his mother both looked a lot like Nannie.

Once, I asked my father why he and Dot had parted company, and why we had not joined him in Los Angeles. He told me to ask my mother.

When our week ended and we departed for Alabama, we took the direct route, across the Mojave Desert. Cars traveled with canvas bags of water slung across their grilles. The wind blowing across the damp canvas cooled the water for drinking and there was plenty for the radiator, which was important in the desert.

Our last day out was rainy, and about forty miles from home Nannie let the Nash wander over the road's edge, where the tires encounter soft mud. We completely overturned, ending right side up with the rear wheels in a ditch. Nobody was hurt, and there was only superficial damage to the car. A farmer pulled us out of the ditch with his tractor and sent us on our way.

Dot drove over from Manchester to collect me the next day. I had loved Los Angeles and talked of little else for weeks. I decided that, when I was out of college and had some money, I would go back there for a longer visit and talk to my father a lot, man to man.

8

Once, when I was in my twenties, a friend from Atlanta, Henri Jova, the architect and painter, visited me in Manchester. As I drove him down Third Street, with its neat houses shaded by old oaks and elms, Henri remarked, "Isn't this the town where Andy Hardy used to live?"

It was, and Manchester High School was where Andy went to school, too. After two years of junior high spent in World War II surplus barracks, heated by potbellied stoves, the ninth grade finally arrived, and we moved into the main high school building. Manchester High looked the way an American school should, a solid-looking brick building trimmed in limestone. It had an air of permanence about it, something I can't say for the awful cracker box that replaced it a few years after I graduated. Like the old grammar school buildings, it had been built soon after the town's founding. It was apparent earlier generations had been educated there because, on my first day, I sat at a desk upon which some lovesick youth had carved my mother's name inside a heart.

Those of us from the town side of Manchester were now

joined by the kids who had spent their grammar school years in the Callaway Mills school across town, so there were lots of new friends to make. There were sixty in my class and 350 in the school, all white. The Black kids went to school in a dilapidated building not far away. In 1954, the *Brown v. Board of Education* decision was handed down from the Supreme Court, causing, if no immediate effect, something of a stir. Many adults seemed worried about it, but most of my contemporaries didn't seem to think it would be such a big deal to go to school with Black kids. It would be long after my graduation, in 1955, that it finally happened.

My freshman year I went out for football, but after a few days the coach made it clear that he thought I was more of a liability than an asset on the field, and I slunk home. For the next two years my athletic career consisted of being cut early from the basketball team, then becoming one of four on the tennis team, mostly because I owned a racquet. My junior year, spurred on by strong evidence that football players were getting the best girls, I went out for the team again. This time I persevered, playing one year of B-team ball and spending my senior year warming the varsity bench. A boy named Norman Collins and I spent two years locked in a contest to see who would become the worst football player in the history of the school. Norman never had a chance.

I can remember only one compliment from my senior year coach, Joe Coffey; he was lecturing us on the physical requirements for various positions. "The mark of a good blocker," he said, "is not, as many people believe, broad shoulders, but a big ass. Now, if that were the *only* qualification, Woods over there would be an all-American tomorrow."

We had a number of pretty good players, but the most talented was a boy named Billy, who had moved from North Carolina. He was both big and fast, an unusual combination for a high school backfielder in Class B football, and he started the season as our quarterback. He had a problem, though: when passing, he tended to get nervous under pressure from the opposing line and overthrow the ball. Our second-string quarterback was a scrawny, scrappy kid of about five feet five inches and 130 pounds named Buck Phillips. He may have been a lightweight, but Buck was cool under fire. He could complete passes and move the ball down the field, so Coach Coffey made Buck move to quarterback and moved Billy to fullback, where he excelled. We only lost one game my senior year. If Buck Phillips hadn't beat him out at quarterback, nobody would ever have heard of Bill Mathis, but at fullback, he got a scholarship to Clemson and went on to become a ground-gaining running back for ten years with the New York Jets (né Titans), on the same team with Joe Namath. I always thought that Bill owed Buck a debt of gratitude.

By this time, Sex had reared its head—which was about as far as it got. The girls were all serious Baptists and Methodists and had been taught to be concerned with their reputations. There were a couple of girls who were less concerned, but they were very busy.

When I was sixteen things took an interesting turn. An Atlanta girl was coming to visit some relatives, and everybody knew that big-city girls were *fast*. I had my driver's license by then, and I took her to a movie. Then I drove her out to our local lovers' lane, a beautiful lake called Parkman's Pond, which was contained by an earthen dam, which was crossed by a dirt road. I drove up onto the middle of the dam and stopped. There was a moon, there was music on the radio, and for the first time in my young life, I had met a girl who was willing to have at least some of her clothing removed.

It was the fashion for girls to wear blouses with about two hundred tiny buttons down the back, and I worked my way through those before I encountered those little flat hooks that secure a brassiere. In male clothing, we have buttons, snaps, and zippers, but nothing like these devilish things. She was perfectly willing to have it unhooked, but she was not willing to help.

In the midst of all this flailing about, the car was suddenly flooded with light, and I looked up to find that a Georgia State Patrol cruiser had arrived on the dam, nose to nose with my car, its blue light flashing on top.

Panic ensued. Clothing was located, and I somehow got the car started and slammed it into reverse. I neglected to back up as far as the road, though, and drove down the side of the earthen dam instead, ripping out the exhaust system. We drove noisily away.

The next day, two things happened: My stepfather made me go back, find the exhaust system, and have it reattached. And I visited the stockroom at my grandfather's store, wherein resided a truncated dummy clad in a Gossard girdle and brassiere. I examined the brassiere's hooks carefully, then practiced—first with one hand, then with two—unfastening them. I remain an ace at bra hooks to this day.

MANCHESTER HIGH SCHOOL WAS, FOR its time and place, a very good school, though Latin was dropped from the curriculum, replaced with Spanish. Why would I ever need to speak Spanish, I wondered. Also, all the boys were required to take two years of agriculture and shop classes. In agriculture class, I excelled at the identification of chicken breeds. I can still point out a Rhode Island Red or a Leghorn when I come across them. My achievements in shop, however, consisted of one wobbly bookcase and a lamp that fell over if you tried to turn it on.

I did, however, being my mother's son, show some affinity for music. When a school band was formed, I was denied the greatly desired trumpet and assigned to the clarinet, an instrument I found boring. Later I would switch to the drums, which were much more fun. I saved up for a set of drums—snare, bass, tom-toms, high hats, and two other cymbals, and played along with Artie Shaw and Louis Armstrong on the phonograph.

Then we got a new band director named Bob Decker who played good piano. He formed a dance band, and I played in it. Soon, I got together a couple of my mother's musician friends, a pianist named Cliff and Harold Guy on C-melody sax; we located a good guitarist and a terrific trumpet player named Cliff from another town, and I sold us to Fletcher Gill for Friday nights at his roadhouse, Gill's, up at Harris City, a few miles north. I got fifteen bucks a night and gained a lot of experience. I used my newfound income to buy my first dinner jacket.

My schoolmates and I were a pretty musical bunch. Apart from singing in the glee club we played four-handed piano ("Chopsticks" and "Heart and Soul") and we sang all the time—on football game buses, at church and Sunday school, and at recess, sitting in the shade of a tree. I don't think kids sing anymore, and it's a pity. We derived a great deal of pleasure from it. We had the time, because TV hadn't taken over our lives, and radio stations were both scarce and boring. At the teenage club we danced to the music that our parents had loved—78 rpm records of Artie Shaw, Glenn Miller, Harry James, and Tommy Dorsey. On Saturday nights in winter, we went to square dances at the county seat, Greenville, music provided by a hillbilly band. And on summer nights, we traveled fifteen miles to F. D. Roosevelt State Park, on Pine Mountain, to a mountaintop restaurant called the Tavern, which had an outdoor flagstone dance floor and a big jukebox. Kids from other towns came, too, and we danced to Tony Bennett, the Four Freshmen, and, for the first time, to Black rhythm and blues outfits, like Big Joe Turner, with "Shake, Rattle and Roll." Elvis was still driving a truck in Tupelo.

In school, we had good teachers—Miss Irma Phillips, in history; Mr. Jim Woodall, in geometry; and Miss Catharine Pope, in algebra. My mother, who wanted some company when A.D. was traveling, rented our front room to teachers, and Catherine Pope was among them. Her proximity didn't improve my math grades, though, and algebra remained seen as through a glass, darkly. Our English teacher was Catherine Chastain, who drilled into me the rudiments of grammar, and, although I was terrible at diagraming sentences or any other technical skill, I gained a grasp of how the language should be written and spoken. I also enrolled in a typing class, which taught me how to think and type at the same time, a skill that would come in very handy.

An important experience for me came when I was given two weeks to do a book report on a piece of fiction of my choice. Following my usual approach to anything academic, I waited until the day before the report was due, then charged up the stairs to the school library and demanded to know where the short novels were. The shortest one I could find turned out to be F. Scott Fitzgerald's *The Great Gatsby*. I loved the novel. By the time I had finished it, I realized that I knew the story, having recently seen the Alan Ladd version of the movie. The book was a lot better, though.

My love of the movies had begun with the Saturday-morning westerns of Gene Autry and Roy Rogers. We had a very nice little movie house called, rather grandly, the President Theatre, after Roosevelt. (Lots of things in our county were named after Roosevelt.) It was Art Deco in style and must have seated three or four hundred, including the balcony, which was reserved for Black people. As a small boy, I used to love to sit in the balcony with my nurse, but the greatest thrill came when the projectionist, Charles Traylor, who lived across the street from my grandparents, invited me to sit in the projection booth and watch the movie from there. Before the movie started Charlie played records, or rather one record: *Artie Shaw and His Gramercy Five*, playing "Cross Your Heart" and, on side 2, "Summit Ridge Drive." It became my favorite, and today I have it on my iPhone. It was the first jazz I ever heard.

I went to the movies *all the time.* The program changed twice a week and on Saturdays, and I never missed anything. As part of our training in history, in school we were lined up and marched downtown in pairs, holding hands, to see *Gone With the Wind,* which may not have been great history, strictly speaking, but, after all, it was set in Georgia. This love of movies would have a great deal to do with the way in which I would write fiction later on.

In high school I was required to earn my two-dollar-and-fifty-cent allowance by cutting the grass, a job that I hated. Eventually, my grass-cutting and my moviegoing came into conflict. I wrote about it, and, on July 30, 1981, the following piece appeared on the op-ed page of the *New York Times.* I called it "A Pain in the Grass," but that was too racy for the *Times,* so they changed it.

THE COUP DE GRASS

I am perfectly aware that there are many otherwise rational people who regard grass as merely a benign, even attractive ground cover, but I know better. Grass is going to kill me someday. It has already blighted my youth, attempted to geld me, and cost me the best job I ever had. Why should it stop now?

When I was a boy, my parents built a house and planted grass all around it. Wherever you looked, there was grass. As I approached puberty, I was taken aside and told not about the birds and bees but about the grass. (It would be many years before I learned about the birds and bees; grass took all my time.) It was imparted to me that if I expected to continue to pull down a $2.50-a-week allowance, I was going to have to keep a Saturday afternoon appointment with a lawn mower.

This was my first major experience with an injustice that occurs unnoticed all over the United States each summer—that of a boy having visited upon him the sins of his father (his father planted the grass). It was not as though the grass were some joy shared by all the family; it had never done anything for me but conceal rocks and chiggers from my unsuspecting bare feet. No, sir, this was clearly *their* grass, but the lawn mower, predictably, turned out to be *mine*. Now, this was a great iron monster of a machine, with a huge gasoline engine, a blade that turned over and over instead of around and around, and with the stentorian roar of a major piece of earthmoving equipment. It started reluctantly and would operate at nothing less than full throttle.

Its blades would chew rocks into small pieces and fire them at me with the force of shotgun pellets; its exhaust would leave me dizzy with carbon-monoxide poisoning; its overheated cylinder would go out of its way to burn my bare legs; and if my vigilance flagged for but a moment it would whip quickly about and catch me in the crotch with a handlebar, leaving me groveling on the front lawn, while it went off in search of innocent azaleas. For years, it turned the backyard into a battleground every Saturday afternoon, and I never won an unconditional victory.

Then appeared salvation. Our local picture palace, the President Theatre, offered me the position of ticket-taker at the Saturday kiddie shows. There was no money, but I could go to the movies free, as often as I liked (every day), and have all the popcorn I could eat, as long as I brought my own bag. Who needed an allowance? My joy at the time could be duplicated today only by an announcement that medical science had found a way for baldness to be cured by overeating.

During the euphoric weeks that followed, while I enfeebled my eyesight and clogged up my digestive tract at the movies, the grass, of course, continued to grow. Then, on my fourth Saturday in the film business, my stepfather showed up, took me into custody, and returned me to the tender mercies of the Great Iron Lawn Mower. It hurts to admit having peaked at 13, but it really was the best job I ever had.

A couple of years ago, I took a deep breath, mortgaged myself to the hilt, and bought a house. The first words I said to the real estate agent were, "No Grass."

"You mean low maintenance," she said.

"You don't understand," I replied, taking her by the lapels and fixing her with my gaze. "I mean *no* maintenance."

I must have got through to her because she found me a house situated on a steep hillside in a little ravine, in thick woods, where no grass could possibly grow. There were leaves, to be sure, but if you don't have a lawn, there is no reason to rake them. You just let them lie there.

My neighbors all live in houses surrounded by expanses of the green stuff. Every Saturday morning now, as I lie in bed eating chili, reading the papers, and watching old movies on TV, I can hear lawn mowers cranking up on three sides of me. When the scent of new-mown grass reaches my room, I get up and close the windows.

I have a true story, a life lesson, for those of you who own more tools than a dentist, who have enslaved yourselves to a horticultural phenomenon that cannot be eaten, smoked, or employed in any other remotely useful manner—that has bound you to a life of unceasing manual labor.

This story is set at Oxford's Christ Church College, some years ago. An American tourist came upon an ancient gardener in the quadrangle, tending a lawn that was flatter, softer, fresher, and greener than anything he had ever imagined. Staggered by the beauty of the man's work, he approached the gardener. "Excuse me," he said, reverently, "but how do you get your grass to look like this?"

The old gardener straightened from his task, scratched his head, and looked about him. "It's simple, really," he says. "First you prepare the ground, then you sow your seed, then you roll it and cut it and roll it again . . . for three hundred years."

And that, my green-thumbed, permanently exhausted neighbors, is what you have to look forward to.

I had originally written the piece for the magazine section of the *Atlanta Journal-Constitution*, but the editor turned it down, and it gave me great satisfaction to see it appear in the *Times*. It had at first been four thousand words long, if you can believe that, and the *Times* asked me to pare it to fourteen hundred; it ran as nine hundred words. The assigned editor was a young lady named Allison Silver, who, I later learned, is the sister of the movie producer Joel Silver, who will appear later in this volume. I believe the lady is in the movie business now, and I certainly hope so, because she nearly drove me crazy with her pickiness. ("Father" in the piece had originally been "wicked stepfather.") Later, the *Reader's Digest* ran the piece, condensing it to four hundred words, a ninety percent reduction of the original, but remember, they condensed *The Holy Bible*, too.

9

Graduation from high school came in May of 1955, and I had
already been accepted at the University of Georgia, the only
college to which my stepfather was willing to pay to send me,
because it was so cheap. It was also easy to be accepted: if you
lived in Georgia and had a high school diploma, or the promise of
one, you were in. While I had graduated in the upper third of my
class with a respectable B-plus average, my study habits, such as
they were, had hardly made me Ivy League material, and anyway,
Harvard and Yale might as well have been on another planet;
nobody from Manchester had ever gone to college that far afield.
I spent my summer working as a lifeguard at the brand-new
swimming beach at Callaway Resort & Gardens, fifteen miles
away on Pine Mountain. And in early September, I presented
myself in Athens, Georgia, to be educated.

Dot and I were driven to Athens by our friends the Wolfes,
who owned a trailer that would hold my footlocker and belongings. George Wolfe drove way too slowly for my tastes. By the
time we arrived in Athens, Georgia, I was beside myself with excitement, but Dot and the Wolfes insisted on lingering to inspect

my room in Reed Hall, the freshman dorm, and to meet my roommate, Charlie Horton, who had also been a lifeguard at Callaway Gardens, and whom they already knew, anyway.

Finally, they were gone, and I experienced a feeling of personal freedom that I have seldom known since. I was out in the world, on my own, unfettered. Within the limits of my forty-dollars-a-week allowance, which had to pay for meals as well as fun, I could do anything I wanted, as long as I attended classes, passed my courses, and escaped the attentions of the school's disciplinary authorities. Then came Rush Week.

Fraternities were important on the UGA campus, perhaps too important. To be pledged to a good house was to achieve instant social acceptance, something that was inordinately appealing to a seventeen-year-old small-town boy. Two frat boys from Manchester, Jimmy Kirkland and Jack Taylor, both extremely nice fellows, had arranged for me to be invited to the Sigma Alpha Epsilon house for a weekend my senior year in high school and, for all practical purposes, I was recruited at that time. I was very impressed with the handsome, antebellum Greek Revival mansion and with the well-dressed, clean-cut boys who were members, so although I received invitations from a couple of other good houses, I accepted the bid from SAE with no qualms. Thus I entered the halls of the largest and, many thought, best fraternity on the campus. Before I graduated, I would come to have very mixed feelings about fraternities in general and the Georgia Beta Chapter of SAE, in particular.

To a boy who had not been away to prep school, college was the first gateway to adulthood. God knows we were only kids, but we tried to behave like grown-ups—with many noticeable lapses. Alcohol was prohibited on campus and in the fraternity houses, but you wouldn't have noticed. The beer and the booze ran freely, imported personally by the trunkful from Atlanta and also sold locally by bootleggers. An ancient Black man named Doc Banks was the butler at the SAE house, and he ran a quiet little booze operation out of the cellar, where he secreted his supplies. Many a time some drunk brother would tear the cellar apart looking for Doc's stash, but nobody ever found it. After fifty years, Doc retired with a nice nest egg of bootlegger's profits, which he had invested in local businesses.

My first rite of passage came with a visit to Effie's, an old-fashioned brothel of many years standing on the wrong side of the Athens tracks. Seven or eight of us piled into a freshman's illegally possessed car and found our way there. We were greeted by the sight of a half dozen young women in slips and nightgowns sitting around a seedy living room watching TV, apparently bored out of their skulls. Everything moved very quickly; I was last through the door and missed out on the one really beautiful girl. Instead, I entrusted myself to a short, plump, blasé young lady who relieved me of, in short order, my five bucks and my virginity, with hardly a pause along the way. After years of raging hormones, I was awfully disappointed with the way things had gone. As we were leaving Effie's I turned to my new friend and fraternity brother, Chip Wood, and remarked, "If that's all there is to it, I'll stick to masturbation." I didn't, though.

As the end of my freshman year approached, I dropped by the campus employment office to see if there were any good summer jobs going. The best thing available was waterfront director of a summer camp. Having gotten my Red Cross instructor's rating in a phys ed class and, I think, being the only applicant, I got the job. The camp was in the beautiful North Georgia mountains, near Dahlonega, and it was for Camp Fire Girls. Apart from the camp handyman, I would be the only male among several hundred campers and a couple of dozen counselors. The mind boggled.

My job was to create and run a swimming instruction program, to teach the senior girls myself and to lifeguard during the swimming periods. I had no other duties and a lot of time to think about girls. The campers were, obviously, off-limits, and most of the counselors were older than I. But before I could choose among those who were eligible, one of them chose me. She was called Scotty, and she was a neat girl—one of my swimming staff, tomboyish, with an impish sense of humor. I had a cabin of my own, of course, and late at night, after everyone was asleep, Scotty would make her way through the darkness to my cabin, creep into my bed, and—having dated Georgia Tech boys back home and thus being more experienced than I—teach me the rudiments of love. She was an awfully good teacher.

Another late-night activity for the counselors, after their campers were asleep, was to sneak over to the dining hall and steal milk from the dispensing machine. Apart from my sessions with Scotty, this was as racy as it got.

Then one night, something peculiar happened. I walked over to the dining hall and, turning on the kitchen light, surprised Scotty and another girl, Fran, who were sitting on a big butcher-block table drinking milk. I turned off the lights and sat between them. It was pitch dark. Scotty and I began to pay a great deal of attention to each other. Suddenly, there arose a terrific clamor; a stack of empty milk cans on the back porch came crashing down, making a noise a lot like a nuclear explosion. Scotty and I, clutching our clothes, raced into the night. Fran, too. The camp authorities said nothing about it, though, and after some discussion, Scotty and I agreed that the cats who lived under the dining hall must have knocked over a can, setting off a chain reaction. We had gotten away with it. Sighs of relief.

Then, when the first term of camp ended, we looked forward to a few days off, and most of the counselors made plans to go to Atlanta. We were warned, though, not to leave camp before the last camper had departed. Scotty and Fran ignored this order, got a ride with some Atlanta parents, and were, for this act of insubordination, fired and told not to return.

The rest of us returned to camp on time with no knowledge of this event, and the camp's directors, two women, called us to a meeting in the dining hall and addressed us in grave tones. Two members of the staff, they said, had violated the rules of the camp in a flagrant manner and were being dismissed. As they continued with a lecture about behavior, responsibility, and morals, I looked around the hall and noticed that Scotty was not present, and it began to sound very much as if the camp directors were talking about Scotty and me. Maybe it had not been cats who had knocked over the milk cans, or maybe somebody had been listening to our late-night groans outside my cabin, which had only screens for windows.

As the lecture droned on, I began to sweat. I had visions of returning home and explaining to my mother that I had been fired from the camp for having sex with a girl counselor. I was sitting on a table, gripping the edges, my knuckles turning white. Finally, a camp director came to the denouement: "The two counselors who are being dismissed are Scotty"—I held my breath and steeled myself for the blow—"and Fran." I let out my breath in a whoosh, and everybody in the room turned and looked at me, sweat pouring down my face, breathing hard, looking terrified.

During the second session of camp, I missed Scotty terribly. I don't know where she is today, but I thank her for the pleasure of those wonderfully educational weeks.

AT THE END OF MY sophomore year I returned to the employment office and got the best job available to a student. Benson's Bakery, an Athens institution, baked fruitcakes the whole summer long, for sale by civic clubs all over the country, who made a buck a cake for their local projects. During the summer, a dozen college boys were hired and given territories around the United States; I was

awarded New York, Massachusetts, Vermont, New Hampshire—
and Maine, if I could get to it in the time available. My job was to
travel to every town of more than five hundred people in each of
these states, locate the president of the Kiwanis or the Jaycees, give
him a sample of the cake and impress him with its quality and
fundraising potential. Somebody from headquarters in Athens
would then phone him and close the sale. I did pretty well at it
and was among the better salesmen that summer, but what the job
did was show me that there was another part of America with real
people living in it, and that, except for their accents and the nature
of their relations with Black people, Yankees were just like the
folks back home. It was a revelation.

Best of all, the job got me to New York City. There I hit the jazz
clubs, got my picture taken with Gene Krupa, and sat in tiny
Birdland and had my ears pinned back by the roaring Count Basie
Orchestra, who were practically breaking the glasses on the tables.

My JUNIOR YEAR I WASN'T doing too well, and, although I hadn't
actually flunked out, it was suggested strongly to me by my
mother that I should take a quarter off and think about things. I
got a job at the brand-new radio station in Manchester, called (predictably) WFDR—The Magic Voice of the Magic City. (Manchester
is called the Magic City because of a peculiar naturally occurring
phenomenon, a hill outside town called Magic Hill. You parked
your car at the bottom, turned off the engine, released the brakes,
and the car rolled up the hill, all by itself. No kidding.) My job was
to put WFDR on the air every morning at five, play records and
read the farm news off the UP ticker until lunchtime, then spend
the afternoon selling radio spots to local merchants.

My big moment came when, at a celebration of the fiftieth anniversary of the Georgia Warm Springs Foundation, I got to interview Eleanor Roosevelt. We talked about my great-uncle Stuart

Chevalier for a moment. "Ah, Stuart," she said, then gave me that wonderful smile, and moved on to the next interviewer. I also got to interview Dr. Jonas Salk, who did not wish to be interviewed. As part of the festivities, the *Today* show, with Dave Garroway, and *Queen for a Day* were broadcast from Warm Springs, and the Elliot Lawrence big band played. There was a dance at the country club that evening, played by a pickup group of musicians from the band, and I was really enjoying the music. During an intermission a beefy guy who had been playing trumpet sat down beside me on a sofa, and I told him how much I liked his playing. He stuck out his hand. "My name is Butterfield," he said. I was stunned. Billy Butterfield had played the trumpet solo on Artie Shaw's recording of "Stardust," which I had danced to so many times, and he had also been part of Shaw's Gramercy Five, whose recordings of "Cross Your Heart" and "Summit Ridge Drive" were the first jazz I ever heard. We had a nice chat, and I went home very happy indeed.

Back at the University of Georgia, though, trouble lay ahead.

10

By the middle of my junior year I had become somewhat disil-
lusioned with fraternities. Although I had made many friends
among the hundred or so members, there were a half dozen or so
that I disliked and who returned the favor. The whole university
being lily-white, racial discrimination never really came up, but
something else did. A boy I knew from Atlanta, Mike Rich, whose
family were the founders of Rich's department store, was at another college, and the SAE chapter there wanted to pledge him.
Problem, though: Mike was Jewish. In fact, he had converted to
Christianity in high school and was an active Presbyterian, but
the national fraternity had a rule that a member must be ". . . fully
acceptable throughout the fraternity," a blatant concession to the
racism of Southern chapters. The chapter wishing to pledge Mike
canvassed other Southern chapters for their endorsement.

A chapter meeting ensued at our house that remains the worst
meeting of any sort that I have ever attended. While the Atlanta
boys, who knew Mike well, were in favor of him being accepted,
a lot of others were rabidly against it. A boy from Augusta, a
premed student I had always liked, stood up and actually made a

motion that we should propose to the national fraternity that . . . only members of the Aryan race" be admitted to any chapter. I and a dozen other people were on our feet, protesting, and only the firm management of the chapter's president kept the whole business from degenerating into a brawl. Finally, a vote was taken, and it went narrowly against Mike Rich.

I was shaken that such a thing could happen. I knew as well as anyone that there were Jewish and Gentile fraternities on campus and that there was little or no mixing of members, but it was a situation I disliked. I felt guilty about belonging to an organization that discriminated against anybody. That a group of young men I knew so well could do such a thing rattled me badly. From that time on I spent less and less time at the fraternity house. To this day I ignore any communication from the fraternity, although they manage to track me down whenever I move. I wish I had resigned at the time and made a lot of noise about it, but the sixties were still around the corner, and there wasn't much in the way of protesting on the campus.

Then, in my junior year, I fell in love. Nancy was the daughter of the housemother at my dorm. She was bright, funny, and best of all, thought I was, too. She was also more than ready to bestow her virtue on the appropriate young man, and I was IT. We spent our time in back seats, on blankets by the river, in a bedroom in her sorority house (closed for the summer), and once in a hammock, which believe me, is dangerous. I counsel you against it.

Later in the summer her mother, who was justifiably afraid that we might immediately get married, spirited her off to visit relatives in San Diego, where Nancy fell in love again, this time with a young naval officer. When she came back, things were not the same. Though we remained friendly, we parted company. Her mother had won. (Years later, after I had been published, her mother took me to lunch at the Capital City Club, in Atlanta, and was very nice. I left mystified as to why she had asked me.)

During my senior year, much of the time I had spent at the fraternity was taken up with two new and absorbing interests. First was the university theater. I had spent three years at Georgia thinking that one had to be a drama major in order to try out for a play. When I discovered that this was not correct, I tried out for the part of Captain Fisby in *The Teahouse of the August Moon*. I didn't get the part. The director, Dr. Leighton Ballew, took me aside and told me he had wanted to cast me, but he had a senior drama student who had never had a lead, and he gave that student the part. I did land the role of Mr. Hokaida, the chief of police in the Okinawan village. All my lines were in Japanese, which had to be learned phonetically, and my big moment was the wrestling scene, in which I made a great deal of noise when I hit the floor, drawing gasps from the audience.

We had a bit of drama offstage, too. A week before we opened our leading man *and* his understudy drove to Atlanta to hear Sir John Gielgud read, and on the way home both were badly injured in an automobile accident and out of the play. Panic ensued, but Dr. Ballew found a podiatrist from South Carolina who had played the part in little theater and could still remember his lines, even the Japanese ones.

Nothing I have ever done since has given me such satisfaction in interacting with a group of people as did that production of *Teahouse*. I think that if I had discovered the university theater in my freshman year I might have wanted to become an actor—in which case I would now be waiting tables in Greenwich Village—or perhaps, I would be a playwright. I forged friendships that, although they lasted only until the end of our run, are memorable. Our Lotus Blossom went on to marry into a great American fortune and, I hear, divorced rather well; another, Curtis Taylor, went on to act briefly in movies before being murdered by a young man to whom he had made advances. His killer went free.

Ever since that time I have always enjoyed the company of actors and envied them their relationships in a theatrical company.

MY OTHER GREAT INTEREST IN my senior year was jazz. I wrote a jazz column for the *Red and Black*, the college newspaper. I also got together a group of musicians and found bookings for us at fraternity parties, weddings, bar mitzvahs, and whatever other parties we could find. I played drums and, if I had had enough to drink, sang. We made fifteen bucks a night, each, and we had a good time.

The most fun I had, though—and the most trouble I got into—was when I and some friends formed the University of Georgia Jazz Society. A mention in a column I wrote for the *Red and Black* attracted fifty or sixty people to an organizing meeting; we named the group, and I was elected president, with the intention of producing jazz concerts with both big name groups and more local bands. When word of this new organization reached the university authorities, I was informed that I needed permission from the school to form any new organization, and I was called into the office of the director of student activities, one John Cox, for a chat. I knew Cox slightly and liked him; he seemed youthful and interested in the students.

I settled into a chair and began answering questions about what we intended to do in this new society. When he heard my answers, he became serious. He told me, explicitly, that we were not to stage any event which involved Black and White musicians playing in the same band. We could have Black bands or White bands, but no mixed bands. I'm afraid I laughed out loud. I reminded him that, only a year or two before, Louis Armstrong had come to the campus with a racially mixed band, and that no riot had ensued. I reminded him that jazz was, after all, a Black art, which was also practiced by White people. And that one of the great things about the music was that it brought Black and White people together. This was exactly what he did *not* want to hear. He told me that I had a choice—either no mixed bands, or no jazz society. Finally, beaten, I agreed to his terms. It was 1959, a couple of years before the college would be integrated.

At the root of this problem, though no official ever mentioned his name to me, was a man named Roy Harris. Harris published a racist newspaper in Augusta; he was a state senator and a political power in Georgia; and he was a vocal and influential member of the Board of Regents of the University of Georgia and terribly concerned that no Black student should ever, ever attend the institution. In short, every official of the university was scared shitless of him, and none of them was going to do anything that might give him the slightest excuse to learn their individual names or to visit the university waving the banners of white supremacy.

The ground rules established, we got to work. I persuaded a number of local businesses that had a lot of student customers to loan us a few hundred dollars for producing a concert; the money was to be repaid from the profits. The money secured, I established contact with a booking agent named Willard Alexander, with the William Morris Agency, in Miami, and told him we were in the market for jazz groups. I told him up front about the racial restrictions that had been placed on us, and he understood. He offered us one of my great favorites, the Four Freshmen, for fifteen hundred bucks, and we were in business. One of our two faculty advisers was a graphic designer, and he put together a nice, silk-screened poster. We printed tickets, publicized the concert on the radio and in my *Red and Black* column, and we packed the Fine Arts auditorium, which held fifteen hundred people. And we repaid our loans.

With a big success in hand, Alexander offered us the Dave Brubeck Quartet—another of my favorites—consisting of Brubeck on piano, Paul Desmond on alto sax, Joe Morello on drums, and Bill Crow on bass. We cranked up our production engine and got going. A couple of weeks before the concert date I got a package from the William Morris Agency in the mail, containing publicity photographs. I remember I was standing in the hall of the fraternity house, where I got my mail. I opened the envelope and there was the Dave Brubeck Quartet staring me in the face. And the bassist was Black. Unbeknownst to Willard Alexander or me, Bill Crow had been replaced by Gene Wright. I shoved the pictures back into the envelope in a hurry and looked around to see in anyone had seen them. I was safe.

Now I was faced with a dilemma about what to do next. My strong instinct was to say nothing to anybody and to continue as planned. I thought that, when the curtain went up, nobody would be fool enough to bring it down in the middle of a concert. And when it was over, I could claim I had been as surprised as anyone to see Gene Wright on the stage. I knew the authorities would, quite rightly, not believe me, but I believed I could brazen it through without getting myself thrown out of school or see the Jazz Society terminated.

The former prospect, however, worried me. I knew the authorities were already nervous about us, and I didn't want to give them an excuse to shut us down. I sought advice from our two faculty advisers, Bernie Bell, the designer, who had played trombone with the Gene Krupa Band in his extreme youth, and a wonderful, jazz-loving English professor, whose name I cannot for the life of me remember. I knew they would both be on my side.

They were, but they advised caution. Why not go to the director of student activities, John Cox, explain the situation—that we had innocently booked the group, that we had already hired a hall, had posters and tickets printed, and had paid a large deposit—and ask him to let us proceed as planned, just this once. It was, after all, the honest thing to do, and we all thought it would work. It didn't. In a millisecond, Cox told me to cancel the concert forthwith, and he would brook no further argument.

I left this extremely short meeting depressed and angry, as only a very young man can be angry at authority. I went to the Co-op, the student drugstore, sat down in a booth with some of my Jazz Society comembers and told them what had happened. Everyone, predictably, was outraged. We ought to get up a petition, somebody suggested. Better yet, I said, we should get up a petition in the form of a telegram, an apology to Dave Brubeck and Gene Wright for the stupidity of our superiors. I left the table, found a typewriter, and in seconds wrote a telegram that stripped a large piece of hide off the backside of the university administration, in general, and Roy Harris, in particular. I returned to the Co-op and, in a matter of minutes, had three hundred signatures on the document, with each signer chipping in a quarter to pay for the telegram. I was on a roll.

Inside half an hour, my roll screeched to a halt. A breathless messenger appeared at my side and told me that the director of public relations for the university, Bill Simpson, wanted to see me in his office immediately, if not sooner. I knew Bill Simpson pretty well. He was very popular with the students; I expected a sympathetic hearing from him. Once again, I was wrong. As soon as I sat down in his office, he told me that I could not send the telegram. I told him to watch me. He argued gently with me for a few minutes, and when I still insisted on sending the telegram, he brought me up short. "If you send that telegram," he said bluntly, "I promise you that there will never again be another jazz performance of any kind on this campus." I said he must be kidding. He said he was not.

I left his office and spent the afternoon trying to get an audience with the president of the university, one O. C. Aderhold. He declined to see me. That evening, beaten again, I trudged dispiritedly over to the local radio station where the student disc jockey, my friend and the trumpet player in our group, Morris Knight, was conducting his regular evening jazz show. I told him about what had happened, and we commiserated for a few minutes. Then the phone rang. It was the Associated Press, calling to confirm some local story. Morris covered the receiver. "It's the AP," he said. "You want to tell them what happened?" You bloody well bet I did! Here was my chance to expose the racism and hypocrisy that had stopped me from producing the Brubeck concert! I took the phone and poured out the story to the AP man, sparing no nuance or detail. I could hear him typing as I related the events of the day. It was my first experience with how wrong the press can get a story.

The next morning, newspapers across America, and across the world, for all I knew, carried a story strongly implying that the student members of the University of Georgia Jazz Society, upon hearing that a Black musician would appear with the Dave Brubeck Quartet, had canceled the concert. The piece named me as the principal perpetrator of this injustice. My name was spelled correctly, though.

All hell broke loose. Daily, for a couple of weeks, the Society's mailbox and mine were crammed with irate letters from people all over the country, condemning us and me for the outrage we had committed. Someone sent a clipping from a San Francisco newspaper by their jazz columnist attacking me personally. In the beginning I tried to answer all the letters, but I soon learned how very nearly impossible it is for an ordinary citizen to correct a wrong news story about him. Not one news organization made any attempt to get my response. The only letter writer who liked what he had read in the AP story was an Alabama Klansman, who wrote to compliment me for my superior White judgment. He had a few words to say about the Supreme Court, too.

I produced a few more concerts, most notably one with the Woody Herman Herd, a great evening that attracted a meager 175 ticket buyers, but my years at Georgia ended with more of a whimper than a bang. I had to attend summer school my last quarter of school to make up for the quarter I spent in the radio business, and I discovered that, because of my decidedly mediocre academic record, I needed an additional five credits—one course in anything—to get my BA in sociology. I ran over to the Center for Continuing Education to sign up for a correspondence course in short-story writing. The woman administrator I spoke to told me that I was a day late for registration and that I could not take the course. In a panic, I went directly to the professor who taught the course and got his permission to register, going over the administrator's head. With great ill humor, she registered me.

It was the only writing course I ever took. I got pretty good grades for my stories, but when I went to the office to get my final exam grade, the hostile administrator told me I had earned an F and, as a result, I could not graduate until I made up the course. Stunned, I tried to contact the professor, but he had already left the campus for his summer vacation. So that night, disconsolately, I packed up my belongings, rented a trailer, and slunk off to Atlanta, where I planned to start some sort of career, though I wasn't sure what. I had wanted to write since childhood, but everyone I knew had repeatedly told me I could never make a living at writing.

There was a postscript, though. When the professor returned for the next quarter, I called him to find out why I had failed the course. Surprised, he told me that he had awarded me a B-plus for my final exam story. The female administrator, miffed that I had gotten into the course over her head, had falsified my grade, causing me to miss the graduation ceremony. (I trust God punished her.) Many years passed before I was able to persuade the University of Georgia that I had graduated in 1959 instead of 1960, and to have a correct diploma issued. (My first wife kept it when we were divorced.)

So, ready to be a grown-up, I drove through the night toward Atlanta, wondering what would happen next.

11

Atlanta had always been the Big City for me. Except for my one weekend foray into New York and my week in Los Angeles, Atlanta was the largest city I had ever visited, and it was very exciting to be there on my own. I had friends there—particularly my old housemate and fraternity brother, Lindsey Hopkins, and my last roommate and another frat brother, Dent Acree—but I had no real idea of what to do with myself, except to find a job.

During my senior year I had met with a dozen company representatives visiting the campus to recruit. Without exception, the future they presented seemed flat and dull. Now, on the suggestion of various friends, I began to call the personnel offices of various Atlanta businesses for interviews, and those I had were alarmingly like those back at UGA.

Anyway, I still had a service obligation ahead of me. The draft was still in effect, and a hitch in some branch of the armed services awaited practically every young man leaving college. I had done the two required years of ROTC at college and had intended to do the last two years, get a commission, go to flying school, and spend three years in the Air Force. However, as I finished my sophomore year the three-year requirement was increased to five years, and that seemed too long. When I got out, my contemporaries would be way ahead of me in their careers.

Finally, I opted for Officer Training School, which would give me a nonflying commission and a three-year obligation. They flew me down to Maxwell Air Force Base in Montgomery, Alabama, gave me an elaborate physical, told me I was qualified, and told me to go home and wait for a starting date. In the meantime, I fell back on old skills: I got a job selling men's clothing at Parks-Chambers, an old-line, Brooks Brothers sort of establishment, working in what was called the Bachelor & Benedict shop at the new mall, Lenox Square, one of the nation's first. I worked for a bright young man named Ham Stockton. This gave me a living, and I enjoyed Ham, who took his work seriously. He taught me a lot about how good clothing is designed and made.

Then, after a wait of some weeks, I heard from the Air Force: all the applicants who were to be in my class had been given the wrong physical exam, and these would have to be redone, a few applicants at a time. OTS was postponed indefinitely, until this could be accomplished. It was going to be months, rather than weeks, they said. Bored with the waiting I joined the Georgia Air National Guard, accepting an obligation of two months of basic training, four months of technical school, and eight years of weekend meetings—plus, two weeks of camp every summer. I also decided that retailing seemed the only work I was qualified for, so I decided to take it seriously and applied for the junior executive training program at Rich's department store, an Atlanta institution. I was accepted, to start upon my return from my military training. Just before I departed, I was informed that the ANG quota for the tech school had been canceled and that I would receive only basic training; not bad, I thought—satisfying my military obligation with only two months of active duty. Little did I know.

I arrived at Lackland Air Force Base in San Antonio, Texas, in

March of 1960 for basic training. A couple fellows I had gone to college with, Tom Young and Bob Tolleson, were in my barracks, and we looked forward to getting this over with. Our drill sergeants were loud and scary, and it was clear they weren't going to be much fun. On the first day they picked out the biggest man in the unit and made him the acting barracks chief. This would have been all right, but as the week wore on it became obvious to all of us that this guy was as intellectually lame as he was big, and that we had to do something to keep him from being made permanent in the job.

Finally, taking a deep breath and my life in my hands, I went to the barracks office and requested permission to speak to the two growling sergeants, neither of whom was more than five feet six inches tall. I was received with snarls and told to speak up and get out. Nervously, anxious not to annoy them further, I explained that some of us in the unit were concerned about our temporary barracks chief becoming permanent, and that we thought we would perform better if lead by someone else. This request was received, at first, in stony silence. Finally, I was asked who I would suggest might be better? I suggested that Bob Tolleson, who had been the cadet colonel of the ROTC at Georgia, might be ideal. Then I was told, abruptly, to get the fuck out. I returned to my bunk, sweating, and told the others what had transpired.

The following day, five of us, including Tom Young and Bob Tolleson, were called into the sergeants' office and told that four of us were element chiefs and that I was the new permanent barracks chief.

Having never before been suspected of having any leadership skills, I was flabbergasted. It must have shown, because the sergeants felt it necessary to explain that I had been given the job because "It took guts to come in here and tell us what you did." I was learning that it was a good idea to keep your mouth shut in the military.

Being barracks chief had some advantages, though. For one thing, I got to assign people to work details, and I always managed to assign myself to some duty during physical training, which, as always, I detested. Our sergeants turned out to be a lot better than any of us had suspected. Our flight did very well; week after week we won the "honor flight" designation, which gave us a TV set in the barracks and weekend passes. We rubbed the competitions' nose in it by erecting a barracks sign that had another plaque added for each week we won. I was doing more and more of the administrative stuff, which gave the sergeants more time off. One of them tended to get loaded at the NCO club and not show up for morning roll call, and I, standing in the predawn darkness would yell out "All present or accounted for," pretending to be him. I had basic training pretty well taped.

Then things went wrong. Apparently because our flight was consistently making all the other flights (and their sergeants) look bad, both of our sergeants were suddenly replaced. I groaned inside, not looking forward to the prospect of training new sergeants. Almost immediately, I was stripped of my high position and returned to the ranks; the reason given was that my dodging PT had been discovered. The last couple of weeks were hell; they were just like basic training.

Finally completing basic, I arrived back in Atlanta ready for my exciting new position at Rich's. I was assigned as junior assistant buyer in the bedding department, and it didn't take long to learn that mattresses weren't as much fun as they sounded. My boss had suffered a career disaster in outdoor furniture and, for his trouble, had been parked in bedding, and he wasn't great company.

When I was a senior in high school, I had read a piece in the paper by Edith Hills Coogler, the women's editor, and I had written her an amusing letter about it. She replied, saying, "I don't know who you are, but you should be a writer." Learning that I was a student, she invited me to call her if ever I was in Atlanta.

I suddenly remembered this, so I called her. She immediately said she would see what she could do at the paper about an interview. And then she began to include me in her circle of friends, who were very amusing company. Edith said that, if I were patient, she would find something for me at the paper. I wasn't patient; I quit my job at Rich's.

My social life improved in Atlanta. I was sharing an apartment with an old friend from UGA, Rutledge Carpenter, and I met a girl we'll call Gloria, who completed my instruction in Sex-Ed 101. She was the mistress of a Coca-Cola high executive, who had parked her in a very nice apartment where she was supposed to wait for him to call. Sometimes, she didn't feel like waiting, and she called me instead, and we covered the rest of the course materials over a period of weeks. This did a lot to prepare me for living in New York later.

Then John F. Kennedy got the Democratic nomination, to run against Richard Nixon, and I signed on for the Georgia campaign.

I was very excited about this young and attractive senator, who seemed not all that much older than I. Georgia being one of only four states, at the time, that allowed eighteen-year-olds to vote, I suggested to those above me that we should make a special effort to attract student votes. I was given an interview with the Georgia cochairman of the Kennedy campaign, Judge Griffin Bell, who would later become attorney general of the United States in the Carter administration. I told him my idea about seeking the votes of the youngest voters. He asked me and a classmate and fraternity brother at Georgia, Jay Cox, to be cochairmen of a college campaign, I in Greater Atlanta and Jay in the rest of the state. I attacked the job with relish. I visited every college in Greater Atlanta, speaking to students and getting a good reception. As we moved into autumn, though, I was out of money. I had been writing short stories and sending them off to the *New Yorker* and the *Saturday*

Evening Post (the same stories to both, which shows you how dumb I was) and just as regularly, getting rejection slips back.

One morning in late September, when I had borrowed about as much money as I could from home, a rejection slip from the *New Yorker* arrived. In what I can only describe as a fit of pique, or perhaps, an act of furious desperation, I called Judge Bell, resigned from the campaign, sold my car, bought a one-way ticket to New York, and never looked back.

Now, finally, real life was about to begin.

12

I phoned a friend in New York from UGA, Hugh Rosenthal, with whom I had worked on the Jazz Society concerts, and he was kind enough to offer me a bed for a few days.

My first night in New York, Hugh was busy, so I got myself to Greenwich Village, though I had a hell of a time finding a cab. (I later learned that it was Rosh Hashanah, and half the cabdrivers in New York at that time were Jewish.)

I was wandering down Bleecker Street when a door opened and closed, and I heard a snatch of a jazz pianist at work.

The place was called the Surf Maid, and I went inside to find a nine-foot Steinway grand with bar stools around it. So I took a seat and ordered a drink.

The pianist's name was Kenny Watts, and he was accompanied by Gene Ramey on bass. Occasionally, a customer would sing something, and after a couple of bourbons, I asked if I could sing. Kenny had once worked for singers like Ella Fitzgerald, and I had never sung with anybody that good. For the next few years I would be in that place a couple of nights a week, along with a dozen or so talented amateurs or failed professionals, singing my heart out. (The manager of the place, who was always seated at the cash register, was a woman named Elaine Kaufman, who would later open her own, eponymous restaurant uptown and become world famous.) She was handcuffed to the cash register, so we never met until years later.

Hugh was living with a roommate in a studio, which in New York means one room with a kitchen and bath. I slept on the sofa for a couple of nights, then Hugh gave me a copy of the *New York Times* and told me it was time to find a home. In almost no time I had sublet a very nice studio at 49 East 63rd Street, near Park Avenue, which was pretty elegant, with high ceilings, a tiny kitchen, and two Danish-style sofas, one of which represented the master bedroom. I rented a typewriter, wrote up a résumé, and started making phone calls to newspapers and magazines; everybody was firing, not hiring.

The Barbizon Hotel for Women, sometimes known among young men as the Tower of Flesh, was a block away and they had a little coffee shop where a fellow could go and find a sandwich and a cup of coffee and, with a little luck, a girl. Things were pretty good; except I was running out of money again.

I met a guy in advertising who told me that ad agencies had training programs for people like me, though I was unlikely to get a writing job because you needed an uncle in the copy department to arrange that.

Realizing that my résumé was pretty skimpy, I typed out a two-page, single-spaced letter highly recommending myself as a talented and hardworking young man, then signed my own name and sent it to a list of agencies the adman had given me. Now they actually had me in for an interview before they told me to go away, and at BBDO (Batten, Barton, Durstine & Osborn) I got an offer to join their training program at the princely salary of seventy dollars a week. (It is a mark of my value to the agency that my secretary was making eighty dollars a week.) I was installed in a cubicle in offices apparently designed in the 1930s, given a Remington Noiseless typewriter, a calculator, and a sheaf of raw data, and instructed to start tabulating the results of a study done by a client. I labored over this for about ten days. When I turned in the finished product it was discovered that I had misplaced a decimal point or something, and the resulting numbers showed the opposite of what they were supposed to show. This event had the sort of happy result of convincing my betters that I was un-suited for such work, and they started looking for another way for me to prove myself.

While they were doing that, I read a copy of *Madison Avenue* magazine, a slick trade journal, and discovered something inter-esting. They had published eight photographs by famous photog-raphers and were holding a contest: readers were invited to write an ad for any product or service, inspired by one of the photo-graphs. I chose a still life of foods by Irving Penn, I think, and wrote an ad for Campbell's Soup Company, a BBDO client. The only line I remember was "Newify your noons."

To my astonishment, I was one of the winners, one for each photograph, and we were promised a fabulous lunch at an ex-pensive French restaurant for our efforts.

This attracted some attention in the copy department at BBDO, since a number of its writers—including the copy chief—had en-tered the contest and not won. As a result, I was given something called a copy test, which was a lot like the photo contest without the photos, and it was sent to Jim Jordan, a hotshot copy super-visor who was reputed to be rising fast. He had just been made a vice president of BBDO, the youngest in the agency. He agreed to give me a try on the Schaefer Beer account.

I began to churn out thirty-second television commercials to be read live by a sportscaster named Win Elliot, who was under contract to Schaefer, and who would stand at a racetrack, a ball park, or a hockey rink and read my copy from a teleprompter, while holding up a bottle of beer and pointing at it.

The tagline for Schaefer Beer, in all its ads and commercials, was: "In the best of circles, it's Schaefer all around." There followed standard body copy which included a line I liked better: "Schaefer is the one beer to have when you're having more than one." At a meeting in Jim's office, I pointed out the line, which had probably been written by Jim, and said I thought it was much better than "Circles," and that it should be the tagline. The group exchanged glances, which made me think that either somebody had already suggested that or wished he had. It turned out that a secret poll authorized by the agency had discovered the interesting fact that eighty percent of all beer was drunk by twenty percent of beer drinkers. Suddenly, I had science on my side.

The agency's jingle-writing team whipped up a tune for our new tagline, and shortly, it was being heard in commercials all over town. Not only that, but it became responsible for my becoming acquainted with some of the jazz giants of the day.

An arranger, a bass player named George Romanis, wrote a dozen arrangements of the tune in different band styles, and I got to spend several days in a recording studio with a big band that included trombonist Urbie Green, trumpeter Clark Terry; a rhythm section of pianist Hank Jones, bassist Milt Hinton, drummer Ossie Johnson; and several other big names. I was in hog heaven.

Between takes, Hank, Milt, and Ossie agreed to back me while I recorded an up-tempo version of "The Whiffenpoof Song." I kept that tape for decades, before it finally disintegrated. Hank and I became good friends, and I would go and hear him play in the bands of the big variety TV shows, like Jackie Gleason and Perry Como. I got free tickets from BBDO and the best seats. They would first do a dress rehearsal, then follow it later with a taping of the show. There were guest stars like Harry Belafonte and others, so it was a good evening's entertainment. Hank and I would get some dinner between the dress rehearsal and the taping, and one evening, walking down Broadway, we ran into someone he knew, a small Black man wearing a sharp suit and a porkpie hat. "Stuart," Hank said, "this is Coleman Hawkins." He was only about the best tenor sax player working at the time. I was nearly speechless. Nearly.

The other members of Jim Jordan's group were Bob Miller, my supervisor on Schaeffer; Charlie Healy, who, while studying for the priesthood, had bailed out of the seminary at the last possible minute; and Ed Gallagher, whose best friend was Bob Newhart, a hot new stand-up comedian. They had known each other in Chicago, where Bob had worked as an accountant, and they began doing comedy routines at parties. Someone in the record business heard them, edited out Ed, and sent Bob to Dallas to work a couple of weeks in a nightclub. They recorded his performances, and the result was a monumental bestselling LP called *The Button-Down Mind of Bob Newhart*.

When Bob came to New York to make his Carnegie Hall debut, he invited our group to attend, and we went to a big party afterward. The opening act for the evening was the Chad Mitchell Trio, one of his backup singers being an unknown named John Denver.

When the sublease on my apartment was up, I moved to another sublease, then I found an apartment at 11 West Ninth Street, in the Village, a place a friend of mine said had "a certain seedy elegance," sharing it with a guy named Roland Michaud, an illustrator in the BBDO art department. Roland was also a gifted cartoonist, his work running in national magazines. I also had to transfer from my Georgia Air National Guard unit in Atlanta to a New York Air National Guard unit in Roslyn, on Long Island, the closest to New York, so I did my weekend training there.

About a year after I moved to New York, one night in the

autumn of 1961, I was singing in the Surf Maid, and when I finished, I heard a snatch of news on somebody's portable radio that mentioned my NYANG unit in Roslyn. Nobody else seemed to have heard it, so I went to the phone booth and called WNEW Radio and asked for the newsroom. That was how I learned that, because the Soviet Union had built the Berlin Wall, my unit, including me, had been recalled to active duty in the United States Air Force and was being sent to Germany.

So much for the bachelor life of an adman in the big city. I gave up my new apartment, stored most of my clothes and other meager possessions, quit my job, and reported for duty on faraway Long Island.

13

Our unit, the 152nd Tactical Control Group, was ostensibly a highly trained team that controlled fighter aircraft from radar screens on the ground in combat situations. In fact, the controllers were working on Korean War–era radars, and nobody in the unit seemed to know much about anything, except a few full-timers who worked every day at the Roslyn station.

Nobody had expected to get recalled to active duty, and our officers were scrambling to figure out what to do next. What they did first was give everybody a physical and inoculate us with guns that mixed vaccines for a dozen diseases. The next morning, I was itchy and discovered that most of my body was covered with a bright red rash. Our unit's doctor sent me to a dermatologist at a nearby naval hospital. My examiner gave me some antihistamines and some lotion to apply, then he said to me, "Do you want out?"

"Out of what?" I asked.

"The military. It's clear that you have a serious allergy to something, and that is disqualifying, if that's what you want. This will happen again."

I was taken aback. Of course, I wanted out; we all did. In fact, a couple of guys had already used family or political connections to get out. I thought about it, but I had given up my apartment, quit my job, and stored my possessions. Jim Jordan and my copy group had thrown a farewell lunch for me at the Waldorf. I couldn't go slinking back and explain that I had gotten out of serving because of a rash.

"No thanks," I said. "I'll stick it out."

The doctor shrugged. "You're a patriot."

A MONTH LATER, HAVING VOLUNTEERED for an advance party of sixty or so who were to prepare barracks for our unit, I boarded the top airliner of the day, a Lockheed Constellation, the Air Force version with web seating, and we took off from Floyd Bennett Field in Brooklyn for our refueling stop in the Azores. Almost halfway there, we lost one of our four engines and were told to turn around and fly to back to Virginia. As we flew up the East Coast, weather began to worsen and closed all the airports along our route, one after another, until we finally were able to land at Gander, in Newfoundland, where we waited a day for a new engine, then took off to fly directly to Kaiserslautern, in Germany. From there we were driven to our new headquarters on an Army base in Mannheim.

Our barracks had been built during World War II by the SS of stone and concrete and featured very large rooms which would easily contain four double-decker bunks and eight large, steel lockers. My job was to assemble these lockers from kits. I have never been of a mechanical bent, and I always seemed to have a few screws and bolts left over.

Once the whole unit arrived, I was assigned to be the chaplain's assistant, a job nobody else wanted. The chaplain was a nice man, but there was little to do; we didn't even have a chapel. Shortly, I was reassigned to the motor pool. I didn't know the first thing about maintaining vehicles, but I knew how to drive them.

For a while, I was assigned to be the driver for our commanding officer, Colonel Magalhaes, who in civilian life was a public relations officer for the New York Telephone Company.

I was given this assignment because nobody else in the motor pool wanted to wear a Class A uniform every day. They were all grease monkeys and preferred fatigues.

The 152nd was an odd group. There were seventeen lawyers among us, none of whom ranked higher than staff sergeant, and none of them were assigned to do anything involving the law. One sergeant I knew had been, in civilian life, the boss of a man he now reported to in the Air Force. He had an easy life.

Our radar screens were installed in a large tent on another part of our base. Suddenly, these ANG controllers were doing exercises with real airplanes, and the results were, shall we say, uneven. One day we had a surprise inspection by a brigadier general from Air Force headquarters, and I drove him and my colonel to the big tent, then waited a couple of hours while the general conducted a surprise inspection. Finally, the two of them got back into the car. There was a long silence, then the general said, "Tell you what, Colonel. We'll have another surprise inspection at ten a.m., a week from Thursday."

I was often sent other places to deliver or pick up officers or supplies. Once I was tooling down the autobahn in my Air Force Ford station wagon, doing about 110 mph, when I passed a Mercedes sedan as if it were standing still, practically blowing its doors off. A moment later I checked my rearview mirror and saw the car gaining on me, flashing its lights. I was baffled, but I pulled into a rest stop.

The Mercedes followed me, and I could see that it contained a man, a woman, and two children. I got out of the station wagon to be greeted by a red-faced man of about fifty wearing civilian clothes. "May I help you, sir?" I asked.

He whipped out an Air Force ID card, which identified him as the director of transportation for the U.S. Air Force in Europe. He chewed me up one side and down the other, while I stood braced at attention, sweating. Finally, promising to turn me in to my commanding officer, he got back into his Mercedes and proceeded down the autobahn at about 60 mph, while I followed about half a mile back, careful not to gain on him.

Soon I became the envy of the motor pool because everybody suddenly wanted my easy job, and I found myself in fatigues, sanding trucks for painting with sandpaper dipped in gasoline. My friend, the allergy, returned, and the doctor excused me from that duty because of the rash on my hands. I had learned something, though: the gasoline supply in our motor pool came from a big tanker truck, and we drew fuel from that as needed, filling five-gallon jerry cans from a huge stack. The fuel from the truck was unmetered, and no records were kept of gasoline usage.

I had by this time discovered the lovely town of Heidelberg, ten miles away down the autobahn. I hung out at a fourteenth-century bierstube called Zum Seppl, in Hauptmann Strasse, where the beer was good, the waitresses were charming, and the food was excellent, as long as you liked red cabbage with everything, and I did. I occasionally rented Volkswagen Beetles from a guy with a small lot. One day he asked me if I could get him some cheap Air Force gasoline from the PX filling station. A larcenous light popped on in my head.

I tell you this only in the certain knowledge that the statute of limitations on this activity expired sixty years ago. Hans and I entered into an arrangement whereby, when the motor pool was deserted except for me, as it often was, I would fill a bunch of jerry cans with gas from the big tanker truck, put them into the back of a one-and-a-half-ton truck, drive them to Heidelberg, exchange them for empty cans, then drive back to the motor pool. As a result, I had the use of a Beetle every weekend for the remainder of my tour.

If I had been caught, I would probably still be in Leavenworth.

.14

Suddenly, I realized that I was, for the first time, in Europe, which was full of places I had only dreamed of visiting. I got some leave and lit out for Paris. I hitched an airplane ride to an Air Force base near a French village called Laon, about eighty miles north of Paris in the Champagne country. From there I caught a train for the big city. I bought a map, found a cheap hotel, and set out to see the sites. All this was on short notice, so I was ill-prepared.

The only contact I had in Paris was that BBDO, my New York employer, had a new office in the city. I dropped in and was introduced to the newly appointed managing director, a man named Jean Chevalier. I mentioned that my middle name was Chevalier, and we became brothers. Jean, apparently with time on his hands, insisted on taking me to lunch. I had never heard of the restaurant he chose, Brasserie Lipp, in St. Germain des Pres, an artsy neighborhood

Jean was greeted by the maître d' and we were given a table in what I later learned was whatever the Parisian opposite was of Siberia. We were surrounded by beautiful and interesting people from the film, publishing, and art worlds. The food was Alsatian, and excellent.

Jean explained to me that his real work was as a fashion photographer. He wasn't sure why he was offered the job at BBDO, but I guess the money was good. Then he told me a story:

"Some years ago, I got a call from a magazine wanting a cover photograph of a mother and daughter. I had cast the mother, but I was having trouble finding a daughter who looked good with her. Then I remembered a family I knew who had a lovely sixteen-year-old, so I called her mother and asked if she could pose for me. She was against it, but finally agreed, as long as it was only once. She didn't want a lot of attention for her young child. The magazine ran, and I began to get calls from people I knew in the film and modeling industries, demanding to know who the girl was and how to find her. Finally, I called her mother and persuaded her to let me have one producer speak to her at home. Reluctantly, she consented, and the producer sent his assistant to the house to interview the girl.

"When he rang the bell, the girl answered the door, and lightning struck. The assistant's name was Roger Vadim, and the girl was Brigitte Bardot. I don't think her mother ever forgave me."

I have been to Brasserie Lipp dozens of times since, though it took me a while to earn a table in heaven, instead of being sent upstairs with the tourists.

I HAD THREE NIGHTS IN Paris, all but exhausting my meager funds, then I got on the train back to Laon, and once there, called the Air Force base to hitch a ride. I was told that there were no flights available, and what was more, there was no bed available in the transient enlisted men's quarters. I could call back the following day.

I walked out of the station and looked around. Laon seemed

a dull place, until I turned around and saw a huge hill rising out of the flat plain, with a cog railway going up its side.

I bought a ticket and after the steep climb was deposited in a beautiful old village atop the mountain, and shortly I found a suitable hotel. The place was run, almost single-handedly, by an elderly man whose English was good. After dinner that evening he bought me a cognac and regaled me with stories of fighting in the Resistance during World War II. It surprised me that the war had touched such a small town, far from Paris or Normandy.

"Where did you find weapons?" I asked.

"We fought with our *fingers*," he replied.

This was brought home to me when I visited a square where there was a memorial to sixty men, women, and children, who had been lined up against a wall and machine-gunned by the Nazis.

Two DAYS LATER I GOT an Air Force flight back to Germany and arrived back at the 152nd before they could list me as AWOL.

MY OTHER GREAT ADVENTURE AROSE from my thus-far short career in New York advertising. Our ANG headquarters, back in New York State, shipped our CO a 16 mm silent movie camera and a crate of film and told him to have a film made about our group, which had a half dozen smaller units scattered around Germany.

The colonel, in his wisdom, passed this off to a young lieutenant who had previously mentioned that he had fooled around with home movies, and the lieutenant, whom I had driven somewhere once, remembered that I was a writer of films, albeit very short ones. The colonel gave us the trusty Ford station wagon and some per diem and told us to come back with a movie.

Armed with a list of our scattered units and a Michelin road map, we set off into Germany, an unexplored territory outside the gates of our base. Over a period of about ten days, we drove to each of the units, from Bavaria to near the North Sea, presenting ourselves to the local COs and asking permission to film. Nobody turned us down; I suppose the colonel had warned them we were coming.

We had a wonderful trip. All these bases were located outside small towns, many of them charming. We found rooms at local *gasthauses* and dinner wherever we could. We filmed for a day, then moved on to the next base.

When we returned with an unholy mess of unrelated scenes, a guy named Hal, who was a film editor for a New York commercial studio, cut it into something resembling a narrative, though without a narration. I cobbled together a script which followed the narrative, then we shipped the whole thing back to head-quarters and let them deal with finishing it. I heard later that they had loved it.

I had had a tour of out-of-the-way Germany that most tourists never see, all on Uncle Sam's dime, and I had freed myself from the drudgery of the motor pool for the duration. I went back to stealing gasoline.

My FINAL PLUNGE INTO THE unknown came when I ran into a girl I had known at the University of Georgia, named Marilyn Eckberg, who was working at Ramstein Air Base in a clerical job. I had made several trips there, ferrying people and goods, and we had dinner. Marilyn told me about a special Army train that ran daily between Frankfurt and Berlin, carrying only military and government personnel. Easter was around the corner, and we decided to go.

Back at my base I made inquiries, learning that the train existed, and began filling out the voluminous paperwork necessary to secure two seats, which had to be submitted to the Army and then to the Russian authorities in Berlin. All this had to be accomplished without typos or erasures, which was one of the Russians' ways of harassing us. If you made a mistake, you had to start over.

Finally, we had it together. We met in Frankfurt and boarded the train, the commanding officer of which was a first lieutenant from Tennessee. He told us that when we crossed the border into the Berlin military zone, the Russians would board the train and meticulously check everyone's papers. If they were not perfectly executed, the offender would be yanked off the train and sent back to Frankfurt on the return trip. He also told us that the Russian guards were fond of girlie magazines and liked to trade.

I had picked up a *Playboy* at the Frankfurt station (only for the articles, of course), so when we creaked to a halt in some lost station on the edge of Berlin, I was ready for the Russians. I exchanged the magazine for a star from a Russian Army cap, and the Russian soldier got the best of the bargain. Our commander, the lieutenant, told us that once, somebody had traded a bottle of cognac for an entire Russian Army uniform, including boots, and since the soldiers were issued only one uniform, somebody that morning had showed up for assembly in his skivvies. Everybody thought this was a hoot except, possibly, the semi-naked Russian.

Berlin was a surprise. It seemed more like Paris than I had imagined, with broad boulevards and outdoor cafes. An old Georgia friend in New York, Lee Jordan, who was the theater critic for the local CBS radio station, had introduced me to an American named Mark White, who was head of the Voice of America station in Berlin, and he had booked us rooms at the Hilton at a rate that even I could afford. He took us to dinner and gave us suggestions for entertainment, one of which was a concert being given by the jazz vocal group Lambert, Hendricks & Ross in a Berlin suburb.

They were great favorites of mine, and we took a cab to the theater and loved every note they sang. When the concert ended, we found ourselves in a deserted area of the city, with no sign of a cab. There was, however, a U-Bahn (subway). We had been briefed before our departure and told that travel on the U-Bahn was permitted for us, but not the S-Bahn (the elevated railway), because the S-Bahn went into East Berlin, carrying essential workers, and didn't come back.

I asked the ticket seller if the train went to the *stadtmitte* (the city center), figuring we could get a cab from there to our hotel. He replied in the affirmative, and we boarded the next train. Our fellow travelers looked like essential workers. Now and then, the train stopped, and passengers got off, but none got on. Finally, we came to a station called Stadtmitte. When the train stopped we rose to get off. The other passengers, who had ignored us up until then, raised their hands and shouted, *"Nein! Das ist Stadtmitte!"* I in my, shall we say, incomplete German told them that the *stadtmitte* was where we wanted to go. *"Nein!"* they shouted back. *"Das ist Ost-Berlin."*

I understood that all right. We had also been told that we could travel to East Berlin only on military tour buses, and that to do so, all military personnel had to be in full uniform. Since I had forgotten to bring my uniform cap, I didn't have a full uniform.

"What are we going to do?" Marilyn asked, as the train began to move again.

"We were told that, if we found ourselves afoot in East Berlin, we were to report to the nearest Russian military installation, since the U.S. does not recognize the government of East Germany, nor its police force." This news did not cheer her up.

After several more stops, the train ground to a halt at a station with an unfamiliar name, and everyone aboard got off. Last stop.

We got off, too, since the alternative was probably to be arrested if we remained aboard, and we climbed the stairs to the street. We emerged into a leafy residential square, and there was a taxi stand at hand, with a single cab waiting for a fare.

"Here we go," I said, taking Marilyn's hand and loading her into the taxi.

"Sprecken zie English?" I asked the driver.

"*Jah*," he replied.

I drew a deep breath. "Please take us to the nearest Russian military installation."

He gazed at me with his brow furrowed. "But that's in East Berlin," he said.

"Aren't we in East Berlin?" I asked.

"*Nein*. West Berlin."

I finally let out my breath. "Please take us to the Hilton Hotel," I said. Apparently, the train we had ridden passed into East Berlin, where essential workers would get off, then continued in a loop, back into West Berlin.

We would sleep in soft beds, instead of on iron cots.

15

I found, after returning from my leave in Berlin, that only one interesting thing had occurred in my absence: a representative of the American intelligence community, presumably, CIA, had addressed my assembled unit and explained to them that the number of American divisions stationed in West Germany was a small fraction of the Soviet divisions stationed in East Germany. And, in the event of an invasion from the east, it would take perhaps two or three days before Mannheim and our unit would be overrun by the Russian Army. Food for thought.

Everything else that happened was much like what had preceded my Easter holiday. So, when July arrived without Soviet tanks in the streets of Mannheim, everyone was relieved to be told that we had completed our mission, i.e., frightening the Soviets into staying on their side of the border, and (they apparently had not heard about our surprise inspection) we were going home.

Dreading the long, upwind flight aboard a Constellation, we were delighted to be herded aboard the new Miracle of the Skies, a Boeing 707, the first American jetliner, which would make the flight in eight hours or so. I looked forward to enjoying the view of the Atlantic Ocean, but it turned out that the Air Force cargo version of the 707 had no windows. It was like flying in a submarine. It also had only enough airline-type seats for the officers. I managed to get some sleep atop a tightly packed rubber life raft.

We landed at Andrews Air Force Base, in Maryland, where I expected long lines for processing. To my surprise, I walked up to a long table, turned in my Air Force ID card, and was handed my discharge from the Air Force (but not from the NYANG), an airline ticket, and some cash for ground transportation. Then, after a cursory look into my duffel bag at U.S. Customs, I found myself on the sidewalk, a civilian once again. Anxious to complete the process, I changed into civvies in the men's room, called a friend in New York and begged for a couple of nights' lodging. Then got a cab, an airplane, and another cab to New York City.

By early evening I was having a beer at Malachy's, which had moved uptown from East Sixty-Third Street. The following morning, wearing my only suit that wasn't in storage, one purchased at the Mannheim PX, I delivered myself to BBDO. Hardly anyone noticed. I was given yet another cubicle and another Remington Noiseless typewriter, with which to ply my trade. In due course, I was given a raise to eighty dollars a week. I had caught up with my secretary. I didn't ask if she had gotten a raise in my absence; I didn't want to know.

After a few months of this it came to my attention that Madison Avenue was home to many advertising agencies, and some of them paid better than BBDO. I had enough completed work, by then, to put together a portfolio, and though not terribly impressive, it got me a better job at a smaller, but highly creative agency called DeGarmo. My two bosses were Adrienne Claiborne, a former writer at Doyle Dane Bernbach, and Bill McCauliffe, an art director. The agency did sterling work and demanded better from me than BBDO, and I made a couple of thousand dollars a year more. I could now actually pay my rent, and I moved into a tiny, under-the-eaves apartment at 69 West Tenth Street in Greenwich Village. It was upstairs over a tiny Russian restaurant called Alex's Borscht Bowl, owned by a tiny Russian chef, and, on the second floor, Ruth's Poodle Shop, which specialized in the laundering and barbering of tiny dogs.

I furnished my apartment with cast-off furniture from my neighbors that had been left on the street for trash collection. I set about becoming a slightly bohemian Villager and bought a motor scooter on which to get around. My sex life improved. Adventurous young women abounded in Greenwich Village.

It could be exciting at times. One evening while adjusting the rabbit ears on my new TV, I looked out the single rear window, which overlooked the roofs of buildings behind mine, and saw a man who was, well, lurking, and peeking into the apartment of some girls I knew, who were having a party. I didn't have a phone yet, so I ran downstairs, around the corner, and up their stairs and knocked on the door. A girl opened it and invited me in.

"Don't look out the rear windows," I said. "There's a man lurking out there. Call the police and continue as you were."

She gave me a drink and did as she was told. I wandered around, occasionally casting an eye at a rear window, and wondered where the hell the cops were. They turned up in about a half an hour, two uniformed patrolmen, and I followed them out onto the roof terrace. I got a glimpse of the furtive man as he saw who was coming for him, then he turned and, in a couple of bounds up a drainpipe, leapt onto the roof above and ran like a deer. To my absolute astonishment, one of the cops drew his .38 and fired two shots at him, apparently missing.

"But he wasn't *doing* anything," I said. "Just lurking."

"Okay," the cop said, reholstering his pistol, "we'll call it in." And they left.

I had a couple of more free drinks, then tottered back to my place. I had been a denizen of Greenwich for less than a week, and I had seen shots fired!

In due course (I'm sorry to keep using that expression, but it is, after all, useful), I moved on from DeGarmo to Cunningham & Walsh, a larger, but less exciting agency, for a five-thousand-dollar raise. This was fun! It was the golden era of advertising, and a kid with a decent portfolio could walk across the street and get a five-thousand-dollar raise! I went apartment hunting.

I wanted more space for my money, and it became clear that I wasn't going to find that in the West Village, which was the high-rent district, so I ventured into the East Village, where I found just the spot at 28 St. Marks Place, which is what East Eighth Street is called in the East Village. It had a large living room, a bedroom, a bath, and a decent kitchen, and it had, of all things, a garden!

The term "garden" is used loosely in the East Village, but it was, I like to point out, outdoors. Across a concrete patio and up a couple of steps and you found yourself ankle-deep in crabgrass, which I thought grew only in the suburbs. It had a tree, too, really a giant weed, which occasionally produced a spidery covering of a disgusting white substance.

I had my cast-off sofa reupholstered and found a carpentry shop on the Bowery that made me some bookcases. In no time I had found a round dining table and some chairs, had the floors stained, hung some pictures, and voilà, a home!

Later, I rented an elderly grand piano, which I couldn't play much, but it was great at parties, as long as I invited a piano player.

I settled into St. Marks Place, which had been, the year before, an area populated by Russian and Polish immigrants, with a few Puerto Ricans thrown in for seasoning. There were still, too, a few old Jews, who had been there longer than anybody, and they ran businesses like the corner candy store and the barbershop, where an eighty-year-old gentleman named Sam would give me an occasional, smooth shave with his straight razor.

Across the street from number 28 was an old Polish social club, called the Dom, which somebody bought and turned into the Electric Circus, the first, I think, electronic disco.

Thereafter, the block was filled every night with tourists from Queens and New Jersey, and fairly quickly, the Russians, Poles, and Jews were edged out by gentrification.

Fortunately, my apartment was in the rear of my building, behind a head shop, so the noise didn't penetrate my perch. Once I came out my front door and was astonished to see a couple of thousand people crammed into my block, listening to a very noisy rock band on a truck bed. I hadn't heard a thing inside.

I had interesting neighbors, too. One day I walked out onto my rear patio, and a garden-level window in the building next door was, for the first time, open. A very beautiful girl was standing at the sink, doing the dishes, facing my patio. I immediately, if lamely, engaged her in conversation. Turned out she was a visitor, not the resident, and the lessee of the apartment was Abbie Hoffman, who was out of town, protesting the Vietnam War, or whatever else was available.

She soon finished the dishes, closed the window, and that was that. I never laid eyes on her again, nor on Mr. Hoffman.

16

After a modest stretch at Cunningham & Walsh, I got bored, and entrepreneurship raised its head. I knew a young man we'll call J., who had his own, tiny ad agency, and I ran my idea by him. Somebody—in Boston, I think—had started what I believe was the first computer dating service. I thought to start one in New York, which, with its zillions of singles, practically yearned for it.

J. thought it was a good idea. I called a few friends, who each contributed a thousand dollars, and found a computer service company that could do the computing. A lawyer friend from my Air Force days, Herb Fisher, created a corporation. And finally, I found a shrink who agreed to collaborate with me on a questionnaire in return for some of the stock. I rented a small office suite, leased some furniture, hired two young women to handle the questionnaires when they came in, and voilà, we were in business. I called it *Click!*, and an art director friend, Carol Nelson, turned that name into business stationery and designed the questionnaire.

I bought a little ad space from the *Village Voice*, which had a youthful audience, then wrote an ad with the headline:

WE'D LIKE TO SAY A FEW WORDS
ABOUT HETEROSEXUALITY:
IT'S COMING BACK.

This explained how you called a number to be sent a questionnaire, filled it out, then mailed it in with a check for something like five dollars. The questionnaires were turned over to the
computer service, who tabulated the answers, and their IBM 360
compared the answers of one to all the others, then printed out a
list of compatible people of the opposite sex and their phone
numbers. After that, it was up to them.

The response was remarkable. Hundreds of questionnaires
poured in, and we were, in a small way, profitable. I continued to
run the ad, but with weaker results, as we used up the *Voice* read-
ership. I got an airline stewardess (as they were then called) to put
questionnaires in the individual mailboxes of her coworkers, and
that did well, too, until we used up that idea.

Clearly, we had to expand our reach, so I called the *New York
Times* and tried to place my ad. No dice. Apparently, some years
back there had been a bunch of people operating as matchmakers,
who charged people thousands of dollars and rarely produced
any matches. As a result, all the New York daily newspapers had
banned them as advertisers. They wouldn't listen to my argu-
ments that we were different.

So, I watched as my little business dried up and blew away.
My investors lost their money, and I filed for bankruptcy. J. sued
me. My debt was seventeen thousand dollars, which seemed a
hell of a lot, since my salary at C&W had been fifteen thousand.

I sent my portfolio to the copy chief at Young & Rubicam, an
old-line agency known for excellent creative work. He hired me
for seventeen thousand dollars a year. Bankruptcy had relieved

me of J.'s lawsuit and my debt, so I personally signed up to buy the office furniture at a big discount, moved it into my apartment and, eventually, worked off my debts.

Life at Y&R was wonderful; it was the best agency I'd worked for, and my work was good. After a while, I discovered that the agency had a London office, so I went to my boss, the copy chief, Al Frankel, and volunteered to give up my vacation time, if he would allow me to work for a couple of weeks in the London office. He said no. I loved the city, though, having been there only once. Thwarted, I happened to meet the president of Y&R International at a meeting and proposed my idea to him. He thought it a good one and sent me off to London.

I had a great time working there, made some friends, and managed to stretch my stay to six weeks. When I got back to New York, Al Frankel waited a few weeks, then fired me. He had loved my work, until I went to London. He had a bulletin board where he posted ads that he particularly liked, and he had put one of mine on that board. It was for Arrow Shirts, and contained a photo of a Tattersall checked shirt, explaining how a famous jockey, Richard Tattersall had, upon his retirement from the track, founded a horse sales business, where the buyers all wore waistcoats and the horses blankets made of Tattersall checked fabric. My headline read:

WE FOUND THIS CHECK
IN A LONDON HORSE MARKET.
A HORSE WAS WEARING IT.

Al had loved that, but he didn't love me anymore. Many years later, we happened to have dinner together, after I had spoken at the Ninety-Second Street YMCA, and he said he had no memory of ever firing me. I figured I could start lying about that on my résumé.

One of the odd things about my life is that nothing bad has

ever happened to me that didn't result in something better happening. This time, I read in the trades that Ron Rosenfeld, generally thought to be the best ad writer in the business, had joined J. Walter Thompson, a staid old agency that wanted to be thought of as creative, so they had hired Ron to start a new group. Ron had been a star at Doyle, Dane, Bernbach, the most creative agency in town, and J. Walter wanted some of that.

I knew Ron, having worked for his ex-wife at DeGarmo, and I called him immediately. We had a meeting, he liked my portfolio, and hired me. In college, I thought if I earned ten thousand dollars a year by the time I was thirty, I would consider myself a success. Ron and J. Walter paid me the princely sum of twenty-five thousand dollars a year. I bought a couple new suits.

One day, some weeks after I had joined Ron's group, his secretary walked into my office and said, "Go home and pack a bag. You're going to Scotland."

"When?" I asked.

"At two p.m.," she replied.

I packed a bag and at two p.m. I found myself aboard an airliner to Glasgow, in the company of a young art director called Tom. We had been sat down at the office and told that our task was to rejuvenate a new Scotch whisky called 100 Pipers, which had been introduced by an ad campaign that had failed.

We flew to Prestwick, in Scotland, where we were met by representatives of Chivas Brothers, now owned by our client, Seagram's. We were then given a tour of their blendery at Paisley where blenders sniffed at hundreds of Scotch whiskies in sherry glasses, dozens of which were selected to create a Scotch like Chivas Regal or 100 Pipers, which had been created as a sort of junior blend. They never tasted the stuff, convinced that tasting would ruin their palates.

From Paisley, we were loaded into a private aircraft and flown to the Scottish Highlands, where we visited various distilleries and admired the glorious scenery, which was, to the astonishment of its inhabitants, going through a sunny spell.

On the way back to New York I had a beautifully simple idea for 100 Pipers: we would photograph a bottle, above which ran a three-word headline: SON OF CHIVAS. That said it all, Tom and I were convinced, and we prepared ourselves to be greeted as returning heroes.

"Yeah," said the account executive we presented our idea to. "That's the third one of those we've seen. The client hated it."

Nobody had told us that we were the fourth team to try to crack that particular nut.

Things were changing back at J. Walter. There were rumors that Ron Rosenfeld was not getting along with top management, and that shouting matches had ensued.

There was a telephone technician now permanently working on the junction box in our hallway. Once, while chatting with Ron's secretary, I asked if I could use Ron's phone. He was out of the office.

"Yes," she had replied, "but be careful what you say on that telephone."

That should have brought me up short, but I had thought she was just joking. She wasn't.

The following morning I arrived at the office to learn that Ron Rosenfeld had been fired from J. Walter Thompson. We were all stunned. How could these Philistines fire the best writer in New York?

That afternoon I got a call from a friend who worked at *Madison Avenue* magazine, wanting to know the inside story of what had happened. I told him what little I knew.

"Can you find out more?" he asked.

"Well, I can sit here and wait for the rumors to arrive."

"If you find out, will you write a piece for us about it?"

"Sure, if I hear enough."

An hour or so later, I got a call from the administrative head of our department, wanting to see me immediately.

I walked into his office and was instantly fired and handed a check for my severance pay.

I began to wonder what that telephone tech had been doing at that junction box all that time.

It was a couple of days before I got a call from Ron, who told me his experience had been not unlike mine. We commiserated for a bit, promised to have lunch together, then hung up.

I was shocked to hear, a few years later, that the wonderful communicator, Ron Rosenfeld, had suffered a massive stroke and later died in a hospice without regaining his speech.

17

Word travels fast on Madison Avenue. When I got home there was a message from my friend Susan Friedman, who worked for Judy Wald, the hottest headhunter specializing in the ad business. She was calling from London.

Her agency had just opened an office there, and the city was ripe for an American invasion, so I should come quickly. The next day I was on a plane. Every day I would drive down Charles Street, where the Judy Wald office was located, and Susan would run alongside the car with a list of appointments for me.

I had interviews at, among others, Grey Advertising, a New York agency with a good-sized London operation. I met with the London creative director, Dick Karp, who was planning a permanent return to New York, then with the chairman, William Turnock. On my return to New York, I was interviewed by a senior creative executive named Sam. Then Turnock called and offered me a job as associate creative director, the idea being that I would replace Dick as creative director when he returned to New York. I accepted.

Every year for many years I had thrown a New Year's Eve Eve

party, on December 30. It was always well-attended because nobody had anything else to do on New Year's Eve Eve. The 1969 party was among the best: big crowd, my friend Ray Bryant, a brilliant pianist, playing the rented grand. I sold most of my furniture to friends, hanging on to my stereo equipment and records, my Eames lounge chair and ottoman, my Mies van der Rohe coffee table and all my books.

The following morning, the movers arrived, packed my stuff—all of it, since Grey was paying the bill—and my friend Lee Lawson, an actress, rode with me in the limo to the airport. I had ten pieces of luggage, half of them cardboard boxes, and a porter spotted it immediately as my stuff was unloaded. "You need special help," he said, and led me to a first-class counter. He exchanged a few quiet words with the airline representative, I slipped them each a fifty, and there was no charge for the extra weight. I kissed Lee goodbye and boarded. I asked the flight attendant to bring me a little bottle of champagne at midnight, then I fell asleep immediately after takeoff, still a little worse for wear from the New Year's Eve Eve party.

At midnight, as requested, she woke me, opened my champagne, and I celebrated New Year's Eve, almost alone in first class.

The following morning, January 1, 1970, I arrived at London Heathrow and was immediately detained by the authorities. It seemed that, not only did I not have a work permit for the U.K., but Grey had not even applied for one. The subject had never come up in my talks with them, and I was ignorant of the process.

I managed to get Bill Turnock on the phone out of a meeting, and he promised to give the matter his immediate attention. I spent four hours on a hard bench, waiting for his attention to bear fruit, and finally, it did. Grey's application had been received, and I entered the United Kingdom on a temporary work permit.

I settled in at Grey, met my creative partner, a talented art director named Terry, and began to learn to be a Londoner. It helped that I had friends from my Y&R time in London, and one of them had a sister who was an estate agent, who found me a delightful apartment in a delightful square called Ennismore Gardens, in Knightsbridge. It was the cellar of a larger apartment, and to reach it I had to first use my key to the beautiful, private gardens, then walk down a flight of stairs to my flat's entrance. It had a fireplace and was nicely furnished, and I managed to squeeze in my Eames chair and Mies coffee table.

I regarded owning a car in New York as a form of insanity, but London was different, offering neighborhood parking with a permit. I bought my first car in ten years, a new MGB-GT, and practiced driving on the wrong side of the road. (Watch out for that first right turn, or you'll end up in the wrong lane and meet a large, red bus coming the other way.)

I was earning the equivalent, in pounds, of twenty thousand dollars a year—less than in New York, but London was a *lot* less expensive. I was fitted for my first tailor-made suit at Blades, which cost one hundred guineas, or about $250, and a dozen Turnbull & Asser shirts. More than fifty years later, T&A still makes my shirts, and I have avoided a heart attack by never asking what they cost.

London restaurants were at least as good as those in New York, and my friends took me to their favorites. David Tree, with whom I had worked at Y&R in '68, was particularly kind about this, as was Matthew Neville-Bell. Matthew had been a practicing dentist in his youth, but he had made some money in real estate and given up dentistry.

(He told me a story about a female dentist friend of his who had done the same thing. One day she had an appointment with a new gynecologist and was on the table, in stirrups, while he conducted his examination. They fell into conversation, and he asked her what her work was.

"I used to be a dentist," she said, "but I found it boring and gave it up for real estate."

"Yes," he replied, examining away. "I never understood how some people could spend their entire careers looking into other peoples' mouths."

She laughed so hard, she fell off the table and had to reschedule.)

I found Englishwomen enchanting—warm and funny. One told me what women of different nationalities said, immediately after having sex. "A German girl says, 'Gut, now let's have something to eat.' A French girl says, 'You weel improve wiz practice.' An English girl says, 'There, dear. Is that better?' And an American girl says, 'Now you must think I'm awful.'"

I grew very fond of English girls.

A few weeks after my arrival at Grey Advertising, I came to work one day and got a call from the chairman, Bill Turnock, telling me that someone from the New York office had been sent to take over from Dick Karp as creative director. This came as a surprise because I had been promised the job when I was hired. Shortly, we were called into the big office to meet with our new boss. It turned out to be Sam, who had interviewed me in New York. Turnock told me it wasn't his choice, that New York had sent him. If he knew why, he wasn't telling.

Sam proved difficult to work with from the start. He never liked anything Terry and I showed him, but never had anything better to offer. We began avoiding him when we could.

I traveled to Newcastle, home of one of our biggest clients, Proctor & Gamble, to meet with their advertising team. Turnock led the charge, with Sam and me, finally, bringing up the rear. P&G had a horrible reputation for ruining good ideas by imposing their own, long-standing rules of how their products should be pitched, always gutting anything new or fresh.

I presented a TV commercial that we were proud of, and they

began to pick it apart. Finally, I said, "What you have suggested is like mixing apples and oranges—with nuts and bolts." This got a laugh, even from their ad people, and the commercial was saved.

On the way home on the train, Turnock complimented me, while Sam maintained a stony silence.

My year's lease on my flat came to an end, and my upstairs landlords wanted my flat back. He, the son of a viscount, had received a portion of his late father's estate, and they no longer needed the income from my rent.

I had some friends who lived across the street in Ennismore Gardens, expat Americans Bill and Susan Blackburn. I had met Bill in New York, and they had been very kind to me after I arrived in London, introducing me to Mimi Kilgore, Susan's sister, of whom I became very fond and still see when we find ourselves in the same city—usually New York or Houston, where she maintains homes.

The Blackburns had just bought a town house and were moving out of their large and handsome flat at No. 12A, on which they had a year left on their ninety-nine-year lease. (London flats are often sold as long leaseholds.) I paid what is called key money for some of the furnishings, they moved into their house, and I moved into the flat. I toured the street markets and found enough affordable furniture to make the place look inhabited. It was great for parties. I and a New York friend in London, Sandi Butchkiss, threw a party for our mutual friend Jerry Della Femina, a spectacularly successful New York ad agency owner, who had written a spectacularly successful book, *From Those Wonderful Folks Who Gave You Pearl Harbor, Front-Line Dispatches from the Advertising War*, and was in London to promote the book, which it is said to have inspired the TV series *Mad Men*.

The party was a spectacular success, too, because people

wanted to meet Jerry. Everybody who accepted our invitation showed up and brought a friend or two. It took a couple of days to clean up the flat.

WINTER CAME, AND I WENT skiing with some friends in Davos, where we stayed with some friends of theirs, Ralph and Kristin, a Swiss couple who owned a nice hotel there.

Days, we skied, sort of. I was on the cusp of moving up from the kiddie slopes to the intermediate class when my holiday time was up. That evening, we played poker and drank Steinhäger, a schnapps, washed down with beer. It was exhilarating.

The following morning, I said my sad goodbyes, left my newly acquired boots and sweaters in storage with Ralph and Kristin for a later visit, and got on the train to Zurich. This journey required a change of trains halfway there. One switched to the Zurich train, while the other continued to a town named Chur. I fell asleep and missed the change, waking up in time to read the name, Chur, on the station platform.

Having missed the Zurich change, and with no trains to Zurich available, I took the train back to Davos, arriving after dinner. I walked into the sitting room, where a poker game was in progress. Everybody took one look at me and burst into laughter. They gave me food, and I sat in on the game.

This was Sunday night, and I was due at the office for a big meeting with a client on Monday morning, so that wasn't going to happen. The following morning I couldn't reach Sam, so I asked Terry to tell him what had happened; only I had concocted a story about having been involved in a traffic accident and being required by the police to stay for a court hearing. It wasn't very good, but I thought it was better than telling them that I had slept through my stop and gone to the wrong town.

When I finally returned to London, later in the week, Sam

called me into his office and fired me. There was no conversation, so the meeting lasted about ten seconds.

I went to see Bill Turnock, who commiserated but said it was out of his hands, as Sam reported to New York. I was given a generous golden parachute and return airfare.

I put Judy Wald and Susan Friedman back to work, hunting down a spot for me. I was soon hired by an English agency, Dorland, as one of two assistant creative directors, under Royston Taylor. I worked fairly happily there for a year or so, then got into an interoffice imbroglio that I couldn't handle, my office political skills being poor at best.

What happened was that our head of TV production had hired a TV production company that he wanted, instead of the one I wanted for my group's commercial. I had already discussed the job with Tony Scott, the brother of Ridley Scott, with whom I had done three commercials for Dubonnet. Then I heard that Bob, let's call him, had overruled me, treading on my territory.

The same day I had had a phone call from a TV producer I had worked with at Grey, telling me that Bob was on the take. He had hired the new production company, because they were willing to pay him, personally, a percentage of their fee to get him to hire them. This is called a "kickback," and it is highly unethical, maybe even unlawful.

I went to my boss, Roy, and explained things. He said he'd look into it.

The following day, I had a meeting with Roy. He told me he had decided to go with Bob's choice of a production house.

I received this in disbelief. It was like a kick in the gut. We discussed this, rather hotly, for a few minutes, when I realized I was not winning the argument. I said that, rather than accepting the situation and work with Bob, I would resign.

Roy, who by this time was as angry as I, invited me to do so.

I returned to my office, typed up my resignation and gave it to Roy's secretary for delivery. Then I went home for the day and out for the evening.

I think I had a little too much to drink at dinner because I awoke the following morning with something suspiciously like a hangover. And, it occurred to me, I was unemployed.

Back at the office, things were very civil. Roy asked me to work a couple more weeks, to smooth the way for a replacement, and I had a couple of weeks of vacation coming, too.

Then came one of those weird turns in life that, after a series of coincidences, changed my life.

18

Here, I have to introduce coincidence to this story. I have always believed in the power of coincidence to suddenly change one's life, for better or worse, and that if you line up enough coincidences in a row, it's called Fate. I'll walk you through the coincidences and introduce you to Fate.

Dorland had a new client, an airline called British Lion, which was assigned to the group I led. One of the client's executives said to me, "Get to know the airline. Fly somewhere."

"Where?" I asked.

He gave me a list of their destinations. "Anywhere you like," he said, "as long as there is space available."

I chose Rio de Janeiro. Before the day was out, I got a call from the client. "Rio got fully booked," he said. "Choose something else."

I chose Genoa.

Later that day: "Sorry, fully booked."

I made another choice with the same result. "Look," I said. "Why don't you just tell me what's available, and I'll pick something."

"Only Las Palmas," he replied.

I had never heard of it.

"It's on the island of Mallorca," he said. "Spain. And there are plenty of seats."

That's three coincidences right there. If some traveler had canceled his reservations to the first three destinations, my life might have turned out to be just as good, but it would certainly not be better.

I accepted the booking, with a departure the next day. That evening, I attended something called the Justice Ball, a social evening for barristers, at the Savoy Hotel, as the guest of my friends Richard and Elfrieda Fallowfield. It was all very grand, black tie, and I was seated with the Fallowfields at a table of ten. Choosing a moment when conversation had flagged, I said, "I need your help." They all turned and looked at me. "Tomorrow morning, I'm getting on an airplane to Las Palmas, in Mallorca, a place I had never heard of until today, and which I know nothing about."

"All you need to know about Mallorca," someone said, "is Nora Cumberlege."

That's a fourth coincidence. You'll see.

"Of course," the Fallowfields said. "Nora is British and owns a guesthouse in Cala Ratjada." Richard whipped out a notebook, jotted down a number, and handed it to me. "Just call Nora as soon as you land. She'll take care of you."

I tucked the number into my pocket.

THE FOLLOWING MORNING, SAFELY LANDED in Las Palmas, I found a telephone and spent a few minutes figuring out how to use it and what coins it liked.

"Hello?" A woman's voice. I asked for Nora Cumberlege.

"Speaking."

"I'm a friend of Richard and Elfrieda Fallowfield. I've just landed in Las Palmas, and they told me to call you."

"Do you have a car?"

"Not yet."

"Rent one." She gave me directions, and I rented a car.

An hour later, I pulled into a large, lovely house with a sign outside reading: SEA CLUB.

Nora found me, introduced herself, her beautiful daughter, Claudia, and her son, Mistral, called "Misty," and I was soon unpacking in a large, airy bedroom on the ground floor adjacent to the front porch, looking out on the Mediterranean. Over drinks, I heard Nora's story. It is a short one.

She had arrived in Mallorca for the first time in the early 1930s, in the company of the Prince of Wales—later, for a short time, King Edward VIII. While anchored next to another largish yacht, they were invited aboard to dinner. Their host was Admiral Cumberlege, the youngest naval officer of that rank since Horatio Nelson.

Nora and the young admiral took to each other immediately, and at the conclusion of the evening, she accepted his invitation to remain aboard with him. The prince returned to his yacht alone, and Nora never left Mallorca again.

The admiral took retirement; they married, bought a house, produced two children, and, at his death, many years later, she turned their home into the Sea Club.

I met a couple that evening, Merrick Coveney and his girlfriend, Janet, who invited me to play tennis the following day. They produced a fourth, an actress I had recently seen on the BBC, portraying a nun, and thereafter, I had a hard time thinking of her except in a habit.

I saw a great deal of the couple during my stay, and they invited me to come and visit them at their home in Ireland, a house in the courtyard of a stately home, Lough Cutra Castle. Merrick was single, but not divorced, his Irish wife being a devout Catholic. Janet was twenty-eight, the age of his daughter, Anthea, a model I knew in London, and they seemed the perfect couple. I admired Merrick's prowess with such a beautiful and much younger woman.

Fifth coincidence. You'll see how meeting them changed my course.

I was having dinner in their home one night before my departure, when Merrick was called to the telephone. He left the table for a few minutes and returned, looking stunned.

Janet was concerned. "What has happened?"

Merrick took a swig of the Rioja and recovered somewhat. It turned out that his estranged wife, a superb horsewoman who rode to the hounds in Ireland, had been killed in a riding accident. Thus, Merrick was simultaneously a free man and a wealthy one, inheriting his estranged wife's considerable estate.

After a decent interval, Merrick and Janet were married.

I RETURNED TO LONDON FROM my Sea Club adventure and earned my living as a decent freelancer. When things got tight, I sold my car and bought a motor scooter. Then my landlord let me know that my lease in Ennismore Gardens would be up in a month, and they weren't considering new leases.

A little about the London real estate market at that time: if you owned a lease the landlord couldn't put you on the street until he had offered you equivalent shelter somewhere else. I was ignorant of this. Had I known, I might have stayed on for years, making my life completely different. I learned that my downstairs neighbors, whose lease was also up, stayed on permanently, declining equivalent lodging.

A sixth coincidence.

I began thinking about the novel that had been on my mind, since the age of about ten, when I discovered a policeman's badge in a shoebox in my grandmother's closet. It was half shot away with buckshot, and there was still dried blood on it. It was explained to me that he, Will Henry Callaway, had been the local chief of police, and he had been killed in the line of duty.

The story stayed in my mind. Occasionally I would think of something else from my hometown and family history to add to it, until it burgeoned into a collection of three novellas, with a continuing set of characters. All of this was unwritten, of course, and I couldn't afford to get another apartment in London without working full time. I decided that the time to write the novel had come. But where could I write it that gave me low rent and part-time employment nearby?

I remembered what Merrick and Janet Coveney had told me about their home in Ireland. I phoned them and asked if there were any good rental properties near them. They said there were properties on the very estate where they lived, and that I should come and see them and have a look. They also said there were ad agencies in Dublin.

I INVITED AN AMERICAN EXPAT couple, Phil McHale and Barbara Danielson, to go with me. Barbara and I had been class partners at London's Le Cordon Bleu cooking school in the autumn of 1972.

I added a few things to my portfolio, and the three of us flew off to Dublin, where I had a couple of work interviews. I managed to convince the managing director of Irish International Advertising that if I were paid what a good writer was worth, I could do five days' work in two days, and he believed me.

An income ensured, the three of us drove down to County Cork to a country hotel called Ballymaloe, which had a legendary chef. We spent a couple of glorious days there, then Phil and Barbara took a flight from Cork back to London. I drove on south to County Galway, where Lough Cutra Castle lay just outside a village called Gort, which I later learned had six hundred people and thirty-eight pubs.

There was a fetching thatched cottage on the estate, but in a state of disrepair, and they also had a nice flat available in the courtyard overlooking the castle and Lough Cutra itself, the largest privately owned lake in Ireland.

After another couple of glorious days with the Coveneys, I flew back to London and contacted the castle's owner, Timothy Gwyn-Jones, a young Welshman in his thirties who had made a fortune in London real estate. We came to an agreement about my renting the cottage, after it had been restored. In the meantime, I would live in the flat.

I bought a Mini from my friend Sandi Butchkiss, sold my motor scooter, and ran an ad in the *Times*, offering my furnishings for sale, mentioning my Eames chair and my Mies coffee table. The flat was flooded with prospective buyers, and virtually everything was sold on the basis that buyers would pay now and collect their purchases on my moving day. This worked like a charm, except that the check written by a well-known member of parliament bounced. He apologized, saying he suspected that I would leave town with his purchase and sent me a check that didn't bounce.

AND SO, ON A RAINY day in February of 1973, I drove my tightly packed Mini down to Wales and took the car ferry to Cork, then drove on to Lough Cutra. Incidentally, the thatched cottage never got restored—at least, not while I was there—so I moved into the stable yard flat.

THIS COMPLETES THE STRING OF coincidences, for the moment. Fate still lurks.

THE
SAILING YEARS

As you may know, I wrote a memoir, *Blue Water, Green Skipper*, that covers the years I spent in Ireland and the sailing experience that sprang from that. Having re-read it, I thought it was pretty good and that I couldn't improve on it. I see no reason to impose the will of an elderly gentleman on this retelling. Therefore, I am suddenly thirty-five again, so here we go. Don't worry, I'll get old again later.

The book is exactly as it was when first published, except that I have restored a half dozen pages that were excised by the British publisher concerning my disagreements with the boatyard, which ceased to operate decades ago.

19

Some Sort of Beginning

I stood in this place for the second time in forty minutes, a small, neat bay, surrounded by low hills, white cottages, a ruined mansion, and an unspecified number of dairy cattle, chewing their way through the morning. This choppy stretch of water was covered by a churning gray sky and contained a half dozen small plastic buoys and an old stone pier. Perhaps "stood" constitutes sloppy use of the language, for about forty knots of wind had me leaning at an unnatural angle to the perpendicular and the hairs on the leeward side of my body standing at an equally unnatural angle to my skin. I had not yet learned that a mild, sunny beginning to an Irish morning does not obviate the necessity for a sheepskin coat and gumboots at a slightly later hour, and I could not, for the life of me, see the Galway Bay Sailing Club.

I drove back to the Thatched Pub in Oranmore and explained my problem to its keeper. As he had already done twice on that morning, he began patiently to direct me to Rinville Bay. I interrupted to explain that I was certain I had found the bay but could not find the clubhouse.

"Ah," said George the innkeeper, with the raised eyebrows of the enlightened, "there's not a club*house*, y'see; there's just the *club*, like."

I gaped at him uncomprehendingly, unable to shake my preconception of the neat building, the flagpole, and the ruddy-faced chaps gathered in the net-draped bar. George leapt into the silence, which every Irishman abhors: "There's just the club, and I'd say they're not likely to be out just yet." It was March, I had to give him that, but it was a Sunday, too, and the paperback I had read had led me to believe that your enthusiastic yachtsman, if not actually on the water nowabouts, would at least be varnishing or splicing something in preparation for the event, and if not that, knocking a few back and talking about it at the very least.

George fixed his gaze on the Guinness pump handle before him, trying hard to be helpful. "Pierce Purcell," he said, looking relieved. "You'd want to speak to Pierce Purcell, he's the secretary or one of the people, like, and you'd find him in the book."

The Irish Department of Posts and Telegraphs, because of the small size of the country, the low density of the population, and its own extreme reluctance to provide any of them with a telephone, has managed to gather all the nation's telephone listings into just one directory, which is, in size, roughly equal to the combined bulk of the Old Testament, the New Testament, the *I Ching*, and *The Joy of Sex*. It proved to contain at least a page of closely spaced Purcells, far too many of them P.'s, P. J.'s, and even Pierces, and none of them in Galway. George tried again.

"Ferdia O'Riordan," he said, this time with real conviction. The book offered us even more O'Riordans than Purcells, but no Ferdias in Galway. "The Bank of Ireland," said George with finality. "That's where he works, at the branch in Salthill." But in

Ireland only the pubs are open on a Sunday, so I thanked George and postponed my search for sailing yet another day.

Sailing had been wafting around the hindmost part of my head since the summer of 1966, when friends had invited me to their summer home in Castine, Maine, and, back in my native USA, taken me sailing every day the wind blew. I had been enchanted with the notion that one could move across the face of the waters, fueled by nothing more than the wind, and I had resolved that if ever I were domiciled in any reasonable proximity to the sea I would learn to sail upon it. I thought, even, that since so much of the world was covered with water and since it lapped against so many interesting places, that I should like to sail right the way round, stopping everywhere.

Eventually, I finished a ten-year hitch in New York advertising, did another three in London, and then, propelled by a lifelong desire to write A Novel, hied myself to the west of Ireland, to County Galway, to Lough Cutra Castle, near Gort, where I resided not in the castle but in the adjacent stable yard, in a flat. I spent two days a week in Dublin, writing television commercials and ads for an advertising agency, and the rest of the time in County Galway, writing my novel or, at least, thinking about it.

Lough Cutra was an ideal place—four hundred acres of grounds, twelve hundred acres of lake, and enough peace and quiet to make it very difficult to find an excuse not to write. To live this sort of existence you have to be either very lucky or very single. Looking back, I still find it difficult to believe I was able to get away with this for two years.

Soon after my arrival in Ireland, in early 1973, I perceived that it was surrounded by water, and the sailing notion, so long displaced by an absorbing career and an athletic social life in New York and London, began to winnow its way into my frontal lobe. I bought a book which suggested that the way to go about learning to sail was to start with a small dinghy, then work up to larger things as desire and funds dictated. For several winter weeks I scoured the west, looking for a small boat to buy or someone who knew where to buy one or someone who knew someone who knew. Just when I was beginning to think that I was the only person in the counties Galway, Clare, and Mayo who realized that Ireland was an island, a friend in Galway, who believed that water should be fished in and not sailed upon, admitted that he had heard of the existence of a sailing club in or near Galway City.

He was pretty cagey about it all, but still, I had managed to penetrate the alleged club's apparent security arrangements to the point where I now had an actual name and an actual telephone number to call. Journeying to the public telephone in Mrs. Piggot's Grocery Store in Gort, I gave the operator the number, inserted the required coinage into the instrument, and waited the customary seven minutes to be connected. To my surprise, there really was a Ferdia O'Riordan at the Bank of Ireland in Salthill, and he very generously invited me to join him for a sail the following Sunday, behaving as if the Galway Bay Sailing Club were common knowledge and had nothing whatever to hide.

During the week which followed I reread my book on sailing and bought another, wishing to be as *au fait* as possible without actually having set foot in any sort of boat for seven years. The Sunday arrived and I again found myself at Rinville. Nothing had changed, except that the wind was blowing slightly less hard and the temperature had crept up a degree or two. The place was still deserted, and I sat in my battered Mini, chatting idly with Fred, a four-pound, five-week-old example of the golden Labrador breed, who graciously permitted me to share my flat with him. At last, a car materialized next to mine, towing a boat covered with canvas. From this car emerged Ferdia O'Riordan, his very pretty wife, and two irresistible little girls, with whom Fred evidenced an immediate empathy. Leaving the two children and the puppy rolling in the grass, we removed the canvas from the boat, revealing a gleaming example of the GP Fourteen class, erected the mast, bent on the sails, and trundled the lot at breakneck speed down the rocky shore. Ferdia and I stripped off our shoes and socks, rolled up our trouser legs, and waded into the icy water. In a trice, I was experiencing again that giddy sensation of motion over water which had so mesmerized me in Maine seven summers before.

We thrashed about Rinville Bay, Ferdia issuing a steady stream of calm instructions, I trying to remember what I had read during the last week, while shifting my weight about in such a way as to keep us upright, and endeavoring to cope with sheets, cleats, and centerboard. "We're nearly planing now," Ferdia said at one point. I made a mental note to find out what "planing" meant. It had a familiar ring.

Back on shore, while gathering my wits about me again, Ferdia, who turned out to be the club secretary, produced a membership form and relieved me of a check. We discussed what sort of boat I should buy and the consensus seemed to be a Mirror, a ten-foot-ten-inch plywood dinghy whose design had been sponsored by the newspaper of the same name, which could be bought ready-built or in kit form, and which was the most popular boat in the club.

Considering that in an entire year of woodworking classes in high school I had produced only one wobbly bookcase and half a lamp base, I thought the ready-built form of the boat appealed most, although I was assured that twelve Girl Scouts had once built one in eight hours. (Twelve Girl Scouts represent a multiplication of my woodworking talents by a factor of twenty-four.) Since demand for these little boats was high and supply slow, I would probably have to wait a bit for delivery, but the club, it was disclosed, owned two Mirrors for the use of members who did not themselves own boats, so I would be able to sail in the meantime. Also, the club was holding a boat show in a couple of weeks' time, and there I would be able to peruse a number of other craft before purchasing.

During the time remaining until the boat show I dropped by Rinville several times more, and on one occasion was invited out for a sail in a twenty-foot dayboat by a rumpled fellow of about my own age, who looked as I imagined a Galway fisherman looked and, to my American ear, sounded. It is a measure of my discernment in these matters at that stage of my Irish experience that he turned out to be the minister for local government.

The First Annual Galway Boat Show took place in the car park of the Salthill Hotel. On display were a dozen assorted dinghies and powerboats, some fishing and diving gear, and other water-oriented paraphernalia. Also on display was a gleaming new Mirror dinghy, which was being raffled as a fundraising project for the club, and which I did not win. However, a large Dutchman and I unearthed one of the club Mirrors from Ferdia O'Riordan's garage and, after an hour or so of puzzling over fittings, rigging, and sails, got it afloat.

We pottered about between Black Rock Pier and the Margaretta Buoy in the middle of Galway Bay, tacking and jibing the little boat in a lovely breeze. My reading program was paying off handsomely, things making a great deal more sense than they had on my first outing with Ferdia. I had another short sail with another member, and then dropped him off at the pier.

My recent reading had included Sir Francis Chichester's book *Gypsy Moth Circles the World* and Joshua Slocum's superb account of his three-year circumnavigation in the last century, the first by a man alone. No doubt these had served as some sort of inspiration, for I pushed off in the little dinghy and sailed her single-handed out to the buoy and back, ajangle at the newness of it all and terrified of capsizing the thing in sight of the crowd on the pier. This was a kind of high several notches above sailing with somebody else. Now, for better or for drowning, I had the thing all to myself, my first command, as it were, and I relished the experience. Tacking around the buoy went much as the book had said it should; the dinghy scooted across the water, seemingly in defiance of, rather than in harmony with, the laws of nature, and I returned to shore light-headed, as if having breathed an enriched atmosphere.

I felt it was some sort of beginning, though of what I wasn't certain, and to my distant fantasy of sailing around the world was added the even more fantastic notion of doing some part of it alone, and although the next time I sailed a boat alone the circumstances were much more exotic and the possible consequences far more serious, the special euphoria of that first, short, single-handed voyage remained unrivaled.

20

Learning a Bit

Carol, Fred, and I arrived at Rosturk Castle on a Friday evening in June, the club dinghy in tow behind the Mini. Carol, an old friend from both New York and London days, was passing through Ireland on her way back to live in the States, and we had been invited up to County Mayo for the Westport Show. The dinghy, much used and a bit battered, was for sailing in Westport Bay, for Rosturk Castle is situated on one of the most beautiful inlets of that very beautiful body of water.

Sunday we went sailing, which was not as simple as it sounds. The inlet on which Rosturk stands habitually dries out twice a day, when the tide recedes, leaving a quarter-mile or so of lovely golden sand to replace the water, which ends up some distance from the castle. Since our time of rising and breakfasting coincided with low water, it was necessary for someone to come with us down the long strip of sand to the water's edge in the Mini and, after the dinghy had been launched, return to the house with the car and Fred, who, in the two or three times I had sailed since my debut, had shown himself to be not much in the way of a yachtsman. He either fell asleep with his head on the tiller or strolled about the decks until he fell into the water. He was, at least, good for man-overboard drills.

We successfully launched the dinghy and sailed off into an already increasing breeze. Westport Bay is filled with islands, reputedly 365 of them, and it had been our intention to sail among them for a sufficient number of hours for the tide to allow us to sail right up to the doorstep of the castle. However, on the water everything looks a bit different; the wind blows a bit harder, the waves are a bit steeper, and, on top of everything else, it was starting to drizzle. I am not sure if I had confided the state of my experience to Carol, but she seemed willing to sail wherever I wished, so I probably hadn't.

We beat out from behind an island and the wind and waves both grew in strength—not to an alarming state, but sailing the boat required great concentration. There was little time for absorbing the beauties of Westport Bay. Carol, incredibly, managed to light a cigarette. We agreed that a shorter sail than originally conceived was in order. We sailed around the island and headed into the channel separating it from the shore where the castle stood. Then we were running, that is, the wind was directly behind us, and so were the waves. We began to surf in a small way, which was exciting, and then we "broached to," which was a little too exciting. When a boat is running broaches, it appears suddenly to change its mind about the direction in which it is sailing and to attempt to change its course, swinging abruptly around and abeam to the wind. This action, in proper concert with a passing wave, can cause the occupants of a dinghy to become swimmers. We were wearing buoyancy aids, but these did not make the prospect seem any more inviting. We broached twice before I learned to anticipate the movement and keep us on a straight course.

We drove on up the inlet until the boat touched the sand, then we hopped out. We were still a quarter-mile from the castle. I sent Carol up for the car and trailer while I got the sails down and stood in the water, holding the dinghy. The tide was coming in quite fast now.

Carol arrived with the car and backed the trailer down to the edge of the water, which was still several yards away from the Mini. I unhitched the trailer, pushed it down to the dinghy, and asked Carol to help me lift the boat onto it. This seemed to take no more than a minute or two. I turned to start pulling the trailer toward the car and saw, to my horror, that water was lapping at the hubcaps of the Mini. The tide was moving faster than I had realized.

I dropped the trailer, dived into the car, and started the engine. I breathed a sigh of relief. I put it into gear and tried to drive out of the water. The wheels promptly buried themselves in the sand. The front axles were now resting on the bottom. I sent Carol back to the house for help, while I tried vainly to rock the car out of the sand by shifting alternately into first gear and reverse. The wheels spun happily back and forth but remained in precisely the same position. I got out of the car and looked around for help. Far up the inlet, perhaps half a mile away, I saw a man driving a tractor, towing a trailer-load of seaweed across the sand. I jumped up and down and waved. He seemed not to see me. I blew the horn of the car repeatedly, but clearly the sound would never penetrate the noise of the tractor engine. There was no one else in sight.

I got back into the car and raced the engine; it seemed terribly important, somehow, to keep it going. Then I began to blow a signal on the horn—dot dot dot, dash dash dash, dot dot dot—SOS, the only Morse code I had ever been able to learn. The water continued to rise, and I continued to honk my signal. I could see Carol; she was not quite halfway to the castle, tired already from her first hike back for the car. The water was now beginning to creep over the door sills. I considered abandoning ship, but continued to honk. Far up the beach a figure was running toward the tractor, pointing my way. The tractor changed direction. Now it was a question of which would arrive first, the tractor or the tide. The tide seemed to be winning. The carpets were now underwater.

The tractor moved faster than I could have believed possible and arrived accompanied by a German guest at the castle, who had been awakened from his nap by the sound of my Morse SOS. Thank God the German Boy Scouts did a better job of teaching its members Morse code than, in my experience, the American branch. Just at the point when I was about to be sailing a Mini instead of a Mirror, the car came free of the sand. It even ran for a couple of miles before dying. The salt water had eaten away the fuel pump and one or two other essentials. If anybody knows of a more graphic way for a budding dinghy sailor to be taught about the tides I don't want to hear about it.

The next thing I learned about sailing was that some boats, for no readily apparent reason, go faster than others. I learned this in the most embarrassing possible way for an adult, from children.

While I waited for my new Mirror to be built and delivered, a period of ten weeks, I tried racing the club Mirror in the regular Sunday- and Wednesday-afternoon events. In the beginning I had had no interest whatever in racing, but I soon found that cruising in a dinghy was not especially appealing, particularly if the wind died and the bloody thing had to be paddled home. So, having memorized about three of the several dozen International Yacht Racing Union Rules, I grabbed a passing teenager for a crew and thrashed my way around the buoys, losing to everybody except two tiny individuals who had capsized and retired. Fortunately, I had a number of excuses with which to console myself: the club boat leaked like a sieve; the sails were old and worn; the bottom was rough with age, and so forth. I bought a dinghy pump, and this kept my feet drier, but my ego remained damp. My new boat would solve all this, I was sure.

The new boat helped. I collected it, all dark blue and shiny, and named it *Fred*, in the hope that it would like the water as much as the puppy. It liked the water, and I finished third in my first race, but that was as high as I could scramble for several weeks. I began to investigate all the go-fast fittings and ideas allowed by the measurement rules of the Mirror Class Association. I grew accustomed to being handed small brown-paper bags in yacht chandleries, while a supercilious clerk intoned, "That will be thirty pounds, please." I began reading the specialist books on racing and poring over the yachting magazines, looking for that elusive instruction which would send me surging to the fore of the fleet. And lo, I began to improve. I began to beat the smaller children. Progress.

A big problem, of course, was that I did not have a regular

Racing *Fred* in Galway Bay.

crew. Most grown men who race in the smaller dinghy classes breed sons and daughters for this purpose, lashing them to the boat as soon as they are old enough to be shouted at. In my bachelor state I was so far behind in this game that it would have taken six or seven years to catch up. So I had to be content to borrow the odd kid when Dad was away or too hungover to make the start. Adults were too heavy, learned too slowly, and had too low a humiliation threshold for crewing a Mirror dinghy. Once, at a two-day meet on Lough Derg, I persuaded a grown-up acquaintance new to sailing to crew for me. In the first race we did miserably, our combined weight destroying us in very light winds. In the second race, after a lunch at which we consoled ourselves with a liter of plonk, a huge wind appeared from nowhere, capsized us, and left us riding to anchor in the half-filled dinghy, drinking still more plonk and waiting for the crash boat to come and take us away. His wife phoned the next day and said he wasn't well and couldn't make races three and four.

So for the rest of the season I found crews wherever I could and continued to chase, and occasionally even beat, the leaders, all of whom were in their mid-teens except my archrival Dr. Tom Coll, an alleged adult with an enthusiastic younger brother for a crew. We exchanged good-natured abuse ashore and afloat, and whenever I beat him he would pretend to sulk for a week.

The highlight of the season was the national championships, a weeklong event held at Lough Derg. I arrived crewless, as usual, but found a twelve-year-old Dublin girl named Caroline, who was small for her age. She turned out to be a shrewd and experienced dinghy sailor, and her small weight helped make up for mine. We finished thirty-ninth out of a fleet of sixty. With luck we could have done better, but still, I had never before beaten twenty-one boats.

It ended the season if not on a high note, at least on one which would hum through my mind all through the following winter.

21

Hooked

I was thirty-five years old when I first sailed that Mirror dinghy—in my late youth, one might say. My figure had assumed those slightly more generous proportions so attractive in a person of my age, and just a tiny bit more of my scalp was exposed to the sunshine than had been true a few years before. (Someone once described me, unkindly, as "balding." This is not strictly true. I am balding only if you are taller than I am and stand behind me.) This is a time of life when a man has a duty to his family, his society, and probably the United Nations to go forth and painfully extract seventy-five or a hundred thousand dollars a year from his nation's gross national product and then plow back about twenty-five percent more than that into mortgage payments, insurance premiums, school fees for his children, analysts' fees for his wife, and quadraphonic sound and electrocardiograms for himself. It is a known fact that unless everybody does this there will be another Depression and a Communist Takeover, followed shortly by a Nuclear Holocaust. I know that it was terribly irresponsible of me, but at this critical juncture of my life my existence was ruled by the compulsion to find a way to make a ten-foot-ten-inch plywood dinghy go faster than that of the thirteen-year-old kid down the street. I know this is no way for a grown man to behave, but I couldn't help it. I was hooked.

This confusing condition becomes even more inexplicable if one examines my career in sport up to that time, which, believe me, will not take long. In my school days in Manchester, Georgia, I fought a pitched battle for two years with a co-student to see who could become the worst football player in the history of Manchester High School. He never had a chance. Every winter for four years I went out for the basketball team and was cut from the squad after the first two weeks of practice, which the coach considered a decent interval, given the state of my native ability. I did, however, make the tennis team in my senior year—mostly, I believe, because I owned a tennis racket and only three other boys went out for the team. I was instrumental in the loss of every doubles match we played that year, and for my efforts was awarded a school letter in track. The coach said something about having ordered too many track letters and not enough tennis. When I lived in London I played tennis about twice a week in Battersea Park, where I could acquit myself fairly well in mixed doubles if the girls were bad enough.

And now, in the middle of my life and with that record behind me, I found myself consumed by and even achieving a kind of competitive mediocrity in a new sport. And when the season ended things got worse. I pored over every yachting publication available, taking notes. I trudged up and down the aisles of chandleries examining the available equipment minutely, buying everything which held the promise of that extra tenth of a knot of speed. I read ever more advanced books on technique—books about roll tacking, spinnaker handling, eliminating weather helm. I ordered a new mast from Collars of Oxford and new sails from Jack Holt. I memorized the yacht racing rules. When spring came I started screwing and bolting the fruits of my winter's search to the dinghy.

And then a wonderful thing happened. Harry McMahon bought an Enterprise. An Enterprise is a larger, heavier boat than a Mirror, and Harry needed a larger, heavier crew to help keep it upright. This size requirement shanghaied Harry's bemused wife into action and his eldest son, Dairmuid, out of it. Dairmuid had all of the qualities I could have wanted in a son of my own. He was eleven years old, skinny enough to help make up for my bulk, and had been shouted at by his father for two seasons in a Mirror. He knew more than enough to keep me out of trouble, and he wasn't big enough to yell at me when I made a stupid mistake. The day Harry showed up with the Enterprise I offered to adopt Dairmuid. Harry compromised by offering to lend him to me for the summer in return for a good price on my old Mirror sails. Everybody was happy except, possibly, Dairmuid. Nobody asked him.

At last I had a regular crew of my own. At last the boat was light enough to sail in light winds. At last the spinnaker was being used well. At last I was being beaten by adults instead of children, and a lot of the time I was beating the adults. Life was full of meaning.

Dairmuid and I campaigned the boat hard that summer, going to as many open and regional meetings as we could manage. We sailed fast but too often made one gigantic, unforgivable mistake in a race—enough to put us fourth or fifth instead of first. Still, it was hugely satisfying and a wonderful excuse for not writing, something every writer desperately needs.

We looked forward eagerly to the Mirror National Championships, when boats from all over Ireland (and some from England) would congregate at Sligo for a week of battling around the buoys.

Championship week arrived, and so did Dairmuid's appendix. Dairmuid was desolated. I was suicidal. Harry offered to take his son's place.

A fully rigged Mirror weighs 150 pounds, which means that Harry and I weighed a lot more than twice as much as the boat. This disadvantage, combined with the fact that Harry and I were both used to skippering and not crewing, giving orders and not taking them, made things a bit tense. In the first race I completely screwed up the rather complicated gate start, to the extent that we started the race about a hundred yards behind the last of the other seventy boats. This seemed to annoy Harry. Then the wind went very light, and, since we weighed so much, we had little chance of catching up. We retired from this race, because, as I explained to Harry, I would rather have an "R" on the scoreboard next to my name than a "71st." Harry had a number of brief but incisive comments to make about this and other of my decisions during the race. The second race went a lot better. I screwed up the start again, but there was more wind and we managed to work our way up to about twenty-fifth. Our relationship as skipper and crew was improving, too. Harry threatened to get out and walk only once.

Then came the third race and, with it, the wind. The wind blew and the waves got bigger—ideal conditions for Harry and me with our weight, and bad for the small kids. Wonderful. We started well but then sailed off on a tack by ourselves. Still, we seemed to be doing fairly well, concentrating hard on keeping the boat as upright as possible and sailing fast. As we rounded a mark and relative positions became a bit better defined I looked around to see how we were doing. "Harry," I said, "I know this seems odd, but an awful lot of those boats seem to be *behind* us." Harry shot me a look of withering disbelief and looked around. His face unfolded like a rose.

"Jesus," he said, "I think you're right." We finished eighth out of seventy boats, better than either of us had ever done at a National, and we were now in a position where, if we finished well in the fourth and last race, we might place in the top ten overall, a circumstance beyond our most lurid fantasies. But the wind continued to rise, and finally, because there were so many small kids involved, the last race was canceled. But there was still glory. We were given a prize for being the oldest and heaviest crew and we had finished twenty-ninth out of seventy boats. It was my finest hour.

22

Hooked Anew

There had been talk of Fireballs for some weeks now. A Fireball is a high-performance racing dinghy with a big sail plan and a trapeze for the crew. It was a different kettle of fish from a Mirror, but four of us were pretty hot on the idea. I assembled costs on everything from the hiring of a mold (we were going to build them ourselves) to spars and sails, but, one by one, people dropped out, and, anyway, something else happened that pointed me in a new direction. Dave Fitzgerald asked me to go sailing with him.

Dave owned a Snapdragon 24, a tubby little cruising yacht of some age but of considerable charm, at least to me. He had sailed her to France earlier in the summer and was bringing her back in stages. The final stage was from Valentia, an island just off southwest Ireland, to Galway, and he invited me to join him and his regular crew in bringing her up. I suspected that he had run out of people to ask who actually knew what they were doing aboard a cruising boat and had been reduced to accepting a dinghy sailor, but I leapt at the chance, having never actually *been* anywhere on a sailboat. I had spent two summers sailing triangular courses, and the idea of floating from one place to another was enormously appealing. This was much closer to sailing around the world.

We drove down to Valentia on a Friday evening, the plan being to set out from Knightstown, on the island, early the next morning and sail to Kilronan, in the Aran Islands, and then on the Sunday into Galway. It was a long drive to Valentia, but we moved quickly, it being important to get to Knightstown before the pubs closed. We slept quite comfortably on the boat (*Pegeen*, she was called), and we got up early enough for the morning BBC marine weather forecast. Five minutes later we were asleep again, as the BBC was forecasting a possible gale Force eight, which seemed to be more wind than Dave wanted to face with a hangover. We passed a sunny day idly, and the gale never materialized. Next morning, after another night at the pub, we overslept and got away later than planned. We had to beat out through the Blasket Sound in a short, choppy sea and, having been anxious about the possibility of being seasick on my first coastal passage, I had taken a seasickness pill, which rendered me semiconscious for the first couple of hours. I recovered by mid-morning and found us broad reaching up the coast with a nice Force four southwesterly breeze behind us.

The company was good. Dave was a large man with a meaty nose who has been known to sign autographs for Tommy Cooper, and when he is not sailing he runs the Tynagh Mines in County Galway. Philip, his other crew, is smaller than Dave and his nose is less meaty, but he is working on that. They are both very Irish, which is to say they never drink between eight and ten a.m. and never stop talking. There was a constant stream of banter in the manner of Robert Newton playing Long John Silver. Great care was taken to impress upon me at all times the infinite knowledge, skill, and courage required to sail a cruising yacht, as opposed to a dinghy. I kept expressing my surprise at how much easier everything was on a larger boat.

It went on like that all day, until Dave announced that he had made a command decision not to continue to the Arans, our late departure having made it impossible to reach Kilronan before the pubs closed. Instead, we would divert to Carrigaholt, in the Shannon estuary, where the state of the tide and the closing hours were more in harmony. We did so, and sailing into the estuary Dave showed me how to use a hand bearing compass to plot a position on a chart, my introduction to the art of coastal navigation. We berthed the boat at the village pier, then moved on to the pub to wait for Dave's attractive and patient wife to collect us for the drive back to Galway. When we returned to the boat to pick up our gear I discovered another facet of cruising the west coast of Ireland: the rise and fall of the tides. In practice this means that you can tie up nicely level with a pier, trot up to the pub for a few pints, and return to find the boat fifteen feet down from its previous level. Negotiating this distance with a full load of Guinness can be tricky. The following week in Dublin I purchased a new item for the inventory of *Pegeen*: a rope ladder. How Dave and Philip had survived for so many seasons without one was beyond me.

The following weekend we journeyed back to Carrigaholt and sailed on to the Arans under spinnaker, with a stiff following breeze which blew us right to the pubs—all of the pubs—on landing. I forget how many we visited, but the largest had two bars, and the smallest was the tiny sitting room of an Aran cottage. We lazed about Sunday morning and then sailed into Galway as the sun set. Everything all those songs say about the sun setting on Galway Bay is true. The place seems to be arranged to show the sun at its best—long summer twilights, just enough cloud to catch and color the light and the shining waters of the bay itself. It is best seen from a boat, and it is breathtaking.

All this yachting had quite turned my head. Thoughts of Fireballs vanished. Visions of cruisers now appeared. I just might be able to scrape together enough from my two-day-a-week income to buy something small.

In the meantime, there was more sailing with Dave. Next was a new event, the Round Aran Race, starting from Galway on a Friday evening and sailing around all three of the Aran Islands and into Kilronan, a distance of about sixty miles, with a nice night passage thrown in.

After that came the Galway Bay Sailing Club Regatta. Dave felt that an event of this stature required a prerace conference on tactics, and this was duly held at Moran's (also known as the Weir), a lovely little thatched pub on the Kilcolgan River, which empties into Galway Bay. We sailed *Pegeen* up the river, dried her out alongside the pier in front of the pub, and all concerned, plus a few others, gathered there. I will not place too much emphasis on the condition of the crew the following morning; suffice it to say that we ran aground three times on a falling tide en route to the starting line in Rinville Bay. At one point, half the crew were over the side in water up to their thighs, pushing *Pegeen*. Recovery was rapid enough for us to win the coveted Sonia Cup that afternoon, and we repaired once again to Moran's for a suitable celebration.

There remained but one weekend before the end of the season—that is to say, before *Pegeen's* insurance coverage expired—and it was a memorable one. Racing was finished and, Philip having allowed his work to interfere with his sailing, Dave and I took a short cruise.

We sailed down the river and into the bay in about a Force four breeze, with the full mainsail and the big genoa set. As we entered open water we looked across to the north of the bay and saw a line of heavy-looking squalls racing toward us. "Shall we shorten sail, Skipper?" I asked.

"Ah, no," replied Dave, laconically, at his most Irish. "She'll be all right."

The wind freshened quickly and the first puff of the squall, a big one, struck. There was a loud crack like a rifle shot; Dave was at the helm and I was sitting near the coach roof bulkhead to keep out of the wind. I instinctively ducked under the main hatch just in time to see the mast go, like a felled tree, into the water. The wind was up to about Force seven now, and *Pegeen* wallowed in the troughs as we struggled to get the mast and rigging back aboard. Dave quickly warned me not to start the engine until we were sure the rigging was clear of the propeller. While Dave lashed the badly bent mast and the boom to the deck I got the sails below and bagged them. *Pegeen* was rolling a lot, with no way on, and by the time I got back into the cockpit I was turning a bit green. The engine, bless its heart, chose to start first go, and we motored back toward Galway, the squalls gone and the sun shining again, I trying not to let on that I was queasy. Before I could object Dave had thrust a glass of dry sherry into my hand and was fixing himself a much-deserved gin and tonic. I hadn't wanted the drink, but to my astonishment, at the first sip, my queasiness instantly vanished. A couple of other people have told me that dry sherry works for them, too, and it's a lot more fun than pills.

With *Pegeen* having been safely berthed in the trawler layby, Dave treated me to an end-of-season dinner at the Great Southern Hotel, in the heart of Beautiful Downtown Galway. It had been quite a season for me; I had had the best of both worlds. I had raced the Mirror for a full season and still managed to get quite a lot of time in on *Pegeen* at the tail end. Meanwhile, three weeks before, another event had taken place that was to contribute to a radical redirection of my life. My grandfather, who was a major figure in my life and whom I loved very much, died. It was not a tragic death, for he was eighty-five and quite prepared to die. Well into his late seventies he was doing an hour's calisthenics and running two miles every morning—he had been mowing his lawn when he was struck with his final illness and died only two weeks later. Still, I was sad; my memories of him were sharp and sweet from my earliest childhood, and I miss him even as I write this.

But he was as kind and generous to me in death as he had been in life, and with a riveting suddenness, I realized that I could now afford to buy a small yacht. Then, on the Sunday morning following this realization, I went into the village for the papers and read in the *Observer* that entries were beginning to come in for the 1976 Royal Western/*Observer* Single-Handed Transatlantic Race.

If I had been a comic-strip character, a lightbulb would suddenly have appeared above my head.

23

On the Brink

O n the face of it, this was a ridiculous idea. In fact, it was entirely possible that it was a ridiculous idea right down to its very toes. My total sailing experience (not counting the week in Maine eight years before, when I was a passenger) consisted of not quite two seasons in a ten-foot-ten-inch plywood dinghy and something less than half a season as third hand on a twenty-four-foot bilge keeler. *Pegeen* was the largest boat I had ever set foot on. My total navigation experience consisted of using a hand bearing compass maybe three times. I was thirty-six years old and, apart from a little tennis in London and sailing the Mirror, had not had any real exercise in fifteen years. It seemed a meager chronicle of assets.

But I had others. I was reasonably bright; I had a little money; I had about nineteen months to find a boat, learn to sail it, learn to navigate it, and to get fit; and above all, I was, just about as much as any man can be, free. That was a very important consideration.

When I was very young, I wanted to get married very badly, but I got over it. I had a couple of close scrapes, mind you, but I managed to stay out of serious trouble. We are all taught that, generally, when between the ages of twenty-one and twenty-five, each of us will meet some Wonderful Person for whom we are destined, then marry, live in a nice house with two cars in the garage, have 2.5 children, and live happily ever after. During my twenties, by a process I can describe only as luck, I managed to become gradually disabused of this notion, and by the time I was about thirty it had occurred to me, first, that there was a possibility that I might, indeed, never get married; and second, that that might not be an unbearably unpleasant way to live. I try to keep an open mind about this, but nothing has yet happened to change it.

So I was free, that is to say, single; neither did I have any burning professional ambition beyond finishing my novel, nor was I burdened with unmanageable debt. My mother being a good businesswoman who had just inherited the family business, I had no one to support but myself, and I had been doing that nicely in just two days a week for some time. I was a fortunate man.

Perhaps I was also a slightly insane one. I thought a lot about what my problems would be. I could meet the physical demands, I thought; I could become fit. But what about the emotional demands? Could I spend several weeks alone at sea in a small boat without the top of my head coming off? Well, I had taken a rather cold plunge moving from Knightsbridge in London to Gort in the west of Ireland. It had taken some getting used to, but I now spent the greater part of my time alone, working on the novel or reading, mostly about sailing. The two days a week in Dublin kept me in touch with real life and the opposite sex, but basically it was a solitary existence.

Most of all, it seemed to me, I faced two things: a problem of organization and an intensive learning experience. There was a lot to bring together in a short time, but I am a compulsive organizer, being a Capricorn; I find it intensely satisfying to bring order out of chaos, and I am good at it. Lately, the only outlet for this compulsion had been the Galway Bay Sailing Club, to the bemusement of its membership. But what about the learning? Quite apart from boat-handling technique, there was a considerable amount of academic knowledge to absorb, particularly celestial navigation, which involved mathematics, and I could not count to a hundred without stopping to think. I had been a slightly better-than-average student at Manchester High School and no better than average at the University of Georgia. Still, I had learned enough about several score of products and companies to be able to write advertising for them; in New York I had become a competent amateur photographer; in London I had learned more than a little about wine. Neither was an uncomplicated subject. If I was enthusiastic about the subject, I could learn.

I wrote to the Royal Western Yacht Club for the rules of the race, and I began to look for a boat. Finding nothing in the Irish newspapers, I decided to return from Dublin to Galway the long way and make a few stops. I drove south to Wicklow, stopping at Neil Watson's boatyard. When a boat changes hands in Ireland, Neil Watson often has a hand in the deal. He is the country's most enthusiastic yacht broker and a nice man as well. Neil showed me a variety of craft in his yard. There were a couple of Trappers (not enough interior space, not enough beam), a French Etap (too small), a pair of Irish-built fiberglass boats called Kerrys (interesting, but freeboard a bit low), and a Comfort 30, a half-ton cruiser-racer, also built in Ireland. This, I thought, was more like it, but it was too expensive, even secondhand. On top of the original cost of the boat there was a lot of extra equipment to be bought. I would have to make do with something smaller.

I drove on to Cork, partly to stop at a favorite country hotel, Ballymaloe House, and partly to see what I could find out about a young New Zealand yacht designer, Ron Holland, about whom I had been reading in the yachting press. He had designed a successful one-tonner, *Golden Apple*; had followed her with a half-tonner, *Golden Shamrock*; and now a production version of *Shamrock* was to be built. Ron Holland was not listed as having a telephone, and I couldn't remember the name of the boatyard which was building his design. It turned out to be Southcoast Boatyard, and I eventually found a small office building, a large shed, and the beginnings of some sort of construction behind the office.

In the office I was directed to the foreman, George Bush, whom I found in the shed, deploying workers around the upside-down wooden hull of a boat in building. George, who wore glasses and a permanently astonished look, explained that Ron Holland was in the United States. He showed me the hull he was working on, which was to be the "plug" around which a mold would be constructed for the new glass-fiber boat, and gave me a look at *Golden Apple*, which was resting on a cradle near the river. He was very proud of *Golden Apple*, as well he should have been. We talked a bit more, and I left the yard with a clutch of xeroxed typed pages about the new boat and a promise from George that he would tell Ron Holland of my interest in the boat when he returned from the States. But a production *Golden Shamrock* cost £9,700 and was out of my range.

I continued to West Cork, to Skibbereen, to visit Fastnet Yachts, which turned out to be another tin shed, seemingly in the middle of a farm and nowhere near any water I could see. But there was an astonishing number of boats crammed into this shed, among them a Hurley 24, which interested me. It looked good, and it was within my budget. It was suggested that I have a look at another Hurley 24 in Monasterevin, near Dublin, which had been at the Dublin Boat Show. I did, a few days later, and was very interested.

Not having any objective information about the Hurley, I telephoned *Yachting World* magazine in London and was connected with David Pelly, the assistant editor. He told me that Hurley was a reliable firm that, due to business difficulties not connected with the quality of its product, was in receivership. He spoke well of the 24, calling it a very seaworthy boat for its size and well designed. I telephoned Hurley's in Plymouth and talked with the sales manager, learning that they had sent the Monasterevin boat to Ireland for the boat show, where it had not been sold, and in the meantime, the company had gone into receivership. The receiver was insisting that the boat be either sold soon or brought back to England. I began to smell a genuine, gold-plated bargain.

Back in Galway I noticed in the Royal Ocean Racing Club's magazine, *Seahorse*, that a Hurley 24 had been sailed in the Round Britain race by Captain Ewan Southby-Tailyour of the Royal Marines. Hurley's gave me his telephone number, and I rang him, slightly uncomfortable because I was not quite sure how to pronounce any of his names. He turned out to be an enthusiast in general and, in particular, about his Hurley 24, *Black Velvet*. He was planning to do the OSTAR in her.

I had in my hand a copy of the rules, which had just arrived in the post. I mentioned a rule that was worrying me. The committee, it said, was unlikely to accept anything under twenty-five feet overall on deck for the race. Ridiculous, said the captain, they had said the same thing about the Round Britain Race, but he had been accepted. I felt better about it now, and we talked of meeting in London at the boat show in January. Nevertheless, after I hung up I wrote to the committee, asking about the acceptability of the Hurley 24 and reminding them of Captain Southby-Tailyour's performance. I received a courteous note back from the club secretary, saying that they knew Ewan Southby-Tailyour well, but he felt it was unlikely that the committee would accept the Hurley 24. I wrote back and asked for a ruling, remembering that the committee had, in past times, been known to reconsider an entry.

In the meantime, the negotiations for the Monasterevin boat began to heat up, and I was made an offer which would be very difficult to refuse. I held off, though, waiting for the committee to meet and rule on the boat. While I was waiting, a letter came from Ron Holland. George Bush had told him that I was interested in a fast cruiser, he said, and he would be happy to talk with me about it.

I had forgotten about Ron Holland's boat in my enthusiasm for the Hurley, and anyway, the *Shamrock* was out of my price range, but I telephoned him and told him what I was thinking of doing and asked him whether he thought a *Shamrock* would be a suitable yacht for the OSTAR. He thought it would. It was an easy boat to sail, and with its wide beam and high freeboard would be very seaworthy. I asked what modifications, if any, he would make to better suit the boat for its purpose. He'd add a skeg, maybe, to make the boat a bit more directionally stable off the wind and to help the self-steering, which would have to be fitted for the race. I told him I'd think about it.

I still had not made a definite decision to attempt the OSTAR project. I didn't know exactly how much money was going to be available, and wouldn't until I went home for the Christmas holidays, and I still hadn't heard from the committee. Still, I knew I was going to buy some sort of cruising boat, and there were some steps I could take. I heard about a Leonard Breewood, who had started a school of navigation. I rang him up and learned that the full course for the Yachtmaster's Offshore Certificate required three weekends of classroom instruction (forty-eight hours), plus considerable study in between. I signed up for the first weekend of the course.

I drove down to Len Breewood's place in Tralee, a new house on the south shore of Tralee Bay, which he and his wife had built as a combination guesthouse/sailing and navigation school. It was in a beautiful setting, and Len turned out to be a man of many parts. He had started as a shipwright's apprentice in the Royal Navy and had later taken degrees in both marine engineering and naval architecture.

He was lecturing in mechanical engineering at a college in Tralee while building up his sailing-school business on the side. A small, wide-eyed man with a dapper beard, he was also an experienced yachtsman and, of course, navigator. My fellow pupil was a native Corkman who was home on leave from his job, which was, improbably, detective inspector in the Hong Kong police force. We spent all day Saturday and Sunday penetrating the mysteries of compass variation and deviation, chart symbols, tidal streams, the buoyage system, the rule of the road, flashing and occulting lights, passage planning, and two or three dozen other subjects, all brand-new to both of us. On Sunday afternoon we plotted a mythical weekend cruise off the south coast. I plotted my course straight through two islands, but apart from my supposed loss of the yacht and my probable fatality, all went well. Sunday night I phoned Ron Holland.

Monday morning I drove to Cork and went to Southcoast Boatyard. I arrived a bit early and occupied my time by taking a ladder around to different boats in cradles on the quay, climbing up to deck level and peering inside. Shortly, I was approached by a rumpled, unshaven figure, wearing jeans and a beat-up sheepskin jacket. Uh-oh, I thought, one of the lads has been sent to tell me not to mess with the boats.

"Hi," he said, "I'm Ron Holland."

24

Things Begin
to Get Out of Hand

Wᴇ sat in the sunny dining room of the Grand Hotel in Cross-haven, with a view of the river and, in the distance, the kelly-green hull of *Golden Shamrock*, the prototype, riding at her moorings. We had the place entirely to ourselves, business not being so hot in November, and our very own waiter hovered about. We had tried to get out to *Shamrock* to have a look at her but couldn't get the club ferry started, so we had repaired to the hotel for some lunch.

Now I was explaining to Ron Holland what I was thinking of doing. I was careful to explain just how little experience I had. It seemed very important not to give him any sort of inflated impression of my state of knowledge. I had, by now, read maybe a dozen books on single-handing, cruising, yacht design, etc., and it is all too easy to bandy about a few technical terms and give someone the impression that you know more than you do. This is done every day in yacht club bars.

I poured out every thought I had about the race, the kind of boat I thought I needed, what I thought I had to do to get ready, what sort of equipment I would need. He was the first person I had told about this in any detail, and somewhat to my surprise, he seemed not to think I was mad and was actually agreeing with much of what I said. I suppose I had expected him to take a more skeptical view, perhaps even to try to discourage me, but this was not happening. Ron suggested we go to the boatyard and talk with the managing director.

Driving down to Crosshaven before lunch, Ron pointed out a large Georgian house on the other side of the river and said that he lived in a flat on one side of the house. Now, driving back toward the yard, past the house again, I mentioned that I had often thought that this area would be a nice place to live, what with so much good sailing, but I thought that I could never find as good a situation as I had at Lough Cutra Castle.

"Let me show you a place we almost took when we came to Cork," he said. "It didn't have quite enough room for us, since we're expecting a baby in the spring."

We drove around to Coolmore, as the house was called, and stopped for a few minutes. Ron's flat was four or five enormous rooms on the south side of the house, and his working space was on the large stair landing. We looked at the original drawings of *Golden Shamrock* and compared them to the production version. The new boat was to have a slightly higher and longer coach roof and a more comfortable interior, but the hull shape was to be identical to that of the prototype.

We met the owner of Coolmore, who looked very much the Master of the Hounds, which, it turned out, he was. He gave us the key to the place Ron wanted to show me, and we drove along a rutted, very muddy road beside the river until we came to a small clearing, where we parked the car. We walked a few yards and came to a lovely old stone cottage right on the banks of the river at a bend called Drake's Pool, so named because Sir Francis Drake is supposed to have eluded the Spanish by hiding there. Because of the double bend in the river they thought it was petering out and went back to search for him in Cork Harbour. The Owenboy River has scoured out a deep pool there, and it is a perfect yacht anchorage. There was an empty mooring directly in front of the cottage. We looked inside: a large living room, a large bedroom, a small bedroom, a kitchen, and a bath. The place had been newly plumbed and wired for electricity. I felt a bit giddy; things had begun to move very fast. I looked again at the mooring as we left. It came with the cottage, Ron said.

At the boatyard we encountered the skepticism from its managing director, Barry Burke, that I had half expected from Ron. He wasn't sure that the boat was suitable for a transatlantic passage. Ron said that he'd crossed the Tasman Sea in a similar-sized boat. I pointed out that the OSTAR in '72 had been done by David Blagden in a nineteen-foot Hunter and asked if he didn't think his boat would be as strong as a Hunter 19. Ron said he'd given the boat more of a bashing in the 625-mile Fastnet Race than I'd give it in a transatlantic. We talked about making changes to the standard design. Burke was reluctant to slow his production line down with modifications to a standard boat. Pull it off the line, said Ron, and put a couple of men on it. Burke wasn't sure. He asked when I would want the boat. Easter, I said. Impossible, he replied. He'd already sold nine boats. The earliest delivery date would be July 1. I did some quick mental calculations. The OSTAR rules required a five-hundred-mile qualifying single-handed cruise no later than three months before the race. I figured that if the boat were ready on July 1 I could just about get her and myself ready for a qualifying cruise before the end of the summer, if I sailed on as many other boats as I could in the spring and early summer. We made a list of the possible modifications to the boat, and Barry promised to let me have an estimate for them. I had hoped that he might agree to some discount, since the boat would undoubtedly receive a lot of attention if it were entered in the OSTAR, and I hoped to do a book about the experience; that would give it even more publicity. Barry didn't seem inclined to give a discount. We left it at that, and I invited Ron to have dinner with me, where we continued our discussion of the yacht and the race. "What would you change about the boat if you were not building to the Rule?" I asked. (The International Offshore Rule is a rating system so complex that it is understood only by computers, which, in turn, explain it to yacht designers and yachting magazines, which publish incomprehensible articles about it.)

Ron looked thoughtful. "Maybe raise the freeboard a little," he said. The freeboard is the amount of hull between the deck and the waterline, and, so my reading had told me, was a principal factor in seaworthiness.

"Suppose," I said, "we put a two-inch slice of teak between the hull and the deck? That would raise the freeboard and also give me another two inches of headroom in the cabin." We were talking about how to change the yacht slightly to make it a fast cruiser instead of a flat-out racing boat. We had already talked about sawing the racing-type cockpit out of the glass-fiber-molded deck and building a more conventional cruising cockpit with seats and lockers.

"I think that's a rather intelligent solution," he replied. I glowed at the thought of having contributed an original idea. We talked about what might be squeezed into the interior. Southcoast had hired a Swedish designer to do the interior, and I was considering doing my own layout with Ron's help, since my requirements were different from the man who might race the boat on weekends, then take an occasional family cruise. I wanted no bunks forward in the boat. I wanted a large, empty forepeak for sail stowage and nothing else. It seemed to me that all the other boats I had seen with bunks forward always had the forepeak filled with wet sails anyway, so why have bunks?

Our evening was drawing to a close, and over coffee we had returned to the subject of a novice attempting to learn enough in a short time to sail the race successfully. I outlined what I thought I had to do in the remaining time. Up until now everything had been a big maybe, but I had been encouraged by my practically daylong talk with Ron. Finally, I said, "I think I can do it." Ron said, "I think you can do it, too. I think it's an exciting project, and I'd like to be involved in it."

I think at that moment the basic decision was made.

Back at Lough Cutra there was a letter waiting from the OSTAR race committee. They had decided to accept Ewan Southby-Tailyour's Hurley 24 entry because of his performance in the Round Britain Race but would accept no other Hurley 24s. Had the boat been of that size but of a more experimental nature, they might have considered it more favorably. I didn't understand that last part, but anyway, my mind was now galloping off on another tack and the *Shamrock* had replaced the Hurley in my thinking.

Now I began, with no credentials whatever, to become a yacht designer, at least on the inside of the yacht. I pored over the layouts of dozens of other yachts, picking the features I liked best. First of all, since I didn't want berths in the forecabin, that could be smaller and the saloon and toilet areas correspondingly larger. Then I crammed into the space available every feature I had heard about, read about, or imagined, and, to my astonishment, it all seemed to fit. A letter arrived from Barry Burke, with an estimate for fitting a skeg, rebuilding the cockpit, raising the decks with my teak sandwich idea, and building a custom interior to my specifications. It came to £1,600 above the cost of the standard boat. This was daunting, but maybe it could be lowered a bit by negotiation.

I had a telephone conversation with John McWilliam, the Crosshaven sailmaker who had clothed *Golden Apple* and *Golden Shamrock*. He had been out of town during my visit to Cork, but he had since talked with Ron and was enthusiastic about the project. We talked about a possible sail plan, and he sent an estimate. Another £1,600 or so was added to the budget.

About this time I felt enough committed to the project to begin to let my friends in Galway know what I was thinking. A friend from Dublin came down to Lough Cutra for the weekend, and I invited Harry McMahon and his wife to join us for dinner. At some point during the evening I mentioned, as casually as possible, that I was thinking of buying a Ron Holland half-tonner. The last boat I had mentioned to Harry had been the Hurley, and I hadn't mentioned any plans for it beyond some coastal cruising. "What would you do with a half-tonner in Galway?" he asked.

I took a deep breath. "I'm thinking of sailing it in the *Observer* Single-Handed Transatlantic Race," I said. Harry looked stunned; his wife burst out laughing. That was to be fairly typical of the reactions of people who knew me as a Mirror helmsman in Galway. I would just have to get used to it.

In early December I went back to see Ron in Cork. He looked at my sketch of the interior and explained, as patiently as he could, that this would not fit, because the sides of the boat did not go straight down but curved inward. On a cruising boat with fuller "sections" it might be possible, but not on a hull designed for racing. Together we drew up a compromise of what *might* be possible. He did, however, agree with my idea of pushing the saloon bulkhead (wall) forward by making the forecabin smaller. Ron pulled out the drawings of a three-quarter-tonner he had designed for production in glass fiber, called the Quest 32. The company that was to manufacture it had gone under. We all agreed that it was a great pity that it would not now be built. Ron was at a stage of his career when he needed several boats in series production, just about the only way a yacht designer can make any real money.

Ron Holland was born and grew up in New Zealand, sailing from an early age. After secondary school he served an apprenticeship in boat building and, as a part of that, took some drafting and design courses. He then went to the United States and worked in California for a well-known designer, Gary Mull, and later, in Florida, for Charley Morgan of Morgan Yachts. He met the sailing-oriented family of Carlins there and married their daughter Laurel. In 1973, sailing his own boat, he won the world quarter-ton championships. The boat was called *Eyghtene* (after the Australian pronunciation of "eighteen"). After the world championships Ron was living aboard the little twenty-four-footer in the Hamble River in England when he was approached by a young Cork businessman about designing a one-tonner. Ron and Laurel came to Cork to talk about it, fell in love with Ireland, and stayed. *Golden Apple* performed brilliantly but erratically in the world one-ton championships in 1974, but she was obviously the fastest boat there and caught the attention of everybody, including the yachting press, and Ron's reputation soared.

Back in Cork, Southcoast Boatyard, which had built *Golden Apple*, asked him to design a half-tonner to be built in time for the world half-ton championships at La Rochelle, in France. The boat, the original *Golden Shamrock*, was rushed to completion and arrived in La Rochelle barely in time for the first race. Because of a stretching of rigging which had occurred on the passage to France, and the lack of time to replace it, *Shamrock* was dismasted in the first race. Somehow, another mast was obtained immediately, and the crew stayed up all night rigging the boat. After that, she performed spectacularly, even in survival conditions, and the decision was made to put the design into series production in glass fiber. Now Ron had another one-off design, a two-tonner intended for the Irish Admiral's Cup team, and the biggest boat he had yet designed. This, he hoped, would be as important a boat as *Golden Apple*, but he still wanted more designs in series production. The dying of the Quest 32 was a blow.

In Cork I also met John McWilliam, the sailmaker, and had another talk with Barry Burke at Southcoast. I also had a talk with Ron's landlord, and told him I was very interested in the cottage. He seemed amenable to having me there.

A few days later, as my Aer Lingus flight took off from Shannon Airport, headed for New York, then Georgia and the Christmas holidays, a broad plan had come together for the project: move to Cork in February, study navigation all winter and sail during the spring on any boat whose skipper would have me; the boat would start building May 1 and be launched July 1; then sail her intensively, going out to southwest France and northwest Spain or perhaps even the Azores with friends, then sail back to Crosshaven, single-handed, for my qualifying cruise. (I wanted to sail more than the minimum five hundred miles, hoping that a longer qualifying cruise would count with the race committee against my inexperience.)

The cottage would have, within a five-mile radius, the boatyard, the designer, and the sailmaker. Both Ron and John McWilliam had promised me as much time as they could spare in tuning the boat and helping me to learn to sail her. The only big question mark was the money, and that would be resolved, one way or the other, when I arrived in the States.

It seemed a very neat program. I could only hope that, in my ignorance, I had not made it too neat, had not failed to take some hugely important factor into account which, when it emerged, would wreck the whole project. If my own funds wouldn't cover the cost, then there was the possibility of commercial sponsorship. I felt that if I had to I could probably do a better job than most in attracting commercial attention, since I had spent all of my working life in advertising, dealing on a daily basis with the sort of people I would have to approach.

The novel would have to wait a couple of years, but then, a novel can always wait, as any novelist can tell you.

The project was all there, in outline; I could do nothing more until January, except think about it. And until January I would think about nothing else.

25

Things Begin to Gel

Manchester, Georgia, is a town of about six thousand people, located about seventy miles south of Atlanta, the state capital. It is, perhaps, two hundred fifty miles from the nearest body of salt water, and the populace is not made up of sailing enthusiasts. A boat is something you row or propel with an outboard motor and is used in the catching of largemouth bass and catfish. To my mother, who is not interested in fishing, boats mean even less.

Dot, which is short for Dorothy and what I have called her ever since I learned to talk, did not quite seem to get it when I explained to her what I planned to do. I spread out the plans for the boat and explained it all again. Still, I don't think the penny dropped until a few days later. We were sitting in her car in a supermarket parking lot, about to drive home with the groceries, when she asked suddenly, "Are you really going to do this?"

"Do what?" I asked. We had not discussed the subject since the day before.

"Sail that little boat across the Atlantic Ocean by yourself."

"Yes."

Gene Spain, our family life insurance man, happened to be strolling through the parking lot at that moment. Dot rolled down the car window. "Gene, I want you to come by the house," she said. "I want to talk to you about some insurance." Gene forgot about his grocery shopping.

A few minutes later the two of them had worked out the details of a fairly hefty policy on my life, over my strenuous protests. "What do I need with insurance?" They ignored me.

"Do you want double indemnity?" asked Gene. "There's only a small additional premium."

"How much is treble indemnity?" asked my mother.

After that she seemed resigned to the idea. She learned long ago that it is difficult to talk me out of something I'm excited about. We met with the family attorney to sort out my grandfather's estate, and I discovered to my astonishment that my estimate of what he had left me was short by half. Now I could afford the *Shamrock* and all the necessary equipment.

I had to cut my stay short by a few days in order to get to London in time for the tail end of the London Boat Show. I stopped off in New York for a day and managed to see a half dozen old friends, then flew to Shannon. Harry McMahon met me the next day at Lough Cutra, and we drove to Cork to catch the ferry to England. But first I had two things to accomplish in Cork.

First, I went to Southcoast Boatyard and, after some discussion, worked out a deal with Barry Burke: I would buy the standard boat at the full price, then the boatyard would carry out any alterations I wanted and maintain the boat until the start of the race at cost for materials and at cost plus ten percent for labor. The boatyard would also obtain any extra gear I required at trade prices. We signed the contract; Barry gave me a letter outlining the alteration and main-tenance and equipment agreement, and I gave him a £500 deposit. We agreed on half the remaining price being paid at the time of molding, May 1, and the remainder on launching, July 1. Harry witnessed the contract. I was delighted with the arrangement and felt it was a good one for both of us. Barry seemed to think so, too.

Next, I called at Coolmore, to finalize arrangements about the cottage. By noon the next day we were at the London Boat Show.

We were like Babes in Toyland. Galway had no well-equipped chandleries, and Dublin, at that time, was not much better. When we wanted a piece of equipment a complicated mail-order pro-cedure was involved, and often a battle with the transport services and customs. Now, spread before us, were two huge floors packed with everything anyone could possibly want for a boat, from the smallest cleat to the tallest mast. There were only two and a half days left of the show, and I had to buy or at least research virtually every piece of equipment that would be needed for my yacht. I bought a sextant, instruments, a hand bearing compass, a VHF radio-telephone, clothing, a wet suit, books, and much else from a long list. I carefully researched life rafts and inflatable din-ghies, emergency radio transmitters, self-steering, and electronics. Whenever possible I approached manufacturers about possible discounts on equipment.

On my return there were still one or two things to do before the move to Cork. I talked to some of the cruising people in the club, and we agreed to ask Len Breewood to come up to Galway for three weekends during the winter to teach the Yachtmaster's Offshore navigation course. Len agreed to come for one weekend a month starting in February.

The other thing was to talk with Commander Bill King. Bill King is a retired Royal Navy submarine commander, in fact, the only submarine commander in any navy, he believes, who started World War II in command of a submarine and who was still alive at the end of it all. He had one hell of a war and has written about it in his own excellent book, *Adventure in Depth*. After the war, annoyed by the Royal Navy's recalcitrance in adopting modern methods, he spent some years in ocean racing and sailing his own boat, then went to farm in County Galway and remained there in contentment with his wife, the writer Anita Leslie, until the late 1960s. Then he began planning a long-held dream to sail around the world, single-handed, nonstop. the *Sunday Times*, hearing about this, offered a £5,000 prize and a trophy, the Golden Globe, for the first man to complete the voyage. Bill's boat, designed by Angus Primrose, partner of Bill's wartime and postwar ocean-racing friend, the legendary John Illingworth, and by Colonel "Blondie" Hasler, who designed the Chinese Junk rig, was named *Galway Blazer II*. Bill set off alone, opposing Robin Knox-Johnston, Bernard Moitessier, and others, to race around the world, alone, without stopping.

About a thousand miles southwest of Cape Town, South Africa, *Blazer* was rolled over in 120 knots of wind and dismasted. Bill sailed her to Cape Town under a jury rig and shipped her back to England for repairs. Those completed, he set off again, and had to put into Gibraltar because of rigging problems. The yacht was once again returned to England, and he set off again. By this time, Robin Knox-Johnston was, beyond doubt, the winner of the race, Moitessier having continued to sail on to Tahiti after rounding Cape Horn, and the others having turned back or lost their boats. But Bill King was determined to complete his voyage for his own personal satisfaction.

On his third attempt, he was sailing two hundred miles off western Australia when the yacht was attacked by a great white shark and badly holed. In a magnificent act of seamanship and personal courage, Bill temporarily plugged the hole and sailed into port. Repairs completed, he finished his voyage without another stop, arriving back in Galway in early 1973, shortly after I had moved there. I had met him socially once or twice and had told him of my long-range plan of doing some deep-water sailing. He invited me to come and talk with him about it.

At the boat show I had been delighted to find that the Multihull Offshore Cruising and Racing Association (MOCRA) had organized a race to Horta, in the Azores, for August 1975, the very time I had been thinking of sailing there. I signed up immediately. Now I went to see Bill King and asked if he'd like to come. He had not sailed at all since returning from his circumnavigation, but two years had passed and he must have been getting itchy for the sea. He accepted immediately. He would sail out with me and one or two other people and would hitch a ride home on another yacht while I sailed back single-handed. He also offered to come to Cork when the yacht was building and share his enormous experience. I was delighted.

That accomplished, I packed my things into a furniture van and moved to Drake's Pool Cottage, Coolmore, Carrigaline, County Cork.

Drake's Pool Cottage. The mooring is right in front.

26

Waiting on Spring

Driving back to the cottage from Carrigaline, about three miles away and the closest village, it occurred to me how isolated I would be at Drake's Pool. The road to Coolmore wasn't really on the way to anywhere, except Currabinny, and that just barely qualified as anywhere. I thought the isolation would be good for work on the novel but not so good for social life. Still musing on my remove from the rest of the world, I arrived at the cottage to find a *Watchtower* magazine on my doorstep. It seemed that, to the Jehovah's Witnesses, nobody was isolated.

The following day I was sitting among my unpacked books, typing a letter, when two pretty girls appeared at the front door. Terrific! Not so isolated, after all! They turned out to be the Jehovah's Witnesses. Still . . . I invited them in and we got into a hot religious discussion. I was annoyed by the ease with which they backed up their convictions with seemingly ambiguous quotes from the scriptures, so I dug a Bible from one of the tea chests and fenced with them for a bit. I scored no points in this debate. There was always a ready scriptural reference, there to be taken literally. Finally, I asked how they felt about sex—outside marriage, I meant. Oh, no. Against the rules, and a couple of suspect verses were quoted. I asked if they believed in a just God. Oh, yes, certainly. Well, I said, I didn't think a just God would require me to remain celibate just because I had happened not to get married. They made an excuse and left.

Worth Newenham, my new landlord, and his wife turned up with a gift bag of turf for the fireplace and stayed for a drink. I asked where I might get a bookcase built in the neighborhood. Books follow me about relentlessly wherever I go, multiplying steadily. When I had left London for Ireland I had given most of my library away, but the few I had brought with me (only about four packing cases full) had done their multiplication trick. The cottage would not be livable until I got them out of the boxes and into a bookcase, a large bookcase. Worth suggested I talk with Nick Roe, who was living on an old trawler on a mooring in front of the cottage, rebuilding it. Nick Roe was to become a very important part of my project before it was all done.

Nick stopped by later with his brother and girlfriend. They were all living on the boat, which was quite, quite large. Nick was very busy with his work, but he agreed to build the bookcase for me.

Gradually, things got unpacked, and I settled in. Ron dropped by now and then. I visited the boatyard, where the new factory for the series production was now complete and the first hull and deck was being molded. The factory looked good, and I felt more confident about the building of the boat. I had conversations about alterations to the boat with the production manager and with George Bush, who would be in charge of the extra work.

On the sponsorship front, I started with the *Irish Times*, perhaps the best of the Irish national newspapers. I had a meeting in Dublin with a member of their management and their advertising agency, and they expressed interest in sponsoring the project, perhaps in concert with another Irish company, yet to be found. I started looking. I tried Guinness first. They seemed a logical place to start, and through an acquaintance, they gave a logical reason for not sponsoring: they had cut back on all but existing sponsorship. They had just turned down a pub in Waterford for a trophy for their darts championship. They could hardly turn them down, then have the lads see on TV that they were sponsoring a yacht, could they?

To save time in explaining what I was doing, I wrote a description of the project and had copies run off. I began sending these to prominent Irish companies, since I intended being an Irish entry. A rule of the race stated that the nationality of the entry would be the nationality of the skipper. In December, when I had written to the committee formally reserving a place in the race, pending the qualifying cruise, I explained that although I was an American I had lived for some time in Ireland and had learned to sail there from Irish yachtsmen on Irish boats, and I requested that an exception be made and I be allowed to become an Irish entry. I had received a letter from the Royal Western Yacht Club saying that would be fine. Shortly after reserving my place I noticed an article in the *Observer* by yachting correspondent Frank Page, giving the number of entries by nationality. No Irish entry had been mentioned, and I dropped him a note saying that there would be an Irish entry, and since I was looking for Irish sponsorship, could he please say so sometime in his newspaper?

My race number of twenty-four was also confirmed. This number might pose something of a problem, since it had to be displayed on the sails, hull, and deck, and I was also entered for the MOCRA Azores race, which might assign me a different number. The problem was solved by asking MOCRA to make me entry number twenty-four in their race, and by asking the Irish Yachting Association for the sail number IR 24; both requests were granted.

The new two-tonner, which would be called *Irish Mist II*, was quickly taking shape at Southcoast. When introduced to Archie O'Leary, the owner, I offered to crew on any delivery trips he might be making when his own racing crew was not available. He promised to keep me in mind.

I found myself extremely busy, although my boat had not yet begun building. I was hustling about, ordering equipment and trying to ensure that it all arrived in time for the launching of the yacht; I was working hard on the sponsorship problem; I was writing to manufacturers, asking for discounts.

Also, I was negotiating with a publisher about a book describing the project. Ron was working on a book for Stanford Maritime, and he and his editor stopped by the cottage for a drink. After hearing about what I was doing, he expressed interest, and eventually we signed a contract. Finally, I still wanted to do some advertising work in Dublin.

I was trying to do all of this with no help whatsoever from the Irish Department of Posts and Telegraphs. In Galway it had taken me fourteen months to wrench a telephone from their grasp, and they had assured me that, as an existing subscriber, when I moved to Cork there would be no problem getting a telephone immediately. (The word "immediately" has no meaning in Ireland. It's just a word.) However, when I arrived in Cork, although my application had preceded me by more than a month, nothing was happening. Finally, after weeks of telephone conversations (they never, never actually wrote any letters, although I would periodically receive a printed form telling me that my problem was being dealt with) they finally told me that nobody who lived more than a quarter of a mile from an existing telephone line could be provided with service, and that I lived 175 yards beyond that distance. Although I clawed my way through what seemed like the entire Irish Civil Service, the situation remained frozen for months.

Other communication systems were, however, working. One bright Sunday morning I awoke to find that, having left the reversing lamp on my car on all night, the battery was completely dead. Being some distance from a telephone, I had another idea. The VHF radio-telephone which I had bought at the London Boat Show was a self-contained one, having its own power supply. Technically, the radio was not supposed to be operated except on the yacht, and only after having been licensed. The boat did not even exist yet, and I had not even applied for a license, but I got out the list of Irish coastal stations and the instructions for transmission procedure. I studied them for a few minutes and then switched on the radio.

"Cobh Radio, Cobh Radio, Cobh Radio (the Cork Harbour station), this is Woodsmoke, Woodsmoke, Woodsmoke (a tentative name for the yacht). Do you read me?" Silence for two minutes, the instructions said. Then if no reply, try again. I tried again.

I jumped about a foot when a clear voice said, "Woodsmoke, Woodsmoke, Woodsmoke, this is Cobh Radio, Cobh Radio, Cobh Radio, what is your position? Over."

"Cobh Radio, I'm at Drake's Pool, uh, ashore, uh, and I have a problem with my car. I wonder if you could possibly telephone the AA for me? Over."

Silence. He probably didn't think he was hearing properly. Then he came back. "Woodsmoke, we don't ordinarily do that sort of thing, but we're not too busy right now, and I've been in that position myself. How will the AA find you? Over."

"I'm at Drake's Pool Cottage . . ."

"Cottage!" he interrupted. After all, this was supposed to be a ship-to-shore radio.

"Ah, yes, there's this cottage, and my car is parked there." I gave him the complicated directions for finding me and we signed off.

An hour later an AA man appeared, scratching his head and saying that he'd never had a call like this one before. I had half expected the police, but a minute or two later the car was started. I never used the VHF ashore again, though.

The Dublin Boat Show rolled around, and I used the trip to Dublin to check on what was happening with the *Irish Times*. Nothing, apparently. However, Exide had agreed to donate the batteries for the boat. It was the first equipment I had been given, and was a lift to the spirits. The Dublin show seemed small after the London one, but it was interesting, and I bought an outboard motor for the dinghy and a few small things.

Back at Southcoast, the first deck went onto the first hull of the new series. It was the first glimpse I had of anything like the complete boat, and I was impressed with what a pretty craft she was going to be. The first and third boats in the series were being sent out unfinished, in kit form, but the second boat, a bright red one which would be finished in the factory, was getting under way, and I was looking forward to seeing it take shape.

Then Fred vanished. He was grown now but still very much the puppy at heart, and he missed the dogs and children at Lough Cutra, especially the children. He had taken to walking the mile or so to the main gate of Coolmore, where a group of small kids gathered to play, and one night, he didn't come home. To make matters worse, his collar and name tag had disappeared the day before, so nobody would know where he came from. As the days passed with no sign of him I took to driving around the countryside looking for him. He had been stolen twice as a puppy, but recovered, and I was increasingly worried about him. He was the only company I had in the cottage, and good company he was, always making me laugh, bringing me sticks to throw into the river for him to retrieve. He liked swimming better than walking, being a Labrador. I put notices up in the post offices in the surrounding villages. He was seen at Ringaskiddy, then Currabinny, then Douglas, eight miles away. There were apparently a lot of golden Labradors about. Since I didn't have a phone, Ron was taking the calls, and they were coming in at the rate of two or three a day. I got one from Kanturk, twenty miles away, but it turned out to be a different Lab. Finally, I put an ad in the *Cork Examiner*, and someone in Douglas called. They had had a strange Labrador about for days. I went to Douglas. It was Fred. He had been gone for two weeks. The minute he was home he had a stick in his mouth, ready for his swim. He got a new collar and ID tag the same day.

Fred, bored with chasing sticks, takes on a tree.

27

Organize, Organize, Organize

In late March we had the second of our navigation classes in Galway, and I managed to get a lot into the weekend. I had dinner with Harry and Lorna McMahon, and although Bill King was away (skiing), his wife, Anita, joined us. What a delightful woman she is. We talked about her bestselling book, *Jenny*, based on the life of Winston Churchill's mother. Anita's grandmother was Jenny's sister, and Anita had known Lady Randolph Churchill as a child. The television series based on the book was running at the time, and talk centered on that. She mentioned that Bill was looking forward eagerly to the Azores trip. I asked Harry to come as well, but he was doubtful whether he'd be able to manage the time. I had already invited Ewan Southby-Tailyour, but he wasn't sure whether the Royal Marines would give him time to do the Azores race and the OSTAR in successive years.

Our navigation class went well, and we agreed to spend our

final weekend, in April, cruising to the Aran Islands and back, putting our newfound knowledge into practice.

Back in Cork, it was time to place my order for sails, and John McWilliam and I sat down to discuss this. Getting John McWilliam to sit down is no small feat. He is the only person I met during the whole of my stay in Ireland who is visibly energetic about his work.

John McWilliam is a northerner, from the Six Counties, and after engineering school did a spell with the RAF, doing individual aerobatics with the famous Red Arrows stunt team at air shows. After that, he did an apprenticeship with the Australian sailmaker Rolly Tasker in his Hong Kong loft, then opened a Tasker branch in Ireland. By the time I arrived, he had gone out on his own, making his sails on the main floor of an old stone mill on the hill behind Crosshaven, and living in a handsome flat on the top floor.

Visiting the McWilliam Sailmakers loft is an experience. You can feel the glass vibrating before you even open the door, and inside, sound strikes with a physical force. There is a souped-up stereo system driving a series of huge speakers, and the noise which comes out is overpowering to all but the demented teenyboppers with whom John McWilliam shares his musical taste. Through two more sets of sliding doors and into the loft proper, one comes upon Mr. McWilliam, loping about the varnished floor, carpet slippers on his feet, foam rubber taped to his knees, with a grace of movement not seen since the actor known as Stepin Fetchit plied the silver screen. John moves much faster, though, and constantly.

John is also very bright, and a first-rate man on a racing yacht. He is probably the only one of the world's top three or four sailmakers who still cuts every sail himself, assisted only by his right-hand man and a harem of local girls, who, even while bent over their sewing machines, giggle and blush constantly. John makes up for being in an out-of-the-way place by delivering his sails to customers all over the British Isles and Europe in a twin-engine Piper Apache, the flying of which gives him enormous pleasure. He probably gives his customers a more personal and more effective service than some sailmakers located in hotbeds of sailing activity, such as the south coast of England. He claims to charge less, too, and his sails are nearly as good as he says they are.

The sail plan we worked out for my boat was made up of a mainsail, a large genoa (foresail), a number-two genoa (slightly smaller than the large one), a medium-weight spinnaker for all-round use, a floater spinnaker for very light winds, and a smaller "starcut" spinnaker for reaching and for running in heavy winds. (Later we dropped the starcut, because I realized I wasn't about to set a spinnaker, single-handed, in strong winds.) There would be no smaller headsail than the number-two genoa, because I intended to reef that sail rather than change down to a smaller one. This would be done by virtue of a device called a Dynafurl. It works this way: the sail, instead of being set on an ordinary wire forestay, is set on a grooved, solid rod forestay, called a Twinstay. In ordinary, crewed racing, a sail can be set on this stay while another one is still drawing, giving an advantage over conventional sail changing. The Dynafurl consists of two swivels, one at the top of the stay and one at the bottom. When reefing the sail, a rope is pulled and the sail wraps itself tightly around the forestay, displaying progressively smaller area. It can be reefed right down to storm jib size in this fashion.

My reason for choosing this system was twofold: (1) I reasoned that in a three-thousand-mile race, an awful lot of time could be spent changing sails in changeable conditions, and the boat would be slowed during sail changes; (2) If the only sail change I had to make was from the number-one genoa to the number-two genoa, this would keep me off the foredeck in heavy weather, when it can be a very dangerous place. My only sail change would be made in less than fifteen knots of wind.

The mainsail, instead of having roller reefing, where the sail is rolled up around the boom, would have slab reefing, in which the sail is simply tied to the boom by a row of cringles (eyes) sewn across the sail. This would be faster single-handed, and the sail would set better as well.

Later, we would add two other sails to the wardrobe: one, a duplicate number-two genoa, so that twin headsails could be set when running in fresher winds, and so that I would have a spare for my principal working sail. Twin headsails are easier to control than a spinnaker and have self-steering properties, too, which would be a help in strong winds. The other addition would be a drifter, or very light large genoa, made of nylon. This would help considerably when beating or reaching in very light winds. Much later, the need for a storm jib would present itself, but I'll get to that later.

With the sails ordered and a delivery date promised to coincide with the boat's launching, I set about selecting other gear. I chose the well-known Hasler Windvane self-steering system. I must admit I chose it with a minimum of research. Mike Ellison, of the Amateur Yacht Research Society, which had done much research, recommended it, and so did Ron Holland. The difficult decision to make was whether to order the small or medium size of the unit. My boat fell in a gray area where the small unit might be big enough and might not. But the larger unit was twice as heavy and twice as expensive, so I took the chance and went for the smaller one. I would not know until the boat was launched whether I had made the right decision, and I was plagued by doubt.

I chose the Avon four-man life raft and the Avon Redcrest inflatable dinghy as my tender. Both were well proven, and I had been impressed by Avon quality at the London Boat Show. Life raft stowage was going to be a problem, because even a four-man raft is rather bulky, and no place had been designed into the Shamrock for it, a mistake, I felt, and one which I communicated to Ron on more than one occasion. I chose Brookes & Gatehouse electronic instruments, simply because, from everything I could gather from every source I could find, they were considered to be the finest in the world. I ordered their Hornet unit, which combines, in one control box, wind speed, wind direction, magnified wind direction (a fine display for beating to windward), water speed, and distance covered. To this I added the Hound water speed amplifier, which gives a finer display of small changes in speed and is invaluable for fine sail trimming.

I also, after much soul searching, ordered the B&G Horatio unit, which offers several functions. Once a course is set into an electronic compass on the deckhead, steering can be done by keeping a needle on a dial straight up, instead of steering a compass course, which demands more concentration and is more tiring. The unit also has an off-course alarm, which can be set for either twenty or forty degrees, important when the boat is under self-steering and will change direction automatically if the wind direction changes. Finally, there is a constant digital readout of the number of miles sailed to either port or starboard of a set course. This would be valuable when setting a course when about to go to sleep. On awaking, I would know how far off course I might have sailed. Horatio was an expensive piece of equipment, costing as much as the complete Hound, but I felt I might genuinely need it.

I also chose the B&G Homer/Heron radio receiver and radio direction finding compass, and the shortwave converter for the radio, which would enable me to pick up radio time signals at sea.

To the Brookes & Gatehouse equipment I added the ubiquitous Seafarer depth sounder (at the suggestion of B&G, because I wanted to economize) and the Seavoice VHF, already mentioned, made by the same company. (I later exchanged the self-contained model for the ordinary model, because I was having difficulty finding room for the extra bulk of the first unit.)

Finally, I added, as a backup radio receiver, the American Zenith Trans-Oceanic Portable, probably the best of its kind, and a Philips car stereo radio/tape player, purely for entertainment. At home I am never without music playing, and I would have missed this terribly at sea.

That was a lot of electronic and electrical gear, but it all got used. I have always had a thing about being well equipped, and the boat would be evidence to this part of my character. In defense, I must say that I felt my lack of experience made electronic help all the more important. A lifelong sailor might guess at the wind speed or direction accurately, but I could not. I felt I needed all the help I could get. This feeling, it turned out, was entirely correct.

I had to choose an engine as well. The choice was between the Yanmar 12 and the Farymann 12 diesels, the Farymann having hydraulic drive. The Yanmar has a good reputation, and I was offered a nice discount on it, but I chose the Farymann because of its compact size and the versatility of installation of the Hydromarine Hydraulic Drive. This equipment is manufactured in Ireland, and Hydromarine offered me, at no extra cost, a heavy-duty unit more suitable for running for long periods without a load, as when charging batteries. They were later to give unstintingly of technical help and advice.

On March 27, Laurel Carlin Holland gave birth to a daughter, Kelly, much to the astonishment of everyone, since triplets, at a minimum, had been expected. Ron was completely bemused by the idea of being a father, and we had a celebratory dinner at Ballymaloe.

My social situation took a turn for the better when a letter came from Ann O'Donahue, a London friend, in response to an invitation issued in January. She would be arriving in early April for a visit. I was looking forward to that. The only people I knew in Cork were my designer, sailmaker, and boatbuilder, none of them very pretty.

Ann arrived on Monday afternoon and we renewed our acquaintance over dinner at Arbutus Lodge, Cork's best restaurant and, many think, Ireland's. Having Ann about the place made an enormous difference. We had the Hollands and Barry and Mary Burke over for dinner and, confirming conversations we had been having, Barry promised to mold my boat next, making it number seven instead of ten. She would be launched, said Barry, around June 1. This was an enormous relief to me. The red boat was only now being completed, and I had been increasingly worried about having the boat ready for the Azores race. Now I would have a month more to sail her than planned!

The red boat was finally launched on April 11. In the water she was very pretty, and we arranged to go sailing on her with Ron and John McWilliam on Sunday.

We were joined by Harold Cudmore, a dinghy sailor, now becoming a helmsman in offshore racing, and a nonstop talker about sailing, Cork, and anything Irish. The boat was a delight to sail. I was astonished at how quickly she tacked. We sailed about Cork Harbour, while Ron ceaselessly tuned the rigging and McWilliam admired his sails. Ron never seems to stop moving on a boat. He is everywhere, dressed in a pair of white painter's overalls, or something equally awful, completely indifferent to what the fashionable yachtsman is supposed to be wearing, and always with tools in his hands. Sometimes he will deign to wear a battered pair of seaboots. Ron seems vaguely uncomfortable in anything new, or even pressed.

McWilliam, on the other hand, is extremely neat, though not given to fashion, as such. He always seems ironed and starched, even on a boat. I think his wife presses him before he leaves the house.

Cudmore, a rangy fellow with a lot of thick, red hair and a native capacity for Guinness, enjoys giving instructions in a manner which manages to be, at once, quick and easy. Both Ron and Harold are good teachers on a boat, each having a large fund of knowledge on every detail of the sailing of a yacht, and a willingness to share it. McWilliam, on the other hand, although possessed of at least as much information, seems to assume that anyone who is over the age of seven has a native understanding of everything that makes a yacht work, and an equal knowledge of things mechanical. Once, when I interrupted him, puzzled by a discourse on load factors or something, he said to me, "You know, it's good training for me to talk to you about things like this; your mind is so . . . so . . ."

"Unsullied by knowledge?" I volunteered.

He grinned. "That's it."

Everything about this first sail in a Shamrock was an eye-opener for me. First of all, it was, at this point in my experience, the largest boat I had ever sailed on; second, it was my introduction to what my own boat would be like, and I was both a little awed by the height of the mast and the sail area, and relieved, in that the yacht didn't seem unmanageable. Ann, who says of her ability on a boat "I do what I'm told," was enjoying herself, too. At least nobody was yelling at her. She tells of a sail down the Channel once with a male companion who became Captain Bligh on a boat. She abandoned ship in Weymouth and took a train back to London.

Sailing back to moorings in front of the yacht club, Cudmore gave me a real workout. Harold would rather sail anytime than use an engine (I saw him sail up to a mooring under spinnaker once, in a riverful of moored yachts), and he decided we would short tack up the river, against the tide. Ron and McWilliam quickly found something to do on the foredeck, and I had to man both winches, with Ann tailing the sheets. I was wiped out by the time we reached the mooring, and after three months on my exercise program. It occurred to me that had I tried that in January I would have collapsed after the first four or five tacks.

Back at the Royal Cork, we ran into Hugh Coveney in the bar and got into a discussion of boats' names. Hugh's *Golden Apple* name came from Yeats . . . "The golden apples of the sun and the silver apples of the moon . . ." The "Golden" handle had continued with *Golden Shamrock*, and I thought I'd like to keep it going, combined with something Irish but a bit more elegant than *Shamrock*. The harp is the Irish national symbol, and that of the Royal Cork Yacht Club as well. *Golden Harp* seemed a good possibility. Hugh liked that, and I think from that time on, though I thought about other names, the yacht, in my own mind, became *Golden Harp*.

Ann flew back to London that afternoon, and I was alone again. Still, my boat was about to begin building, and I was about to make my first passage of the season and my first to England. *Golden Apple* had been sold, and Hugh Coveney had invited me to sail on the delivery trip.

28

My First *Golden* Cruise

The next two weeks were mostly occupied with final meetings about the molding of the boat. I think we had at least three final meetings. I was beginning to have doubts about some of the modifications planned for the boat. First, I abandoned the idea of replacing the whole cockpit and decided just to make the existing one deeper. Then I was talked out of that, because of doubts about the cockpit draining properly when heeled. Finally, George talked me out of raising the decks with the teak sandwich idea. He was concerned about the possibility of leaks around the hull/deck join. I gave in on the custom interior, too. I would accept the Swede's standard interior and simply add extra stowage space.

A letter came from Mike Ellison of the Amateur Yacht Research Society, who was helping to organize the Azores race. When Harry McMahon and Ewan Southby-Tailyour had not been able to get enough free time to do the race, I had told Mike I'd consider taking a girl crew, which the committee had suggested entrants do. Now Mike had two candidates for me, and the following day I received a letter from one of them, Shirley Clifford. She sounded fine, but she was married to Richard Clifford, a Royal Marine officer who had done the last OSTAR, and I wrote her a frank letter explaining that I had not expected inquiries from a married lady, and that I didn't want any angry Marines buzzing about. I didn't, either.

Golden Apple departed about one o'clock on a Friday afternoon, Hugh Coveney having come down to provision and fuel us. The rest of the crew were Ian Hannay, skipper, an English airline pilot and, as it turned out, a former British Olympic helmsman in the Dragon class; Richard Edwards, an English medical student; and Killian Bush, George's son. Killian worked at the yard and had crewed on *Apple* the year before. I'd had some sort of mild bug since the day before and was feeling rotten, so as soon as we set sail at Roche's Point, at the mouth of Cork Harbour, I turned in until time for my watch. It annoyed me to feel poorly at the beginning of a trip to which I had so looked forward; it was my first sail out of sight of land.

I was awakened later by the sound of the engine starting. It was a sound I would grow to hate during the next three days. The wind had been light when we set sail, and now it had dropped to nothing. Motoring on a Ron Holland one-off racing yacht is not like motoring on anything else. Instead of the purr of an engine, muffled by soundproofing, we had a deafening chug, muffled only by a panel of sailcloth between the quarter berth and the engine. Soundproofing is too heavy to be used on a superfast Holland design. We motored on through the late afternoon and into the evening, picking up, at some point, an exhausted pigeon who perched on a spreader, hunkered his head down, and fell into an apparently dreamless sleep, stirring himself from time to time to shit on the deck below.

Dawn came slowly, and we found ourselves motoring onward in a haze that made it impossible to judge distance. The sun shone weakly through it. The effect was one of being anchored in one place with the engine running, there was so little sensation of movement in the haze. By late afternoon things had cleared enough to sight Land's End, my first landfall in a yacht, and that was exciting. That lower-left-hand corner of England was abeam by 20.00 hours, and I turned in after my three-hour watch, looking forward to nine uninterrupted hours of sleep. Motoring was curiously tiring, and I still felt rotten. I was awakened by Hannay at 03.00 after only six hours of sleep and told that I was on watch. (Often on a yacht when racing, or when cruising in heavy weather, the skipper and/or the navigator does not take a watch, but saves himself and is awakened if there are problems.)

It was now clear and very cold (it was only April, remember) with a huge full moon lighting everything through the haze. As I took the helm, Richard gave me the course and said he hadn't sighted the Lizard light and thought we had probably passed it in the fog, earlier. I settled down in my long underwear, jeans, two sweaters, offshore jacket, lined mittens, and my balaclava. The balaclava was the best idea I'd ever had, I thought, keeping me nice and warm inside my jacket's hood.

Half an hour later I sighted two flashing lights slightly off the starboard bow. This was very peculiar, according to the ship's light patterns I had studied in the yachtmaster's course. A larger ship will have two mast lights, one high, aft, and one lower, forward. But they do not flash. The only thing that flashes is a lighthouse or a buoy, and besides, I couldn't see the red and green port and starboard lights which a ship should be wearing. I switched on my pocket torch (always necessary on a night watch, I had discovered) and had a look at the chart. We were past the Lizard, we thought, and the lights were too high to be buoys. I turned to port to avoid the thing, which seemed to be moving.

The two lights continued to flash, and the whole thing made no sense, so I decided to call the skipper. I didn't feel too bad about waking him up, anyway. I shouted "Ian!" a half dozen times but got no reply. Finally, I lashed the helm, stuck my head down the companionway, and yelled "SKIPPER!" This message did not reach Ian, but Richard stumbled, shivering, out of his sleeping bag. We regarded the flashing lights together, through the haze. Finally, Richard dug out *Reed's Nautical Almanac*, consulted it briefly, and timed the lights.

"Well," he said, finally, *"one* of 'em is the Lizard," and went back to bed. I corrected my course quickly, having been steering toward a large and very solid part of Cornwall for the past five minutes. Sure enough, as we drew abeam of the thing, the light-house became visible. The second flashing light appeared to be caused by the light striking another, smaller tower of some sort behind the lighthouse. Later, what seemed to be Falmouth appeared and receded.

That afternoon came the highlight of this exciting voyage on the world's fastest one-tonner. We put into Salcombe for more fuel. We had no dinghy and only one jerry can and the petrol stations were all closed, but the kindly harbormaster quickly arranged for us to buy ten gallons from the local ferry operator, and we were on our way again faster than if we had had a dinghy and more than one jerry can and if the stations had been open. Moreover, after crossing the bar at the mouth of the harbor, we found that rare thing, a breeze, and got a couple of hours of sailing in before it died and we had to go back to the engine.

I was on at midnight, then again at nine on Monday morning (the skipper was saving himself again). It was quite foggy, and we were approaching the Needles, the group of rocks at the western end of the Isle of Wight. Ian fiddled with the Radio Direction Finder, did some calculating, and said, "You'll be hearing the Needles fog signal soon." Soon, indeed, the mournful sound came out of the fog, and shortly afterward, the proper buoy appeared on the nose. I was impressed.

We were in the Lymington Yacht Marina by eleven, cleaned out the boat, cleared customs, rang Avis for a car, and by one I was in bed at the Angel Hotel, dead asleep. It had been the most boring and most exhausting three days I have ever spent on a boat, before or since. So much for exciting delivery trips in fast sailing boats.

The following evening I met for the first time, in person, both Ewan Southby-Tailyour and Shirley Clifford. Ewan (it is pronounced Uwan, I discovered, and Southby, as South) looked more distinguished than his years would suggest, and Shirley looked just like her photograph. Everybody was a bit restrained when we first met at my hotel, two-thirds of the group being British, but after our arrival at a Poole restaurant and the subsequent wine consumed, relaxation prevailed, and I may even have been forward with the lovely proprietress. The evening ended, I think, with an aura of goodwill, in the officer's mess of the Poole Royal Marine base at three a.m. Shirley reassured me that it would be okay with her husband for her to sail with two strange men to a remote island in the North Atlantic. She was a victim, she said, of the "marry your crew and give her hell" syndrome and could not occupy the same floating object as her husband.

Next day, I visited some chandleries and called in at M. S. Gibb in Warsash and Kemp's in Titchfield. Gibb makes the Hasler Windvane self-steering system, and I met Robert Hughes, their marketing manager and resident self-steering expert, who kindly showed me where and how the things were built. I left almost understanding how the gear worked.

At Kemp's I went over the mast order, and Peter Cartwright and his people made a suggestion or two which seemed useful. Earlier in the day, James Kirkman, sales manager at Brookes & Gatehouse, had spent some time explaining the workings of the instruments I had bought, so my time on the south coast was well spent.

I dashed up to London and spent a day or two taking Ann to the theater and gaining weight, then flew back to Cork, anxious to see my newly molded hull and deck.

It hadn't been molded. Somebody's brother had died, or something, and they promised to have it done and out of the mold on the following Monday, a week later. I was extremely annoyed at the delay, especially since Bill King was coming down for a visit, hoping to see the boat under construction, but I gave the yard my next installment on the boat, £5,500. It was the largest check I had ever written. As long as I was writing big checks, I thought I might as well give John McWilliam some money, and as something extra he threw in a free ride on *Irish Mist II*, which had just been launched.

I leapt at the chance, and soon was crouched on the tiny afterdeck behind the helmsman, getting my first look at what goes on on a big boat. Quite a lot went on, and it would not be long before I got considerably more experience on the big two-tonner.

Bill King arrived on schedule, chugging up to the cottage in a tiny Fiat, and we grilled steaks in the backyard, American style, while we talked about boats—his and mine. Bill is a firm believer in Blondie Hasler's Chinese Junk rig, which does have its advantages. It can be reefed in seconds without the skipper bothering to come on deck, and it is quite possible to cross an ocean in such a boat without so much as donning oilskins.

The following day we went to the yard and Bill saw everything, from the molding to the joinery. He pronounced himself impressed with the design and spent a long time talking with the various foremen and with George Bush and Barry Burke. We had a good day, and I came away feeling that his trip had been worthwhile, even if we couldn't see my boat. The following day, we went over my charts and made a list of what else was needed for

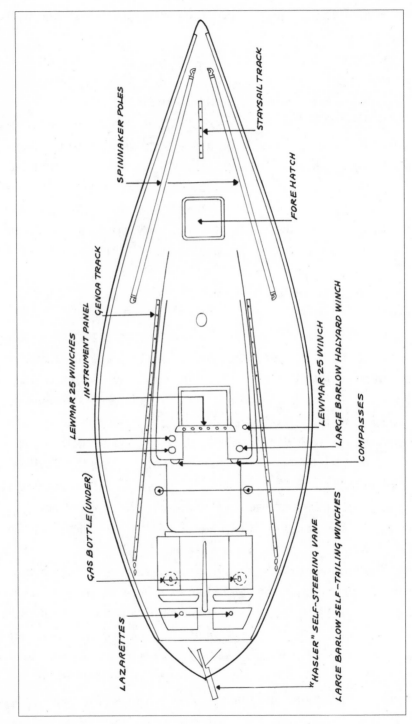

STAYSAIL TRACK

SPINNAKER POLES

FORE HATCH

GENOA TRACK

INSTRUMENT PANEL

LEWMAR 25 WINCHES

LEWMAR 25 WINCH

LARGE BARLOW HALYARD WINCH

COMPASSES

GAS BOTTLE (UNDER)

"HASLER" SELF-STEERING VANE

LARGE BARLOW SELF-TAILING WINCHES

LAZARETTES

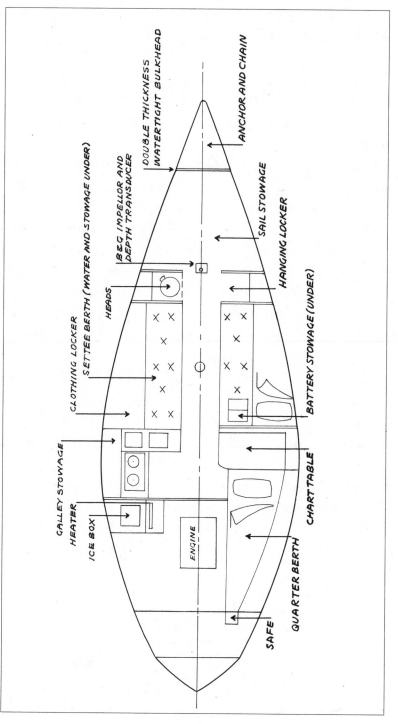

the Azores race. It was startling, the number of charts and publications necessary for such a passage. I had only about half of what was needed.

A local diver came and had a look at my mooring that day, too, replacing some chain and a couple of shackles which had rusted beyond safe limits. I would be ready for the boat long before she would be ready for me.

I spent the weekend in Galway, where Galway Bay Sailing Club was holding its annual boat show. I had worked on the one the year before and was interested to see how the new edition looked, and surprised to find my old Mirror, *Fred,* on display and for sale. The local doctor to whom I had sold her in the fall had never even sailed her.

By Tuesday, back in Cork, my boat was finally molded but not yet out of the mold. I had signed on for a week's cruise on *Creidne,* the Irish Training Ship, the following week, and before I left, Ron and I went down and worked out the deck layout and gave the instructions to the fitting-out foreman. Basically, all the winches and controls were grouped as closely to the cockpit as possible, so that they could be reached and managed by one man. This differed from the standard deck layout, where halyard winches are operated by crew on deck rather than one man in the cockpit (see diagrams on pages 184 and 185.) We also had a long talk with the joinery foreman about changes to the interior layout, mostly the addition of extra stowage place wherever possible. That done, I drove to Dublin and joined *Creidne* in Dun Laoghaire.

29

A *Mist* Opportunity

Aboard *Creidne,* which is a fifty-foot Bermudan cutter, purchased by the Irish government as a temporary training ship during the planning and building of a new eighty-foot brigantine sail trainer, I was delighted to find Ian Mitchell, an old friend from the Mirror racing circuit. Eric Healy, a toothy, tubby, chatty gentleman with vast experience in sailing vessels all over the world, is *Creidne's* permanent skipper, and he assigned Ian and me as duty skippers for our planned voyage to Holyhead, across the Irish Sea, in Wales.

First, though, we did a few drills in Dun Laoghaire Harbour, picking up moorings under sail, man-overboard drills, and power handling. Then, up at an early hour for the passage to Holyhead. We had a pleasant and uneventful crossing in lightish winds, and Ian and I both learned the importance of judging tidal streams, for Holyhead turned up on the port instead of the starboard bow, where it should have been.

The trip back on the following evening was more exciting, with the wind blowing Force five and six. Several of our crew had tanked up on beer the night before and, in the short, steep seas we now encountered, they paid the price. Both our watches were shorthanded as a result, and we got little sleep. We underestimated the tide again, and had to put in a half hour tack to clear the Kish light, just outside Dublin Bay, all the while dodging the Dublin–Liverpool car ferry, which seemed awesomely large from the deck of even a fifty-footer.

Back in Dun Laoghaire we changed crews for the second cruise of the week, only Ian Mitchell and I remaining from the first group. We sailed down to Wicklow, then Arklow, then back to Dun Laoghaire. The week had been especially valuable experience for me, doing everything from foredeck work to cooking to skippering, and giving me experience with the cutter rig, which has two foresails. At Dun Laoghaire, Captain Healy let me bring *Creidne* alongside under power, which happened without incident but perhaps a bit slowly. In his evaluation of my week, Captain Healy mentioned that I should be more patient with the crew when skippering, and that I needed more experience under power. I didn't tell him I had never handled a boat under power before.

Archie O'Leary had asked me to come along on the delivery of *Irish Mist* to Lymington the following weekend, and I busied myself with the final details of rounding up equipment for my boat. Manufacturers can be remarkably slow sending equipment, even when it has been paid for in advance, and I was constantly having to chase orders to see that everything arrived in time for the launching.

Quotes for insurance came in, and I chose the one from Hinson & Company in Dublin, the official insurance agency for the Irish Yachting Association. Their quote was no lower than another company's, but I had been impressed by the personal interest shown. I was paying £200 for coverage in British and Irish waters, single-handed, and another £150 for the Azores race and the single-handed return.

One piece of equipment required by the rules of the race was an emergency radio transmitter which would operate on two civil aviation frequencies, to be used in case of losing the boat and taking to the life raft. This signal would be picked up by a commercial airliner, then the rescue services would use the beacon to help locate the raft, which would be very difficult indeed if it had to be located visually. Blondie Hasler, one of the founders of the OSTAR, would probably not approve of this equipment, since he was against any competitor making any use of the rescue services. He has been quoted as saying, a competitor who got into trouble ". . . should have the decency to drown like a gentleman and not bother the rescue people." I was perfectly happy to have the transmitter aboard.

I was becoming increasingly concerned at the lack of progress on the boat. Barry Burke, who is the second most charming man in Ireland (the most charming man in Ireland, and the nicest, is Dr. Eamonn Lydon, of Oranmore, County Galway), would, whenever I would come to him, perplexed about the boat's progress, place a fatherly hand on my shoulder and say, "Now, Stuart, your boat is the most important boat being built in this yard, because of what she has to do, and you just can't rush a boat like that."

Everything else seemed to be moving along on time, however. One day a few weeks before, the area engineer for Lucas, the electrical equipment people, had turned up at the yard unexpectedly and said he had heard from Hydromarine, the engine people, that I needed a second, larger alternator. He said that Lucas would be happy to provide it and any technical advice I needed, and now the engine had arrived, the big alternator bolted into place.

Now came the passage to Lymington on *Irish Mist II*, and it proved to be all that the *Golden Apple* delivery had not. We slipped our moorings at Crosshaven in the early evening on Friday, May 31: Archie O'Leary, the owner; Pat Donovan, a Crosshaven publican and regular winch grinder and cook on *Mist*; Peter Walsh, a Cork gynecologist (just in case); and a student who was studying yacht design in Southampton, to whom I shall refer as The Kid.

We were soon close reaching in a steady Force six, gusting seven, as darkness closed. In these conditions, watches were being kept in pairs, and Archie put me with him, obviously anxious about my lack of experience.

Harp with the lid off.

I had made a point, from the beginning, of communicating to the people I sailed with that I was new to larger boats, because I did not want anybody to overestimate my skills, but lately, this was beginning to become a problem. By the time we sailed on *Mist* I had some twelve hundred miles of offshore experience and had taken an extensive course in coastal navigation, plus about ten days of practical instruction, a week of that on *Creidne*, a larger boat than *Irish Mist*. This was probably more than your average weekend yachtsman would do in two whole seasons, and I could now do, competently, just about anything that needed doing on a boat, barring mechanical and electrical repairs, for which I showed little talent. Certainly, there were things I didn't know how to do on specific boats; I had never worked with slab reefing, for instance, which *Mist* had, but it was simply a matter of becoming familiar with a particular boat's equipment.

Bill King checks over a Shamrock in the factory.

I had also discovered two marked advantages which I possessed, both quite accidental and unlearned, but advantages nevertheless. I didn't get seasick, apart from an occasional queasiness, and I was not frightened on boats.

I felt, and still feel, a kind of apprehension before beginning a passage—in the earliest days this had been partly a fear of being seasick, or, perhaps, a fear of being frightened, but I was not subject to the kind of demoralizing, even paralyzing fright that I had sometimes seen in others on a boat. Even now, while we were sailing to windward in the biggest winds and heaviest seas I had yet experienced, I felt nothing but excitement and exhilaration. If Archie hadn't been on deck with me I think I would have been singing or shouting at the top of my lungs into the wind.

Mist bucked into the seas, sending the occasional wave racing down her flush decks to hit us full in the face like a bathtub of water. For some reason, this struck me as funny, and I laughed a lot. I think Archie thought I was hysterical. The two hours of our watch passed very quickly, broken only by the passing of a large, brightly lit ship, probably the Cork–Swansea car ferry, the *Inisfallen*, which flashed "K" ("I wish to communicate with you") at us. We had our hands full in this weather, but after looking up what "K" meant, The Kid answered her, with what signal I'm not sure. I think she just wanted to know if we were all right in the heavy seas; it was nice of her to worry.

Below, *Irish Mist* was, at times, as wet as it was on deck. The main hatch leaked a lot when a wave raked the decks, pouring water into the lower, leeward bunk, rendering it unusable. There was a spacious galley but no handholds, these being judged by Ron Holland as weighing too much, and we had a tendency to ricochet about the main cabin when trying to move around. (When Ron Holland dies and goes to hell, his punishment should be to spend eternity inside one of his own designs with no handholds, sailing to windward in about a Force seven.) If you could stay wedged into a bunk long enough to get the leecloth tied, then you could sleep in reasonable comfort, though. The boat contained the aforementioned galley, two lower and two upper berths in the main cabin, a single and a double berth in an after area, and a chart table right aft, where the navigator could, in theory, speak to the helmsman through a small hatch. The rules require certain comforts on a racing yacht, but still it was quite a spartan interior, which Ron thought to be a new high in luxury. (Ron was once quoted by a yachting magazine as saying that all he required for the interior of a racing yacht were facilities for lying down and boiling water. He denies this. I believe the magazine.)

I had a look at the course plotted by The Kid, who was navigating us, and wondered aloud if he were allowing for tidal stream, leeway, and surface drift. He saw no point in bothering with these, and as a result, we ended up twenty degrees below our proper course, had to put in an unnecessary tack, and sailed fifty miles farther than necessary to reach Hugh Town, St. Mary's, in the Isles of Scilly, our first stop.

I was greatly taken with Hugh Town. We were met by the customs/immigration official and advised about anchorages. At one point he asked Archie, "If you're an Irish ship, why aren't you flying the Irish ensign?" Archie had a ready and truthful answer.

"My designer thinks flagstaffs weigh too much."

We visited the local pubs for a few pints and walked through the village, a very pretty one. I resolved to get back here again, maybe single-handed. That would be a good trial for *Golden Harp*. It was about a twenty-four-hour sail from Crosshaven (on the proper course) over open water, without too much shipping about, and it seemed a very pleasant port in which to spend a couple of days.

We had had a bit of excitement coming into the port when the gearbox seemed not to be working. When we were ready to drop sails the engine started readily but seemed not to be going into gear. In Hugh Town we discovered that the propeller had fallen off, and Archie decided to sail directly on to Lymington without another stop, since getting in and out of ports would be awkward without the engine.

We weighed anchor early the next morning and began a fast passage, reaching and running down the Channel, sometimes flying a spinnaker. By midnight we were past Start Point and headed for Portland Bill and its infamous tidal race. The Kid, for reasons I never understood, had plotted our course *inside* the race, saying something about it being on the rhumb line to the Needles. I had long since given up talking with him about the navigation. The Kid was very good indeed on sailing the boat, nearly as good, I think, as he believed himself to be, but I had grown very weary of the patronizing advice he had been constantly giving, and he and I were not getting along very well.

Now we sailed into Lyme Bay with a following wind of about Force three, on The Kid's course for the inside of the Portland Race. Archie was already worried about going inside and gave Peter Walsh and me explicit instructions not to sail too far out of the bay and, thus, get us into Portland Race. "Don't get too far in, either," he had said. "Jibe if you have to, to maintain your course, but for God's sake *don't* get us out into that race. It's one of the most dangerous places on the south coast of England."

We sailed on peacefully for a while, and then the wind began to back, and we were having to sail ten degrees above our course to keep from sailing by the lee, that is, with the wind coming from a direction where the boat might accidentally jibe. Soon, we were twenty degrees above our course, and I suggested jibing to Peter. He was doubtful, Archie having given instructions not to sail too far in. Why didn't we sail on the other jibe for half an hour, then jibe back and sail for another half hour, and so on? Peter finally agreed, though reluctantly. We jibed the boat in the gentle breeze, and Archie was on deck like a panther, in his underwear, roaring about "jibing for the sake of jibing . . ." I think that, under normal circumstances, he would not have reacted quite the same way, but he was clearly anxious about sailing inside the Portland Race, and he would not listen to any explanation of why we had jibed.

Dawn came and Portland Bill was before us. As the wind had backed it had increased sharply, and was now blowing a Force seven, gusting eight. The seas in the race were huge and close together, with waves breaking everywhere. In addition to the normal problems of negotiating the race, we had wind against tide, and a lot of both. Archie was at the helm, and we had to go within fifty yards of the rocks in order to stay out of the race. It was very exciting sailing, with the boat sometimes reaching ten knots when surfing down the big waves, and we made it safely through. Archie, a former international rugby player, admitted having been scared. "It's like just before playing for Ireland against England," he said. "It's running down your legs."

After the Portland Race, though, Archie would not let me take the helm again, as a kind of punishment, I think, for my sinful jibe of the night before.

The wind now veered, and as we approached the Lymington River, we faced the prospect of beating up the narrow channel against a falling tide and with the car ferry to the Isle of Wight threatening to leave at any moment. We hailed a couple of smaller yachts, asking for a tow, but nobody could hear us, so we started up the river under sail. This involved a lot of very short tacking, and with a group who had never tacked the boat at all.

In her crew cockpit, *Mist* has a grinding pedestal linked to the two huge winches, and Pat took charge of that. Peter and I each tailed a winch, and The Kid stood in the pulpit, yelling "TACK!" whenever he thought we were getting too close to the edge of the channel. It would be very embarrassing to run the beautiful new yacht aground on a falling tide in one of the most densely boat-populated rivers in England. It went well, though, the boat tacking remarkably quickly and accelerating fast. At times she seemed to be pointing straight into the wind. Finally, approaching the marina, a large yacht gave us a tow for a hundred yards or so, and The Kid cast us off with what he thought was enough way on to drift into a berth. He had misjudged, though, and we began to drift backward with the tide, with no steerageway. Pat Donovan had the presence of mind to throw a line to somebody on a berthed boat, just as The Kid panicked and threw the anchor out.

We began to clean up the boat and stow the gear, but The Kid, it appeared, was not yet finished with my education. I came very near to throwing him overboard when he began to explain ". . . how we fold a sail."

I thanked Archie for the best sail I had ever had. I had been very impressed with the way he had brought us around the Bill in such awful conditions and with his skill in tacking us up the river. I had learned a lot and, surprisingly, was not nearly as tired as after the *Golden Apple* delivery, although the passage in *Mist* had been much more arduous. Now I left *Irish Mist II*, and clambered onto the dock and into the arms of Ann, who, clever girl, had driven down from London.

We had a pleasant evening in Lymington, and next morning, after running a few local errands, we embarked on the car ferry to the Isle of Wight, which I had never visited. The purpose of the trip was to discuss the rigging of my boat with Ben Bradley of Spencer's, the riggers, but we did some shopping in Cowes's narrow High Street first. It was there I discovered one of the most comfortable of sailing garments, the Javlin Warm Suit, which is a sort of thermal underwear, retaining heat and preventing condensation under oilskins. This would prove to be a valuable purchase.

At Spencer's, Ben Bradley and I agreed on the size and composition of my boat's rigging—Ron had suggested wire rope rather than the standard solid rod rigging, which was fine for offshore racing but didn't last as long. We also went a size up on the standard, for extra strength.

Next day, I rang Shirley Clifford in Poole, just to see how she was and to report on the progress of *Golden Harp*, and she reminded me of something I had forgotten. The Azores and Back single-handed race (AZAB), sponsored by the magazine *Yachting Monthly*, was starting on Saturday from the Royal Cornwall Yacht

Club in Falmouth. She and Richard would be there, and so would Ewan Southby-Tailyour. Why didn't I come down? Why not, indeed? I hired a car, and on Thursday afternoon took off for the West Country.

I arrived at the Royal Cornwall to find fifty yachts preparing for the next day's start. Almost immediately I bumped into Robert Hughes, the Hasler self-steering expert from Gibb, who had at his disposal a very fast speedboat, with which he could go from yacht to yacht, offering advice and helping to solve problems. Having never so much as seen a single-hander's boat this was a marvelous opportunity for me, and I made mental notes on layout, control lines, etc.

Richard and Shirley Clifford turned up with their children, and I met Frank Page, the *Observer*'s yachting correspondent, and his lovely wife, Sammie; Liz Balcon and Angela Green, also from the *Observer* staff; Angus Primrose, the yacht designer who was sailing one of his own designs, a Moody 33, in the race, and his wife and daughter, Murlo and Sally; Andrew Bray of *Yachting Monthly*, who was sailing his Pioneer 10 in the race; and briefly, Clare Francis, the girl who had already done a transatlantic crossing in a Nicholson 32, and now had an Olsen 38 at her disposal, courtesy of her sponsors, Robertson's jams.

I had dinner with Richard and Shirley, and the following day, Murlo and Sally Primrose and I joined Robert Hughes and his brother, Brian, on whose fast boat we would watch the start of the race. The wind was very light, so there was little drama before the start, but shortly after the start we all became very annoyed with a French spectator boat which was sailing behind Clare Francis flying a spinnaker, thus taking Clare's wind and making it difficult for her to get her own spinnaker to fill. We roared up to the French yacht and, after a few loud words, they bore away and left her alone. It had been a rotten thing to do.

The fleet slowly drifted toward open water, and after a final goodbye to Angus Primrose on *Demon Demo*, we roared across the bay to my favorite village in Cornwall, St. Mawes. Then, back to the Royal Cornwall, now strangely empty, and the drive to Fowey, farther up the coast, where I was meeting Richard Clifford and Ewan Southby-Tailyour at a Royal Cruising Club rally. I arrived in the pretty village and got a ferry out to Ewan's yacht, *Black Velvet*, only to discover him drinking on another nearby boat. We passed a pleasant afternoon, and Richard arrived from Falmouth in *Shamaal II*, his Contessa 26, single-handed. There was then one of the nicest sights I have ever seen on the water. Three of the larger yachts at the rally were tied together in the river, and a very large and exuberant cocktail party took place in the lovely twilight. I added Fowey to my list of harbors to visit.

Richard Clifford invited me for a Sunday-morning sail in *Shamaal*, and I accepted with pleasure. We just went out of the river for a bit, then back to a mooring, but it was the first time I had ever sailed on a single-hander's boat, and it was nice to see how expertly Richard handled her. We followed our sail with a lunch of fresh mackerel.

Richard, as I have mentioned, is a captain in the Royal Marines, and takes great pride in his fitness. He climbs the mast of *Shamaal* without benefit of bosun's chair or steps, just right up it like a monkey. He also takes pride in sailing *Shamaal* without an engine of any kind and handles her with great flair and confidence.

He gave me something to think about when he said that during the last OSTAR, he had been swept overboard by a wave, saved only by an arm which caught a guardrail. He said that, after struggling back on board, he sat down in the cockpit and wept. I thought, if this hard, tough, superbly fit Marine officer, trained to endure the worst of hardship, had been reduced to that state by exhaustion and terror, what the hell would happen to me under similar circumstances? I could only hope that I would never have to find out.

Back in Cork, the launch was set for June 28. I wrote out a launch invitation and a press release. I had them both printed, and I mailed about fifty invitations to friends and people who had contributed equipment or help on the boat, and I sent press releases to all the Irish newspapers, plus the television service RTE, along with an invitation which also invited everybody to a post-launch celebration at the Royal Cork. I also gave invitations to a half dozen of the foremen and workmen in the yard who had been particularly helpful, and to the office staff, all of whom had been very nice. Then I placed an invitation in the hands of Pat Hickey, a director of the yard, and handed one to Barry Burke.

30

Launching

Normally I sleep like a stone, but for the rest of June prior to the launching, I slept badly. Nor could I read. Even absorbing books like Adlard Coles's *Heavy Weather Sailing* couldn't hold my attention. Every time I read of some heavy weather maneuver I began thinking about how *Golden Harp* would react under the circumstances.

But there were bright spots. Vincent Dolan of J. B. Roche, a Cork chandlery, donated a twenty-five-pound CQR anchor and eight fathoms of chain to the project. Alan Best of Croxon & Cobbs, a Dublin chandlery, gave me a trade discount on any gear I wished to purchase from him—they were particularly good on charts— and Western Marine, in Dalkey, gave me a generous discount on the four very expensive Beaufort life jackets I wanted for the boat. Cotter Electronics, a Cork instrument installation company, came and did a first-class job of fitting the Brookes & Gatehouse equipment and the other electrical gear, and gave me a very low price for a great deal of highly skilled work. And George Hayde and his people at Lucas came through on their promise of technical help, doing all the wiring on the batteries and alternators. They also contributed the splitting diodes and isolating switches for the batteries, a generous contribution, indeed, coupled with the expensive, marinized alternator.

There were disappointments, too. A Dublin sailmaker who had, three months before, agreed to send a man down to measure the boat for its very important spray hood now doubled his price in a transparent effort to get out of doing the job. He succeeded. Then a west coast sailmaker agreed to do the job and never showed up for the appointment, after keeping us waiting an entire afternoon. He didn't even bother to phone to say he couldn't make it. John McWilliam, from the heights of the international racing sailmaker, would not stoop to such mundane work, either, but at least he had made it clear months before that he wouldn't touch the job with a fork, and he didn't waste my time the way the others had. Before the summer was over, I would suffer from the lack of that spray hood.

I drove up to Tralee and spent an intensive two days with Len Breewood, studying celestial navigation and trying to cram two weekends into one. Len very kindly made me a gift of a light meon anchor which he had made himself. I had been unable to find one like it in Ireland.

Then I drove to Galway and spent an enlightening morning learning how to make a diesel engine behave itself. I had never seen one up close before, but even I understood and came away with a large donation of expensive engine spares. (A few days later, an extremely heavy parcel arrived in the post. Hydromarine had sent me a spare propeller, a very expensive chunk of brass!)

Back in Cork, visible progress was being made on the boat. The keel had been fitted, as had the stainless-steel brackets for the self-steering, and I watched as the deck was dropped onto the hull and fastened in place. At last, it looked like a boat!

Acceptances and regrets began to come in for the launching. Sadly, Ann would be working (she designs sets and costumes for films) and could not be in Cork. But other people were coming from all over the country.

At McWilliam Sailmakers, another last-minute flap. I had designed a "Betsy Ross" (the lady who designed and sewed the first American flag) spinnaker, in honor of the 1976 Bicentennial celebrations in the States, and this called for a circle of thirteen stars on a field of blue. The problem was that John had, instead of making five-pointed American stars, made six-pointed Israeli stars. Wrong celebration. I had to spend an hour soothing him and telling him how easy it was to make five-pointed stars, and he still charged me three quid apiece for them.

Launch day dawned. Nick and I were at the yard early to find the boat now hauled out onto the quay. The gathering for the launching was scheduled for eight in the evening, and the boat would be open to visitors for an hour before launching at nine, on the high tide.

At about eight-thirty, people began to arrive and, suddenly, it all came together. By a quarter-to-nine *Golden Harp* bore every resemblance to a finished boat, her loose wires tucked away and the floorboards and dining table suddenly in place. She was nothing if not a fine actress.

John Smullen, my insurance agent, arrived from Dublin with a lovely young lady and the gift from himself and Alec Hinson of a handsome visitors book, embossed with the yacht's name. It was a psychic thing, for I had not been able to find one in Cork.

Rapidly, its pages began to fill. Ron Holland and John Mc-William were the first signators; George Kennefick, admiral, and Raymound Fielding and Harry Deane, vice-admiral and secretary, respectively, represented the Royal Cork Yacht Club, now

Harp's home club; Ferdia O'Riordan and Michael Healy turned up to represent the Galway club, while Harry McMahon, though we did not know it at the time, was at Dublin Airport, having come from a medical conference in Edinburgh, trying to persuade Hertz to hire him a car without a driver's license, which he had forgotten; Worth and Pasha Newenham came, so did Len and Margaret Breewood; friends from all over were suddenly there, admiring my boat. Nick had miraculously got the tape player going, and the music added to the festivities. Tom Barker from the *Cork Examiner* was there, and although RTE had had to divert its one Cork camera to a fire, or something, Irish radio was represented in the person of Donna O'Sullivan, a redhead of whom I would see more.

Now all my anger and frustration vanished under a wave of euphoria. It was just as though the boat was actually finished. This moment, which I had dreamed about, but of which I had begun to despair, had finally come. It was all exactly like a real boat launching.

Finally, George mounted the crane, swung the yacht over the quayside, where she paused, her decks level with the stone. Barry Burke, who was not able to be present for the launching, had provided a bottle of champagne, cleverly scored several times so that it would break at the first blow. It is supposed to be terribly bad luck if the bottle doesn't break the first time. Laurel Holland, terribly conscious of her responsibility, said, "I christen this ship *Golden Harp.* God bless her and all who sail in her!" and swung mightily at the bow, missing the boat completely. She hadn't actually touched the boat, though, so no harm done. On her next swing the bottle smashed just the way champagne bottles are supposed to at yacht launchings, and *Golden Harp* dropped into the Douglas River with a fat splash.

It was all so perfect: the water of the river turned to shimmering gold by a huge setting sun, the crowd gathered to wish the boat well, the lovely weather. I made a short speech, thanking Ron and other people who had contributed to the effort thus far, and we adjourned to the upper deck of the Royal Cork for a bit of champagne.

Toward the end of the evening George Kennefick made a few kind remarks, and in my response I was able to thank George Bush, whom I had stupidly forgotten to thank at the launching. George had been in charge of the most difficult of all the work, the modifications, and his work would prove to have been done well.

An hour before the launching.

I hit the bed that night like a felled tree. I don't think I've ever had a better evening.

The following morning, Nick and I drove to the yard with as much equipment as we could manage, and we began to load the boat. George persuaded me to wait for the afternoon tide, to give him time to do a few more things, and I agreed.

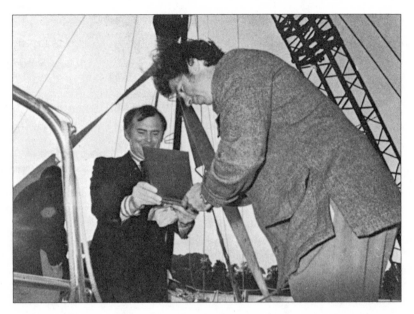

Ron is first to sign *Harp's* visitors book.

"God bless this ship and all who sail in her!"
Laurel Holland christens *Golden Harp* on her second swing.

As we were preparing to cast off and the last workman was hastily gathering his tools to avoid a trip down Cork Harbour, I glanced into the shallow bilges and noticed water there. "Where did that come from?" I asked.

"I don't know," he replied, shaking his head. "I've mopped her out every morning since she was launched, and there's still water coming in."

Golden Harp, four days after her launching, was leaking.

31

The Race Before the Race

The next three weeks were a whirling potpourri of rage, outrage, relief, elation, depression, and exhaustion.

Ron came down to Drake's Pool and shouted from shore that he was leaving for Norway the following morning to compete in the World Three-Quarter-Ton Championships in his design, the Nicholson 33, *Golden Delicious*. The delays in finishing the boat had robbed me of one of the most important elements of my plan, the presence and advice of Ron, helping me to learn to understand and sail the yacht. Before we sailed for Portsmouth and the MOCRA Azores race, he would be able to spend only three hours on the boat.

That evening Ron, John McWilliam, Nick, and I took *Harp* out into Cork Harbour. Ron did some tuning on the rigging, and John flung up the spinnakers for the people in the clubhouse to see. It was immensely satisfying and a bit unreal finally to see the boat under sail, even if the only headsail we could set was the light genoa, because the headsail reefing system had not yet been rigged. I would not see much of John on the boat, either. His earlier enthusiasm for the project had now been overtaken by a busy sailing season and a full order book for sails.

Harp returned to her mooring in Drake's Pool, where she would spend most of her time until the Azores trip. Killian, George Bush's son, turned up to work on the boat as a freelancer, and things began to pick up. He and Nick began working their way through a list of a hundred jobs. In the rare moments when she was not being worked on, I tried to sail *Harp*. Finally, on a Sunday afternoon, we left Cork Harbour for the first time, even if only for Oysterhaven, a few miles down the coast. I tried my first single-handed maneuvers, jibing and tacking. On the way back up the river we stuck on the mud once and had to swing the boom out and heel the boat to get off. The passage to Drake's Pool was a bit dicey at low water. There was a lot of water in the bilges when we got home.

Nick was ill for two or three days, but Killian made progress. He had made up with the yard now, and occasionally George dropped by with a forgotten bit of gear or to do some small job. He investigated the leaking and said the boat would have to go back to the yard for a haulout to be repaired. He also casually mentioned that the nuts on the keelbolts were not the specified stainless-steel ones; the yard had been out of those when *Harp*'s keel was fitted. It was depressing to contemplate delivering the boat into the hands of the yard again, but there seemed no other way.

Two weeks to go. Bill King and Harry McMahon came down on Saturday night for a day's sail on Sunday. We had dinner at the Royal Cork and met a Dutchman, Eilco Kasemien, who was about to set off for Iceland on his wishbone ketch for his OSTAR qualifying cruise.

The day of Bill's and Harry's arrival had not been without incident. Killian didn't turn up to work on the boat, as it was raining. It was spring tide and there was a southeasterly wind blowing, which pushed *Harp*'s stern in toward shore. As the tide receded, her rudder grounded on the last bit of a shelf, which was usually underwater. Nick and I rowed out and got as much weight forward as we could to see if she could be floated off. She was stuck fast. We sat in the pulpit with the life raft and the anchor for three hours waiting for the tide to turn. The rudder moved freely when she floated, and we breathed a sigh of relief that no apparent damage had been done.

Sunday morning dawned, chilly and foggy. Bill, Harry, and I motored down as far as the yacht club and picked up a mooring to wait for the weather to clear. Later in the afternoon we poked a nose into the harbor to find three hundred yards of visibility and foghorns everywhere. We repaired again to Drake's Pool, having never set a sail. Bill felt, though, that he had at least had a good look at the boat and would not feel quite so much a stranger when we left for England. He and his son, Tarka, a Guards officer in London, would arrive on the twenty-third to help prepare the boat for sailing on the twenty-fifth.

On Monday George came by and we arranged that I would take *Harp* to the yard on the morning tide on Thursday (it is possible to get over a bar to the quay at the yard only two hours before or after high water). Killian did more work one day and didn't show on another. A man came and examined me for my radio-telephone license and very helpfully searched out some additional information on billing for telephone calls and telegrams via shore stations. On Wednesday a brief letter arrived from Eve Palmer. She and her husband, Alan, had been among my closest friends in London. Alan and I had worked together as co-creative directors at an advertising agency and had remained close after we had both left the agency. The letter read: *Dear Stuart, my dear*

Alan died of a heart attack on Monday, the 7th. Love, Eve. Alan was a year older than I. I sat in the car in front of the post office and reread the letter for half an hour. Its meaning would not change. I would have difficulty thinking about anything else for days.

On Thursday morning Nick and I motored up the river to the boatyard. Hauled out and perched on a cradle, *Harp* had that stranded look that all pretty yachts have when they are out of their element.

There was a crack in the epoxy resin which bound the keel to the hull, and daylight could be seen between hull and keel. I left George with a list of jobs to do, told him I had to have the boat back on Saturday, and left.

The day got brighter when the book contract and a check arrived from my publishers, and Joe McMenamin, who had just bought the Lipton's supermarket chain, promised me some free groceries if an earlier request to the Quinnsworth chain was not favorably received. And a letter had arrived from Quinnsworth saying that they were interested not just in groceries but in sponsorship! Sponsorship was a constant thorn in my side, what with the recession cutting everybody's advertising and publicity budgets, and this interest helped me to forget for a while the condition of the boat. I rang their offices in Dublin and made an appointment for Monday afternoon to meet with their board of directors to tell them about the project. My mood was further improved by a visit to the yard on Friday, when I found a full crew working away on *Harp.*

I should have known all this was too good to last. On Saturday morning I arrived at the yard to collect the boat. I had brought my checkbook, as I knew there was another four or five hundred pounds outstanding, and I hoped that, after much pressing, the yard would have the bill ready for me. They had. John Harrington, the office manager, presented me with a bill for something more than £2,100 and told me that he had instructions that the boat should not be put into the water until it was paid in full. I asked if he expected me simply to write a check for that amount without checking over the bill carefully, which would take a day or two, at least. He said that those were his instructions. Barry Burke and his associate Pat Hickey were "unavailable" for discussion of the matter. Steam coming from both ears, I wrote a check for the full amount and dated it for the following Wednesday, so that I would have time to make some arrangements with my bank manager. I collected a bill of sale, the boat was put into the water, and we departed. On the trip back down the river I looked quickly over the bill and saw at least three hundred pounds in overcharges and a great many items about which I had questions to ask, but I would have to go over it with a fine-toothed comb later. At Drake's Pool Lieutenant Bernard Tofts of the Irish Naval Service was waiting to swing my compasses, a job that took the afternoon.

Sunday we went sailing, and the boat leaked. I went to George's home in Crosshaven that evening and told him the boat was still taking water. He said there was still something they could do about it with the boat in the water, and he would send somebody to do it early in the week. I told him that if the boat still leaked on the passage to England that I would have it repaired at Camper & Nicholsons and expect Southcoast Boatyard to pay the bill. We were sailing on Friday and had no more time.

Monday morning, on the train to Dublin, I went carefully through the bill. It was, quite simply, full of holes. At one point, when I had been pressing him for a final estimate on the boat, Barry Burke had said to me, "Don't worry, we're not going to charge you twelve thousand pounds for the boat." The cost, in fact, exceeded the estimate Barry had given me when I was considering a custom cockpit, a custom interior, and raising the freeboard of the boat, all of which I had decided against on grounds of cost. I would have a number of questions to ask about the bill.

At Quinnsworth I met Don Tidy, managing director; Jim Blanchard, financial director; and Des O'Meara, head of their advertising agency. We sat down around a conference table and exchanged pleasantries, then I talked for half an hour without taking a breath. I told them about the history of the race and about my boat and my plans. I told them everything I could think of. When I had finished they all asked questions, then Don Tidy excused himself for a few minutes. When he returned he said that, in association with a sister company, Penney's, he thought they would like to sponsor my entry to the tune of £10,000. First, though, he would like me to meet separately with the two advertising agencies involved, explore the opportunities for publicity, and have them report back with their opinions. I canceled my return train reservation and booked a late-night flight back to Cork, then went to Des O'Meara's offices with him. We were unable to reach the Penney's ad man, as he was out of his office at a conference, but Des and I went through the whole project with his public-relations manager, and they pronounced themselves satisfied that the opportunity was a good one for Quinnsworth. They would meet with Penney's man and describe the project to him. I had to get back to Cork, as we were sailing in four days and there was a lot to be done. I left the offices of Des O'Meara Advertising in a trance of elation.

I telephoned a young lady of my acquaintance, Noelle Fitzgerald, and told her I would trade her a good dinner in return for a lift to the airport. Noelle, who knows a good offer when she hears it, accepted, and soon we were ensconced at the Bailey, dining on Dublin Bay prawns and Puligny Montrachet '66. At the airport I was in far too good a mood to leave Noelle in Dublin, so I took her with me. We abandoned her car in the Dublin Airport car park, I got her a ticket, and we were off, she without so much as a toothbrush.

In Cork the next morning I first went to see a solicitor, Frank

O'Flynn, recommended by my bank manager. He advised me to write to Barry Burke, stating my questions and objections on the boatyard's bill, then stop payment on the check. I asked what that could lead to if we could not reach an amicable settlement. Frank said I could then deposit the full amount jointly with him and the yard's solicitor, and the matter could be put to arbitration later, under the terms of my contract with the yard. I saw my bank manager again, John Rafferty of the Bank of Ireland in Douglas, an immensely helpful man, and made arrangements for funds in the event I should need them. I then wrote a polite letter to Barry, itemizing the points which I wished clarified on the bill and asking him not to deposit my check until we had met to discuss them. I then stopped payment on the check, following Frank O'Flynn's advice. I took the letter to Southcoast Boatyard, knocked on Barry's office door, placed the letter in his hand, and asked him to telephone me when he had had a chance to read it. He said he would do so.

That afternoon, Noelle and I plundered the Quinnsworth supermarket at the Douglas Shopping Center. Don Tidy had rung the manager and told him to give me £200 worth of anything I needed. I had intended to buy our food in England, where it is cheaper, to Shirley Clifford's meal plan, which she had already prepared. Now, in the absence of a meal plan and in the presence of a license to shoplift, I tooled down aisle after aisle of the splendid store, grabbing whatever looked interesting for Shirley (not I) to cook, while Noelle trotted along in my wake with a stenographer's pad and a pocket calculator. A couple of hours later I was checking nine shopping baskets past a bemused cashier, the whole thing coming to £199.74. At one point I heard a little girl say to her mother, "Mummy, that man must have *lots* of children."

Back at Drake's Pool I worked with Nick until nine on the boat, while Noelle cooked dinner for us. We all slept well that night.

Next morning, Noelle, bless her heart, boiled ten dozen eggs for five seconds each to seal them, then went through the medical kit to see that everything was in order. Then I dropped her off at the airport and picked up Bill and Tarka King at the bus station. We spent the rest of the day working on the boat, cleaning her out and fixing as much as we could. By nightfall she was ready to be loaded. We had dinner and went to bed early.

The following morning, while Bill and Tarka began loading food and gear, I visited the boatyard to talk with Barry Burke about the bill. He had not telephoned me. When I arrived I was told that Barry was home with a bad back, but a moment later he rang, and I was able to speak with him. I explained that I was there to discuss the bill, and in his absence I suggested that I go over it with John Harrington, pay him for whatever we were in agreement on, and defer any other discussion and payment until my return from the Azores, when we would have time to sit down together and talk about it. He said that would be quite all right. We chatted for a few minutes about the coming race and his plans for Cowes Week, then said goodbye.

I sat down with John Harrington and went carefully over the bill. We found £390 in overcharges, which John agreed to. I gave him a check for £760, leaving a balance of about £1,100 to be settled on my return from the Azores. I left the yard in good spirits, vastly relieved that we had reached at least a partial settlement without a fight, and hopeful that we would be able to thrash out the rest amicably when I returned.

Ron came sailing with us in the afternoon for an hour, and in the Force six and seven winds blowing in the harbor we all managed to glean new information from him. We set Fred, as I had begun to call the Hasler, self-steering, and he pointed us unerringly at a perch across the harbor, sailing right up to it. Ron pronounced himself impressed.

We spent the remainder of the day packing food into plastic

shopping bags and stowing it on the boat. Things were moving well for our planned departure mid-afternoon the next day, Friday. I sometimes wonder what would have happened if we had left on time, whether things would have turned out differently. Maybe so, probably not. When enough small coincidences pile up and affect circumstances, it is called Fate.

As it was, we finished our loading on Friday in time to sail, but we were tired. We had planned to stop and rest for a day in the Isles of Scilly, but we hadn't been able to get a large-scale chart of the islands in time, and Bill was worried about going in without it, so we stayed in Drake's Pool for another night, and were invited to Coolmore House for a drink before dinner by Worth and Pasha Newenham.

Pasha and Bill King had known each other since Pasha was a Wren and Bill a submarine commander, both stationed in Ceylon, during World War II. We sat in the handsome drawing room of Coolmore, bathed and shaved, sipping sherry and listening to Bill and Pasha reminisce. The boat was ready. I felt a lovely sense of completion and contentment and expectation.

I was just beginning to daydream about what the Azores would be like when Mark Newenham, Worth's elder son, came in and said that Nick wanted to see me outside. I thought that, for some reason, he wouldn't be able to come to dinner, and I was already feeling disappointed as I walked out the door. But Nick's face was grave. "I hate to be the bearer of bad tidings," he said (oh my God, I thought, the boat's aground again, or sinking!), "but John Harrington is down at Drake's Pool on a boat with a solicitor, a court official, and a policeman, and they plan to tow your boat away." They had been trying to slip the mooring when Nick had rowed out and asked them to wait until I could be summoned.

Thanking heaven that I had prepared for something like this, I rang Frank O'Flynn, and he promised to come straightaway. I had another glass of sherry, then went down to the cottage. The two boats were tied together, and they were all sitting out there, chatting with Nick. They declined to come ashore when invited; I declined to go out to the boat until Frank O'Flynn arrived. I sat down on the riverbank with Bill and Tarka, and presently Frank appeared.

We rowed out to the boats, and an extremely calm and civilized discussion took place. It was agreed that I would give Frank my check for the full amount of the yard's bill, and he would pay the money into the court for safekeeping. When I returned from the Azores, the matter would be settled. I was happy with the arrangement, as long as it kept the money out of the yard's hands. As we were preparing to go ashore, I took John Harrington aside and asked him what the hell was going on. Hadn't we discussed and settled all this? Hadn't Barry agreed to the arrangements? If he was unhappy, he had had a day and a half to contact me and discuss it. Why hadn't he done so?

John was acutely embarrassed. He had simply been instructed by Barry that he was putting it into the hands of a solicitor; he was given no details. Now *Golden Harp* was under arrest, a court order taped to her mast. At least they hadn't nailed it to the aluminum.

Frank told us to go ahead with our dinner plans, while he and Donegan, the yard's solicitor, adjourned to Rosie's, the local pub, to discuss the details of the transaction. We trooped into town to start our belated farewell dinner, and an hour or so later Frank stopped by to say that all was well, we could sail the next morning. We phoned John Rafferty to stop payment on my earlier checks to the yard and to ascertain that funds were available. All was well there, too.

Next morning, after final stowage and the taking of many photographs, we motored down to the yacht club, had lunch and took on ice, then fueled and were off. (On the way out of Drake's Pool we had scraped our keel across a mudbank, nearly losing Bill over the pulpit, at the exact moment somebody, probably Theo, had fired a parachute flare from the woods in farewell salute.)

As we motored down the river out of Crosshaven, a single Mirror dinghy followed for a time in our wake. The sight brought back a rush of memories. Roche's Point was soon abeam and, after a lot of sail trimming and adjusting, *Harp* sailed herself for all of the night, as we began to become accustomed to her.

Tuning up.

32

On to Portsmouth

We spent a fine day sailing, fiddling with Fred (who was reluctant to steer on a beam reach), bailing water (which seemed to be coming from forward somewhere, maybe from the long hull fitting), and continuing to build the boat. Tarka finally divulged that he had spent a year as an apprentice with Hickey Boats in Galway when a lad (he had been fired when the foreman found him making a model airplane during his tea break), and he took on the bulk of what had to be done. Bill navigated and I bailed, using the Jabsco electric bilge pump, which had been fitted for just such an occasion. The shape of the hull precluded any more than about two inches of bilges, so two gallons of water could make the interior a miserable place.

We were at Land's End in time to see a beautiful moonrise above Cornwall. By midnight Wolf Rock was abeam, and we altered course for the Lizard, the southernmost tip of Cornwall. As we approached it the tide turned against us, and although we were registering several knots on the speedometer clock, we seemed to be standing virtually still. I spent long periods of my midnight-to-three watch sitting on a cushion on the pulpit, my safety harness clipped to the forestay, watching the moon and the water and the night while Fred steered. It was one of the most beautiful nights I have ever spent on a boat.

By midday Monday we were motoring in a flat calm, and I was using the VHF radio constantly. The Dynafurl had revealed a maddening tendency to separate into two equal halves, and although it could be repaired easily, it was causing us worry; water was entering the boat in increasing quantities, and we were now bailing hourly; and every other fault which had been built into the boat was now surfacing, my own mistakes surfacing, too. During the afternoon a puddle of hydraulic oil collected in the bilges. The trouble was found to be a leaky inspection meter which I should have removed. I sent a telegram to Jeremy Rogers's Boatyard, the English agents for Steam, who made the Dynafurl, asking for a replacement to be ordered from the States immediately by telephone. Then I rang Camper & Nicholsons and asked for a haulout and repair of whatever was leaking when we arrived in Gosport. The radio hummed all afternoon with such messages. Bill had flatly refused to sail for the Azores unless we could get the leaking stopped in Gosport. I was in full agreement with him. We motored on.

We also used the radio for social purposes. We made a lunch date later in the week with Angus and Murlo Primrose and, since Ann was in France and would not return in time for our departure for the Azores, I spoke with a young lady whom I had met at another sailing event earlier in the season and invited her down to the south coast for a night later in the week. This young lady shall be known in this tale as The Bird.

By mid-afternoon on Tuesday the Needles were abeam and

we entered the Solent to find it seething with yachting activity. Cowes Week was due to start on Friday, and the narrow body of water was full of boats practicing. Spinnakers, tallboys, bloopers, and every other sort of sail were everywhere, and it was a very pretty sight indeed. We sailed slowly in light winds past Cowes and past Norris Castle, where Bill's wife, Anita, was staying with friends. Although I had sailed into the Solent before on de-livery trips, never had I seen it so dressed with sail. It was very beautiful.

Late in the evening we berthed at Camper & Nicholsons Marina in Gosport. The next day would be Wednesday. The race started on Saturday, and there seemed to be at least two weeks' work to do on the boat. Moreover, we were asking for Camper's help at the worst possible time. The first race of Cowes Week was happening on Friday, and the yard was choked with yachts being readied for the world's premier week of yacht racing. We wolfed down a takeaway Chinese meal and got the last solid sleep we would have for a week.

Early Wednesday morning I waylaid Camper's repairs manager, John Gardner, as he drove through the gate. We went over *Harp* together, and within the hour she was high and dry, sharing Camper's crowded apron with the likes of *Morning Cloud*, *Golden Apple*, the giant Rothschild yacht, and numberless other French yachts, their bottoms being diligently rubbed down by their crews and their skippers complaining loudly (the French are very good at this) to anyone who would listen. A foreman and crew were assigned to *Harp*, and by noon her keelbolts had been loosened to let her dry out in preparation for resealing the keel. Tarka had found a leak in the forward bulkhead and the trouble was quickly located. Every time the yacht hit a wave, water was forced through a gap in the glass-fiber seal and into a dead air space under the anchor well, from which it ran through a leak in the "watertight" bulkhead into the forepeak.

In the afternoon Bill and Tarka left for business in London, to return Friday, and Shirley Clifford rang to say that she would arrive the next day. Robert Hughes from Gibb turned up and spent four hours tuning and refining the self-steering system and refused to accept a penny. Staggering with fatigue, I took him and his wife out for dinner. I slept on *Harp*, high on the apron, a most peculiar sensation.

I was up at the crack of dawn to let the workmen on the boat and spent most of a frantic day shopping for gear I hadn't been able to find in Ireland. Shirley turned up in the afternoon, and I gave her a list of things to do. The Bird was not far behind. I had not been able to find a decent place to stay in Gosport, and since I had to go to Lymington anyway to exchange a broken meter at Brookes & Gatehouse and collect the new Dynafurl from Jeremy Rogers, I booked us in at The Angel there. We made a mad dash for Lymington in her car in order to get there before closing time and just made it. Bill Green, Rogers's man in charge of Dynafurls, broke the news that the replacement hadn't arrived, then gave me tools and instructions on repairing the existing unit. I left instructions to send the replacement on to the Azores so that it would be there when we arrived.

On top of this, The Bird was unhappy. She was unhappy about the sleeping arrangements, unhappy about being in Lymington, and only moderately appeased by a good dinner at Limpets. Next morning she was unhappy about waiting at the post office to see if the replacement Dynafurl would arrive at the last minute, and she pitched a fit when I kept her waiting at a chandlery while I bought other last-minute gear. The drive back to Gosport was completed in stony silence, and our farewell was very abbreviated. That night I noted in my diary, ". . . sometimes I am a very bad judge of women."

Angus Primrose joined us for lunch at the local pub (Bill and Tarka had returned from London) and gave us a soothing account of his part in the Azores and Back race. The wind, said Angus, had never blown more than twenty-five knots and he had been supremely comfortable throughout. He made a suggestion or two about gear arrangements, and then we were hard at work again. At closing time Camper put *Harp* back into the water. She looked in very good shape, but we still had ahead of us the job of re-stowing all her gear and the food. That evening Bill, Shirley, and I took the hovercraft to the Isle of Wight for the prerace party in Bembridge. There were twenty-four hours before the start of the race, and it was the first time the three of us had been together.

Tarka and Anita met us at the party, and we relaxed for a bit and chatted with some of the other competitors. Mike Ellison, of the Amateur Yacht Research Society, was competing in a bor-rowed trimaran, and I met Bill Howell of *Tahiti Bill*, the Australian dentist, and Brian Cooke of *Triple Arrow*, the sailing bank manager. Both were OSTAR veterans, and I had been looking forward to talking with them about the race, but with time so short, that would have to wait until our arrival in Horta.

Bill returned to Norris Castle with Anita and Tarka, and Shirley and I got the last ferry off the island. When we arrived at the marina we found Richard Clifford asleep on *Harp*'s deck and invited him in. Ominously, Shirley was complaining of not feeling well, but I was too tired to take much notice.

Next morning, she was worse and running a temperature. We put her into a pilot berth and worked around her. Richard tackled a dozen jobs on deck while I emptied the boat of her stores and prepared to restow them. Shirley had pared down our Quinnsworth groceries to what we would need for the three of us, plus some for my trip back to Ireland. Bill and Anita arrived and Anita sat on the dock, resplendent in a large sun hat, and took notes for a stowage plan as I hustled grub onto the yacht. Bill pronounced himself uneasy about the whole thing. Richard kept looking at the shambles and shaking his head. "You'll never make it," he kept saying.

Tension mounted. Then the committee types began coming round and muttering about Shirley's illness. She was refusing to see a doctor, and they didn't like it. I discussed it with Shirley and Bill and proposed a solution. Shirley had been looking forward to the race for weeks, and I was reluctant to disappoint her because of what might be only a twenty-four-hour bug.

"Look," I said to the committee, "we'll take her down the Channel with us. She'll probably get better. If she gets worse, there are a dozen places we can quickly put her ashore. If she's not better by Plymouth we'll put her ashore there." The committee didn't like it. I pointed out that we weren't violating any race rules. The skipper of a yacht is responsible for deciding who races with him. Bill pointed out that *he* was the skipper and he had agreed to this plan. The committee said we'd be disqualified if we arrived in Horta without the minimum specified crew of three. They offered us another girl as crew. I pointed out that we would be disqualified if we changed crews within twenty-four hours of the start, and the start was five hours away. They said they'd overlook that. I asked why then wouldn't they overlook the three-crew rule? *Harp* was built as a single-handed boat; two could handle her easily enough. The rule was obviously aimed at some of the bigger multihulls. They hemmed and hawed. I was beginning to get annoyed. We had much to do and little time to do it. They were wasting what we had left. I finally told them, as politely as I could, that we had made a decision which did not violate the rules and that that was it, so to please go away and let us get on with it. They finally did.

Bill and Richard were still expressing doubts about our being ready for the start, and finally I exploded. "Look," I said, "we have five hours to finish what has to be done. If we don't make it, we won't start, but let's stop wasting time and get on with it. Don't anybody say to me again we won't make it, okay?" Everybody went back to work.

The race was to start at seven o'clock in the evening. Incredibly, by five-thirty we were finished. Everything was stowed and Richard had accomplished a lot of absolutely essential work on deck. We had just time to dash for a shower. That finished, we pulled up at the fuel dock just in time to catch the attendant before he left for the day. We took on diesel, then left Richard on the fuel dock. We would not have made it on time without him. We motored out to the line with the main up and immediately found a fouled genoa halyard. I had to go up the mast to clear it but, fortunately, the sheltered waters were flat and motion at the top of the mast was minimal. I took a moment for a look at the view. There were fourteen yachts on the line, only two of them monohulls, *Harp* and *Gypsy Moth V*, being sailed by Giles Chichester, Sir Francis's son. There were a number of large multihulls, in the fifty-foot range, and a number of smaller cruising types. It was a very pretty sight in the late-afternoon sun.

We started badly. The seaward end of the starting line was to

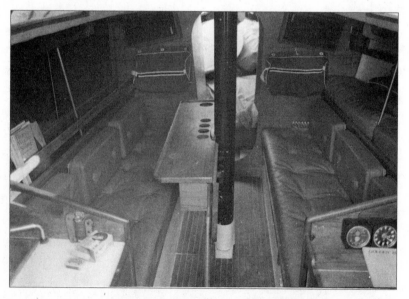

Harp's main saloon from the hatchway, with galley to port and chart table to starboard. Sail stowage in forepeak.

be an anchored trimaran, the committee boat. However, there was also another trimaran anchored nearby, a spectator boat, and we mistook that for the committee boat. We started third from last. But we had started.

Main hatch viewed from the saloon.

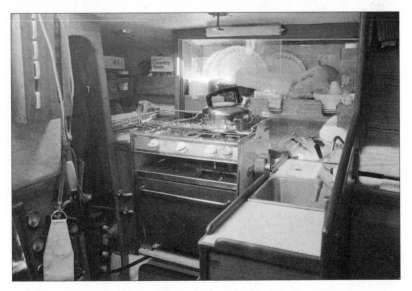

Harp's gourmet galley. The central heating unit is visible to the lower left of the cooker.

The well-equipped navigation area.

33

On Our Way

As soon as we had altered course down the Solent we found the light wind behind us and got up the Betsy Ross floater. *Harp* began to move. With about five knots of wind showing on the B&G meter, her speed increased from two and a half knots under main and genoa to four knots under spinnaker. We began to overtake multihulls.

Just before Cowes, as we passed Norris Castle, we heard explosions from shore. "They're saluting us!" Bill shouted. Sure enough, Tarka and Anita were firing the castle's cannon in our honor. As we approached Cowes, the little town's lights began to come on in the dusk. We passed the Italian tall ship *Amerigo Vespucci* at anchor, and astern of her, the Royal Yacht. It was too late in the evening for an exchange of salutes, but as we passed, a small, dark-haired woman waved a handkerchief at us from the ship's afterdeck. I think it was the tea lady!

By the time we'd passed Cowes, we had overtaken four catamarans and trimarans, and, shortly afterward, we passed another. Mike Ellison's voice came out of the darkness: "Your navigation lights are excellent!" He was referring to our very bright Marinaspec masthead light, and it was comforting to know we could be seen from a distance. We were facing heavy traffic in the Channel and God-knew-what in the Atlantic, and I had no wish to experience being run down by shipping. We continued to pull away from Mike's trimaran and, shortly, were hot on the heels of a big cat, both of us doing everything possible to put on speed so as to make the Needles light before the tide turned foul in the Solent and trapped us there in light winds. Then the wind began to freshen and the catamaran pulled slowly away from us, although we could see his lights until after midnight.

We got the featherlight floater down in the freshening winds and continued under the genoa, both of us too exhausted to set the heavier all-round radial spinnaker. Each of us slept soundly when off watch that first night.

We sailed most of the next day with the boomed-out, big genoa, still too tired to get a spinnaker up. The weather was sunny and warm, and we let Fred steer while we lay on the decks and rested. Shirley felt better for a time, then returned to her original condition. She refused all offers of aspirin to lower her temperature, and by late afternoon Bill was saying that we were fast approaching the point where we would have to decide whether to put her ashore in Plymouth. It was not much of a decision. Shirley was only a passenger in her condition, and her condition wasn't improving. We altered course for Plymouth.

Our vague plan had been to sail the boat somewhere pleasant after we'd dropped Shirley, if it came to that, somewhere that I could sail back from single-handed in order to qualify for the OSTAR. But now I was very dissatisfied with this notion. I put it to Bill that we go on to the Azores. After all, the boat had been repaired, we were thoroughly overprovisioned for the passage, the boat was easily managed by two, and our exhaustion was beginning slowly to slip away. Bill readily agreed, to my ever-lasting relief. I would have been very unhappy if, after all this preparation, we had been forced to change our plans. Now we began to plan how to lose as little time as possible in Plymouth. Our first plan had been to pick up a mooring in front of the Royal Western Yacht Club or to put into the Mayflower Marina and get a night's rest before continuing. But since deciding to continue to Horta we were in more of a hurry. I got on the VHF and contacted Rame Head Coast Guard as we approached Plymouth. They said they would arrange for the pilot boat to take Shirley off at the breakwater and would ring Richard to collect her ashore. We pressed on.

Near midnight, as we approached Plymouth breakwater, we were able to contact the Plymouth pilot boat directly on the radio-telephone, and they soon spotted us, sailing slowly under main only, with the deck lights on. They came skillfully alongside and took off Shirley, her suitcase, and an incredible number of plastic shopping bags. As we prepared to get under way again there was a shout from the pilot boat. Shirley had forgotten a shopping bag. We repeated the performance, tossed the last bag over, then were free. Bill took the first watch and set a course for the point where we had left our original course. Our plan was to return there before continuing to Horta, keeping a record of our lost time in order to appeal to the committee in Horta to subtract this from our elapsed time. We would also appeal not to be disqualified.

When I came on watch Bill reported that we had been sailing through thunderstorms with gusts up to Force seven and that he had reefed everything and been up the mast twice to retrieve or sort out halyards. I had slept through everything. On my watch little happened except a fishing boat that wouldn't go away, and I spent an hour making sure we didn't hit him or foul his nets.

Later in the day I telephoned a committee member and reported our loss of crew and lodged our request to remain in the race and be credited with the eleven hours it had cost us to put Shirley ashore and return to our original course. He said they would let us know in Horta. I then telephoned my mother in the United States and Ann, who had returned to London, to let them know of our progress before we were out of range of Land's End radio. I don't know what the Land's End operators say when they ring a telephone number, but it never fails to astonish anybody who is getting a telephone call from sea. They can never quite believe that it is possible for a small boat out of sight of land to make a telephone call. It is great fun.

It was now Tuesday afternoon, August 5 (we had started at seven p.m. on August 2), and the wind was freshening and heading us, an experience which was to be repeated ad nauseam for the rest of the passage. We reefed and began to beat. We did not know it at the time, but nearly two weeks later we would be still in identical conditions. At three a.m. the preceding morning I had been wakened by Bill. I was beginning to understand that not only was he a natural pessimist, but that he actually seemed to *enjoy* it when things went wrong. When anybody else would have been depressed and cursing his fate, Bill seemed stimulated.

"What?" I mumbled, rolling over and trying not to let any heat escape from my sleeping bag.

"Bad news," Bill chirped. I was sure I could see his teeth in the darkness. I was sure he was grinning. The engine battery had shorted and was completely flat. I was sleeping on the hatch to the battery compartment. I struggled out of my sleeping bag and got at the battery. An untaped lead had rubbed against something. I taped it, switched the battery leads to start the engine, and began to disappear into the sleeping bag again.

"I've been thinking it over," Bill said. "I think we should turn back." I woke up again.

"What?"

"I'm old and weak," said Bill. "You're young and strong, but inexperienced. We've had this battery trouble and the Dynafurl is going to break at any moment. It's your decision, but I just want to put my view to you. If you decide you want to go on to Horta, we'll do so."

I was silent for a moment. "Old and weak" was not a new theme. Bill King is a small but wiry man, and he is well muscled from manual labor on his farm. I suspected that he was stronger than I. In reflective moments he would bemoan his old age, referring to himself as ". . . nearly seventy." He was not yet sixty-four. Once, over dinner, he'd remarked how well he was feeling, how youthful. I'd pounced: "But a couple of days ago you were practically on your deathbed."

"Ah, but now I've had half a bottle of wine," he replied with a grin.

I thought that now I detected a trial balloon of some sort, but I was too sleepy to give him the persuading he seemed to want. "I'll sleep on it," I said, "and we'll talk about it in the morning, okay?" I knew that we would cover another fifteen or twenty miles while I slept.

The next morning the sun was shining and *Harp* was going well to windward. Bill remarked what a seakindly boat she was. "She goes to windward so much more comfortably than *Galway Blazer*, with her big spoon bows for running in the Southern Ocean," he said admiringly.

"Listen, Bill," I said, "everything's going well now. The batteries are fully charged, and if the Dynafurl breaks again it's simple to fix with our new tools. We're both feeling better every day. I think we should go on."

Bill nodded. "Right. We'll say no more about it."

We went on.

34

Hard on the Wind

A week out. I was sitting in the cockpit in the late evening, enjoying the view. There is nothing, absolutely nothing, as beautiful at sea as the sky at night. There seem to be at least four times as many stars as on land, and the Milky Way is just that, a great white swath across a black universe. Then I heard a new noise.

Sailing is not as quiet a pastime as many people seem to believe it to be. Every sailboat is accompanied by a constant little concerto of sounds—water sweeping past the hull, halyards flapping against the mast, the leach of a sail shaking in the wind. A new sound means that something, however small, has changed. The sound I heard now was coming not from the boat but from the water. I looked over the starboard rail and saw, lit by its phosphorescent progress through the sea, a torpedo coming straight for the boat.

It is amazing how many thoughts and images can pass through

the mind in a second or two. I saw the yacht erupt in the explosion, and myself flying through the air, then I thought, Nonsense, nobody would torpedo a small boat; anyway, I can see that the torpedo is a living thing. It was a great white shark or killer whale. Bill King had been attacked by one in the Southern Ocean, now it was happening to us. I saw the boat, holed and sinking, while we scrambled into the vulnerable life raft and the creature circled the crippled yacht, waiting. Inches from the hull, the great white "shark" veered sharply away from the boat, as if he had ricocheted. I discovered that I had been holding my breath.

The great white shark/torpedo was a dolphin, the first I had ever seen at night. Now I saw that there was a pair. They did their torpedo act again and again, driving at the yacht, then veering away at the last possible second. Since they provided their own lighting in the phosphorescence, I could clearly see their shapes and features, their smooth gray skins. I sat, transfixed, for nearly half an hour as they played their game, having the time of their lives, then they were gone.

We had altered our watch-keeping system now, and we were both well rested. After passing over the continental shelf and leaving the trawler fleets behind, we were in much less danger of collision, being off the most heavily traveled shipping lanes. Now one of us would stay dressed all night, ready to go on deck if necessary but not keeping a constant lookout. One night, when I was on watch, I was dozing lightly in my berth, when I became aware that Bill had awakened and was going on deck. I returned to my doze, thinking he had gone up to pee, but suddenly the yacht tacked. A moment later Bill came below again. "I think I must have developed some sort of ESP in submarines during the war," he said. "I just woke up and knew I had to go on deck. We were on a collision course with a very large ship." I looked out of the hatch and saw the enormous thing about three hundred yards astern by then. I made a mental note always to sail with people who were former submariners, and I wondered if I would ever become that attuned to what was happening around the boat.

We settled into a routine aboard, a routine ruled by the constant strain of being hard on the wind. When a small yacht is beating to windward she will suffer more fore and aft motion and heel more sharply than on any other point of sailing. *Harp's* motion was very kindly for a yacht of her size, but it is the heeling of the boat which is the most tiring feature of beating. When the boat is heeled at, say, a constant angle of twenty degrees from the vertical, life aboard becomes a continuous struggle with the law of gravity. One is always traveling either uphill or downhill and never on a level path. Ordinary tasks, like eating, become much more entertaining and exciting. I had equipped the galley with some very attractive American dinnerware, each plate of which had a rubber ring around the bottom which, the ad stated, kept the plate from sliding off the table even at a thirty-degree angle of heel. The ad was absolutely correct; the plates did adhere at that angle. But what the manufacturers had neglected to point out was that, while the plate would remain firmly in place at a thirty-degree angle of heel, the food slides off the plate into your lap. We learned to eat everything from bowls and to hold firmly on to them. They might not tip over or slide when heeled, but the suspense was unbearable.

We ate well. In spite of the rigors of beating, I cooked a hot breakfast every morning until the bacon ran out, and we had a hot dinner every night and shared a bottle of wine. Bill, who had a firm rule of no alcohol when single-handing, relaxed this stance when sailing in company. I think it made us both better company. In the evenings we talked endlessly and listened to tapes from the Monty Python TV series. Bill had never heard of Monty Python, Irish television not having worked up enough courage to broadcast the series to the west of Ireland, and we were both often convulsed. We had a broad range of audio entertainment at our command—the

Python tapes, music ranging from Vivaldi to Simon and Garfunkel, and, of course, the BBC World Service on shortwave. We even got Radio 2 until we were about eight hundred miles out.

We remained fairly busy, apart from sailing the boat. I practiced my celestial navigation, comparing my positions with Bill's, and they began to come close. I read a lot, too, getting through Anita's excellent biography of Francis Chichester and a couple of novels. Occasionally, a ship would turn up and we made efforts to communicate. Since the range of our little Seavoice VHF radio-telephone was only about forty miles, we could not communicate directly with land, so I had an idea for sending telegrams via other ships. Merchant shipping did not keep a watch on VHF, using it mostly for port operations, so I kept the signal flags KVHF ready for hoisting. K is the international signal for "I wish to communicate with you." VHF, I figured, was self-explanatory.

When we saw our first ship, we got the flags up in a hurry and switched on the radio. Nothing. I lit a white flare. Still nothing. We figured we had not seen him soon enough, and since he was abeam, overtaking us, by the time we got the flags up, he probably hadn't noticed.

Another day, a tiny fishing boat turned up from nowhere. He was apparently a tuna fisherman and the boat was so low in the water that it approached us unnoticed. It had not occurred to us that there would be fishing boats this far from land. He ran alongside us for a few minutes, and in spite of the flags and Bill's efforts in French over the loud-hailer (the boat was from a southwest France port) we failed to make him understand that we wanted him to switch on his radio. With lots of friendly waving he disappeared over the horizon.

Our second attempt at a merchant ship bore fruit. We saw it early and had the flags up in plenty of time. I was screeching out "K" on the hooter as the ship came up to us, and soon I had her radio operator on the VHF. She was an Italian grain carrier, the

Mario Z, under charter to the Russians to ferry wheat from New Orleans to Leningrad, and she was on her way to the States in ballast. I chatted with the radio operator, a Spaniard, for some time, and he kindly agreed to send telegrams home for us. All merchant mariners, I believe, are bored out of their skulls and perfectly delighted to pass the time of day with a small yacht in the middle of nowhere. It breaks up their day.

Talking with the ship had made our day, too, and there was better to come. For the first time since leaving England, we were freed. The wind backed and we were, at last, reaching. We had two lovely days of it, screaming along in bright sunshiny weather, clocking up our best runs of the passage. Our very best noon-to-noon run was 148 miles. It began to look as if we would make Horta in time for the competitors' dinner on Saturday night, the sixteenth, and our spirits rose markedly. It had been depressing beating, beating, beating, sometimes laying our course, but even then hard on the wind. This was beautiful sailing, and we began to speculate about what Horta would be like. Bill had sailed past the Azores but had not stopped there, and I knew only what I had seen in a tourist brochure the race committee had sent.

We raised another ship, a German this time, and sent a telegram to Horta giving an ETA of Saturday. Spirits were high.

Then we were headed again. Worse, the wind dropped and we began to experience our first light weather, and from the worst possible place, on the nose. Very depressing. But I was learning an important lesson—that the sea doesn't care when you arrive, or if you arrive at all. The sea is indifferent to the desires of those who sail upon her, and no amount of sulking or swearing will change that. One learns patience at sea, and always the hard way.

Bill got hurt. He had opened a locker under a settee berth and, having forgotten that he had left the lid off, sat down, falling into the locker, the edges striking him around the kidneys. He was obviously in a lot of pain, and I was worried. There was nothing in our super-duper medical kit, at least nothing I knew how to use, which would help a ruptured kidney. We were relieved when Bill didn't pass any blood, and we thought that the worst it could be was a bruised kidney. The worst of the pain passed, and although Bill was very sore and uncomfortable, he insisted on doing all the work he usually did, which was plenty. The only concession he made to his injury was to wear a normal safety harness instead of the length of rope he usually wore around his waist.

We plodded on, tacking back and forth to maintain our course, Bill in pain and I irritable, disappointed with our progress. We had hoped to make Horta in twelve days; now two weeks had passed. We worried that *Gypsy Moth* had already left Horta to return to England. We had hoped Bill would be able to return on her, saving the airfare.

Finally, on Sunday morning, we awoke to find Graciosa, the first of the Azorean archipelago islands on our route, sitting fat and green in our path. Even more remarkable, we had been freed again and were pointing at the port end of the island, right where we wanted to go, with the wind on our beam. We sailed on toward the island, and as we approached, a small motor launch appeared, towing two large rowboats full of men. Up a stubby mast on the launch, a man was clinging precariously, scanning the horizon. These were the Azorean whale hunters, going after the monster sea mammals as generations of Azoreans have, in an open boat, using a hand-thrown harpoon, their only concession to modernity the little launch which towed them out for their hunt. They gave us a cheerful wave and continued their search.

Then, of course, we were headed again and found ourselves pointing at the wrong end of the island, hard on the wind. Graciosa looked very inviting, with thick, green vegetation; tiny, white villages here and there; and beautiful beaches, with an occasional stretch of dramatic cliffs. We beat our way into the channel between Graciosa and St. Jorge, the neighboring island, and pressed

Landfall! Graciosa was our first land for two weeks.

Harp is dwarfed by *Tahiti Bill* in Horta Harbor.

on toward Horta in the shallower, rougher water and freshening winds. We beat all day and all night. I contrived not to wake Bill until he had got some sleep and then turned in at dawn. Sunrise was a relief, for we had been running without lights. About a week out, the Marinaspec masthead light had inexplicably stopped working, and two days before, our spare navigation lights had gone, too. We then ran with the deck lights on, which took a lot of battery charging but at least made us visible. Finally, the deck lights went, too, and our last night out we were completely dark and worried about the possibility of colliding with an unlit fishing boat in the blackness.

At half past seven Bill woke me. I looked across the water and saw the harbor wall of Horta. We put in a final tack and crossed the finishing line at 08.47, local time. We sailed into the harbor and were directed to a mooring. Somebody on shore set off some fireworks. As we furled the reefing genoa the Dynafurl broke again, but it didn't seem to matter now. We were in Horta. It had taken us fifteen and a half days.

35

Horta, Sweet Horta

What we saw amazed me. I had been expecting a brown, arid, rather deserted island. Faial was as lush and green as Ireland, and more mountainous. Horta wrapped around the little harbor and ran up the hillside, lots of trees and white buildings.

Gypsy Moth V was moored nearby. Giles Chichester rowed over and invited us aboard for coffee. We began to pump up the dinghy. A motorboat came alongside and deposited a plump fellow in a bright green shirt aboard, waving customs forms. Funny sort of customs man, I thought. He extended a hand and said, in American-accented English, "Hi, I'm Augie." And Augie he was. Born of an American mother and an Azorean father, August (pronounced "Ow-goost") had spent some time in California before returning to live in Horta. Augie was a mine of information and good cheer. Did the laundry need doing? No problem. The electrics need fixing? Can do. I really began to relax.

We signed the forms, surrendered our passports to Augie, and splashed over to *Gypsy Moth*. There Giles and his crew, Martin Wolford, brought us up to date. *Runnin' Scared* had won the race. We were the last boat to finish, though not last on corrected time (we were also the smallest boat to finish), and three or four boats had retired. Everybody had taken longer than anticipated, so the dinner had been put back to Sunday night. We had missed it by twelve hours. But there was a beach party that night, and probably one every night from now on. The Club Naval, the local yachting, diving, swimming, and fishing organization, had apparently been given a grant from the government tourist office to entertain the race crews and their wives and girlfriends who had met them in Horta, and the club was having a wonderful time spending it. Nobody's feet had touched ground since reaching Horta. Neither would ours.

We staggered ashore under the weight of an incredible amount of laundry for two people, borrowed the staff shower at the Estalagem de Santa Cruz, a lovely modern hotel built inside the walls of an old fort next to the Club Naval, then, cleaner and more closely shaven than we would have dreamed possible, tucked into a lunch of fresh tuna (I had always thought they were born in cans) fried in batter, local grapes and cheese, and a cold bottle of the native white wine, Pico Branco (the local red wine is good, too, if you don't mind your teeth turning blue), all of it a welcome change from the tinned food on the boat.

Thus fortified, we began to lurch about Horta, exploring. We lurched because we had not yet got back our land legs, and the earth seemed to move in the same way the boat had. We found the Café Sport, which is the headquarters for visiting yachtsmen in Horta. The owner, Peter, receives and forwards mail, changes money, lends his telephone, and keeps social intercourse among visiting boats moving at a brisk pace. We renewed acquaintance with other crews over cold beer at the Club Naval and swapped stories about our experiences on the passage out. As it turned out, nearly all the other boats had sailed into a different weather system from the one we had encountered, and while we had had fresh headwinds for virtually the whole passage, they had had free but light winds and had suffered calms, so everyone had been slow arriving.

I got a list of finishing times, did some calculating, and discovered to my astonishment that, allowing for the eleven hours required to put Shirley ashore, we had finished third on handicap, beating *Gypsy Moth* on corrected time. In fact, only *Runnin' Scared* and *Triple Arrow* had beaten us on handicap. But, in spite of our appeal to the committee, we had been disqualified under the three-man, minimum-crew rule, as had been David Palmer, in *FT*, who had put a crew ashore on another island so that he could make a flight back to England. Our good position on corrected time raised my hopes for the handicap prize in the OSTAR, but much would depend on the kind of handicap I would be assigned for that race.

In the afternoon I completely succumbed to the lure of being ashore again and moved into the Estalagem de Santa Cruz, reveling once more in clean sheets and hot showers. The boat was a bit of a mess, anyway, since she had begun taking water through the keelbolts again, and everything was very damp. All the rooms had balconies overlooking the harbor, and I could see *Harp* bobbing gently at her moorings, only a couple of hundred yards away. Bill moved into a hotel on top of the hill and got some much-needed rest.

That evening Club Naval threw a beach party for us and, leaning into twenty-knot winds, we ate fish rubbed with garlic and cooked over a charcoal fire, washed down with Pico Branco. Lots of locals and nearly all of the crews came, and all had a marvelous time.

For the next day or so I wandered around dazed, still unable to believe that I was actually in Horta. Giles Chichester threw a party on *Gypsy Moth*, and two other boats were tied alongside to handle the overflow. The conversation and the wine flowed like water, and before we knew it late evening had come and all of Horta's restaurants were closed. Martin Wolford; John Perry, skipper of *Peter, Peter*, who floated about in a white suit, straw hat, and ten-day beard in the best beachcomber style and who claimed to be a solicitor in London; and a young lady who had flown out to meet a competitor who had subsequently retired from the race, all came to dinner on *Golden Harp*. We ate and drank well and when, in the wee small hours of the morning, the party began to break up and John and Martin offered to deliver the young lady ashore, I said I would do that myself, since I did not wish to disturb her while she was washing the dishes. I saw John and Martin on deck and to their respective dinghies and then settled down with a brandy while the young lady finished in the galley.

When we came on deck for the trip ashore, *Harp's* dinghy was gone, in spite of the perfectly good clove hitch I had tied in the painter. It was now two o'clock in the morning, and we were faced with the choice of shouting until we woke some wine-soaked sailor on another boat and asking him to get up, dress, and row us ashore in the pouring rain, which had just begun to fall, or staying on the boat. The only sensible thing to do, of course, was to stay on the boat. It was all perfectly innocent, really it was; she stayed in her bunk and I stayed in mine. It is a mark of what dirty minds people have, however, that we took a great deal of raucous abuse the following day.

The dinghy was found, blown ashore at the other end of the harbor. I have never been entirely convinced that John Perry did not have a hand in the undoing of my perfectly good clove hitch. I do not think Martin would have stooped to such an action, but you can never tell about a London solicitor in a white suit and a straw hat.

The days drifted lazily by, with the odd bit of work getting done on *Harp* whenever *mañana* arrived. We continued to be royally entertained by the Club Naval. There was a special dinner at the Café Capitolia for the last boats to finish—*Harp* on real time, *Peter, Peter* on corrected time. Augie and Luis, the commodore of the club, always seemed to be inventing a reason for another special dinner. One day I expressed an interest in seeing some of the island, and a taxi materialized in front of the Estalagem for a free tour. Another time, while I was working on the boat, a motorboat came alongside bearing a bottle of the local brandy—another prize for the last boat to finish. There seemed to be no end to it all. John Perry threw a party on *Peter, Peter*, a fifty-foot catamaran which could have served as a floating dance hall. Brian Cooke looked around and remarked that there was probably room for a branch office of the National Westminster Bank.

The moon rises over the seven-thousand-foot volcano on Pico.

Brian, who had suffered a bad fall from the top of the mast of *Triple Arrow* the season before, admitted that his broken back had not healed completely, but said that he was looking forward to the OSTAR the following season, and to his winter project of attempting to beat Chichester's speed record from West Africa to South America, on which he would qualify his new boat for the OSTAR. There was an impromptu dinner with Mike Best of *Croda Way* and David Palmer of *FT* and his lovely wife, Elizabeth. Mike and David were both, as I was, sailing back from the Azores single-handed to qualify, and we had an interesting chat about preparing for the race.

Scrimshaw, etching on whale ivory, is the Azorean art form, and Orthon is its chief practitioner in Horta. Working in a small house crammed to the rafters with whales' teeth and other bones and a great deal of ingenious machinery, most of which he made himself, Orthon, for a modest sum, will engrave the image of a yacht on a polished tooth and mount it. Each competitor was presented with a tooth engraved with the name of his yacht, and these handsome gifts no doubt grace bulkheads in widely scattered places today.

As the week passed, yachts began to sail for England. First to go was *Gypsy Moth*, and she got a send-off of fireworks and hooters. Before leaving for home, Bill Howell laid me out in the cockpit of *Tahiti Bill*, injected me with a painkiller from my medical kit, and reglued a loose bridge which had been rattling around the back of my head since Portsmouth. Bill King found a berth with him for the sail back. The other boats followed one by one, until only *Runnin' Scared* and *Harp* were left. I saw a lot of David and Ann Walsh, who were sailing *Runnin' Scared* back, and they planned a trip to Ireland in the autumn, when we would cruise down the south coast. Most days we took *Harp* along the coast from Horta and anchored for a picnic and a swim. In the evenings, Ann formed the diverting habit of suddenly shedding her clothes and dashing into the pool at the hotel on the hill, while the ancient night watchman railed at us. I was sad when *Runnin' Scared* sailed out of the harbor and left me to enjoy Horta on my own.

But other boats were arriving all the time, Horta being a prime stopover for yachts on transatlantic passages: *Charisma* and *Tenacious*, both members of the American Admiral's Cup team in the recent Cowes Week, came and went; two Canadians sailed in aboard a homemade catamaran; an American couple arrived on a lovely little cutter which sported a square rigged sail; a couple who had briefly been neighbors at Coolmore while building a boat at Crosshaven came in on their way to Brazil; and we all watched with bated breath as the pilot boat took a giant, seventy-five-foot ketch in tow just before she drifted onto some rocks, her engine seized and her sails blown out in a gale. She was *Polaris*, a handsome if weathered old boat, built in Germany in 1914, sailed by a very mixed crew which included an English bank manager turned fisherman turned boat bum, a couple of pretty girls, and a mad Irish skipper. They were great fun for the rest of my stay and, at last report, Shay, the skipper, and Tim, the fisherman/bank manager, were still in Horta, running a discotheque.

An American ex-marine and now merchant marine radio operator named Bob Lengyl turned up in *Prodigal*, a tiny sloop, and nearly worried himself to death when I told him that the race committee was closing the entry list for the OSTAR. He had been preparing for the race for two or three years but had neglected to reserve a place. He got an application in the mail, pronto.

One of the most interesting people to sail into Horta was Laurie, a wiry Aussie with an impenetrable accent and a wide gap between his teeth. He had a story to tell about that. Leaving Virginia Beach, in the United States, for Horta, he had been caught in a hurricane, then come down with an abscessed tooth. Unable to stand the pain, he had sloshed down some whisky, then taken a drill and a self-tapping screw to the roots of the tooth, when it had broken off in attempts to pull it with vice-grip pliers. While he was lying semiconscious in his bunk recovering from that, a supertanker nearly ran him down, scraping his little boat along the entire length of the huge ship's hull and pulling out his mast and most of his stanchions. He had restepped the mast and repaired his rigging at sea, then sailed on to Horta.

Laurie and Len, one of the Canadians, gave me a great deal of help with getting *Harp* ready to sail again, especially with the electrical system, which was performing very poorly. Len had a complete electrical tool kit aboard his boat and worked wonders with a soldering iron.

David and Ann Walsh aboard the *Harp*, anchored off Faial for lunch.

The people at the Estalagem were interesting, too. A writer and photographer from *National Geographic* turned up, doing a story about the Azores, especially about the whale hunting. Then Perry Mason turned up at the bar one afternoon. Or was it

Ironside? Raymond Burr, the actor, for reasons I never quite got straight, owned the lease of the government-built Estalagem. It was very peculiar, at breakfast or dinner, to look up and see Perry Mason/Ironside across the dining room. He gave a reception one evening and is a charming man.

My stay in Horta was stretching pleasantly on, my chief excuse being the nonarrival of the new Dynafurl. There had been some confusion about when and where it was to be sent, and an exchange of telegrams was required before I was notified that it was on its way. Augie and Luis took over from there. They somehow arranged for the pilot of the flight from Lisbon to the Azores to collect the package in Lisbon, then pass it on to the pilot of the interisland flight, thus saving several days in shipment. Augie then walked me through most of the Azorean Civil Service in order to save me paying exorbitant duty on the gear, which was being almost immediately reexported anyway.

A northeasterly gale held up work on the boat for another two days, giving me a breather to enjoy the stories of the anti-communist demonstrations in Ponta Delgado and Horta. At that time Portugal, which owns the Azores, was going through a political upheaval and it looked as though there might be a communist takeover of the country. The Azoreans, who are pro-American, pro-English, and anti-communist, did not like the sound of this at all, and a considerable number of them were talking of declaring independence if the communists succeeded in Lisbon. There were very few communists in Horta, but that was apparently too many. There were large demonstrations in the middle of the night, which I slept through. On one occasion the plan had been to burn the local communist headquarters, but it seemed that a rather nice person lived next door and no one wanted to risk the fire spreading there, so a discussion was held and it was decided to remove the communists' books and papers and burn them outside. The communists retaliated by sabotaging the record player at the local discotheque. On another island a large crowd escorted two communist leaders down to the sea and tossed them in. When they realized that one of the two could not swim they immediately rescued him. The Azoreans are like that.

September had arrived, and I was beginning to worry about getting home before the equinoctial gales started. I had never heard of the equinoctial gales until Bill had casually mentioned their occurrence on the passage out. As I made my final preparations, stocking up on Pico Branco and fresh food from the lovely local market, I checked with the meteorological office at the American air base on another island. There was still a stiff northeasterly wind blowing, and I did not relish the thought of beating back to the British Isles after beating all the way out. The duty officer said I could expect the northeasterly to continue for a day or two, then moderate and swing around to the south or southwest. That wind should hold for a few days, then veer to the northwest. He advised me to sail due north until the wind veered so that I would be in a position to take advantage of the northwesterly. He also said that I probably wouldn't experience winds of more than twenty-five knots on the passage home. As it turned out, he was right about everything except that.

On my last night in Horta there was a dinner party aboard *Polaris*, and then I performed the ritual every yachtsman follows before leaving Horta. I painted a golden harp on the harbor wall next to all the other yachts' names and symbols, hundreds of them, including Chichester's, that have accumulated there over the years. The next morning, September 4, I collected fresh bread and, particularly, banana bread from the Estalagem, gathered my gear together, and, with Len, rowed out to *Harp*. Len helped me deflate and stow the dinghy, had a last look at the electronics, and got a lift ashore. I started the engine, slipped the mooring, and motored past *Polaris* for a last shouted goodbye. I truly hated to go.

I motored through the harbor entrance, nearly in tears, passing the Pico ferry; everybody aboard waved goodbye. I unreefed the genoa, switched off the engine, and started to beat toward Pico in the fresh northeasterly. The seven-thousand-foot volcano was distinctly outlined against the bright blue sky, not wearing its usual crown of clouds. It suddenly occurred to me that I had never, not once, sailed *Golden Harp* single-handed.

I began to consider wintering in Horta.

36

Alone from Horta
to Crosshaven

I began to tune the rigging—adjusting the shrouds until the mast was standing straight on both tacks, something somebody had told me how to do in Horta. It worked, and by the time I had finished, my initial nervousness at sailing the boat alone was gone. I began really to enjoy myself; it was a wonderful feeling of self-sufficiency.

Pico began to recede into the distance as we (I always thought of *Harp* and me as "we") approached Graciosa. As night fell, I navigated from bearings on the many lights dotted about the island. We pointed toward the western end of Graciosa, taking a different route from the passage out, and I rested fitfully, coming up often to check my bearings. I would not really feel comfortable until we had cleared Graciosa and were in the open sea with no rocks to pile up on.

Our first full day out was sunny and clear, lovely sailing, but with the wind still on the nose and dropping. Late in the afternoon I sighted a ship and got my KVHF flags up in a hurry, something I was getting good at. She was the Polish merchant ship *General Madalinski,* and I got the usual warm reception from the radio operator, who agreed to send telegrams to the States and Ireland for me. The captain gave me a position which closely corresponded with my own navigation, a great relief, since that day I had done my very first noon position on my own. I spent the time reading and listening to the American Forces radio station at Lajes Field in the Azores, which was much like listening to a small-town American radio station. The news was particularly nice to hear, since I hadn't read a newspaper or listened to the radio for more than two weeks.

I got my first good night's sleep and awoke to find us nearly becalmed. I set the drifter and had to work all day at keeping the boat moving in the light airs. At my next noon sight we had covered only thirty-five miles, a discouraging figure, but shortly after lunch the wind swung around behind us and I was able to set the Betsy Ross floater spinnaker. The boat's speed increased immediately from two to three and a half knots, more when the wind puffed a bit. Fred steered perfectly, the sun shone, and I had the best sailing I had ever experienced, lying naked on the deck with a glass of wine and soaking up the sun while *Harp* took care of herself. This was a totally sybaritic experience and was the time when I most wished I had someone to share the trip with. Randiness began to set in.

In the afternoon I contacted a Russian merchant ship, the *Alexander* something-or-other, and got the first cool reception in my experience with other ships at sea. They gave me a position and weather report but they didn't seem too happy about it and, since I had sent telegrams the day before, I didn't press them to pass on messages. They divulged that they were en route from Leningrad to Cuba and then signed off.

I went to sleep with the floater still up and woke at midnight to find that the wind had risen and the spinnaker had torn along the starboard leech. When I went to get the sail down, the deck lights shorted again and I had to do it in the dark. I was very sad about the spinnaker since it had become my favorite sail. It was like seeing a good friend with a broken leg, and I folded it into its bag to await the ministrations of John McWilliam in Crosshaven.

Now I had day after day of free sailing. On the eighth I was making six to seven knots in ten to twelve knots of following wind when a very embarrassing thing happened—or, at least, it would have been embarrassing if there had been anybody there to see it. I got a bad spinnaker wrap; my Irish tricolor all-rounder wrapped around the forestay in the middle, while remaining full of wind at the top and bottom, giving the effect of an overengineered brassiere sticking out in front of the boat. I tried everything I could think of to free the sail, but it refused to unwrap and it began to look as if I would have to climb the mast to unwrap it from the top. It was mid-afternoon and I decided that since we were still making a good speed I would leave things as they were until it began to get dark. If the spinnaker hadn't unwrapped itself by then, and I fervently hoped it would, then I would go up the mast and free it. In the meantime, a beer seemed a good idea. After all, I was in the middle of the North Atlantic Ocean, and there was nobody there to witness my humiliation. Why not relax?

Five minutes later a Dutch naval vessel, HMS *Zuiderkruis*, turned up and, after making radio contact, the operator's first words were, "Can we assist you in clearing your spinnaker?" I said I could handle it, and after getting a position and a weather report and ascertaining that they had picked me up on radar at a distance of five miles, I went on deck, shamed into climbing the mast. I waved goodbye to the ship and started up. After ten minutes of swearing and struggling with the bloody thing, it finally came unwrapped, and as the big sail filled I was startled to hear a loud cheer. I swung around to look behind me and found the ship stopped, her entire crew hanging over the rail, applauding. She gave a loud hoot on her horn and was on her way again. So much for privacy in single-handed sailing.

In the middle of that night I got a fine scare. I was sleeping like a stone when there came a loud thumping on deck. Pirates? I charged up the companionway ladder to find nothing. Then, as I was about to chalk the sound up to a nightmare and go below, the thumping started again. A small, needle-nosed fish had jumped into the cockpit and was thrashing about the floor. I caught him and returned him to the sea. I don't know if I really rescued him, for at that moment a pair of dolphins appeared and started into the phosphorescent torpedo act again, and he could have made a midnight snack for one of them. I watched, still fascinated, until they departed, then crawled back into my bunk.

I settled into a deep contentment. I was comfortable, well fed, and doing what I had been planning for months. The nearest problem was eight hundred or so miles away, and I was enjoying my solitude and self-sufficiency. The only fly in the soup was that *Harp* had never stopped taking water, and as time wore on she took more and more. There was so much that it was impossible to isolate and tell where it was coming from.

The electric bilge pump had packed up again and, since the intake for the main pump was too large to collect water in the shallow bilges unless the boat had three or four inches of water inside her, the only way to bail was with a sponge and a bucket, and it wasn't much fun. By now I was taking out about twelve gallons of water four times a day, and anything that touched the floor got soaked immediately.

I continued north, and the barometer began to drop. When it

went down six millibars in four hours I knew I was in for a blow, and I reefed before dark even though the wind had not yet risen; I had no wish to have to reef in the middle of the night with the deck lights not working. By morning we were in our first full gale ever. Fortunately, the wind was still behind us and we were able to maintain our course while running before it with a double-reefed main and the genoa reefed to storm jib size. We were making excellent time.

I settled into a heavy weather routine. This consisted mostly of staying in my bunk, sleeping or reading, apart from a periodic look around the horizon for shipping and a check of the sails and decks to make sure nothing was chafing or coming adrift. And bailing. As the weather deteriorated, the leaking got worse. I began to become accustomed to living in my seaboots, with two inches of water slopping about the cabin. There were two exterior forces as well which made things less comfortable. One was the mini-broaches. When a boat "broaches to" when running before the wind, she suddenly veers and tries to point into the wind, ending up beam-on to the seas and the wind. This can be very dangerous, and *Harp* never quite performed the maneuver. What she did do was begin to broach, then correct. Fred, like any self-steering gear, could not anticipate the action of a following wave the way a helmsman can. He could not correct the boat's direction to allow for a wave which was about to change it. Rather, he would have to wait until he felt the yacht beginning to change direction, then correct. This resulted in a sort of "mini-broach," in which the yacht would start to veer abeam to the wind, then resume her proper course. The effect on the occupant of the boat and the contents was much like that on the occupants of a car which, traveling at, say, forty miles an hour, suddenly and sharply swerves to avoid another car backing out of a driveway, then continues down the street. If I were standing, cooking, for instance, when the mini-broach occurred to port, I would be tossed across the cabin to land on (or under) the chart table. This is not as much fun as it sounds.

The gale moderated after half a day, but we were left with a large, old sea running. Still, we had about twenty-four hours of relative quiet, with winds of no more than about twenty-five knots, and this seemed something of a rest. The most tiring part was the constant bailing.

Then the barometer, after rising a bit, began to fall again. In the first gale it had bottomed at about 1,014 millibars. It was there again when I went to bed on the night after the gale. During the night I dreamed, first, that I was being tossed around in a rubber dinghy. I think this came from being bounced in my bunk between the foam-rubber cushions of the settee back on one side and the lee cloth on the other. Toward morning I began to dream that I was lying on a beach with the sea lapping against the sand a few inches away. When I woke there was, instead, about four inches of water lapping around the inside of the cabin. Thinking for a couple of minutes that the boat was sinking, I began bailing. There is a saying that there is no more effective bilge pump than a frightened man with a bucket. This, I can say from personal experience, is true. Finally, when I had scooped up as much water as possible with the bucket and had to resort once again to the sponge, I realized that the boat was not sinking, that she had merely begun to take more water. During the next three days she took more than three hundred gallons.

When I had recovered enough from my fright to look around me, I found that the barometer had plunged to 1,008 during the night and that there was forty knots of wind blowing outside. While bailing, I had hardly noticed the motion of the boat. Now I did. I could hardly fail to notice it because suddenly the boat committed one of her finest mini-broaches; I was lifted off my feet, flung across the cabin from the chart table, and deposited squarely on top of the cooker. By the time I had disentangled myself from the stainless-steel fiddles on top there was the distinct smell of gas in the cabin. I quickly got into the cockpit locker and turned off the gas supply at the bottle. From that time, when I wanted to cook, I had to go into the cockpit, turn on the bottle, then dash into the cabin and light the cooker before enough gas collected to cause an explosion. Once the flame was burning it seemed to consume any excess gas from leaks, but I used the cooker as little as possible from then on. What really cut back my use of the cooker was the fire.

I had gone through my cockpit/cabin drill, but the disposable cigarette lighter was damp and slow to light. When I finally got a spark and a flame the whole cooker, both burners and the grill, burst into massive flame. My reaction still astonishes me. There was a fire blanket near my right hand and a fire extinguisher at my left knee; either would have quickly extinguished the fire. But instead of using one of these, I simply *blew*. The fire went out like the last candle on a birthday cake. I was very, very careful with the cooker after that.

Force ten in the Atlantic. The waves never look as large in the photographs.

Now, with so much wind blowing, the sea around me became an even more fascinating place. It wasn't very cold and rain was spasmodic, so I would sit in the watch seat in the companionway and watch the gale. Fortunately, the wind had risen slowly and without changing direction radically, so the seas, though large, were regular and from the same direction. Using the mast as a guide, I reckoned the waves were a bit over twenty feet in height, and I watched, transfixed, as *Harp* rose to meet each one. Just when it seemed that a giant sea would overtake us and fall on top of the boat, the yacht would rise to meet it, and the wave would pass harmlessly under us. As the wind rose even more there seemed to be waves breaking everywhere, but never one immediately behind us. When that happens, when a yacht is "pooped," an incredible weight of water falls onto the boat, serious damage can be done and gear washed away. If the main hatch has been left open the cabin can fill with water and the boat founders.

Harp surfed down the big waves, often exceeding her theoretical hull speed of about eight knots. I have one vivid memory of sitting in the watch seat, watching the instrument dials; the yacht suddenly accelerated to nine knots, surfing down a wave, and the wind-speed indicator was registering a steady forty-five knots with the wind dead astern. This meant a true wind speed of fifty-five knots, or more than sixty miles an hour. The noise and spray were incredible, but knowing that I had a good boat under me, it was not frightening but exhilarating.

Now my spare navigation lights failed. On reaching Horta I had found that the masthead light had simply disappeared, blown away on the passage out. Now, with the spares gone, too, I was reduced to one small, battery-operated white light, which I taped to a stanchion so that it could be seen all round. In a lull, when I started to unreef the genoa a bit, the Dynafurl parted again, the top half of the top swivel staying up the mast with the halyard and the bottom half sliding down the Twinstay with the sail. As long as the wind was behind us this did not pose much of a problem, since we could still sail very fast under the double-reefed main only, so I lashed the sail to the deck along with the number-one genoa and sailed on. I would have to climb the mast and retrieve the top half of the swivel before I could set a headsail again. Quite apart from the weakness in the Dynafurl, which would have to be redesigned, this meant that there was a gap in my sail plan. The smallest sail I had aboard was the number-two reefing genoa, which meant that if the Dynafurl failed in heavy weather I needed a smaller sail to set until I could repair it. I would have a lot of rethinking to do when I reached Ireland, but then, that was what the qualifying cruise was for—to expose weaknesses in the boat and her systems. On that basis my cruise from the Azores was already an outstanding success.

The storm continued for nearly three days, with the wind only occasionally dropping to gale force. My reaction to being tossed about was, surprisingly, not fear but anger. I found it difficult to sleep, because when the boat mini-broached and woke me up my anger at being awakened made it difficult for me to go back to sleep. This cut into my reserves of strength, and the constant bailing kept me tired, but I became really exhausted only once.

At dusk on the thirteenth, I went into the cockpit to change the battery for the navigation light and discovered to my horror that both the number-one and -two genoas were dragging in the water, attached to the boat by only a shackle at their tacks. If I lost those sails, or even if they were badly torn, I would have no headsail to set and would be at the mercy of the wind, unable to sail in any direction but downwind. I was afraid to stop the boat and let her lie ahull, abeam to the seas, so I left her on her course, got into a safety harness, clipped onto a jackstay, and crawled forward to the foredeck, where I could reach the overboard sails.

With the additional drag from the two big sails, the boat had slowed to about four knots and was heeled more sharply. Large amounts of seawater were washing over me, and when I began to try to pull the sails aboard I discovered that they seemed hopelessly entangled in the lines, now broken, which had been laced through the guardrails to keep the sails on deck. Also the drag on the sails was incredible. It was like trying to haul in nets full of fish, single-handed.

As if all that wasn't enough, I began to hallucinate. I had read about the hallucinations of single-handed sailors. Joshua Slocum believed he had been assisted by a Portuguese seaman from another era, who appeared when he needed help. Others have written of shouts from on deck when something had gone wrong. Still others have seen and talked with friends or relatives. My hallucination was somewhat more mundane. The telephone rang.

Of course, there was no telephone on *Golden Harp*, but that did not stop it from ringing. What's more, it was a *French* telephone, like the instrument in a cheap Paris hotel room. It rang and rang. It was a bit like being in the bath, hearing the phone ring and being unable to answer it. My thought process went: Dammit, there's the phone, must answer it; no, can't answer it, got to get these sails aboard again; wait a minute, stupid, there is *no* telephone . . . There's the phone, must answer it . . . It went on and on as I struggled with the sails, the same thought pattern turning over and over in my head; I could no more stop it than I could stop the phone from ringing.

It took me more than an hour to haul the sails aboard again and secure them, the whole of the time being drenched, often with my feet dragging in the water as I tried to find a position where I could get a better grip and more purchase on the dragging canvas. Twice I almost lost a seaboot, rescuing it just as it was being washed from my foot. Finally, I had both sails aboard on the foredeck, lying spread-eagle on top of them to keep them from going again. Foot by foot I slid their bulk back toward the cockpit, taking infinite pains to see that no part of them slipped overboard again, because now they were attached to nothing except me. I made the cockpit, pushed the sails in ahead of me, then collapsed on top of them. At last, I thought, I can answer the telephone. It stopped ringing, just as it always does when you've struggled out of the bath and, clutching a towel about you, raced through the house, leaving a trail of wet footprints. Later, when I told a friend about this, she said, "Suppose it hadn't *stopped* ringing." That is a terrifying thought.

I lay in the cockpit for half an hour, not even budging when another squall hit. After all, *Harp* was steering herself, and I couldn't get any wetter. I think that if anything else had gone wrong at that moment I would have been unable to do anything about it. It is that degree of helpless exhaustion which is so dangerous to the single-hander. Sometimes, if you can't cope you can't live. It's as simple as that.

Soon after this delightful evening the storm began to abate and the wind veer. By morning the wind was ahead of the beam, still blowing about thirty knots. We were close reaching under double-reefed main only and our speed was down to two knots. Without a headsail we were going to make little progress, and if the wind continued to veer we would end up pointing at France instead of Ireland. There was nothing to do but go up the mast, retrieve the halyard, fix the Dynafurl, and get a headsail up. I made my first attempt almost immediately; I got about two steps up the mast, a forty-knot squall hit, and I was quickly down and into the cabin again, very chastened.

Next day, Sunday, I tried again. The wind had dropped further, but there was still a big sea running and, the wind having veered, it was now coming from two directions. I got as far as the crosstrees this time before I chickened out and retreated to wait for the seas to go down. Finally, late Monday afternoon, I made one last assault on the mast. I ran the boat off to steady her as much as possible, got into a harness, and started laboriously up the stick, clipping one of the two stainless-steel carbine hooks onto a higher step before unclipping the lower one. That way if I slipped I would always be hooked onto something, although I didn't relish the thought of swinging around like a pendulum from a rope clipped to a mast step. I stopped at the crosstrees to rest my hands, which were already very tired from gripping the steps so tightly, then continued. Step, hook to next step, unhook from lower step, step again. It went that way for all of the mast's thirty-eight-foot height, until finally I was clinging desperately to the top, both arms wrapped in a bear hug around the mast. It was necessary to hold on very tightly still, for the boat was rolling in the confused seas, and the mast was cutting an arc of fifteen to twenty feet at the top. Had I lost my grip there would have been a kind of slingshot effect, and I would have been catapulted off the mast into the sea. I stuck an arm through a mast step so that I would have a free hand, praying that the boat would not do a snap roll and break it at the shoulder, and started to haul down on the halyard.

The whole of the time I was at the top of the mast I thought about two things to the exclusion of everything else. The first was Brian Cooke falling onto the decks of *Triple Arrow* and breaking his back; the second was a teenager jumping from the yardarm of a tall training ship that summer, striking the water and dying instantly from the impact. That was all I could think about.

When I had finally inched my way back down the mast I sat on the deck for fifteen minutes until I could make a fist again, then repaired the Dynafurl and hoisted a foresail. I was nearly as tired as I had been after rescuing the sails. And while I had been doing that, other things had been going wrong. I discovered that when falling off a wave, *Harp* had jammed the log impeller up into the hull, freezing the mileage recorder. This was easily put right, but I had no idea when it had happened, and not knowing what distance I had covered screwed up my dead reckoning mightily. I hadn't had a firm position fix for several days because there had been so little sun, and with my dead reckoning out, I was very unsure of my position and still not close enough to land to use radio direction finding.

Then the engine refused to switch off. I had been charging batteries, and the lever which controlled the accelerator had jammed, corroded by seawater that had reached the engine through the cockpit floor, which was almost impossible to seal properly because of the way it was constructed. No amount of easing oil or blows with spanners and winch handles would free the lever, so now the only way to stop the engine was to turn off the fuel cocks and let it run out of fuel. Then, before starting again, the fuel system had to be bled to get out the air bubbles in the fuel lines.

Next, my last disposable lighter refused to work, and, having no matches on board, I had no way to light the cooker. This meant no hot food, no hot coffee, no hot anything, and I was not looking forward to eating cold tinned food.

Finally, the main alternator failed, but at least I was able to plug in the spare. It would charge only one battery at a time, though, so I had to switch leads to charge both batteries, and I could not run the engine and use the other electrics at the same time. Bloody nuisance it turned out to be, too.

By Tuesday I was over the continental shelf and had a rough RDF position, but I was anxious to contact a ship for a tighter fix. Once, when I had been lying on the foredeck repairing the wiring to the forward navigation light, I saw first one, then four ships, but the engine was running at the time to charge batteries and I couldn't use the VHF. In the early hours of Tuesday morning I spotted a brightly lit fishing boat nearby and began signaling KVHF. He apparently didn't read Morse, so he came over for a closer look. He was soon well within shouting distance, but my electric loud-hailer chose this moment to malfunction, so I was reduced to shouting "VHF—Radio" as he circled and came up about fifteen yards off my starboard quarter, running alongside and slightly behind us. It was a huge steel trawler, a hundred feet or so in length, and she was wearing a German or Dutch name that I could never quite read. I shouted repeatedly, but there was lots of shrugging and shaking of heads by everybody on deck.

Suddenly, the helmsman put his helm over all the way to port—I could see him in the wheelhouse spinning the wheel—and started across my stern without reducing speed in the least. I froze in the cockpit as the enormous trawler came toward us—I was actually looking up at her bows—and waited for the crash. The thought raced through my mind that if I went below to get a life jacket I would be trapped there when the collision occurred, and that there was no time to launch the life raft. So I stood, clutching a winch and bracing myself for the blow. He missed *Harp*'s stern by less than ten feet and took more than ten years off my life. I turned the signaling torch on myself and waved him away. I resolved never again to ask a fisherman for help or advice unless I was really in a bad way.

I got little sleep that night, keeping a watch for shipping, then at dawn I saw a strange shape sticking up over the horizon. My binoculars had fogged up from being wet, so I couldn't identify it, but I thought it must be an uncharted oil rig, and since it seemed to be receding I went below to make a cup of coffee. I had begun hearing jets passing overhead now and figured I must be on the London–Cork air route. A few minutes later I heard a helicopter, a very loud helicopter, and went on deck to find a U.S. Navy chopper hovering about a hundred feet directly above the boat. I looked astern and there was the largest warship in the world, the USS *Nimitz*, a nuclear-powered aircraft carrier more than a thousand feet long and with a crew of five thousand. I knew about her from an interview I had heard on the BBC with one of her officers. She had been on a courtesy visit to England and she was now apparently trying to find out what the hell a small yacht was doing sailing about with no one at the helm. I waved at the chopper crew and they went away, apparently satisfied that there was someone on board. Again, the engine was running and I couldn't call her up on VHF.

Tuesday passed quietly with light weather and occasional rain, but toward evening the wind freshened and I was running at a good clip, on course for Crosshaven, I hoped. I was still a bit shaky on my position, getting good bearings from Old Head of Kinsale and Galley Head, but unreliable ones from Round Island, in the Scillies. I began to plan a landfall about eight-thirty the following morning at Roberts Head, just outside Cork Harbour.

I stayed up all night, waiting for Old Head light to appear, hoping it would be in the right place. To make matters worse, my log had begun to overread, destroying my dead reckoning. It began to drizzle heavily and I worried about visibility as I approached the Irish coast. About four a.m. I sighted the loom of Old Head light. I got a quick bearing on it and settled down for the light itself to appear. Roche's Point light at the entrance to Cork Harbour would appear, eventually, too.

Then the visibility closed in completely. The drizzle obliterated everything, and although I kept a vigil I was never able to raise either light. Dawn came in the most peculiar way. It was not possible even to tell where the sun was rising. Everything just changed from black to ever lightening shades of gray until it was full daylight. All I could see was fog. There was not even a bird about to give me some idea of how far I could see. The terrible thing about fog is that it makes it impossible to judge distance.

I sat in the watch seat with the depth sounder in my hands, watching the water get shallower and shallower. I expected an eight-thirty landfall and the soundings seemed to confirm this. I felt pretty sure that I would sight land somewhere between Kinsale and Cork, a distance of about fourteen miles, but then I could also make my landfall east of Cork. I could only point the boat at where I thought Roberts Head might be and hope for the best.

The sounder read forty fathoms, then twenty, then fifteen, then twelve. Eight-thirty came and went. Still no land. Still no visibility. Then I heard a noise like the engines of a ship. Oh, God, I thought, as if making a landfall in no visibility weren't enough, I've got to dodge a ship or fishing boat. I doubled my efforts to see through the fog. All I could see was a white line on the water just ahead of us. A streak of detergent foam washed out of some river, I thought. Then, less than two hundred yards dead ahead, a large, green cliff appeared out of the fog. The noise had been the sea pounding against it. The white line had been the surf. I had found Ireland; now I had to find Crosshaven.

I jibed very quickly indeed and sailed east along the coast, keeping it barely in sight. Since I wasn't certain where I was, I didn't want to run onto rocks on one part of the coast, thinking I was on another part. The visibility cleared slightly and I saw a buoy, Daunt Rock buoy. After a week without a firm fix and in two hundred yards of visibility, I had found Roberts Head on the nose, and twelve minutes late. I was giddy with excitement.

I contacted Cork Harbour radio and asked them to have customs meet me at the Royal Cork and to ring Nick at the cottage and ask him to help me get into Drake's Pool and pick up *Harp*'s mooring. I sailed along into the entrance to Cork Harbour, still in poor visibility, and picked up Ringabella Bay and Ringabella House on its shore. The hammerheaded water tower on the hill appeared. It was not until I was abeam of Roche's Point that the fog lifted enough for me to see the lighthouse.

As I began to tidy up the yacht and get ready to take the sails down I looked up to see a Mirror dinghy sailing past me out of the harbor. Her skipper was single-handed. I thought, where the hell is he going, single-handed, on a day like this? And then, I wonder if he knows what he may be getting himself into.

I motored up the river into Crosshaven and picked up a mooring in front of the Royal Cork Yacht Club. The place was deserted, apart from a steward and the customs men, who were there to meet me. As the customs men were going ashore, Nick appeared, roaring down the river in his rubber dinghy, standing up and waving both hands. He came aboard and we motored up to Drake's Pool and picked up *Harp*'s mooring. Fred greeted us in a frenzy as we stepped ashore in front of the cottage, and I wondered, How many people can sail thirteen hundred miles and never touch land until their front doorstep? I turned and looked at the yacht swinging peacefully at her moorings.

Golden Harp was home.

Fog begins to lift at the entrance to Cork Harbour.

37

Back Home

Everything seemed very peculiar at home in Ireland. I had the usual problem of stopping the earth from swaying, of course, and the rooms of Drake's Pool Cottage seemed vast after the confines of *Harp*'s cabin, which had seemed so roomy at sea. I staggered about the cottage, babbling incessantly to Nick and Heather. I could not stop talking. We had dinner at a local restaurant. The thing I had missed *second* most on the passage was food cooked by somebody else, served on a white tablecloth, with cloth napkins. I talked all through dinner and straight through till bedtime. By the time I crawled between my first clean sheets and soft bed in thirteen days I was hoarse from talking.

The autumn was a busy time, and the boat was my first priority. The broken log was returned to Brookes & Gatehouse for servicing; Hydromarine sent a man down to recondition the engine; Lucas replaced both alternators and the splitting diode, all of which had been corroded into uselessness by seawater entering the engine bay through the cockpit floor; Derek Holland, a neighbor at Coolmore and a former ship's engineer, rewired the whole boat; Nick fitted my ingenious little heater; and the cooker, which hadn't liked it when I had been thrown on top of it, was replaced. I raced the boat in a Sunday event in the harbor, crewed by a tribe of local Lydens, and she took twenty gallons of water in three hours, so Harold Cudmore and I packed the keelbolts with lifecaulk and hemp and retightened them, and this greatly reduced the water she was taking, though it did not cure the condition.

John McWilliam and I flew to the Southampton Boat Show and I got a lot done there: Marinaspec kindly replaced the blown-away masthead light, explaining that there had been a faulty weld on a few lamps and they had not been able to track me down; I met Jim Nolan of Barlow Winches, who agreed to loan me a pair of big self-tailing winches and a larger halyard winch; and I had a talk with Camper & Nicholsons about bringing *Harp* to England for repairs. On the flight back we had to divert to Shannon, as Cork Airport was closing, and the following morning we had a beautiful, low-level flight over the green Irish countryside, stopping at two small airfields along the way, one of them the front lawn of Kilbritain Castle, near Kinsale.

Before leaving Horta I had asked Luis, commodore of the Club Naval, to write to the Royal Western, confirming that I had left Horta alone; on arriving in Crosshaven, Harry Deane, secretary of the Royal Cork, had also written to them, confirming my single-handed arrival. I had then, as the rules required, submitted a list of my noon positions between Horta and Crosshaven, and on September 29 I received a letter from Lloyd Foster saying that I had been accepted for the race pending only the final inspection of *Golden Harp* in Plymouth the week before the race. This was a monumental landmark for me. I felt that I had now accomplished a great part of what I had set out to do: I had learned to sail, got experience on a wide range of boats, completed one navigation course and half of another, making up in practical experience what I had lost in classroom instruction; I had planned and had the yacht built, equipped her, sailed her fourteen hundred miles with Bill King and thirteen hundred single-handed; I had experienced an enormous variety of conditions, and both the boat and I had stood up to them. All that was left to do before the race was to overhaul the boat completely and make the refinements I had already worked out in my head.

The autumn slipped by in the most pleasant sort of way. David and Ann Walsh from *Runnin' Scared* came over for a weekend sail to Kinsale, followed closely by Ann, who came for several days.

Harold Cudmore, Ann, and I sailed down the south coast of Ireland, stopping for the night and a good dinner in Kinsale, then proceeding to the lovely little village of Castletownsend, where we were joined by Philip McCauliffe for a short passage on to Baltimore. We ate well, slept well, and spent many pleasant hours in the West Cork pubs. After a day in Baltimore the weather went to hell and showed no signs of clearing up, so we got a lift back to Cork and left *Harp* on a mooring there for collection later.

While awaiting *Harp*'s return, Ron Holland, John McWilliam, and I appeared on the Irish version of the TV quiz show *To Tell the Truth,* in Dublin. We all claimed to be me, and a panel had to figure out who was lying. We must have been pretty good liars, because only one of the four panelists guessed correctly. Highlight of the program came when a panelist asked Ron what a centerboard was. "Something that keeps a boat from sailing sideways," Ron answered. The panelist turned to McWilliam. "And what do you have if you don't have a centerboard?" she asked, pouncing on him for an answer. "A boat that sails sideways," replied John. We had a great time.

I had hoped that the television appearance might help pave the way toward finding a sponsor for the race, something that had eluded me so far. (There had been a regretful letter from Quinns-worth on my return from Horta, saying that they had decided they could not participate.) But the recession of 1974–75 had hit Irish businesses hard and advertising budgets, never very big in Ireland, were at an all-time low.

Ron, his design business expanding rapidly, bought a farm-house across the river from the Royal Cork, made plans to ren-ovate a pigsty and turn it into a design office, and hired an assistant. O. H. Rogers, a young man from Florida, had been Ron's first client when he struck out on his own, the resulting boat being called *Cherry Bomb*. Now, after campaigning for a couple of seasons, O.H. was apprenticing himself to Ron, and he would turn out to be a big help to me in preparing *Harp* for the race.

On November 20, O.H. and I motored *Harp* up the harbor and delivered her into the hands of Southcoast Boatyard for her "im-mediate" repairs. On December 1 I left for my home in Georgia, to spend the Christmas holidays there. I stopped by the yard to see how work was progressing. I had a talk with them about it, and they promised to be well along with her when I returned in January.

I spent five weeks in the United States, working on the early chapters of this book, visiting friends at home in Manchester and in Atlanta, looking into the family business, a clothing business rapidly becoming a department store which needed further ex-panding, and just relaxing. Only one event occurred that might have had a bearing on my entry in the OSTAR.

My last week at home I did something to my back which made it very sore—a muscle strain, I figured. Then, on the day of my departure for Ireland, then London and the boat show, I was bending over the sink shaving when something down low snapped, and I was suddenly in excruciating pain. I tried to delay my departure for a day, but the only flight I could get was the one I was already booked on, so, walking in a rather peculiar way, I arrived at Atlanta Airport, struggled up to the Delta Airlines ticket counter, and said in a strangled voice, "Do you think you could get me a wheelchair, please?" The startled girl behind the counter picked up a telephone, spoke a few words, and within seconds a man with a wheelchair materialized at my elbow. My ticket was processed instantly, the gross overweight of my luggage was overlooked, and it was shipped straight through to Shannon Airport against all regulations, since I was stopping in New York.

Moments later, I was being wheeled at a rapid clip down the two and a half miles of corridor to my departure gate (it is *always* two and a half miles to my departure gate), sailing through the security search with hardly a pause, the wind made by our swift pace cooling our passage every step of the way. It occurred to me that I had inadvertently discovered a wonderful new way to travel in airports. I recommend it.

I was put on the plane before the other passengers, made comfortable, given a quick glass of water with which to down the large painkilling pill I was waving about, and given the first drink when the bar opened. At Kennedy Airport, New York, I was met by another wheelchair, my New York–routed luggage appeared in record time, and I was deposited in a taxi without my feet ever touching the ground. I believe I was passed from person to person so quickly because each of them was afraid I would die while in *his* hands.

After a two-day visit with my old friend Carol Nelson (remember our experience with the Mini and the incoming tide?), this entire performance was repeated in the Aer Lingus terminal at Kennedy, at Shannon Airport in Ireland, and, eventually, at Heathrow in London. This, I thought, is the only way to go.

I hobbled through the London Boat Show, stoned out of my mind on painkillers (all the back doctors in London had flu or were out to lunch, or something—it was a week before I could persuade one to see me), tying up loose ends as best I could. I ordered an excellent new suit of oilskins from Morgan of Cowes, the yachting tailors, and four Javlin Warm Suits, in case I decided to take the northern route in the OSTAR. I also bought an excellent signaling torch, and Camper measured the standard *Golden Shamrock* at the show in order to make a much-needed sprayhood for *Harp*. I also had a long lunch with Tim Stearn of Stearn Sailing Systems to talk over modifications to the Dynafurl, and he promised to supply me with a newly designed unit which would solve all my problems.

When I finally got to see a back specialist, he ushered me into a large gilt office; poked here and lifted there, ignoring my screams; then laid me on an altar-like slab in the middle of the room, stuck a needle into my backbone, and lubricated my spine as if it were the crankshaft of a Fiat 128. This hurt only slightly more than my original back problem. I left his office, poorer by £25, clutching an orthopedic back cushion and a prescription for more painkillers.

Fortunately, my back did not hurt when I lay down, which meant I could sleep well, or when I was sitting, which meant I could eat well.

Ann and I toured our favorite restaurants, and I enjoyed the occasional dinner with other old friends. Angela Green of the *Observer*, whom I had met at the start of the Azores and Back race in Falmouth the summer before, joined me for lunch one day and brought me up to date on the race. At the close of entries on December 31, 1975, there had been *197 entries received*, and all hell was breaking loose in the yachting press. Disaster at the start was being predicted from all sides, and there was a lot of bitching about the acceptance of Alain Colas's huge 236-foot yacht, *Club Méditerranée*.

I, for one, was delighted to have the big boat in the race, since it stimulated so much discussion, although I was not going to be sailing across her bows at the start, screaming "Starboard."

38

Reconnoiter

In early March I made a reconnaissance trip to Plymouth and managed to combine business with pleasure. I had never been to Plymouth and I was anxious to have an advance look at the facilities well ahead of the race. Ann joined me for the trip. First, we visited the Royal Western Yacht Club of England, which would be organizing and running the race, and as we walked down the steps to the waterside setting of this famous club, we were greeted with a bit of drama.

A bright red trimaran was in a lot of trouble. He had apparently tried to sail away from a club mooring, had got into irons and drifted dangerously close to the rocky shoreline and to the sea wall in front of the club. He had flung out an anchor, which was holding his bows off, then somebody from the club had thrown him a stern line. That somebody turned out to be Lloyd Foster, secretary of the Royal Western and every OSTAR aspirant's main contact with the race committee. Lloyd turned out to be a calm, boyish-looking fellow, in spite of long naval service going back to navigator's duties on a World War II destroyer. He settled Ann in the drawing room with a magazine and sat me down in his office. I had a dozen questions and he had all the answers: yes, there was a good yard where I could make advance arrangements for any last-minute repairs to *Harp*; yes, there would be a shipping company at Millbay Docks to collect any extra gear from competitors and send it ahead to Newport; no, we could not use our engines at the start, no matter how many boats entered; yes, there would be plenty of space for 197 boats in Millbay Docks, etc., etc., etc.

We chatted for an hour or so, and I was relieved to discover that the committee was unperturbed by all the criticism being leveled at the race. The controversy centered on the number of boats and the fact that a single-hander cannot keep a lookout at all times, which, according to the race's detractors, made single-handing unseamanlike. What the detractors preferred to overlook was the fact that the start would be postponed if there were fog or extreme weather, and that every entrant knew that he would have to stay awake for the first two days of the race until he was across the continental shelf and out of the fishing fleets.

The editorials and letters to the editors seemed to imply that the full burden of avoiding collisions rested on the single-hander, and that merchant ships and fishermen were never at fault in these circumstances. On the passage from Horta to Crosshaven I had once, on a bright sunny day, come on deck to find a large merchant vessel dead ahead of me on a reciprocal course. I had borne away to avoid a collision, and as the big ship sailed past me I never saw a soul on her decks or bridge. This is not an unusual situation at sea, and I believe that if the standard of watch maintained on most yachts, even single-handers, were maintained by merchant seamen and fishermen, there would be few, if any, collisions at sea.

Lloyd seemed to feel that no matter what the committee decided, they would be criticized, so they would simply press on, organizing the race the way they felt it should be done.

We left the Royal Western and had a look at the place where all the OSTAR yachts would congregate in late May. Millbay Docks is a large, concrete tidal basin with locks which open an hour before every high tide and close an hour afterward. It is surrounded by businesses and warehouses, most of which have something to do with shipping or ships and, apart from its size, is not a very impressive place. It is doubtful if the place has ever been drained and cleaned, and there is a story that once, when someone fell into the water, he was, after having his stomach pumped out, detained for forty-eight hours in a hospital for observation. I do not doubt it.

We drove over to the Mayflower Marina and were given a tour of the facilities there, and I booked *Harp* in for the week prior to the deadline for being in Millbay Docks. Finally, we visited Alec Blagdon's boatyard, and I made arrangements for a haulout in case it was necessary before the race. Alec Blagdon is a kindly man with a West Country accent, and we shared mutual friends in Cork. I felt he would be very helpful if I should need it.

I had hoped to take Ann sailing, but on our return to Cork found that the yard still had not finished with *Harp*. A couple of young American students turned up, sent along by Bill King, and I put them to work rubbing and antifouling the yacht's hull. Eventually, we got her in the water. At last she seemed right. I was certain that a lot of detail would still need work, but she was basically watertight and sound. Her keel had been removed, a reinforced glass-fiber "shoe" inserted between the keel and the hull, and the keelbolts glassed in. This stopped the movement of the keel which had loosened the bolts and allowed water to come into the boat. The Brookes & Gatehouse log hull fitting had been replaced, the first one having been incorrectly installed; lockers had

had floors glassed into them to keep bilgewater from entering; the port pilot berth had been enclosed to make a clothing locker— now the heater radiator would warm two dry lockers as well as the boat; a beam had been glassed under the deck to reinforce the inner forestay deck fitting; a pad eye had been fitted to the foredeck and bolted to a bulkhead—I could now set a small storm jib flying without taking down the headsail, just roller-reefing it; the interior of the cabin had been relined with foam-backed vinyl; the windows had been removed, resealed, and bolted on; a new Sestrel Porthole compass had been fitted, which could be read both from the cockpit and from the cabin; all the deck blocks had been removed, resealed, and refitted; the decks had been given a new and better nonslip finish; and a dozen other small refinements had been made.

She was mine again. *Mine.* I had six weeks to get her ready for a May 15 departure for Plymouth. Harry McMahon and I would take a leisurely week to sail her there, the last unhurried time I would have aboard her. I looked forward to it eagerly.

39

A Last Irish Spring
and Final Preparations

That there was much more work to be done on the boat became clear the first time I sailed her. Some friends and I set off for a weekend cruise to Kinsale, and as we were sailing out of Cork Harbour one of the girls asked for a sponge and bucket to do some bailing. Thinking that a little water had been left in the bilges I handed down the bucket, but a couple of minutes later, as *Harp* heeled in a gust, there came a shout from below that water was pouring into the boat. I jumped down the companionway ladder to find a heavy stream of water entering the cabin from the engine bay. I got the ladder and engine bulkhead off and found a bare-ended hose pouring water into the boat at the rate of about twenty gallons a minute. Fortunately, a wine cork was the perfect size to plug the hose, and with a Jubilee Clip tightened around the whole thing, it seemed watertight. But we canceled the cruise to Kinsale and settled for a sail around Cork Harbour, uncertain what other defects we might find.

Harold Cudmore and I planned to sail up to Galway, to arrive in time for the West of Ireland Boat and Leisure Show, now a fixture of the Galway Bay Sailing Club. O.H. and I sailed the boat as far as Kinsale, from where Harold and I would depart for the long cruise down the southwest coast, then around the corner and up the west coast to Galway, but we began to get bad weather forecasts for the west coast and I decided to drive. We left the boat on a mooring at Kinsale, for collection later. A couple of days afterward I was awakened at eight in the morning by the ringing of the telephone. (After six months of clawing my way through the Irish Civil Service, I had finally got a phone by appealing to a politician friend, who wrote one letter and did the trick.) A voice asked if I was the owner of *Golden Harp*. I was. She had broken her mooring and was aground on the opposite bank of the river.

I dressed and made the fourteen miles to Kinsale in record time, my heart in my mouth and pictures running through my mind of *Harp* lying on her topsides, her mast tangled in some tree. I arrived to find that Courtney Good, a Kinsale businessman and owner of another Shamrock, had pulled her off with the club crash boat, and we got her onto another mooring quickly, completely undamaged. It had been the scare of my life, for if she had been damaged badly I would have had one hell of a time getting her right again in time for the race. I sailed her back alone in a Force seven, but it being an offshore breeze the sea was flat. It was only the second time I had sailed her single-handed, and it was very exhilarating.

I drove up to Galway for the boat show, which was bigger and better than ever, and for a last goodbye to the people who had given me my first opportunity to sail, both in dinghies and cruising boats. At the dinner, I was allowed to say a few words, and I presented a cup to the club to be given each year for the best cruise by a member. I was very sad to think that I might not see Galway or any of my friends there for a very long time.

Sometime in April I read that there was a second Irish entry in the OSTAR, Patrick O'Donovan, and that he had just sailed into Kinsale at the completion of his qualifying cruise in a thirty-one-foot trimaran. The next day I was invited to dinner at the O'Donovans' Cork home, where Patrick and I got acquainted and compared notes on our preparations. He mentioned a new marine radar detector which would sound an alarm in the presence of radar signals from another ship, and this sounded a good idea, since the OSTAR rules prohibited radar on the yachts participating. I ordered one immediately.

Patrick had had his problems with getting a boat ready and would have more. He had planned to sail *Lillian*, a fifty-five-foot proa, in the race, and had actually qualified in her, but on a return trip from Ireland to England with *Lillian*'s owner, the proa had capsized in a Force ten and Patrick and the owner had spent eighteen hours in the life raft, tied between the proa's floats, until they were picked up by a fishing vessel. When they returned to look for *Lillian* she could not be found, and they learned subsequently that she had been taken as salvage by a Russian ship, sawn into manageable pieces, and left on a quayside in Cairo, of all places. All Patrick had got back was his passport, forwarded by the British consulate there. Now he had bought my friend David Walsh's trimaran, *Silmaril*, and qualified her. The following morning he stopped by Drake's Pool for a look at *Harp* and more conversation. Patrick, who was only twenty-three, would be one of the youngest competitors in the race. Born in Cork, he was now living in England and was preparing his boat there.

Ron and Laurel Holland moved into their new home, Strand Farmhouse, in Currabinny, across the river from Crosshaven, and for the first time Ron had a proper design office. From his drawing board he had a view of the Royal Cork and the members' yachts moored in the river; he could see all who came and went. Shortly before I left for Plymouth, he and Laurel cruised down to Kinsale with me, the first time they had sailed together in two years, kept apart on the water by Ron's increasingly busy schedule and Laurel's pregnancy. Kelly, the Holland daughter, was a big tot by now, and Laurel was pregnant again.

Now I applied to the Irish Yachting Association to be examined for the Yachtmaster's Certificate, the culmination of a program I had been working on for more than a year. To my astonishment and consternation, I was told that I did not have enough experience to sit for the examination. The Yachtmaster's program called for forty-eight hours of classroom instruction (I had had sixty-four); six days of practical instruction (I had had ten); and five hundred miles of offshore cruising (I had submitted a logbook documenting more than four thousand miles offshore, thirteen hundred of it single-handed). I was incensed to be told that I did not have enough experience even to take the examination. If I took it and failed, fine, but I did not feel I should be denied the examination after so much work. Apparently, the difficulty had stemmed from a report about my training cruise aboard *Creidne*, when Captain Eric Healy, the skipper, had suggested I needed more experience of handling the boat under power, and that I had been impatient with the crew when skippering. I agreed that these had been justifiable, constructive criticisms at the time, but since then I had sailed more than three thousand miles and amassed a great deal more experience, and I did not feel that comments made a year before still were applicable. At the suggestion of a friend, I wrote to the president of the IYA, explaining my position and requesting an examination before I left for Plymouth. I waited nervously for a reply.

My back problem had begun to abate now, after more than three months of pain whenever I stood up or walked for more than two or three minutes at a time. The lower back pain had extended to the sciatic nerve, which runs from the hip down to the foot, then given way to severe muscle cramps which continued for some weeks. I had been to two more back specialists; one had given me muscle relaxant injections which helped somewhat; the other had told me just to wait and it would go away, and he prescribed a very embarrassing, steel-braced corset to be taken on the transatlantic crossing in case the fractured disc slipped out of place again. Having always been extremely healthy and unaccustomed to severe pain, I lived in terror of the thing recurring in mid-Atlantic. My last treatment came from a quack, an Irish farmer who seemed to be able to "divine" and treat the source of pain, much in the way that some people are able to divine water. His treatment had the most immediate and dramatic effect of all, although it did not cure the problem entirely, and I was unable to see him again, as he lived some distance from Cork. So I tucked my corset into a locker on the boat and hoped for the best. I was also very careful about lifting things and favored the injury whenever I could.

At the Easter bank holiday weekend I planned a return to the Scillies with some friends, having been very impressed with the islands when we stopped there during the *Irish Mist* delivery trip the spring before. We spent a delightful, sunny weekend, listening to the local male choir in the pub and seeing Harold Wilson, recently retired as prime minister, strolling on the beach with the giant Labrador which had once nearly drowned him when the dog had capsized the dinghy from which Mr. Wilson was fishing.

Our passage back was pleasant and fast, taking only twenty-seven hours in a good breeze. We had been supremely comfortable on the boat, what with the central heating and the stereo, and after much work the bugs were finally being ironed out. *Harp* was beginning to be something like ready for the transatlantic. No serious water was coming into the boat, although there were one or two minor leaks I hadn't yet located; the new Dynafurl supplied by Tim Stearn was working well in its newly engineered form;

and with the addition of the new storm jib, which could also be used as a reaching staysail, the sail plan now seemed ideal.

Back in Cork my sextant, which had been left with Henry Browne & Son for reconditioning and correction, arrived, not having withstood very well the tender mercies of the British and Irish postal systems, and I packed it back to London with Harold Cudmore, who was setting off for America and Spain on the international yacht racing circuit.

Word came that I would be examined for the Yachtmaster's Certificate after all, and a Mr. O'Gallagher met me at a Cork hotel, examined me closely for more than an hour, and pronounced me passed, to my intense relief. I believe I was the first person to be certified under the program.

I made a final dash to London, where I conferred with my publishers and took care of last-minute details. Ann and I continued our restaurant research, and I had another lunch with Angela Green of the *Observer*, when I learned that Chay Blyth, who had damaged his huge trimaran, *Great Britain III*, in a collision with a ship, would not be participating in the race. All doubts about the entry of Alain Colas had been resolved, though, and he would be sailing his 236-foot *Club Méditerranée*. Colas had nearly severed his right foot when it was caught in an anchor chain the year before, but he had made a remarkable recovery and, wearing a special boot, had made his qualifying cruise in the Mediterranean with a crew of forty. He would do another 1,500-mile single-handed qualifying cruise prior to the race.

Henry Browne & Son, when they saw the state of my old sextant, promptly gave me a new one without charge. *That* is the sort of customer relations that maintains an outstanding reputation, as was also my experience with the Omega Watch Company. I had purchased an expensive Omega wristwatch which had performed erratically; when I got no satisfaction by reporting this to the American importers, I wrote directly to the company in Switzerland, and within a very short time, the Irish distributors had replaced the old watch with a brand-new Omega Seamaster electric wrist chronometer, which performed beautifully. In general, I found that most of the suppliers I dealt with took great pride in their products and were always ready to make adjustments when warranted. Only two or three times in the eighteen months that I dealt with manufacturers was I disappointed by a supplier's attitude. During the whole of the project I was badly let down by only one equipment manufacturer.

My final task in London was to buy provisions for the race, and for this I went to Harrods, that superb department store in Knightsbridge. On the Azores trip I had become bored very quickly with my diet, and I was determined to take more time and plan my menus more carefully for the much longer transatlantic passage. I chose Harrods because their magnificent food halls are stocked with a huge variety of *main courses* in tins. Any supermarket has a lot of canned food, but the choice of main dishes is poor. Harrods has everything, from the simple to the exotic, and I filled four or five large shopping carts with stews, chicken, sauces, cheese, meats, and, best of all, American snack foods I had grown up with, packed in tins to preserve their freshness. It was expensive, but I would eat very well indeed.

Back in Cork I had less than a week to dismantle my life in Ireland and prepare for a new one at sea. Those last days were wildly busy, every moment taken up with packing, paying bills, making arrangements to have mail forwarded and goods shipped to the States. I was very sad at the thought of leaving Drake's Pool Cottage, and even sadder to leave Fred, but he had, fortunately, practically adopted the McCarthy family, who lived near the main gate of Coolmore, staying there whenever I left Cork for a few days. They loved him and he loved them. It is not every dog who has the opportunity to choose his own family.

Harry was arriving on Friday and we were sailing for Plymouth on Saturday. On Thursday night Ron and Laurel Holland arranged a farewell dinner at their new home in Currabinny; John and Diana McWilliam were there; Nick, Theo, and Heather came; so did Derek and Carol Holland and O. H. Rogers—all of whom had done so much work on the boat that I could never thank them sufficiently. Friends Donna O'Sullivan and Carey O'Mahoney came, too, and we had a good dinner and a fine evening, even if it was tinged with sadness for me.

On Friday the removals people came and took away the personal belongings I would be sending to the States, and in the afternoon Harry McMahon arrived. We worked the rest of the day getting gear sorted, had a farewell drink at the Royal Cork Yacht Club and a steak at the Overdraft, and got a good night's sleep. Next morning I took Fred's bed, bowl, and rubber mouse to the McCarthys' and made my farewells there.

We loaded all the gear onto the boat and began stowing everything, tied up next to Nick's boat in Drake's Pool. Fred had been behaving oddly for the last twenty-four hours; I think he knew something unusual was up. The day before he had turned up in Carrigaline, apparently looking for me, something he would not ordinarily do. Now, after my choked-up goodbye, he sat on the stone slip in Drake's Pool and solemnly watched us working on the boat. I had explained to him long before that he would never be allowed on *Harp* until he had learned to use a marine toilet, and after a few instances when he swam in circles around the boat, demanding loudly to be hauled aboard, he had given up, and whenever I rowed out to the boat he habitually departed in a huff for the McCarthys'. He sat there the whole morning, watching. Finally, we had the last bit of gear stowed, we had made our last goodbyes to Nick, and we were ready to leave Drake's Pool for the last time.

We started the engine, cast off Nick's lines, and, as we motored around the first bend and out of Drake's Pool, the last thing I saw was Fred, sitting in front of the cottage, watching.

40

Cork to Plymouth

An hour later we were in a full gale. The southwesterly six-to-seven wind that had been forecast had become southerly and Force eight. Harry, who does not have the world's best sea legs the first day of a cruise, was very ill, and in his bunk. I reefed us down to storm canvas, set Fred (the Hasler Windvane Steering), and relaxed as best I could in the seas. The gale continued all that day and all night, and morning brought little relief and bad visibility. Our first intended stop had been the Isles of Scilly, but I had borne away onto a close reach to ease our motion and keep up our speed, and we made our landfall at Land's End early the following evening. Faced with a hard slog to the Scillies, I decided to turn left and reach to St. Ives, on the north coast of Cornwall, instead. It turned out to be a delightful alternative.

Not having a large-scale chart of that part of the coast, I telephoned the St. Ives harbormaster on the VHF and got excellent approach instructions, and we were anchored in the lovely bay by midnight, ready for a much-needed night's rest. There was no customs officer in St. Ives, but we went ashore anyway the next day, saw the town, had dinner, and returned to the quay to find two police detectives waiting for us at the dinghy. Our identification and explanations were accepted, but it was clear that, the political situation being what it was, the constabulary was taking a close interest in any visiting yacht flying an Irish ensign.

After another night in St. Ives, we beat our way around Land's End in a Force seven wind, Harry now fully recovered, and made our way in moderating weather to St. Mawes, my favorite Cornish village, just across from Falmouth. I had radioed ahead to arrange for the customs launch to meet us there, and on arriving we did a little square dance with them in St. Mawes Harbour as they came alongside us, bending a stanchion or two and the top shaft of the self-steering, but finally we were safely moored.

Two days later we sailed to the entrance of the Helford River, and as we started to motor up that beautiful Cornish estuary, the engine, though it continued to run smoothly, ceased to drive the boat and we had to be towed to a mooring.

The following morning Harry went over the side in a wet suit to see if the propeller turned when I put the engine in gear. It did not, but we didn't know if the propeller was freewheeling on the shaft, or if the hydraulic drive wasn't turning the shaft. The best solution, after several calls to Hydromarine in Galway, seemed to be to continue to Plymouth without the engine and there look for repairs, so we slipped our mooring and sailed to Fowey, enjoying a light-weather spinnaker run along the way. We were able to sail up the river into Fowey and anchor without incident, had dinner ashore and a drink at the Royal Fowey Yacht Club and another on a Royal Navy training yacht anchored alongside us, then sailed for Plymouth the next morning.

It was a beat in fresh winds all the way, but finally we were sailing past Plymouth Breakwater, past the Royal Western, around Drake's Island and up to the Mayflower Marina, where we were towed to a berth. After a year and a half of preparation and dreaming, *Golden Harp* and I were finally in Plymouth together. I could hardly believe it.

It was now Monday, May 24, and there were only twelve working days left before the start on Saturday, June 5. I had carefully planned to be in Plymouth that far ahead to have time to handle any unexpected problems, and a good thing it was, too. My biggest problem was the engine. Actually, the engine in its broken state performed the only function it had to for the race, charging the batteries, but I did not like the idea of having a major piece of equipment not in working order, even if it had to be sealed during the race so that it could not be used as a propellant. Besides, it was still on warranty, and that would have elapsed by the time I arrived in Newport. The plan was for O. H. Rogers, who was driving my car to Plymouth, to bring with him a new tank, which comprised the major part of the hydraulic drive unit. I had described all the symptoms to the Hydromarine people in Galway, and they were sure that it was either the propeller or the tank. I had performed all the tests instructed by both Hydromarine and their agents in Southampton, and they felt it could only be one of the two problems. O.H. should have arrived on the Tuesday, and I had the engineer coming from Southampton on that day, but then O.H. phoned from somewhere in Somerset to say that my car had blown a cylinder head gasket and he would be delayed a day, so the whole operation was put back.

Finally, O.H. arrived with the new tank and the spare propeller pins, and all was ready. The engineer arrived from Southampton, walked under the boat, which we had dried out on the scrubbing pad at the marina, turned the propeller first one way and then the other, and said, "It's not the tank and it's not the propeller; it's the driven pump, which sits behind the tank, and I don't have one with me. Didn't anybody tell you to try turning the propeller both ways? It should only turn one way." Nobody had mentioned this simple test. The engineer promised to see that the proper parts were sent and instructed a local mechanic on how to perform the relatively simple installation.

O.H. and I pressed on with small jobs, assisted by Peter Adams, a local friend of a friend who was very helpful in getting me around the strange city of Plymouth, and in transporting my Harrods stores and Averys wine from the Royal Western office in Millbay Docks to the marina for stowage aboard *Harp*. The arrival of these stores had caused much amusement at the Royal Western. Harrods had packed everything so carefully that the apparent volume of my food was twice its real volume. There were two huge crates and three cases of wine from Averys. Nobody could believe the shipment was for thirty-foot *Golden Harp* and not for 236-foot *Club Méditerranée*.

The slaving aboard the boat was relieved by an increasingly active social life as more and more competitors arrived. The bar at the Royal Western was getting more crowded by the day, and nobody talked about *anything* except the race—especially what equipment different boats were carrying and, most of all, the riddle of which route to take.

There are two main routes taken by most competitors and several variations. The most-sailed route, and the one which had always been sailed by the winning yacht, is the great circle route. Its principal attraction is that it is the shortest, about two thousand eight hundred miles. But it has great disadvantages, too: the weather can be very rough at times, there is the likelihood of icebergs and fog along the way, and, worst of all, a skipper taking this route must expect headwinds nearly all the way, and he must tack back and forth in order to get west, since a sailboat cannot sail straight into the wind. This circumstance can add several hundred miles to the distance actually sailed.

The second important route is the southern, or Azores, route. This involves setting a southwesterly course to and past the Azores, down to about latitude thirty-seven degrees north, then turning west and sailing to about longitude sixty-five degrees west, before turning northwest for Newport. On the face of it this route sounds silly, since it is about three thousand five hundred miles long, but it does have its advantages. In a year of typical weather, a skipper will have a lot of reaching winds and not nearly so much beating to windward as on the great circle route, and thus should be able to sail much faster. Nobody taking this route had ever won the race, but in each race somebody always came close, and often it turned out that boats taking the Azores route sailed fewer miles than boats which had had to tack back and forth on the great circle route. Another major attraction for the Azores route is kinder weather and lots of sunshine, and, of course, the Azores themselves are on the route in case a boat suffers damage or her skipper is injured. The big disadvantage of the route is the big Azores High, which, in addition to providing sunshine, can also provide extended periods of calm, and sailboats do not sail in calm weather: they sit on the sea, occasionally being pushed in the wrong direction by ocean currents.

There are variations, as I have mentioned: there is a high, northern route, where some hope to pick up following winds, but the risk of ice is much higher; and there is the very southerly trade winds route, which offers almost certain free sailing, but which is so long that it has rarely been taken in the race. The big joker in the pack is the Gulf Stream, a strong ocean current which originates in the Gulf of Mexico, runs around the tip of Florida, up the east coast of the United States, turns northeast and continues across the Atlantic toward the British Isles. Anyone trying to sail a route between the great circle and the Azores routes will have to contend with this major, adverse current, and most prefer to avoid it, those on the great circle route remaining north of the stream, and those on the Azores route remaining south of it, until crossing the current almost at right angles when turning northwest for Newport. The excellent chart from the official race program is reproduced here and illustrates all the various routes.

Many people had already made the decision to plunge straight across via the great circle, no matter what; others would not consider any route but the Azores. I was undecided, preferring to wait for the weather briefing the day before the race before making a decision, but I was biased toward the Azores route. *Harp* went well in light moderate airs, and I felt my level of experience was probably better suited to going south.

I had had some advice from the Irish Weather Service, who had kindly sent me some charts and diagrams and reported on some studies of westerly winds in the North Atlantic, but the sum total of all these was that nobody could predict anything about the weather we would encounter with any degree of probability, let alone certainty. So I would wait for the final briefing, in the meantime soliciting as many opinions as possible—and there were almost as many opinions about the route as there were competitors. There was a great deal of caginess in any discussion of route, nobody being willing to commit himself on the subject. If somebody did commit himself he was probably lying and would be taking another route on the day. This caginess always made me laugh, since the whole question was so riddled with uncertainty and the weather on any route so unpredictable that it seemed to make little difference what anybody thought before the race.

On Tuesday night, Richard Clifford invited me aboard *Shamaal II*, on which he lived, for drinks. It was a big party for a small boat, comprising Richard; myself; Robert Hughes, the Gibb self-steering expert; two other Royal Marine officers; the Bulgarian entry, Georgi Georgiev; and two people who were to have a large effect on my life, Mike and Lizzie McMullen. Mike was sailing *Three*

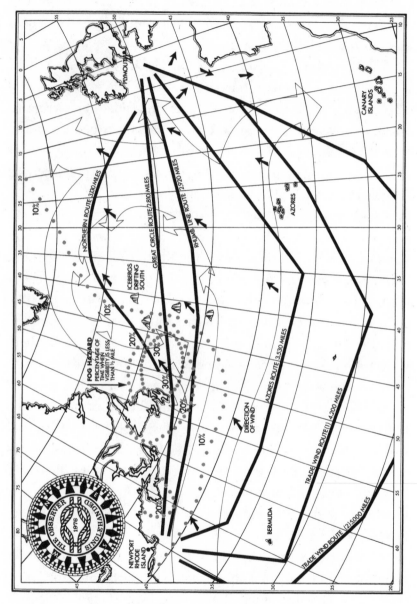

Map of routes across the Atlantic.

Richard Clifford, relaxed and confident at the start.
Quest zooms by in the background.

Cheers, a fast trimaran designed by the very successful Dick Newick. His practice crew, David Hopkins, was also there.

Mike McMullen had sailed *Binkie*, a thirty-two-foot monohull,
in the last OSTAR and had finished well up. While in Newport he
had been invited for a sail on *Three Cheers* by Tom Follett, who had
sailed her in the race. Mike had been instantly attracted to the
boat, although he had never sailed a multihull, and bought *Three
Cheers* and immediately began to sail her in preparation for the
next OSTAR. Lizzie had enthusiastically joined in the project and
they had spent a great deal of time together on the boat during the
ensuing four years. The previous summer they had made an extended cruise to the Hebrides and made a film about it which was
soon to be shown by the BBC. Mike was a tough, former Royal
Marines commando officer and a superb yachtsman, and his
ability, in combination with such a fast and proven boat as *Three*

Cheers, had made him one of the favorites to win the race outright, in spite of the fact that *Three Cheers,* at forty-six feet overall, was much smaller than the other favorites.

I was attracted to Mike and Lizzie McMullen as I have rarely been attracted to any couple, their collective charm, enthusiasm, and total commitment to the race captivating me completely. Mike held forth on his opinions about the OSTAR and Lizzie goaded him from the sidelines; we talked and talked and laughed constantly. Lizzie was a very beautiful girl, and I complimented her on her nose. (There are leg men, etc., etc. I have always been a nose man.) She liked that, and it became our private joke.

We eventually continued the party in the bar of the Royal Western, and by the end of the evening I counted them as close friends, difficult as that may be to explain. For ten days I would see them constantly, then I would not see them again.

Angela Green of the *Observer* arrived to set up the press office, and we began to see a great deal of each other, often meeting Mike and Lizzie in the club for drinks and another discussion of the race.

Harry had flown back to Ireland the day after our arrival, and now O.H. had to leave, too, so I was on my own. I greatly envied those entrants who seemed to have whole staffs of people to fetch and carry and bolt things onto their boats. Even some of the smaller boats had vans full of gear and teams of friends, relatives, or professionals working on their problems. Ann was coming down the Thursday before the race, but until then I would have to get help where I could find it. Robert Hughes, in addition to servicing Fred, was most helpful with stowing my food, and Ian Radford, who was in the marina aboard his entry, *Jabuliswe,* and who was much readier than I, was very helpful. The marina staff did what they could, and Alec Blagdon loaned tools from his boatyard, even though I did not have to take *Harp* there for anticipated repairs. But by the end of the week, although a great deal had been accomplished, my list of things to do did not seem any shorter, and *Harp* would have to be moved into Millbay Docks on Monday night, along with all the other entries, to undergo her three inspections— one for water and stores, one for safety equipment, and one for structural soundness and suitability of gear. She would also have to be inspected by the handicap committee, and the gear lever of her engine would be sealed, so that the engine could be driven only in neutral, for battery charging.

In addition to the list of things I had planned to do in Plymouth, new problems kept cropping up: first, the hydraulic drive problem, then the engine's electrical system. An electrical engineer came aboard and immediately found the problem which had caused my batteries to discharge: one of the battery wires had been led across part of the engine's exhaust system which, when it got hot, had burned through the insulation of the wire, causing a short circuit.

On Saturday night Angela and I invited Mike and Lizzie Mc-Mullen to come aboard *Harp* for drinks. They were tied up until later in the evening, so Angela and I had dinner at Bella Napoli, which was becoming a sort of culinary headquarters for everybody, and went back to the boat to wait for them. They were late, and as we were sitting below having a drink, we heard a commotion from across the marina. I stuck my head through the hatch and looked around. Two pontoons away a large group of dark figures was gathered around another boat, some of them pounding on the coach roof, others pumping up and down on the bowsprit, pitching the boat fore and aft. I heard someone shout above the din, "Aha! We know what you're at!" I went back below, laughing, and told Angela that some poor bastard across the way was having either his sleep or his amorous activities disturbed by his friends.

A few moments later I heard hushed puzzled voices on the pontoon next to *Harp* and stuck my head out again to see what was up. Mike and Lizzie and a half dozen other people were standing there, trying to figure out where *Golden Harp* was. Forgetting that

Harp was an Irish entry, they had asked at the marina office for the American boat and had been directed to *Catapha*, whose skipper, David White, had been rudely awakened by a great deal of noise and commotion. "What really worried me," Mike said, as they all tumbled below and found seats, "was how big that guy was." Andrew and Roslyn Spedding, close friends of the McMullens', had come along, together with David Hopkins and Paul Weychan, designer and builder of *Quest*, a fast-looking trimaran which would be sailed by John deTrafford. There were a couple of other people jammed into *Harp* as well, but in the ensuing joking and laughing I forgot their names. Andrew Spedding had sailed in the last OSTAR, and was one of the scrutineers who would be inspecting *Harp* in Millbay Docks. I tried to keep his glass full.

At one point in the evening I remember Mike remarking, "There's a lot of luck involved in this race." It was a comment I had not heard anyone else make, and I would have occasion to recall it later.

41

Countdown

MONDAY. I spent the morning doing small jobs on the boat. The marina mechanic, Ted, came and changed the engine's water pump, which had been leaking, and installed a new Jabsco electric bilge pump.

Ian Radford volunteered to come with me on the tow to Millbay Docks and help me berth *Harp* there, which might be tricky with no engine and so many boats about. Ian is a young physician who had been practicing in Zululand and who had done a stint performing heart surgery with Christiaan Barnard in South Africa. He had accepted a new job in Miami, Florida, and was emigrating the hard way, via the OSTAR. A cheerful soul, Ian was always ready to lend a hand with no more recompense than a cold beer or two . . . or three.

As we were waiting for the towing vessel to come for us,

Lizzie trotted up, a bottle of whisky in each hand, and invited us to come for a look at *Three Cheers*. The lovely, primrose-yellow trimaran was tied up at an outer pontoon of the marina, where she had just been blessed by the family vicar. The bottles of booze were gifts from friends who had turned up for the ceremony. Nigel Lang of *Galadriel*, one of the little Contessa 26s in the race, joined us, and we spent a pleasant half hour aboard as Mike, with obvious pleasure and pride, gave us a Cook's tour of the boat. I had only been on one or two tris, and I was fascinated as Mike explained the modifications he had made which would make her an even faster boat than when Tom Follett had sailed her. I lifted an upside-down bucket in the cabin and found a small ham-type shortwave radio transmitter. He was keeping the bucket over it, Mike explained, because he had not had time to get a license for it, and anyway, he would only use it in emergencies. Nigel remarked on the absence of stanchions and guardrails on the boat, but Mike pooh-poohed the idea, saying he thought they were unnecessary.

We finished our tour and Ian and I invited Lizzie to stop by *Harp* for a glass of sherry on her way home, since she was passing the boat, anyway. Lizzie, who had been fascinated with all the little comforts on *Harp* compared to the austerity of the lightweight *Three Cheers*, rolled her eyes and said she'd just love to come and see my central heating and listen to my stereo again. I said she could snuggle up to my central heating anytime, and as we left Mike shouted after us, "You watch that fellow. I don't trust anybody who has central heating and stereo on his boat!" We left *Three Cheers*, Lizzie giggling, and strolled along to *Harp*. We had sat and chatted for only a minute when the towing vessel turned up, and we had to cast off. As Lizzie jumped ashore we agreed that Angela and I would try and meet them at the club later that evening for dinner. "Don't forget to bring your nose!" I shouted after her as she ran toward the car park, still clutching the whisky.

She laughed and waved the bottle. I was looking forward to spending another evening with the McMullens.

John, the marina's bosun, towed us slowly around to Millbay, and as the gates were not yet open, we had an opportunity to circle and get a close look at *Club Méditerranée*. From the water she seemed even more massive, with her four tall masts, enormous deckhouse, and huge windcharger propeller aft. Alongside her, *Golden Harp* looked about the same size as the little Avon dinghy we were being towed by looked alongside *Harp*. As we waited for the car ferry from France to dock and the Millbay gates to open, other yachts began to congregate in the area, and by the time the gates opened a dozen or more boats of all sizes were there, this being the final deadline for entering the docks without incurring a time penalty.

Inside, Captain Terence Shaw, former secretary of the Royal Western, who was in charge of docking arrangements, directed us to a berth alongside *Pawn of Nieuwpoort*, being sailed by the Belgian entrant, Yves Anrys, and *Achille*, whose skipper was the young Frenchman Max Bourgeois. Terence Shaw, white-bearded and very salty-looking, did not need a megaphone to issue his instructions, and skippers disregarded them at their peril. Soon, Nigel Lang, in *Galadriel*, and young Simon Hunter, in *Kylie*, another Contessa 26, were tied up outside us, making a raft of five boats, with *Achille* closest to the concrete dockside.

Behind us were the two Chinese lugsail schooners, *Ron Glas* (which is Gaelic for "gray seal"), sailed by Jock McCleod, a Scot, and Bill King's old boat, *Galway Blazer II*, now owned by Peter Crowther, who is just a bit mad. Also there was Angus Primrose in a Moody 33 of his own design, *Demon Demo*, soon joined by Chris Smith in the tiny *Tumult*, only twenty-two feet long.

Millbay Docks was now home to nearly every boat that would start, and the whole place took on a festive air that completely changed the ordinarily drab appearance of the place. Angela and her *Observer* press office were there; Camper & Nicholsons and M. S. Gibb were sharing a portabuilding, and Brookes & Gatehouse were located in a trailer nearby. All the famous boats from past races were there: *Jester*, the Chinese lugsail folkboat which had been sailed in every OSTAR, first by Blondie Hasler and later by Michael Richey; *Tahiti Bill*, Bill Howell's cat; *Vendredi Treize*, the 128-foot giant of the last race, now called *ITT Oceanic*; *Cap 33*, formerly a French trimaran, now sailed by an American from Boston, Tom Grossman. *Manureva*, in which Alain Colas had won the last race, was to have been sailed by his brother, but had lost a float and would not compete.

Lizzie and Mike McMullen.

Among the new boats were *Kriter III*, a seventy-foot catamaran built as *British Oxygen*, winner of the Round Britain Race when sailed by Robin Knox-Johnston (beating Mike McMullen in the much smaller *Three Cheers* by less than an hour); *Pen Duick VI*, Eric Tabarly's boat, built to be sailed in the Round-the-World Race by

Three Cheers under full sail.

a crew of fifteen, now being sailed by Tabarly alone; *Galloping Gael*, a boat designed to the maximum limit of the *Jester* class and sailed by an Irish/Canadian/American, Mike Flanagan; *FT*, also designed to the maximum of the smallest class and sailed by David Palmer, who seemed certain he would take the class prize; *Spaniel*, a hitherto unknown Polish entry, with a bucket seat and automotive steering wheel in her tiny deckhouse; five identical boats designed by Marc Linski, a Frenchman; and four identical thirty-two-foot trimarans designed by Dick Newick especially for the race, one of them sailed by a close friend of Ron Holland's, Walter Green, an American.

With the withdrawal of *Great Britain III* and *Manureva*, only seven boats were entered in the largest group, the *Pen Duick* class. One of the most interesting was a sixty-two-foot trimaran with a truly vast sail area, *Spirit of America*, sailed by Mike Kane, who claimed his boat to be the fastest multihull in the world. The medium-sized *Gypsy Moth* class had considerably more entrants, but by far the largest was the *Jester* class, with about ninety boats, most of them privately owned, nonsponsored boats like *Harp*.

Living conditions not being in the category of wonderful in Millbay Docks, I moved into a hotel until the start. On Monday night Angela and I went to a party given by Tom Grossman of *Cap 33* and met a number of other entrants. Although we knew each other by sight, this was my first meeting with Mike Kane. He was reputed to be a bit cocky about his boat and his chances, and with a few drinks under his belt he was in rare form, talking about the incredible speeds the Lock Crowther–designed tri could reach and how well proven she was. We lingered a bit too long among the congenial company at Tom's party and missed Mike and Lizzie at the club.

"No pictures, please." Mike Kane of *Spirit of America*.

Tahiti Bill Howell.

TUESDAY. THE HYDRAULIC ENGINEER RANG and said that Hydro-marine would reluctantly supply the needed replacement unit, but that they were insisting he come back and install it. I cringed at the cost, but I agreed. I spent the morning rounding up bits and pieces of gear, including two white fishing floats which would have to be painted black to conform to a last-minute rule that each yacht carry two black balls hoisted when the boat was under self-steering with no one on deck, a concession to the criticism from *Yachting World*. I was doing this job when the first of the scrutineers, Walter Venning, arrived aboard *Harp*. "Come aboard," I said. "I was just painting my balls black." Then from behind him appeared his girlfriend, Sally, the other scrutineer. I think I blushed.

They asked to see all the required safety equipment, checking each item off on a list, then chatted for a minute. Walter turned out to be a cousin of Bill King's, which Bill had told me. He is a tomato grower, and once, when Bill was about to make a transatlantic crossing in his first boat, *Galway Blazer I*, Walter gave him a basket of tomatoes which had been carefully selected so that one of them would ripen each day. It had worked perfectly, Bill said, the last tomato ripening on his last day out.

Yves Anrys and I had a chance to talk a lot as we were each doing jobs on our boats. Yves had been a reserve Olympic helmsman in the single-handed Finn dinghy class and was sailing a half-tonner similar to *Harp* but very stripped-out inside and much, much lighter. He is a merchant seaman and was planning to race his boat in the World Half-Ton Cup Championships later in the year.

WEDNESDAY. I WAS A BLUR of motion all the morning, running errands, seeing to last-minute fittings, and filling small gaps in my list of necessary gear. There seemed to be no end to it, and I was beginning to have a feeling of running out of time. While in this somewhat harassed state I got a telephone message from the Royal Western office in Millbay Docks that the McWilliams and the Hollands were arriving at four in the afternoon and please to meet them.

We arrived back at Millbay Docks and were standing outside the *Observer* press office, chatting with some people, when Angela

Angus Primrose.

Yves Anrys of *Pawn of Nieuwpoort*,
Harp's next-door neighbor in
Millbay Docks.

called me aside. "Have you heard about Lizzie McMullen?" she asked. Oh, God, I thought, there's been a car crash and Lizzie's in the hospital with a broken leg or something.

"No," I said.

"There's been a terrible accident. Mike and Lizzie were working on the boat at Mashford's yard this morning when an electric drill fell overboard into the water. Mike shouted for her not to touch it, but she did. They gave her heart massage and artificial respiration for half an hour until an ambulance could get out to Cremyl, but it didn't help. She was dead on arrival at the hospital."

I froze inside; I couldn't believe what she was telling me. Lizzie McMullen, beautiful, bright, delightful Lizzie, could not be dead; it was simply not possible. I asked Angela if she were absolutely sure, if there were any possibility of a mistake. Angela was sure. Lizzie, who thirty-six hours before had been joking about my central heating, laughing, and sipping sherry on *Golden Harp*, was gone. Irrecoverable. Out of anyone's reach. Out of my life. Out of Mike's. Dear God, I thought, if I feel this way, as if somebody had struck me with a blunt instrument, how must Mike feel?

"How is Mike?" I asked Angela.

"I don't know. I'm sure friends are with him. I've sent a telegram." I wanted to send a telegram, too. I sat in Angela's office and thought for a time. There were less than seventy-two hours left before the start of the race. This would have been the most crushing possible blow at any time, but to happen now, after four years of work and preparation together. It suddenly seemed unthinkable that Mike should not sail the race. I found a pencil and wrote, "I only knew her for a week, and I loved her, too. There is no answer to the senseless. Please sail the race and win it." I signed the telegram, gave it to Angela to send, then went out and sat in the car, numb. A man wandered over and began talking to me through the open sunroof about an ice cream seller who had been ejected from the docks because he didn't have the proper permit. I chatted absently with him without knowing what I was saying. Angela came out and we talked for a moment, then I left. I felt I had to keep doing things, that I couldn't stop—not just because I had so much to get done but because if I stopped I would think about Lizzie and, worse, about Mike. So I kept moving, kept ticking items off my list, but it seemed that every two or three minutes I would stop and realize all over again that Lizzie was dead, and it was just like being told for the first time.

I spent most of the afternoon with the Hollands and McWilliams, but in a kind of daze. When they left for the airport early that evening, I went to the club. I found Lloyd Foster and asked if he knew Mike's plans about the race. "I think it will certainly be impossible for Mike to compete now," he said. "Of course, there's the funeral, but there'll have to be an inquest as well. There are just too many formalities to complete before Saturday." I suggested that the competitors might send some flowers, and Lloyd agreed to receive contributions. Later, that didn't seem enough, seemed too transient, and some of us thought perhaps the committee might accept a new trophy for multihulls to be presented in memory of Lizzie. This seemed much more satisfactory, more permanent, and Lloyd said he would bring it before the committee for consideration.

I don't think anyone who knew Lizzie McMullen, however slightly, went to bed with dry eyes that night, and I was more deeply affected than at any time since my grandfather had died. It had been a bad day.

THURSDAY. EVERYTHING BEGAN TO GATHER momentum. There were three events scheduled for competitors: a lord mayor's reception at midday, a competitors' briefing in the early afternoon, and a dinner that evening. In between, I was at a dead run. The hydraulics engineer from Southampton turned up bright and early with the new pump. I spent the rest of the morning running errands and arrived at the lord mayor's event after the speeches. Lloyd Foster called me over to confer with Henry Williams and Colonel Jack Oddling-Smee of the committee, who agreed to accept the proposed Lizzie trophy. Liz Balcon of the *Observer* voiced the newspaper's approval, and both the club and the *Observer* agreed to contribute a substantial amount of money to be combined with the competitors' contributions to purchase a piece of silver. Lloyd asked me to announce the trophy at the competitors' briefing in the afternoon and said he would accept the contributions.

I found Richard Clifford chatting with a very attractive girl and the three of us adjourned to a local restaurant for an hour to rest from the rush of the day. Richard told me that Mike had decided to continue in the race and would be at the briefing. I felt vastly relieved and very happy about that. Yves Anrys had said to me the previous afternoon, "The man's wife is dead, that's one problem. If he doesn't do the race he will have two problems." I thought that described the situation very succinctly, and I was glad that Mike would not have to suffer the additional agony of missing the race. I hoped, too, that competing might have a therapeutic effect.

As we gathered at the Royal Western for a group photograph and the briefing, I found Mike, looking shattered but holding up well, told him what we wanted to do, and asked if he minded if it were announced at the briefing. He agreed readily. When we sat down for the photograph on the club's front terrace, there seemed to be a thousand photographers, and I think most of us were a little taken aback at all the attention, not being used to that sort of thing. I was sitting somewhere near Clare Francis and the crush around us was incredible as all the photographers, as one man, rushed forward for close-ups of the prettiest skipper in the race. A lot of attention was focused on Mike, too, but this was more discreet, thankfully. We filed into the main lounge of the club and were briefed on the starting and finishing procedures; the *Pen Duick* class would start at twelve noon, the *Gypsy Moth* class at twelve-thirty, and the *Jester* class at one o'clock. The finishing line would be a line between the Brenton Reef lighthouse and a nearby buoy, and we were given a chart of the Newport area. A representative of the Ida Lewis Yacht Club of Newport, who was handling the arrangements at the other end, said that an effort would be made to meet as many competitors as possible. Other details were discussed, then I made the announcement about the new prize, to be called The Lizzie McMullen Perpetual Trophy, for the first multihull to finish. It would be a presentation of the competitors in the 1976 race and would be presented in perpetuity. There were a few more announcements, and we broke up to return to our boats.

Ann arrived during the afternoon, and I left her to rest at the hotel while I got back to the boat. Arriving there, I found that the replacement hydraulic unit had blown immediately upon installation, and the engineer was trying to cannibalize the old unit to repair the new one. I got the electrical engineer started on replacing the battery and rewiring the engine bay, working around the other engineer as best he could. This was a time when I had planned to be lounging in the cockpit with a glass of wine, watching everybody else panic. Instead, Yves Anrys was lounging in *his* cockpit, watching *me* panic. The handicap committee came by and had a look at *Harp*. I sat them down and explained as thoroughly as I could that *Harp* was *not* in her present condition a competitive half-tonner, that she was much, much too heavy for that and had larger rigging, steps on the mast and lots of other windage-making gear, such as the Dynafurl reefing. They nodded sympathetically and agreed that she would not rate as a standard half-tonner, and I felt I had made my point successfully.

I raced back to the hotel to change for the banquet, and we made it on time. The atmosphere was relaxed, and although a lot of people looked tired, as I'm sure I did, everybody looked happy. Ann got her bottom pinched by somebody who turned out to be Jerry Cartwright, an American yacht designer from Newport and a friend of Ron's. I asked her if she wanted me to hit him, but she seemed flattered.

We sat with Yves Anrys, Max Bourgeois, and Ian Radford, with Bill Howell at the next table, so we were among friends. Jack Oddling-Smee made a gracious and amusing speech, the new editor of the *Observer*, the incredibly young-looking Donald Trelford, made another, and Val Howells responded on behalf of the competitors. Val had been a competitor in the first race, in 1960, and now he and his son, Philip, had built identical boats for the *Jester* class for this race. The party broke up and everybody went to get some sleep before the last full day we would have before the start.

FRIDAY. WE WERE UP AT the crack of dawn and back on the boat. The two engineers were working away at it, and I sent Ann off in the car for some last-minute shopping while I worked on the boat.

With the two engineers still working it was a mess, and with only a day to go.

Lizzie McMullen was buried in the family plot at the little church in the Cornish village of St. Mellion, a few miles from Plymouth. Mike Kane and I drove up, and Richard Clifford and Clare Francis were there, too. Mike McMullen bore himself in a manner which put us all to shame. "He's taking it better than I am," Mike Kane said.

Mike McMullen invited us back to the house after the funeral, and was everywhere, putting everybody at ease. He showed us around the place, a pair of workmen's cottages he and Lizzie had been converting into a single house, doing all the work themselves. Only one room was completely finished, and it was heartbreaking to see, on a beautiful Cornish hillside with a view nearly to Plymouth, still another project that they had begun but would not finish together. I told Mike how glad I was that he would be sailing the race. He said, "Your telegram just about did it, you know." I said I thought Lizzie would have been pleased, too, and Lizzie's father, who was standing with us, agreed.

On the drive back to Plymouth, Mike Kane and I got to know each other better, and I began to appreciate the pressures he was under, over and above anything I was experiencing. He was being sponsored by the American Tobacco Company, and a crew had been sent to make a film about his project. A camera and sound crew were following him around everywhere he went; they had been in California taking shots of his home and family before he left for England, and there were the usual PR men skating him around the TV and press people, too. He was longing to be out at sea, I think, leaving it all behind.

Ann and I worked the rest of the day stowing gear and tidying up last-minute details. By early evening *Harp* was nearly ready. During the afternoon I met Mike Flanagan of *Galloping Gael*; he came aboard, introduced himself, and asked to borrow my dinghy to do some work on the topsides of his boat. I had heard that Mike was very confident of his chances in the *Jester* class and wasn't shy about it. We chatted for a couple of minutes, and he seemed a nice enough guy.

Mike Kane came to the dockside, camera crew in tow, and we had a shouted exchange of good-natured abuse for the benefit of the television audience. Robert Hughes arrived and replaced the steering vane shaft which had been bent in the altercation with the customs launch in St. Mawes. Everything was finally aboard and fitted; only some stowage remained, and we left that for the following morning.

Ann and I had hoped to have a farewell dinner at the superb Horn of Plenty in Gulworthy, but we finished on the boat too late and decided on dinner at Bella Napoli after a drink at the Royal Western. There we bumped into Jerry Cartwright, the well-known yacht designer and bottom pincher, and a very attractive English girl, Suzy Wassman, who had lived for a time in Newport. They joined us for dinner. Jerry had done the last OSTAR but hadn't been able to complete a boat in time for this one, and we talked all through dinner about the race, the routes, and problems I might encounter. I had missed most of the weather briefing that afternoon, turning up at the wrong place, but everybody I talked to still seemed to think it was a toss-up between routes. Only a smaller-than-usual amount of ice on the great circle made that route seem a possible favorite. I was still leaning toward the Azores route, having heard nothing new against it, but still had not made a final decision. I would not really have to do that until leaving the Channel.

I was also bitching a lot about the handicap I had been assigned that afternoon. Nobody knew what handicapping system the committee was using, but whatever it was, I didn't like it. *Harp* had been given a handicap of nineteen days and some hours; *Pawn of Nieuwpoort*, Yves Anrys's boat, identical in size to *Harp* but

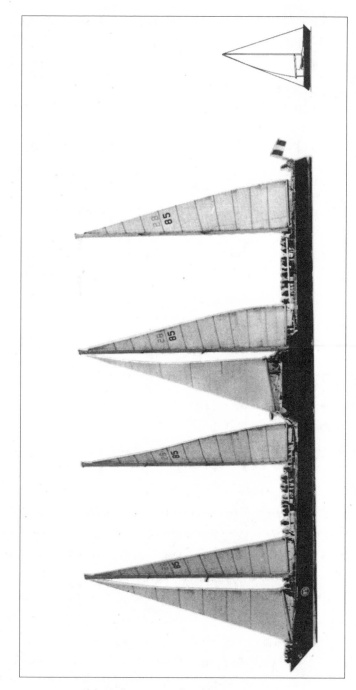

Club Méditerranée and *Golden Harp* to scale.

stripped out inside and much lighter, had been assigned a handicap of twenty-two days and some hours. I was giving Yves three days! Clare Francis, in her thirty-eight-foot *Robertson's Golly*, was giving me only half a day! When Yves and I sat down and went through the list, we discovered still more strangeness. *Harp*, designed as a half-tonner, was actually giving time to a one-tonner! I had written out an immediate protest to the committee, citing a half dozen apparent anomalies, and they had told me I would get a decision in Newport. I was very concerned about this, because the handicap prize was the only one *Harp* had any real chance of winning, being eight feet overall and three and a half feet on the waterline shorter than the class maximum.

In spite of all the shoptalk, the pleasant dinner eased the tension a bit and, since Jerry would be on the press boat at the start, we invited Suzy to join Ann and me on *Harp* for the time before the start. That way she could get inside the restricted zone, where spectator craft were not allowed.

Tomorrow was the day, but I was too tired at bedtime to reflect much about it.

SATURDAY AND THE START. WE were up at six; collected my fresh meat, a week's supply, from the hotel freezer, where it had not frozen; stopped by the fish market for a large bag of ice, which smelled like fish; and got down to the boat. I dropped Ann, the meat, and the fishy ice there and drove to the marina, where Mike Kane had promised me some last-minute weather poop. Mike was late and I had too much to do to wait, so I went back to Millbay Docks, giving Richard Konklowski, the Czech entry, a lift. I hadn't had an opportunity to talk with Richard before, but he was an interesting fellow, sailing his little home-built twenty-four-footer, *Nike*, in the race for the second time.

Since the Czechs have no boat-building industry and import restrictions abound, Richard had had to build his boat from whatever materials he could find, making many fittings himself, even the sails.

Since repairs on *Harp*'s engine had been completed so late, there had been no opportunity for the committee to seal the gear lever, and I was given an acceptance certificate and told they would trust me. (As it turned out, they didn't have to.) This meant that, unlike the other competitors, we had a usable engine for the period before the start and did not have to be towed. So, with Ann and Suzy aboard, we were among the first out of the docks, collecting a round of applause from the crowd gathered at the gates. (Angela told me later that *all* the competitors got a round of applause. I had thought it was just for *me*.)

We motored out to the starting area, stowing gear all the while, and started to look at boats. I don't think anybody got a better look at things than we, with our engine. We motored back and forth through the fleet, dodging hundreds of spectators that could simply not be kept out of the restricted area, in spite of the best efforts of the Royal Marines, buzzing about in inflatable assault craft, yelling at people. There was every possible kind of spectator boat inside the restricted area, most of them small yachts under power, but I even saw two kids in a Mirror dinghy thrashing about among the competitors.

In spite of what sounds like chaotic conditions, everything was quite orderly, the spectators were well behaved, apart from their trespassing, and I did not see a single incident of any kind. Fortunately, it was a light day. In heavy weather things would have been a bit hairier, but then, in heavy weather, there would not have been so many spectators.

Club Méditerranée sailed slowly around at the starboard end of the line, her decks crawling with people (spectators did not have to be off the boats until the ten-minute gun), and *Spirit of America* stayed nearby. I knew Mike Kane wanted badly to start before Colas, and there he was, waiting.

The ten-minute gun went for the big class, and the huge boats started jockeying for position. *ITT Oceanic*, sailed by Yvon Fauconnier, was down at the starboard end of the line with *Club Med* and *Spirit*, and the other large boats were more scattered. Poor Tom Grossman, on *Cap 33*, had been bumped up from the *Gypsy Moth* to the *Pen Duick* class when it was found that his boat exceeded the length for the medium class. He had simply taken the word of the previous owner on her measurements, and now he was in with the big boys, the smallest boat in the class.

Seconds before the gun I saw Mike Kane get *Spirit* into irons nearly on top of the starting line. He just stood in the cockpit shaking both fists in the air until the big tri decided which tack she wanted. Fortunately for Mike, Colas was late, and *Spirit* recovered in time to nip *Club Med* at the line. Then *Spirit* was gone, reveling in the light conditions, while *Club Med* moved sluggishly toward the Channel. It was clear that if it were going to be a light-weather race Mike would probably win it hands down.

Mike McMullen sailed past in *Three Cheers*, and I shouted to him, "Win it, Mike!"

"I'll bloody well try!" he shouted back. He was smiling.

As soon as the *Gypsy Moth* bunch were away, I put Ann and Suzy off onto a spectator boat, switched off the engine, and began to sail slowly around under main only, the reefing genoa furled, and the drifter lashed on deck in case the wind dropped. I have never experienced anything quite like the atmosphere among the competitors at the starting line. Here, in an intensely competitive situation, everybody was wishing everybody else luck! Each time two boats passed there were shouts, jokes, and absurd insults exchanged. I saw and exchanged greetings with Nigel

Lang, Ian Radford, Max Bourgeois, Peter Crowther, Angus Primrose, Andrew Bray, Richard Konklowski, Richard Clifford, Ziggy Puchalski, Mike Flanagan, Simon Hunter, and two dozen or so others whom I had never met but were wishing me luck, anyway.

I saw Angela, aboard one of the *Observer* press boats, and waved goodbye. We were planning to meet in Newport, where she would be running another press office at the other end. I saw the boat carrying Ann and Suzy a couple of times more, and then I heard the ten-minute gun. I had chosen the starboard end of the line, because starting on the starboard tack would give me right of way over boats on the port tack. I ignored all other tactical considerations in favor of playing it as safely as possible. With nearly ninety boats on the line it would be all too easy to collide with somebody and be out of the race with damage before it even started. In spite of my decision to play it safe, though, I felt all my dinghy racing instincts coming back as the minutes ticked away; I stopped thinking about safety and started thinking how to be on the line when the gun went. Suddenly, nothing else mattered.

I made a couple of passes at the line under main only, then settled into an oval pattern near the starboard end, jibing around in circles and watching my stopwatch. At about a minute and a half to go, I found myself being crowded by the Linski boats, all five of them, which seemed determined to start as a fleet. At forty-five seconds I let go the tiller and hauled on the leeward sheet, breaking out the reefing genoa, and started for the line. I crossed exactly thirty seconds late. Lousy for a dinghy start, but pretty good under these conditions. Much better yachtsmen than I started way behind me.

Nineteen months, almost to the day, after my first offshore passage in a yacht, I was starting across the Atlantic, single-handed. I felt as if I would explode. I felt terrific.

Spirit of America nips *Club Méditerranée* at the line
as *ITT Oceanic* prepares to tack.

ITT Oceanic and *Club Med* jockey for position at the start,
as much as one can jockey for position in boats of this size.

42

At Sea at Last

As I crossed the line I overtook and sailed between Richard Konklowski in *Nike* and Michael Richey in *Jester*, with only a few feet to spare on either side. After that I was in the clear and had only to worry about yachts approaching on the port tack. I was making about three knots in the light breeze, very good considering *Harp* was wearing the number-two genoa instead of the number-one. I had set the smaller sail at the start because it would be more manageable in tight quarters.

I sailed perhaps three miles into the Channel in order to lay Penlee Point with plenty of room to spare, noticing that I seemed to be sailing as fast as Clare Francis in *Robertson's Golly*, which was carrying a bigger sail. Just before I tacked, Walter Green, in the Dick Newick tri *Friends*, sailed across my bows, moving very fast. Conditions were ideal for the trimarans, and shortly after I tacked, David Palmer in *FT* overtook me to leeward, having apparently gotten a very bad start. Just after we crossed the line, Peter Adams and his family motored alongside in their small yacht and we made our goodbyes. Now another familiar yacht, *Ruinette*, from Cork, called me on the VHF and wished me luck. It was my last such contact that day, and I felt I was really on my way.

Up to windward Yves Anrys in *Pawn* and Lars Wallgren in *Swedelady* were giving me a boat-for-boat race. Yves, with his big genoa set, began to pull away from us, and *Swedelady* began to change up to a bigger sail. I hung on to the number-two, hoping the wind would freshen, and Yves pulled away from me. Then Ian Radford in *Jabuliswe* appeared astern and began, very slowly, to overtake me. She was a smaller boat than *Harp*, and I knew if I didn't get more wind soon I would have to make the sail change. Because of the furling gear, this was a more difficult change than with conventional gear, and I dreaded losing the time without a foresail during the change. In higher winds when a smaller sail was needed, I would have the advantage, but at the moment, in about a Force three, I did not. Ian was right forward in the pulpit of his boat and stayed there for a long time, apparently making some repair.

Then the wind dropped a bit, and I had no choice but to make the sail change. Once Big Jenny, as I called the number-one, was up, our boat speed increased and we were making a good four knots. Then the wind freshened again and we did even better. About five in the afternoon, off Fowey, we overtook Angus Primrose in *Demon Demo*, a bigger boat, and I knew we were doing well. Ron had said that *Harp* would do better than the Moody 33 on any point of sailing except reaching, and it appeared he was right. Shortly after that, David Pyle in *Westward*, one of Angus's Moody 30s, just nipped me, but when I tacked again I saw that I was pointing much higher than he, and later I was sure that we had overtaken him.

Darkness fell and there were lights everywhere. There was one yacht in particular that seemed to be keeping pace with us and I thought it must be Ian, in his smaller but much lighter boat.

Nobody could sleep that night while we were still in danger of colliding with one another or with shipping in the Channel.

I drank coffee to keep awake, although I had some Dexedrine should I need it, and dined on ham sandwiches and chili con carne that Ann had made in Plymouth. In fact, with a dozen sandwiches and a large pot of the chili, I ate little else for the first three days, except cereal for breakfast. I saw very little shipping, but there were yachts all around us.

At midnight I called Lizard Coast Guard to check the visibility there and was told it was eight hundred yards. By two a.m. it was down to two hundred, but it must have lifted, because I saw the Lizard light briefly at three a.m., then it disappeared. When dawn came, I could see only two yachts as we approached the Lizard, and they soon disappeared after tacking. I did not know it then, but they were the last I would see. The Lizard was really socked in, although visibility on the water seemed about a mile. I came close enough to the headland to hear the fog signal, but I never saw the land at all. It would be some time before I saw any land again.

I tacked away from the Lizard, got the yacht on course, and began making telephone calls on the VHF. It was my last chance to say goodbye to people before I was out of range of Land's End radio. It was still very early morning in the Channel, but in the States it was five hours earlier. I heard a British warship on the VHF to somebody, reporting that some of the larger yachts had been reported at the Scillies, and I chatted with Andrew Bray on *Gillygaloo*. We arranged a calling schedule for noon GMT, but I slept through two of the appointments, and we did not make contact again. I talked with *Chica Boba*, an Italian yacht, which was apparently behind me. Andrew had been ahead. Late in the afternoon I spotted a Scottish yacht, *Sundancer*, not a competitor, called him up, and was told that he had seen *FT* near Bishop Rock, which indicated to me that David Palmer was disregarding his earlier, hotly declared intention to go south.

A large group of dolphins came and played with us for half an hour or so, then darkness fell again and I faced my second night without sleep. At midnight I heard a very clear VHF transmission from a ship called *Arctic Seal*, who was talking with the Coast Guard. When his transmission was finished I called him up and had a long, friendly conversation with the officer on watch, Jerry Miller of Port Arthur, Texas. I could see the brightly lit ship several miles off my port beam and he reported that he could see me on radar at a distance of eight miles, and could see my masthead light as well. This was most comforting. He also gave me a very precise position from his satellite navigational system, which amused me, since Alain Colas had not been permitted to carry that equipment on *Club Med* and had shown a good deal of annoyance toward the perfidious British because of it. I had been able to see *Club Med* for a large part of the first afternoon, and I knew she could not be liking these conditions. I said goodbye to *Arctic Seal* and set a course for the southwest, having made my decision to take the Azores route.

I caught a cold. Coming down the Channel, my throat had become sore and now the whole thing blossomed. This, combined with some queasiness from the rough seas we had begun to experience, made my first week out very uncomfortable. I had little energy and what I had went quickly when I had to deal with some problem, like when the Big Jenny wrapped herself around the forestay. It was worse than the spinnaker wrap had been on the Azores trip, and took a lot longer to get undone.

I was still in radio contact with Land's End and St. Mary's Coast Guard at the freakish distance of 110 miles out, although I could read them better than they me. I tried to relay a message from Lizard Coast Guard to *FT* about this time, but couldn't raise him. This reinforced my belief that he had gone farther north than I.

My radar detector seemed to work, waking me in the middle

of the night once, when a big merchant ship went by. Trouble was, it detected other things, too, like my electric razor, and often came on when the boat was being tossed about. Still, it seemed better than not having the thing at all.

I learned the hard way that no sail could be lashed on deck on the leeward side in any kind of a sea, or even on the windward side when things were rough, without its going overboard. This happened twice, but since the sails were shackled onto the deck at the tack, they were recoverable. It was not nearly so tough to get them back on board in a Force seven as it had been in the Force ten coming back from Horta, but it wasn't a hell of a lot of fun, either, and with the cold sapping my strength, it was exhausting.

We were constantly in fresh winds, usually Force five to seven, and sometimes sailing free, so our daily averages were usually a hundred miles or better at this point in the race, and I felt good about the possibility of achieving my twenty-nine-day goal.

My only brush with the opposite sex at sea, a few dolphins apart, came when I raised the German merchant ship *St. Clemens* on the VHF and found, to my delight, that she had a female radio operator, one Heidi Riedel. Heidi and I chatted for ten to fifteen minutes, both regretting that we could not get together for a drink. She was from Hamburg and promised to take a message to an old friend there for me. It was the last leisurely radio conversation I would have with anybody, because soon after that when I switched on the ignition to charge the batteries, the engine would not start. The trouble was clearly electrical, and among all the things I did not do well, electrics ranked high. I removed the switch panel, checked all the wiring, and sprayed everything with some stuff which was supposed to dispel moisture and improve electrical connections, but nothing. I checked all the connections on the starter motor and sprayed those. Still nothing. I tried jumping the electrics with a screwdriver blade but succeeded only in making a lot of sparks and frightening myself. Finally, all my electrical ideas exhausted, I tried starting the engine with the hand crank. The manual said this was easy to do, even in cold weather. Ho, ho. I cranked the bloody thing until I couldn't stand up anymore, a marline spike stuck under an alternator belt to control the decompression lever. I'd get it spinning well enough, but as soon as I released the decompression lever the engine would stop turning. I thought perhaps a stronger man might turn it further, but I doubted it.

This was a depressing situation, because it meant that when the charge remaining in the batteries was exhausted there would be no electrical power left on the yacht. This would mean no VHF, no cabin lights, no instruments, no stereo tape, and, worst of all, no navigation lights. I would still have radio reception for weather reports, radio direction finding and entertainment on the battery-operated Brookes & Gatehouse and Zenith radios, and depth sounding on the battery-operated Seafarer but no log for speed and mileage recording, no wind direction or wind speed, and no off-course computing from the Hadrian.

I had gone to such pains to ensure that I had the best possible battery charging system, extra-large batteries, two alternators, etc., and now here I was without electrical power because I could not start the engine, a possibility that had never occurred to me. A thousand pounds' worth of electrical and electronic equipment was now useless. I went over the whole system again, afraid that I would arrive in Newport, somebody would point at a loose wire and say, "That's your problem." There was nothing loose, and apart from that I didn't know where to begin. I stopped using everything electrical except the log.

There had been a shortage of sun for the last few days, and I had been proceeding without sun sights to fix my position. Now, as the remaining charge in my batteries faded away, I knew I would soon be without the log, valuable for keeping a good dead reckoning position. Finally, the log ground out its last hundredth of a mile and stopped. I was left with only those navigational aids which mariners had used for centuries: the compass and the sextant.

I had been at sea for eight days when I got the first bad news. Dominique Berthier, one of the two French girls competing, had lost her yacht, *5100,* but had been rescued by a French trawler. I wondered how she could have been near a trawler after eight days at sea, far from the continental shelf. *(Later information: Mlle. Berthier had collided with an unknown cargo carrier and received damage to the yacht's hull. The boat started to take a lot of water and she decided to return to Brest. Nearing France, just off Seil Island, the hull began to break up and she abandoned the yacht for the life raft, watching the boat sink twenty minutes later. Shortly after that she was taken aboard by the trawler and was in Dovarnenez by midnight.)*

I had finally found the radio frequency for the special weather forecast being broadcast for us by the BBC World Service and what I was hearing sounded very bad for the yachts on the more northern routes. Confirming this, I heard the wife of Guy Hornett, who was sailing *Old Moore's Almanac,* on the Jimmy Young show on Radio 2; she said Guy had run into two successive Force nine severe gales. Later in the day the BBC reported that Pierre Fehlmann on *Gauloise* had begun taking water and had retired, and that Yvon Fauconnier on *ITT Oceanic* (formerly *Vendredi Treize*) had broken an arm and that some of his sails were in the water. Jock Brazier, in *Flying Angel,* was also reported to have retired with self-steering problems, and H. G. Mitchell in *Tuloa* was said to have retired. That made five that I knew about. What else was happening up there? *(Later information: Pierre Fehlmann lost Gauloise, and was taken off by another ship under very trying circumstances; Fauconnier and ITT Oceanic were taken in tow by a Russian tug; Guy Hornett and Harry Mitchell finished the race.)*

For three days I was in very thick fog with light headwinds, a very bad combination. I could see nothing, and nothing could see me, but at least there was the consolation that merchant ships would be using their radar, and I had a large radar reflector mounted fifteen feet up on the backstay. In fact, it might be easier to detect my presence that way than by eye, especially at night. My daily average began to drop as I tacked through the soup in the light winds. I did some figuring that at my present rate it would take me forty-three days to finish. That was a horrible thought, but I felt it couldn't go on forever like that, and that we would get reaching winds after the Azores and the turn west. After freshening and freeing us for a few hours, the wind went light again and back on the nose. To make matters worse, there was a very large swell running, the product, I suppose, of the rougher weather farther north. This made it very difficult to take advantage of what little wind there was. I had set the drifter, the superlight nylon genoa, but the violent motion of the boat shook the light breeze from the sails and the boom swung back and forth and had to be tied. It is one thing to sit on a flat sea with no wind. It is quite another to roll about with no wind. Cooking became messy; messier, even, than in rough weather, when there is a kind of rhythm to the seas. I spilled a glass of red wine all over the tennis whites I was wearing and into my bunk. I got even more bruised than I did in heavy weather, especially around the knees and thighs, from bumping into things.

During the days, I read as much as I could, finishing *Alistair Cooke's America* and starting a biography of Thomas Jefferson. In between, I finished Rosie Swale's *Children of Cape Horn*. Rosie had swept through Plymouth, relieving me of £5 for her club of sup-porters building the Swale's new catamaran and leaving me with copies of her two books. I ate well. A lunch might include pâté de canard, Parmesan cheese (with the mold sliced off), Bath Oliver biscuits, and half a bottle of Bâtard-Montrachet. I gained weight. I began to cultivate a mustache.

From the radio news I learned that *Kriter III*, formerly *British*

"Water, water everywhere . . ." Becalmed in mid-Atlantic.

Oxygen, was reported to be breaking up and *Club Méditerranée* had been hove-to for three days, repairing sails. There had been a rumor in Plymouth that Colas could not hoist the sails alone, which meant that if he reefed in heavy weather he would not be able to get them up again. I found it difficult to believe that Colas would put himself in that situation, but the word was that there were no winches available big enough for one man to hoist such a huge sail. Somebody else, I didn't get the name, had been picked up in a life raft.

Then came the really stunning news: there were only ninety-nine competitors left in the race. Thirty-one had retired or been lost. I had, up until this time, heard about only six or seven boats. Thirty-one gone, and it was June 18—thirteen days after the start of the race! A report came that the Soviet tug *Bestroshryy,* which had taken *ITT* in tow, had also taken Yves Terlain off *Kriter.* He had been able to hold the huge cat together just long enough for help to arrive. Tabarly was reported 850 miles from Newport and it was said that he might be there as early as the twenty-first, which seemed utterly impossible to me.

My first two weeks I had covered 1,066 miles, probably sailing fifteen or twenty percent more than that because of headwinds. Poor progress. I missed the electricity, especially the instruments, and it annoyed me that when it got dark I simply had to go to bed. I tried reading with a flashlight, but it was very uncomfortable. I was in my sleeping bag by ten and always it took me at least two hours to get to sleep, not being accustomed to early bedtimes. I listened to Willis Conover's jazz program on the Voice of America, and to the American Forces Radio and Television Service, in addition to the BBC. We were too far out for Radio 2 now, but I was picking up the American station in the Azores again, and getting the first hard news about the coming Democratic Convention in New York. After reading about him for months in the *International Herald Tribune*, I heard Jimmy Carter's voice for the first time. He sounded very familiar, like half the people I'd grown up around in Georgia.

I became very subject to reminiscence, something that had happened to me on the return trip from the Azores, too. I found myself easily moved by memories and by things I read or heard on the radio which brought back memories. The Northern Service of the Canadian Broadcasting Company was replaying a series of old radio programs, *Inner Sanctum*, *The Green Hornet*, and, best of all, Jack Benny. The CBC and VOA also played a lot of music from other eras, and one evening I suddenly found myself in tears, listening to Bob Hope and Marilyn Maxwell, I think, singing "Baby, It's Cold Outside." It's not a very sentimental song, but I suddenly remembered that when I was about six years old I had known all the lyrics to the male part of that song, and a little girl across the street had known the girl's part. I remembered sitting under a tree in my grandparents' front yard on a hot summer day, singing that duet, while we waited for the local fire department to come and rescue a cat which had been chased up the tree we were sitting under by a local dog. What moved me was the memory that I had had a childhood in which firemen came to rescue cats from trees.

On Sunday, June 20, I scored what for me was a navigational triumph. I took my first moon sight, plotted it across a sun sight, and had an instant position without having to wait for a noon sight. It doesn't sound like much of an event, but after a while alone at sea, small successes become wildly elating, just as small problems become hugely depressing. While I was doing the plotting I looked up from the chart table and saw through the windows on the port side the bows of a huge ship. I ran up on deck, waving and pointing at the signal flags I kept flying, which meant "Report me to Lloyds." People on deck waved back and, as I watched, the ship made a ninety-degree course change to port and sailed away. Apparently, she had come up on my starboard side, gone astern of me, and then run on a parallel course on my port side to see if there was anybody aboard. I had been too absorbed in plotting my position to hear her engines, close as we were. I wondered what the outcome would have been if the encounter had occurred at night.

The calms and light winds persisted, but very gradually the sea became flatter, until it was not unpleasant to be sailing slowly. My log for Monday, June 21, read, in part: *Sitting in the watch seat writing this—a lovely evening. I'm wearing only tennis shorts, and the air feels good on my skin. There is what looks like squally showers up to windward; if it will bring a good sailing breeze that's O.K. with me. I have been sitting on the "back porch"—the self-steering platform—trailing my feet in the cool water. It is very blue and extraordinarily clear. A fish about eighteen inches long appears to have fallen in love with the rudder—he has been swimming alongside, almost touching it, for hours. We were almost completely becalmed from nine a.m. to four p.m. . . . Spotted a mooring buoy ahead and after what seemed like a very long*

Harp drifts through the light airs in mid-Atlantic.
The very light drifter genoa kept her moving.

*time, crept abeam of it. It had the number nine on top and the name (I
think) Nancy Egary. The owner can find his mooring at 40°27′N,
27°22′W. Heard on BBC that Tabarly is within a day's sail of Newport.
If it's true he will beat the record by three days. Seems impossible . . . The
Azores are being even more elusive than on the trip with Bill. Graciosa
is still sixty miles away and Flores is a hundred miles further than
that . . .*

I was wearing tennis shorts and not running around naked
because I had been doing just that, and parts of me which were
unaccustomed to the hot sun were complaining. I could sit comfortably only in certain unusual positions. The Azores were,
indeed, taking their time about turning up. On the race the year
before, Bill and I had taken 15½ days and we had considered that
two or three days too long. That night, however, I picked up the
loom of a light on Faial and as I was about to go below to plot the
bearing, I looked astern and saw two enormous red lights from a
position where there could be no land. It was obviously not a ship,
and just when I was beginning to reassess my opinions about
UFOs, I realized that it was the moon rising, only a sliver of it, but
huge and red and broken up by black clouds stretching across it.
It was a few minutes before my pulse returned to normal.

Next morning, I could see things growing in my drinking
water. This was alarming. I remembered an account by a competitor in the last race describing a similar experience with his
water; he had had to put into the Azores to clean his tanks and
change the water. If I wanted an excuse to visit Faial again, here it
was. I decided to wait another day before making a decision about
it. When I checked it again, I found that the contamination was
only in the starboard tank and not the port, and I remembered
that Yves Anrys had given me two water-purification tablets
before the start of the race. I had put them on the chart table and
forgotten what they were. Now they were wedged under the

barometer and crumbling, but I swept up the pieces, divided them equally between the two tanks, and poured a pint of water in after each of them to make sure they did not lodge in the filler pipes. I reasoned that the contamination was probably harmless bacteria, and anyway, the pills were at work now, so I would drink the starboard tank first, before anything new started growing in it.

A day later, the water situation was still on my mind when I rose to find Faial, green and lovely, off my port bow, with a cloud-enshrouded Pico behind. The height of the islands, Faial at 3,500 feet and Pico at 7,000 feet, must make them among the best land-falls in the world, when they are not obscured by cloud. I thought of Horta and the people and places I knew there—Augie and Luis, the Club Naval, Peter and his Café Sport, the Estalagem and the village market—and I resolved to come back when I could combine the excitement of seeing the Azores with the satisfaction of visiting them.

The BBC was now reporting that the race winner was five hundred miles from Newport, but they had stopped mentioning Tabarly specifically. I wondered how Mike McMullen was doing, hoped he was up front, unnoticed, and winning. I had thought about Lizzie and Mike often, and I wanted him to be not just the first multihull but the first boat across the line. I knew that no one else could be as highly motivated.

The water was choppy in the archipelago waters. Faial re-mained in view for nearly a day and a half in the clear weather, and as I was coming on deck for my noon sight on the twenty-fourth, glancing to see if the island was still there, I saw instead a ship coming up fast astern of us. She was *Olwen*, Royal Navy, I think, since her officers were in whites, but there were women aboard, too, and I wondered how the Royal Navy had managed that. She passed me, then circled and came close abeam my star-board side, and I shouted through my Tannoy loud-hailer, "Please report me to Lloyds."

My first flying fish. Not exactly a trade winds breakfast.

"I have already done so," replied an officer from the bridge.

I asked for my position, but he was unable to get the information before his part of the ship passed me, and suddenly *Harp* was *very* close to her, close enough for a rating further aft to ask after my welfare only barely raising his voice. I dropped everything and threw in a very fast tack, and the big ship slid by only a few yards away. That rattled me a bit, and it must have got to her captain, too, for this time he did not circle but hove to and waited for me to come to him. I was not about to go anywhere near the ship, stopped or not, without an engine. He waited for a few minutes, probably trying to get me on the VHF, because an antenna was visible at my masthead, then sailed on. At least my position would be reported, I thought.

That night I heard on the BBC that Clare Francis was a thousand miles from Newport, apparently on the great circle route. I got out the dividers and measured my distance from the finish. I had made my first turn on my course at about 37°30′N,

35°W, and I still had just over two thousand miles to go. Maybe they were having heavy weather up there, but at least they were having wind, too, while I sat becalmed or in light headwinds day after day. But now I was at my southerly turning point, the place where the reaching winds were supposed to be. If they came, and if they were fresh, my daily runs would improve dramatically. And anyway, didn't they have calms on the great circle route? Maybe there was a chance of making a good showing, yet.

43

Going West

I don't suppose I had really expected fresh reaching winds to materialize the moment I reached a point on the chart, but I was bloody disappointed when they didn't. Still, at the end of three weeks I had covered 1,645 miles over the ground, and my daily average was improving steadily.

Life went on in a regular sort of way, my daily routine continuing. I saw my first sea turtle; he measured about three feet across his shell and was covered in barnacles. We sailed slowly past him in light winds, so slowly that I was able to go below, get a camera, and take a couple of shots of him.

Then my eggs went bad. An egg company had given us thirty each, and Yves Anrys had given me his, but for some reason my taste for them had disappeared and I had eaten only two since Plymouth. I had a good time with them now, though. I sat in the cockpit and dropped them overboard one by one, watching as they sank but remained in sight for an amazingly long time in the clear water.

I had passed my halfway point and had begun to get out my large-scale charts of the east coast of the United States and mark them up for future use.

On July 28 the BBC reported that the French Navy had started a search for Eric Tabarly. This seemed ridiculous to me, since he had been out for only twenty-two days, and there were any number of good reasons why he might not have appeared in Newport yet. What seemed more a cause for concern was that sixty-seven of the yachts in the race had not been sighted or heard from either during the past week or since the start. I was glad I was not one of them. It suddenly occurred to me that although I had been seen and my family and friends had news of me, I had none from them and would have none until reaching Newport.

Anything might have happened—someone might be dead or ill—and I would have no way of knowing. It was a facet of single-handing that had never crossed my mind and I found it mildly discomforting. Colas was reported two hundred miles from Newport after putting into St. John's, Newfoundland, for repairs. This was perfectly proper, since the rules stipulated that a yacht could stop anywhere for as long as her skipper wished, as long as he was not towed for more than two miles into and out of port and observed all the other rules.

The following day, the twenty-ninth, I heard that Tabarly had won, crossing the line at nine in the morning, Newport time. Colas was thought to be close behind. I was sorry that Mike McMullen hadn't won, or Mike Kane, but there was still the multihull prize, which I had begun to think of as the "Tin Lizzie." Then, the next day, came the amazing news that Michael Birch, in one of the little Newick trimarans, *The Third Turtle*, had finished third, followed closely by Kazimierz Jaworski in his thirty-eight-foot monohull, *Spaniel*. They were both remarkable performances,

Spaniel's being perhaps the most remarkable since she was a monohull. David Palmer, who had expected to win the *Jester* class in *FT*, had dismissed the Newick trio as contenders, saying that a boat completed this season could not win for lack of time to prepare. It was a classic case of a competitor believing that everyone else would experience the same teething problems he had; of not recognizing that there will always be someone, in a race of this size, whose boat is better designed, better prepared, and better sailed than yours. Considering all the variables, it was not a race to be cocky about. Here we had the boat that everyone had predicted would win in a walk coming second, beaten by a boat designed to be sailed by fifteen men, then two yachts from the smallest class finishing third and fourth, ahead of much larger, faster boats which should have beaten them. It was that kind of race.

From my log of July 1: *I have just dined on sweet and sour ham, with peanuts and raisins, and the Bâtard-Montrachet '70 and am a little bit drunk; Willis Conover is playing very good jazz on the Voice of America and Mike Flanagan is dead. BBC said at midday, as I was eating a ham sandwich, that* Galloping Gael *has been found by a merchant ship, drifting, with no one aboard. Mike is apparently the victim of what I have always thought is the single most dangerous risk of this Race— falling overboard and watching your boat sail away. It is said that drowning is a pleasant death, but it cannot be pleasant to tread water and contemplate it until it happens. When I heard about this my first action was to put down my sandwich, go and sit on the back porch (first clipping my harness to the pulpit) and rig a tripping line to the self-steering. It is now being towed behind with a number of knots and two loops tied into it. It may not be much, but it is all I can do. I didn't know Mike Flanagan well, but he seemed a nice enough fellow and was, I am told, supremely confident of his chances of winning the "Jester Trophy." Now, barring a true miracle, he is gone, a victim of what? The Race? His own self-confidence (vanity)? Or an unavoidable accident? (There are unavoidable accidents.) Now, in the last month, two attractive young people I knew are dead. Why do I feel responsible, or at least guilty? They are not dead because they both knew me, although I may have been their only connection. I have believed from the beginning that someone would die in this Race. Now, someone has. God, let that be an end to it.*

On July 2 I heard that Colas had been docked ten percent of his elapsed time for having someone help him hoist his sails in St. John's. *(Later information: A member of the race committee had telephoned the St. John's Coast Guard to learn the circumstances of Colas's arrival and departure and had been told that on leaving, Colas had taken a party on board with him out of the harbor, thus breaking the most important rule of all, the one about sailing alone. Whether or not he had help with his sails made no difference, and he was lucky to get away with a ten percent penalty.)*

My radar reflector chaffed through its shackle and slid down the backstay, thus reducing my visibility on radar. I plowed through my tinned American snack foods, continuing to gain weight and contemplating the disappearance of my navel.

From my log of July 3: *Becalmed most of last night and until 11.00 hours this morning. When the wind returned it was, of course, nearly on the nose. I have been irritable all day. If I don't improve my daily average it will take me another three weeks to reach Newport, and we've been at it for four weeks today. We seem to sail (hard on the wind) from one calm to another, like traffic roundabouts on the route, each jammed, with movement nonexistent. BBC says that David Palmer and Walter Green finished seventh and eighth (but who was fifth and sixth?). They were both very good performances, finishing ahead of a lot of the Pen Duick and Gypsy Moth classes. Good for them. I hope Mike McMullen was fifth or sixth. Why don't they give us more news? The BBC hasn't had one interview with anybody connected with the Race. Today I am (temporarily) weary of this enterprise, but now that the boat is moving again, in whatever direction, I feel better.*

What I did not write in my log, for fear of giving the idea more credence in my own mind, was the thought that if Mike McMullen were not number five or six, he would not be in Newport when I arrived. I tried to think of all the hundreds of reasons why he might not be among the leaders—broken mast, leaky boat, illness—and still be safe, but the thought would not go away.

As July 4, 1976, the bicentennial anniversary of the founding of my country dawned, I was still thirteen hundred miles from Newport. Shattered was my hope of being in Newport for the celebration, and shattered it had been for two or three weeks, but that didn't make it feel any better. Now I was worried about finishing the race before the fifty-day time limit expired. As we rode out a Force seven on the nose, I listened to reports of celebrations from all over the United States on the Voice of America. The queen was in Newport, hosting a dinner for the president. Pity I couldn't make it. Somebody, probably Protestant terrorists, had planted some bombs in Dublin. I was sad to think that the mindless war was beginning to be felt in the Republic. The Israelis freed the hostages at Entebbe, in Uganda, and I think that was the high point of my day. I stood up and cheered. I read Joseph Conrad's *The Nigger of the "Narcissus"* and then, in a fever of patriotism, wrote a letter to Jimmy Carter, offering to work in his campaign. It would be some time before I could mail it. Thirteen hundred miles to go. Twelve days, with luck. Twice that, without it.

The next day the wind began to rise and back, putting us on course again but hard on the wind. It blew hard all that night, and I was routed out of bed early the next morning to reef right down to storm canvas. The squall hadn't allowed any time for dressing, so I did the job naked. By the time I had finished the wind was blowing a steady Force ten, and the scene around me was very strange. Here we were in fifty to fifty-five knots of wind (I was certain about that, comparing it to the blow on the trip back from the Azores the year before), and the sun was shining brightly. It was very warm, and I sat naked in the cockpit for half an hour or so, watching the enormous seas and delighting in the sunshine. It was delightfully pleasant until the wind increased to the point where the spray hurt like hell, and I had to get below, my skin red as if from a needle shower.

As the storm continued, I began to worry that it might be a hurricane. The hurricane season runs from June to November, but most of them occur in September or October. I got out my *Reed's Nautical Almanac* and began to read up on hurricane symptoms. They all fit. I began to think about jibing, to sail away from the center of a possible tropical storm, which is the standard procedure, but I decided to wait for an hour or so to see what happened to the barometer. I crawled back into my bunk and tied myself in for the wait. A few minutes later I opened my eyes and looked straight up through the starboard window. I could see the cap shroud waving in the breeze. (The mast receives all its lateral support from two wires on each side of the mast. The cap shroud is the outer, longer one. If it goes on the windward side, the mast goes, too.) I ripped the back cushions off the bunk to get at the bosun's bag and a spare clevis pin, found one, grabbed a harness, and got on deck, all, it seemed, in a matter of seconds. It was still blowing very hard, and now I had to brace my feet against the toe rail, hang on to the inner shroud, and try to catch the waving length of wire rope. Finally, I got it, and with trembling hands managed to get the clevis pin in place and secured. I was just breathing a huge sigh of relief when one of the spinnaker poles, which had been secured to the windward side of the deck, hit me in the back. It was another couple of minutes before I had wrestled that back into place and resecured it. Back inside the cabin, shaking like a leaf, I reflected on what might have happened had I jibed a few minutes earlier; the loose shroud would have then been on the windward side and the mast would have gone.

Less than an hour later we were becalmed again. I couldn't believe it. Almost no wind and still a huge sea left from the storm.

Very uncomfortable. But when the wind finally filled in again, it came from the east, which was nearly impossible according to the pilot chart. Not wanting to set a spinnaker in the confused seas, I boomed out the number-two genoa, hoisted the full main, and we flew before the wind, clocking up 140 miles during the next twenty-four hours, our best day's run, and 120 miles the following day, before the wind veered and headed us again. It was now July 9 and there were less than a thousand miles to go.

With the boat hard on the wind again in a moderate breeze, I stretched out for an afternoon nap. I was nearly asleep when I heard a buzzing sound. The Zenith was tuned to the Voice of America and I thought the Soviets were jamming it again, as they sometimes did, but the buzzing grew quickly into a roar, much louder than any noise the radio could make. I charged into the cockpit, knowing that sound could be only one thing. As I came through the companionway, a single-engined airplane roared past our port side, only about fifty feet above the water. I dived back into the cabin for a camera and got back into the cockpit before he could turn for another pass. He turned and started to come straight in toward the boat as I began taking pictures. For a moment I had the feeling that I was about to be strafed, as in those old World War II movies. He flew past and began to turn again. He was Royal Navy, and I figured he must be from an aircraft carrier, because even though he was carrying a large fuel tank under his fuselage, the nearest land was Bermuda, about 450 miles away, and I didn't think such a tiny aircraft would have that sort of range. He came back in again, low, along our port side, and I could see the lone pilot. I felt a curious kinship with him, both of us single-handed in the middle of nowhere. He turned and flew away to the east, and I knew he was from a carrier because there was no land in that direction. Next, I thought, we'll have the carrier along, and I settled down in the cockpit to wait for her to appear.

Fifteen minutes later, there was another, different sort of noise, and I opened my eyes to see a helicopter coming straight at us from the north. It occurred to me that although the first pilot had found me and I had waved, I had given him no indication of whether I needed help, so as the chopper passed I gave him a thumbs-up sign. Two crewmen, sitting in an open doorway aft, waved back, and they were off, back to the east again. I waited for a while longer in the cockpit, but the carrier never appeared. I knew, though, that I had been reported, for the first time in three weeks, and I was wildly elated.

I now found myself low on water. The fouled starboard tank was empty and the port tank was less than half full. There was only one bottle of beer left, too, but plenty of wine and food. I had begun to lose weight, now, the snack foods having run out, and I was in good health and excellent spirits. I expected to be in the Gulf Stream soon, and I began to read up on what Adlard Coles and Erroll Bruce had to say about sailing in that great ocean current. None of it was good. The current normally runs at one-half to one and one-half knots, according to the pilot chart, but what I was reading indicated that in places it could run three to five knots and even reverse its normal southwest to northeast direction. The very warm water temperatures caused very changeable weather conditions, too, and nobody seemed able to predict anything about the Gulf Stream.

On the eleventh, as I was cooking, I looked out and saw through the port window what looked like a big squall. There had been dark clouds down there all day, but we had been making good progress under shortened sail. I started on deck to have a better look but stopped with one foot in the cockpit as a thunderstorm, complete with thunder and lightning, struck us. I have never seen anything like it. Visibility came to an end. The self-steering, about eight feet away, disappeared in a wall of gray water. The sea around the boat turned white, churned into foam

Found! The search plane from the British aircraft carrier *Ark Royal.*

The search plane was closely followed by a rescue helicopter, very reassuring.

by the force of the rain. I pulled my foot back inside the hatch and stood on the ladder and watched. I suppose it lasted for about two minutes, and then I was able to get into the cockpit and reef farther. I felt lucky that nothing had broken, and I figured it would all blow over as quickly as it had come. It did, but it came again and then again. I have never experienced anything as sudden and as violent as these thunderstorms which raked across us for two and a half days. On land there are trees and buildings to break the force of such storms, but not at sea. Even more frightening than the sixty-knot gusts of wind was the lightning. For the whole of the two and a half days I had the feeling of living under a huge, electrically lit sign which, because of some wiring fault, was flashing on and off erratically. It was all the more frightening because *Harp's* mast, thirty-eight feet above the water, was the only tall object in hundreds of square miles, and it was made of aluminum, a wonderful conductor of electricity.

A Gulf Stream thunderstorm about to come roaring in.
Winds exceeded sixty knots during these.

Occasionally there was a lull, when the wind would drop to Force six or seven for a few minutes. During one of these, Fred tacked the boat and put us aback. He had done this several times, when the combination of a gust and a wave would push the boat up into the wind a bit, and I was extremely annoyed with him. I had always talked to him, as if he were a dog or cat, and now I found myself screaming at him as I struggled to get the boat back

The Irish Tri-Color all-rounder—the only time I was able to set a spinnaker.

343

on the right tack in the big seas, "You sonofabitch! You do that again and I . . . I won't oil you anymore!"

About seven-thirty in the evening of the thirteenth the wind had dropped enough to unreef, and for the first time in what seemed like years, the horizon to windward was not filled with dark thunderheads. I released the reefing line to the Dynafurl and started to crank in on the sheet to shake out the reefing genoa, pleased because we were only about four hundred miles out of Newport now, and I was hoping to cross the line on Friday, the sixteenth. That would give me a reasonably creditable passage of forty days—more than I had wanted to take, but not bad. Something stuck. The sail would not come unreefed. Swearing under my breath, I hauled the sheet in as tight as it would go, made it fast, got into a harness, and crawled onto the foredeck, where I began turning the swiveled forestay by hand. Suddenly, the forestay wasn't there anymore. There was a metallic thunking noise and the whole stay, sail and all, flew out of my hands, the aluminum reel at the bottom nearly hitting me in the face. I had been squatting, turning the stay, and now I was dumped back onto my bum, watching the forestay, which supported the mast from forward, waving the number-two genoa in the breeze from the top of the mast like a giant flag. First the stay, now the stick, I thought.

I sat on the foredeck and waited for the mast to go.

44

Drifting in the Gulf Stream

Incredibly, the mast did not break. The wind was down to about Force three, the main was double-reefed, and the inner forestay held everything together long enough for me to charge aft and release the main sheet and start getting halyards forward. Fortunately, *Harp* was equipped with two genoa halyards and two spinnaker halyards, and I got three of this lot forward to the toe rail and winched them tight. The mast would not fall now, but there was the immediate problem of recovering the flailing forestay and sail before the fitting at the top of the mast broke under the strain and sent everything overboard.

After twenty minutes of fruitless effort, trying to haul everything down onto the deck by hand, I discovered the easy way: I put the windward sheet onto one of the big Barlow self-tailing winches and cranked away until the stay was back on deck and under control. Perhaps "under control" is an overstatement, for the aluminum-rod forestay was writhing all over the place like a giant serpent. Finally, I got it shackled to the toe rail and lashed it so that it could not thrash about and chafe things. Next, I got the sail off, with some difficulty, and stowed. This gave me another genoa halyard to play with, and now the wisdom of having the little storm jib made came home to me. I set this flying on the halyard, tacked to the pad eye, which had been fitted about two feet abaft the forestay tack, and once again we had a headsail and could go to windward. We couldn't point very high, but we could go to windward, and that's where Newport was.

Trouble was, now that the wind had dropped and we had been reduced to a double-reefed main and a storm jib, we could move at only about two knots. I was afraid to hoist the whole main for fear of putting too much strain on the halyards and toe rail forward. Making two knots, there was no chance of reaching Newport by the weekend, and this was very depressing. Still, things could have been a great deal worse; we could have lost the mast and really have been in trouble. Our reduced speed called for a reassessment of the food and water situation, too. Food was getting short and water even shorter, so I had to be very careful to see that nothing else happened to delay us, or I would have to go on a very serious diet. I had already started brushing my teeth in salt water, and now I watched every drop. I tried collecting more water in the thundershowers by hanging a bucket from the end of the boom; this worked for a while, then the bucket blew away. But at least we had a main and a headsail and, above all, a mast.

Twenty-four hours later, however, we didn't have a headsail anymore. The halyard on which it was flying parted at the mast sheave, probably because, in an effort to get the luff of the sail tight, I had winched it up too much and it was carrying too much of the weight of the mast. I was afraid to set the sail on another halyard—I was running out of them—and we made little progress during the night under the reefed main only.

I decided to have a go at getting my VHF transmitter working with spare batteries from my signaling lamp. They were six volts each; six plus six equaled twelve, I reasoned, and the VHF worked on a twelve-volt current. I wired the two batteries together, hooked them to the radio, and it worked! At least, I was getting crackling noises. I didn't want to try transmitting until I could see a ship, since the batteries were small and surely wouldn't last long.

By morning it was clear that under the present sail plan we could sail either to Newfoundland or to Bermuda but not to Newport, unless we got a radical wind shift, and I wasn't going to count on that. The only alternative seemed to be to repair the forestay in some way so that we could set a headsail, a job which seemed clearly impossible. It was bad enough that when the stay was unshackled from the toe rail it would start thrashing about again; but the main problem would be getting the stay to stretch enough to reach the forestay tack. I had found the cause of the failure: a deck eye which fitted into the bottom of the forestay had come unscrewed. First, I removed the deck eye from the forestay tack and tried to screw it back into the bottom of the stay. The threads were stripped. It would go part of the way in, then freewheel when turned. I spent two hours, lying on my side on the foredeck, draped over a spinnaker pole, trying to get the thing screwed back in. Finally, using a large screwdriver for leverage, I managed by putting pressure on it and turning at the same time, to get it most of the way in. But I had no way of knowing if the threads would hold and keep the same thing from happening again.

Now I had to try to stretch the forestay far enough to reach its deck fitting. The logical thing to do, of course, was to ease off the backstay, then crank down on the halyards forward, bending the mast until it reached. But I knew that would not get it close enough. O.H. and I, when *Harp* had been relaunched at the beginning of the season, had had one hell of a time getting the backstay to reach under similar circumstances, and that was with two of us pulling on it and no sea tossing us about. I would have to find another way.

My eye fell on the reefing line, which had broken when the stay went. This was a length of flexible wire rope with a rope tail spliced to one end for ease of handling. I took the block normally used for the spinnaker foreguy and shackled it to the forestay tack fitting, then ran the reefing line up through it and tied it around the wire drum at the bottom of the forestay. I took the rope tail back to a winch and cranked it as tight as I could, then went back to inspect the angle at which the line was drawing the forestay toward its fitting. It looked right, but there was still a twelve-inch gap between the end of the stay and the deck fitting. I went back to the cockpit and cranked each halyard down as tight as I could, then cranked on the reefing line again. It was working. I loosened the backstay even more and cranked down on all the winches again. The gap was now only about two inches. Was it possible this was going to work?

I cranked still further and the reefing line parted. It wasn't going to work. I was going to have to sail to Newfoundland and try to keep from starving to death while I was doing it. I ran the line through the block again and retied it, then went back and started easing off the backstay even more, frightened stiff that I would turn the wheel one thread too many and the backstay would go. I eased it about two inches beyond where I thought it would be safe, then, one by one, cranked down on the halyards again, then the reefing line. I went forward to inspect the gap. The deck eye was one-fourth inch from the position where the clevis pin would slip in to secure it. Summoning up all the strength I had, I squeezed the eye into the gap. The clevis pin went in. With trembling hands I secured it with a split pin, and we had a forestay again.

I couldn't believe it. I had done something that two men shouldn't have been able to do in a seaway. Could Robin Knox-Johnston have done this? (Of course he could, and in half the time.) The job had taken me from ten that morning until early evening, and I was too exhausted to hoist a foresail, so we slogged on overnight under main only. The next day was the sixth, the day I had planned to arrive in Newport, and we had drifted thirty-five miles to the northeast, pushed by the Gulf Stream. When the forestay broke we had been about four hundred miles from Newport, on about the latitude of Cape May. Now we were farther north, and I was worried about being headed again, as we would not be able to point high to windward with the present state of the rigging.

On Friday morning I thought I would try to pick up Nantucket Lightship, as we were getting close to being within radio direction finding range. I couldn't hear Nantucket Lightship, but I was picking up another signal loud and clear. I checked the chart in *Reed's*, showing all the New England radio beacons, and none of them matched the Morse code I was hearing. I began running through the lists of other east coast beacons, and in a moment my finger froze. I was hearing a radio beacon on the coast of *North Carolina*, and it had an effective range of *a hundred miles*. Had I, through some navigational blunder, approached the coast in the wrong place? Was I really off North Carolina? I began twirling dials furiously, weak with apprehension. I found another beacon and hurriedly looked it up. Cape Cod Light. I nearly fainted. Apparently, some freak atmospheric condition had allowed me to pick up the North Carolina beacon so clearly. For confirmation, I switched on the Zenith and started looking for commercial stations. The thunderstorms had caused so much interference that I had been unable to pick up anything except shortwave for several days. I found a station in Lynn, Massachusetts. I felt better.

Now my biggest concern was being becalmed. After the violence of the thunderstorms, we were down to about a Force two and it was coming from, of all places, the east. I got up a spin-naker, hoisting the heavier all-rounder, because if the wind rose I didn't want to do another spinnaker change. We ran for most of the day in a light breeze, then, about sunset, the wind began to rise and go around. Soon we were close reaching at about seven knots and I was steering, because Fred couldn't handle the helm under those conditions. I took the spinnaker down at dark and got up the number-two genoa, hoping that the dodgy forestay fitting and the two halyards still taken forward to the toe rail would keep the mast up. We managed an eighty-mile run that day, and I was pleased and relieved. That night, after dark, I thought I could detect a change of color in the water. The edge of the Gulf Stream is easier to find in the north than in the south. The water temperature and the color change very quickly at the edge. Next morning, the color was a dirty brown instead of the deep blue to which I had become accustomed.

A ship's horn at this range is a surefire alarm clock.

Gazing into my last sunset at sea. The mustache, so carefully cultivated, went soon after my arrival in Newport. It made me look less like Clark Gable than I had planned.

We had the mast, we had a foresail, and we were out of the Gulf Stream. Newport lay ahead. We were finally in the home stretch.

45

The Final Dash

Sunday morning, the eighteenth, I picked up a Newport commercial radio station. I could not have been more excited if I had been contacted by a flying saucer. I could hear people talking, and they were in Newport, Rhode Island. What's more, they were reporting race news. Five or six boats had finished during the last twenty-four hours, including Ziggy Puchalski and Richard Konklowski; another twenty-five boats still had not finished, so at least I wouldn't be last.

I had a good lunch and stretched out on a settee berth for a nap. A few minutes later, as I was sleeping soundly, I was lifted right off the berth by the sound of a ship's foghorn at what seemed a distance of about eighteen inches. I landed in the cockpit, ready to dive overboard and swim for it. There, about fifty yards off the port quarter, was a large merchant ship, *Alchemist*. I jumped below to get the loud-hailer, not wanting to use the tiny radio batteries unless absolutely necessary. I started to shout that I wanted to send a telegram, but she was already overtaking us. Someone on the bridge made a hand signal to indicate that they would circle. I tried to wave them off, remembering my close call with *Olwen* some weeks before, but they circled and came up again. I shouted out a telegram to Angela in Newport, giving an ETA of Tuesday, and asked for a position. But we were being overtaken again, and the big ship circled a second time. This time, the radio operator was standing on the foredeck, and as I shouted out my message, he sprinted toward the stern of his ship, writing furiously. Someone on the bridge had an old-fashioned hand megaphone and shouted a position to me. It struck me as funny that I, on my tiny boat, should have an excellent loud-hailer, while they, on their huge ship, should have a megaphone.

They sailed on, promising to dispatch my telegram immediately. My spirits soared now. My position had been reported, my navigation had proved to be perfect, and in two days I would be in Newport. I anticipated arriving between noon and three with the light winds we were experiencing. Then, only a few minutes after the disappearance of *Alchemist*, I looked off the port quarter and saw a yacht, the first I had seen since the English Channel. She was in the far distance, and even with the binoculars I could not recognize her, but I felt sure she was a competitor. She was there for the rest of the day, slowly overtaking us, and during the night she disappeared.

While I was watching her I saw something else in the water, a float of some kind, with a pole and a radar reflector. Then another, and another. This meant I would have to keep a lookout for fishing boats that night and the next, but also that they were using radar to find their floats, so would be likely to spot me, even though my reflector had slipped down to about six feet above the deck.

Darkness fell and I kept a close watch, sometimes lying down for ten minutes at a time to rest but not falling asleep. About two-thirty in the morning, as I was resting, I was suddenly overcome by a violent chill. Shaking uncontrollably, I got up to light the cabin heater but thought I would first have a look around. I stuck my head up through the hatch to find a large fishing boat two hundred yards dead ahead, bearing down on us at about ten knots. I grabbed a torch and signaled him, and he changed course to pass about twenty-five yards on our starboard side. The chill vanished. Had I developed another level of perception, like Bill King? Maybe.

Monday, July 19, our last day out. The wind backed and freshened, and we were tearing along at six knots under our reefing genoa and double-reefed main. My ETA began to change, and, for once, to earlier. We saw no shipping of any sort that day until sunset, when the first fishing boat appeared. At midnight, a huge, brightly lit ship, looking like an aircraft carrier, appeared on the horizon and tore across our wake several miles astern at very high speed.

We had now picked up Gay Head Light on Martha's Vineyard to starboard, and Buzzard's Bay Light was ahead, off the starboard bow. I kept a running check on our position with bearings from the two lights, combined with a check of our depth. At midnight I estimated we were fifteen miles from Brenton Reef Light and the finishing line, but I would not yet see it, even though it should have been visible at that distance. I hoped that one of the infamous local fogs was not enshrouding Newport—that was all I needed. I was taking great care to see that nothing went wrong this close to the finish. I kept thinking about Bill Howell in the last race, about to finish in fifth place, then colliding with a fishing boat. I didn't want that sort of problem now. My ETA was now three a.m. I had not wanted to arrive at night in a strange port and I hoped I would be met at the finishing line, as had been mentioned at the prerace briefing.

At twenty minutes past midnight I saw Brenton Reef Light

flashing in the distance. I abandoned my compass course and began steering for the light, the first time in forty-five days I had a mark to steer for. It was very satisfying. At 01.45, Judith Point Light appeared, and from bearings on the two lights I estimated my distance at seven miles. An hour later, I was almost on top of Brenton Reef Light and looking hard for the flashing red light on the buoy that marked the other end of the finishing line. I could see the lights of Newport arrayed behind the light.

I brought some flares, the signaling torch, and the loud-hailer into the cockpit. I didn't want to waste a minute being found when I was across. The red buoy appeared where it was supposed to be.

On July 20, 1976, at 03.15 local time, 07.15 GMT, *Golden Harp* crossed the finishing line. The second we cleared the line I stood up on the afterdeck and struck a white flare. The yacht lit up as if a dozen klieg lights had been thrown on it. I had never seen such an intense, white light. The flare burned for about a minute, then sputtered out, leaving me with no night vision whatsoever. Gradually, my eyes became accustomed to the darkness again, and there was no boat of any kind to be seen. The wind was dropping very quickly, and *Harp* was slowing, now running dead before it at about two knots. I waited a few minutes and struck another flare. Again, the intense light, followed by equally intense darkness. Still no other boat.

Following the chart as best I could, we started up the narrow entrance to Naragansett Bay toward Newport. The lights of the town and of the large suspension bridge farther up the river made it very difficult to pick out buoys and lights ashore. The wind continued to drop and soon we were barely stemming the tide. We drew abeam of where Castle Hill Coast Guard station was marked on the chart. I could see a large building on a hill, with several exterior lights. I signaled the station, but there seemed to be no one on watch. (The building was a hotel. The Coast Guard station was behind the hill.) I tried the VHF but got no reply either from the

Coast Guard or from Goat Island Marina, where a twenty-four-hour watch was being kept at a reception center being run by American Tobacco. Nothing. Maybe the small batteries were enough for receiving but not for transmitting. I struck another flare abeam of the Coast Guard station. Still no notice was taken of me.

I sat in the river for the rest of the night, fuming at being ignored. Forty-five days at sea and no bands, no fireworks, no dancing girls, not even a rowboat. The river was absolutely devoid of traffic of any kind.

These people did not seem to understand my heroic achievement. Did they think I did this every day? Shit.

Dawn came as slowly as possible. I made a cup of coffee and tried to stay awake until somebody else was up. I wondered what time the local water-skiers got started; there didn't seem to be anybody else stirring. There was still not enough wind to make any headway against the tide.

At six o'clock I heard an engine. Reception committee? Fishing boat. He was on his way out for his day's work, passing a hundred yards to starboard. I hailed him and asked if he would call Goat Island Marina on his radio and ask them to come and get me. He said he would, and I settled down with my coffee again. A couple of minutes later, he had turned and was coming alongside.

"Nobody's up," he said. "Throw me a line, I'll take you in." The only other person aboard his boat was a girl.

"I envy you your crew," I said. "I haven't seen one of those for six weeks." She laughed and made my line fast.

As we moved up the river a huge, red sun rose behind the spires of Newport. I stood on the deck and looked at the houses and green shore. It seemed unreal, a New England Disneyland, constructed of papier-mâché. We approached the marina's fuel dock. A lone figure stood on the pier, holding a towel. I shouted at him to take a line. He did. He was waiting for someone to come and unlock the showers. I called the reception center. No answer;

it had closed the day before. Customs wasn't up yet. No need to wake Angela at this hour. I lurched back to the yacht on my new land legs and puttered around the decks, sorting ropes, then went below for another cup of coffee. I was too excited to sleep. A voice from above. I stuck my head up. A smiling face greeted me.

"I'm Pete Dunning. I run the marina. I think you're the sixty-third boat in. Congratulations."

"Where's Mike McMullen?"

"He hasn't been reported since the start of the race."

I knew it. I think I had known it all along.

46

I had my first hot shower in six weeks, and Angela turned up soon afterward, having been rung by Pete Dunning. I got all the news: 125 boats had started the race; I had finished sixty-third; thirty-six had retired in various stages of damage; five had sunk, but their skippers were rescued; Mike Flanagan was lost and Mike McMullen was missing. Several other boats had not been reported but were eventually accounted for.

There was much discussion about what had happened to Mike McMullen. It was the consensus among those who knew him that he would not have taken his own life, even after having lost Lizzie. He seemed too good a yachtsman and too familiar with his boat and her limitations to have lost her in heavy weather. No collision had been reported. It is my own view that he went in some simple, everyday way, probably falling overboard like Mike Flanagan and like Brian Cooke the year before. That can happen to anybody, no matter how good he is. It is unlikely that anyone will ever know for sure, of course. The only possible consolation for any of his friends is that, depending on the way things really are, he might

At last, a tow into Newport.

be with Lizzie. Anyone who knew them will spend the rest of his
life missing them.

I puttered around Newport for a couple of weeks, getting
small repairs done to *Harp*. My mother had been in Newport when
I arrived and said she was getting tired of the family business. I
had decided to sell the yacht and spend some time reorganizing
things and getting her retired. I had a novel to finish, too, and the
day after I arrived in Newport I talked with Ron Holland about a
new boat for the next race, a bigger and faster boat. It was a very
satisfying experience to finish the race, but I wanted to do it again,
and faster.

Newport is a pleasant and hospitable place. Angela and I saw
a lot of Peter Crowther of *Galway Blazer* and his girl, Pauline, and
David Cowper of *Airedale* and his wife, Caroline. Jerry Cartwright
and his wife, Kay, had a lot of the competitors over for dinner, and
other dinner parties took place on the various yachts and at the
Black Pearl on Bowen's Wharf.

There was much warm camaraderie among the finishers, and each time another yacht finished, there was much shaking of hands and swapping of stories. Most of the early finishers had gone by the time I reached Newport, but many competitors were still there. A lot of them left the day after my arrival to return via a race to Horta, then France. Tom Grossman of *Cap 33,* who had finished fifth, came down on a visit from Boston. The people of Newport invited us to beach parties and made us feel welcome. They had had an active summer, what with the Tall Ships, then us.

Angela came back to Georgia with us for a few days before returning to London and her job on the *Observer.*

The race rules are being rewritten, probably to exclude giant yachts, and that may be for the best. There has been the usual chorus from some of the yachting press that the race be abolished or made into a two-man event. No matter what is said, it seems impossible to make them understand what this race means to the people who compete in it. Many human beings need adventure, real adventure, personal adventure, and, sometimes, as in our case, solitary adventure. Some men and women have always needed that, finding their own physical limits without the aid of bearers and Sherpa guides, searching out their own emotional and spiritual boundaries in places where there is no one to answer to but God. As our society grows and our environment shrinks, there will be more and more little men who will wish to deny us that. Many of them have public or editorial platforms and they will use them to attack this event. They must be ignored.

It is interesting to note that at the start of the race, where chaos had been predicted, not one untoward incident occurred which could be attributed to the size of the race, its organization, or the single-handedness of its entries. During the remainder of the race

Tabarly, now a French national hero.

Clare Francis celebrates her July 4th
arrival in Newport.

only two collisions with ships occurred: one of them not serious, one resulting in the sinking of the yacht and the subsequent rescue of her skipper. Another competitor, Nigel Lang in *Galadriel*, had the truly incredible experience of colliding with another single-handed yacht, not a competitor, hundreds of miles out in the Atlantic. Neither was seriously damaged.

Two lives were lost, the first ever in this event. It was inevitable that it would happen in one of these races, and now it has. Both men knew that it might, though neither probably expected it would happen to him. Both, in a sense, died defending the right of men to risk dying in adventurous living.

No one has proposed, with any effect, that motor racing be prohibited or that men stop trying to climb Everest. It is simply accepted that those who participate in these enterprises do so at their own risk, and good luck to them. Those of us who race single-handed ask no more than that. Leave us alone; ignore us, if you like, but let us get on with it.

Let us, as Jack Oddling-Smee, commodore of the Royal Western Yacht Club, has said, "enjoy and profit by what must surely be one of the last great freedoms granted to us in this ever contracting world."

Afterword

Finishing the OSTAR didn't end my sailing career, although I did sell *Golden Harp*. I sailed in the infamous Fastnet Race of 1979, in which fifteen competitors and four observers were lost (see *Fastnet, Force 10*, by John Rousmaniere for the definitive account), aboard *Toscana*, a Swan 47 owned by my editor and publisher, Eric Swenson. That autumn, I skippered the yacht back across the Atlantic, starting at Falmouth, in Cornwall, and stopping at Horta, Madeira, and Las Palmas and Puerto Rico, in the Canary Islands, finishing at Antigua. Since then I've sailed on other people's boats, and I'm now a partner in a 1935 motor yacht, *Enticer*, and I spend a couple of weeks a year aboard her. When I owned *Golden Harp* I looked upon motor yachts as boats that spilled my drink when they chugged past, making a wake; now I take a more benevolent view, and I enjoy sitting on the afterdeck, a gimlet frozen to my fist, spilling other peoples' drinks. I also operate my own Hinckley 38, *Indian Summer*, in Maine and Key West.

Some footnotes, gained with the passage of time: Parts of Mike McMullen's yacht, *Three Cheers*, were found a couple of years later, encased in the frozen shores of Iceland, identified by the serial numbers on some of the electronic instruments. My opinion of how Mike died has not changed.

The last known sighting of *Three Cheers* was made by my friend George Kennefick, at that time the commodore of the Royal Cork Yacht Club, who was approaching Cork Harbour, under power, in nearly calm conditions when he came across the trimaran, sailing slowly westward. He motored alongside her for a few minutes, chatting with Mike, who, he said, seemed in good spirits, except for the lack of wind. Then the wind came up, and Mike sailed away, obviously headed for the northern route. No one ever saw him again.

Some of the people mentioned have, inevitably, died since the book was finished. Andrew "Spud" Spedding died a few years later of natural causes; Worth and Pasha Newenham are gone, as is Harry McMahon, who died in his fifties of a coronary.

BILL KING, HOWEVER, HAS PASSED his one hundredth birthday and is still sailing. Ron Holland and John McWilliam remain friends, although I don't see them often. Ron is now designing some of the largest, most luxurious sailing yachts afloat. I see Harold Cudmore rather more often; he lives next door to the Royal Yacht Squadron, in Cowes, on the Isle of Wight, where I summered from 1983 to 1993.

Ann Greville-Bell married an Australian architect and lived there for many years, but now they are back in England. I exchange an occasional e-mail with Ann and with Angela Green, who still lives in London.

Fred and I had a riotous reunion in Ireland a year after the race, and, after witnessing this, the McCarthy family insisted that he go home with me. I gave him my American Express card and put him on a flight from Shannon to New York, where he was fed, watered, and emptied by the ASPCA, who then transferred him to an Atlanta flight. He lived to the age of thirteen, charming everyone he met, and he was the best dog I have ever known, with apologies to the three further Labs I have owned since, all named Fred.

THE LATER YEARS

47

I established a routine; on Tuesday mornings, I would rise before dawn and drive to Dublin, a three-hour drive at top speed over deserted roads and unpeopled villages, arriving at the ad agency in time to start the working day. I would spend the night at whatever Dublin hotel had the best rate, work the following day, then drive home to Lough Cutra Castle, arriving in time for dinner. I sustained myself thus.

I got invited to a dinner party now and then; every hostess likes an odd man. I was often paired with a riotous woman in her seventies, Molly Cusick-Smith, or rather Lady Cusick Smith, who lived grandly in one of County Galways finest country houses and was mistress of the East Galway and Bermingham Hunt, probably because she owned the pack of hounds. I occasionally followed the hunt, but did not have the skills to survive riding in it. They would meet at a country pub at ten o'clock on a fine weekend morning and would take on a load of port, presumably for courage, then they would ride hell-for-leather across fields and over stone walls (which required the courage). They would arrive, exhausted, at Molly's home, Bermingham House, for lunch and more drinks.

On one occasion a young priest, new to the county, had ridden with the hunt, in habit, and he walked his mount over to Molly's and said (supply your own Irish accent): "Ah, Lady Cusick-Smith, yer harse is in a fine lather!"

"Father," Molly replied, in her most regal accent. "If you had been between my legs for the past four hours, you'd be in a lather, too!" She was like that.

One day I read in the classified ads in the *Irish Times* that a farmer in County Limerick, south of Lough Cutra, had a litter of Labrador retriever puppies for sale. I phoned him, then drove down there and bought the male runt of the litter, naming him Fred. (I name all my dogs Fred; it's easier that way.) I was given an appropriately sized cardboard box to contain the puppy in the car, and it soon became evident that he did not enjoy the experience. My solution to the problem worked: I picked up two young girls hitchhiking to Galway and one sat in the front passenger seat, with Fred in her lap, a position he found more appropriate to his dignity.

Fred became my constant companion for the rest of his life, except for one year (I'll explain that later). He was extraordinarily intelligent and equally charming, making friends with everyone he met.

I had been training him to empty himself outside, not inside, when one day he walked over to the door, pointed his chin at the sky and howled like a tiny wolf. I opened the door for him; he waddled down the steps, did his duty, and struggled back to the top. He never howled again, but he was now trained, mostly by himself.

Young girls were particularly susceptible to Fred's charms. One evening at Paddy Burke's, a pub on the way to Galway, he sat in a young lady's lap at the bar, and she fed him a few sips of her Bloody Mary. Suddenly, she shrieked and stood up, holding a glassy-eyed Fred away from her. He had peed in her lap. It was a rare social lapse.

When he was around twelve weeks old I took him to Galway with me, as I took him everywhere, to visit a boatyard. Fred ran happily about, greeting people, and when it was time to go, I could not find him. He was nowhere to be seen in the boatyard, and I walked across the road to an encampment of Irish Gypsies (not Romanys), a dozen or so trailers and cars, with household wares on sale. I went from trailer to trailer, asking after Fred, but no one had seen him. I returned home, disconsolate.

I went to Dublin for my working tour, then returned to Galway, where I was having an Irish girlfriend, Maeve, over for dinner. She asked after Fred, and I told her the woeful story. "I'll find him," she said.

She taught at a school near the Gypsy encampment, and she posted a notice on the bulletin board of a little grocery where they shopped, offering a fifty-pound reward. Half an hour later, a small child turned up at her school and said he knew where the puppy could be found. If she'd give him the fifty pounds, he'd take her there.

"I'm not giving you the money until I've seen the dog!" she lectured him, in her best schoolmarm style. He reluctantly agreed to show her.

He led her to one of the trailers, took her inside and took the lid off a cardboard box, and there was Fred, who had, apparently, not left his temporary quarters since the first day of his captivity. Maeve grabbed him up, and the boy's mother said, "We'll have the fifty pounds!"

"I'm not giving you fifty pounds!" Maeve exploded. "You're a thief!" and she marched back to her school, unmolested, where she attempted to give Fred a bath in a bathroom sink. It didn't work very well. When she brought him home, it took another half hour to get him clean in the kitchen sink.

But Fred was home. He remains the only puppy I ever knew who was kidnapped by Gypsies.

48

I now found myself "on the beach," as shipless sailors call themselves, except that I still had *Golden Harp*. I was thirty-eight years old, unemployed, and I had time on my hands. I responded by doing pretty much nothing.

I did a single-handed sail up Buzzards Bay and over to Martha's Vineyard for a couple of days. Arriving there, looking for a berth, I saw a bait shack with a sign offering berths, so I pulled over to their dock and was assisted by a half dozen workmen on the site, who had been attending an elongated lump of something under a canvas cover. One of them pulled it back a bit and introduced me to an enormous great white shark, looking dead. In fact, I had stumbled into the filming of *Jaws II*, which was being shot in and around Edgartown.

The film guys nailed a little of the production's lumber across my berth, so my fenders would have something to rub against, and I had a nice breather on the Vineyard for a day or two.

Back in Newport, I readied for the trip south to Georgia and took on a female crew, a Newport resident and a good hand, for a portion of the trip south. We sailed south around Montauk and headed for Cape May, at the southern tip of New Jersey, intending to sail up Delaware Bay, thence to the Chesapeake Canal, across to the Bay, and down to Annapolis. It was getting late, so we put into the Cohansey River, winding off Delaware Bay and beautiful with marshes, to Greenwich (pronounced the way it is spelled, not the Village). We found a cozy-looking marina and made the turn toward the dock, and as we approached, while the engine continued to turn, the propeller did not. We coasted into the dock. Diagnosis: blown hydraulic drive.

Long story short, the engine went back to Ireland, the girl went back to Newport, and I went south, to Manchester, Georgia, and the family home.

My mother, Dot, had been running the family store, Denham's, after my grandfather's death, and my stepfather passed on around the same time. She wanted to retire from the business, and that left me. I sat in my grandfather's office and wondered what to do next. Selling the store was what, though it took several months. In the meantime, I rented a nice apartment in Atlanta at a development called Cross Creek and put myself on salary at the store—only thirty grand, but it was enough for the moment.

My next step was to set about writing *Blue Water, Green Skipper,* since I already had a contract with Stanford Maritime, in London, and W. W. Norton, who would publish the American edition. I put to work the skills I had learned in advertising, planting my ass in a chair and writing a thousand words a day, whether I felt like it or not.

I renewed old friendships in Atlanta, with my college roommates, Dent Acree, now an attorney who also lived at Cross Creek, and Lindsey Hopkins, heir to a large family fortune, initially based on Coca-Cola stock, and now amusing himself with buying and operating a Buick dealership. Lindsey had always loved cars. There were a couple dozen other friends from the old days, so I had a good social life, and Atlanta had a large population of single women.

My work went well. I finished the book and it was published to some acclaim, which surprised me. Reviews invariably praised the quality of the writing, and having one's own opinion confirmed is always gratifying.

I HAD AN IDEA OF doing a book about the Round Britain Race, which is a two-hundred-yacht race around all of the British Isles, starting and finishing in Plymouth, home of the OSTAR. My editor, Eric Swenson, was an enthusiastic yachtsman, owning and racing a gorgeous Swan 47, and he liked the idea of the book.

I had another plan, too: while driving all over the British Isles, I would do a book about another hobby, country inns and restaurants. Eric liked that, too, so I had two books to support me.

I saw a new, entry-level model from Porsche, the 924, in a showroom; it cost ten thousand dollars. I went into my local bank in Manchester, where I was now established as a main-street merchant, and asked for a car loan. The banker, who I had known all my life, looked at me in astonishment. "We have *never* loaned *anybody* that kind of money for a car," he said.

"Don't you have any customers who drive Cadillacs?" I asked.

"No," he replied.

The next day I was in Atlanta. I walked into the First National Bank in Buckhead, and the manager instantly made the loan. I ordered the car to be delivered to the Porsche factory in Germany, and in due course I collected it there, then tooled around Switzerland and Italy for a week or so. Once on the autostrada, in northern Italy, doing about ninety, I was pulled over by a police car. Two cops got out and signaled me to stay in the car. The two of them walked around the car a couple of times, speaking rapidly and gesticulating, then got back into their car and drove away. The car was, apparently, the first 924 they had seen.

I drove the car to England and was there a few days before the start of the race, long enough to rent a flat as a London base and then visit a few inns for my other book on the way to the southwest of England. Once in Plymouth, I found a few of the competitors I knew from my time in England and Ireland, and I had some conversations that would be useful to me in the book to come.

My friend Spud Spedding, who had won the race with the late Mike McMullen the last time it was sailed, looked at the weather and thought it was ominously calm. He and Mike had won the previous race, by *rowing* their yacht all of the last day and across the finish line.

On starting day there was just enough breeze to get everybody out of Plymouth Harbor and into the English Channel. I drove on ahead to the next stop, in Ireland, and, finally, the fleet appeared, well overdue.

By the time I met the fleet in northern Scotland, it had become apparent that there was going to be precious little to write about, so I called Eric in New York and explained the circumstances.

"The hell with it," Eric said. "Why waste your time?"

"I can still do the country inns book, though," I said.

"Great, go ahead."

Over the next twelve weeks I drove the Porsche twelve thousand miles around the British Isles, gaining weight steadily from all the good cooking.

Back in London I met an attractive young woman, an equine sculptress named Susannah, who lived in a "grace and favor" (free) cottage behind the scoreboard at the Windsor polo field. She was the only woman who played with the national team, and she was sharing the cottage with another young woman who was having a surreptitious affair with Prince Charles.

The two of them threw a party at their cottage one evening to honor the Argentinian polo team, and I was invited and told, confidentially, that Price Charles would be a surprise guest at the event.

That evening, I was chatting with a Canadian investment banker of about my own age, named Jock, when the two of us were summoned to the rear garden of the cottage by the hostesses.

"We need the help of the two of you desperately," Susannah said. "Can you please cut a piece of mutton in half for us? It's too big to fit on our barbecue pit."

Of course we could! We were shown to a shed and, armed with hacksaws, confronted our "piece of mutton." It was an entire sheep, a big one, and we had to saw it in two from end to end. It was also still partly frozen, which didn't help. It took us the better part of two hours, working from opposite ends, to get the job done, and we finished, exhausted and sweaty, our shirts soaked through.

We turned the carcass over to the Argentinians, who would do the barbecuing, and had a few drinks while our clothes dried. It was nearly eleven o'clock before dinner was served, and Prince Charles never showed, the press having got wind of the party and surrounded the place, cameras at the ready.

49

We're in the autumn of 1975, now. I saw some friends for dinner in Atlanta, Sidney and Rebecca Guberman. Rebecca was the former wife of one of my college roommates, Lindsey Hopkins, and she was working on the Jimmy Carter campaign for president. I told her that I had worked on the JFK campaign, and would like to help Carter. She invited me to come up to the Atlanta headquarters and meet some people. Having been living in England and Ireland for nearly seven years, I had no idea who Jimmy Carter was. When I went home for the Christmas holidays in 1975, my mother had to explain to me who he was. After that, he began popping up in the *International Herald Tribune*, now called the *International New York Times*, and, increasingly, in the British and Irish press. I found him increasingly interesting.

The campaign offices were in a large multiuse development—offices, shops, and a hotel—in midtown. I drove up to Atlanta and checked into the hotel for my early-morning meeting the next day. I thought I might get some dinner and see a movie, so I went down to the bar for a drink. I sat near an attractive woman, and we fell into conversation. After the warm-up, she asked, "Would you like a date tonight?"

"I'm going to dinner and a movie," I replied. "Why don't you join me?"

"No, no," she said, "you don't understand." She explained it to me.

I told her that I didn't want to jeopardize my amateur standing. She excused herself for the ladies' room and didn't return. I went to dinner and a movie.

The following morning, I visited Rebecca and she introduced me to Jim King, who was in charge of a chunk of the campaign that included advance work, and to Rufus Youngblood, who ran the day-to-day advance operation. Rufus was the Secret Service agent, now retired, who had thrown himself over Lyndon Johnson's body to protect him during the assassination of JFK, and who had subsequently been promoted to run the presidential protection unit.

Jim told me that there was a new class for advance men starting the next day and asked me to join it. I would be assigned to the presidential schedule at the end of that and would travel a day or two ahead of the candidate to set up a venue, obtain a sound system, and do whatever else was needed to make the appearance a success.

I joined the class, and Jim took us through the routine we would have to follow to ensure that the candidate's appearance went smoothly. He also told us that, if we screwed up—if the sound system didn't work, for instance—we would be given a bus ticket home. We had three very full days of this, including an extensive briefing by a Secret Service team on how we would operate in conjunction with them.

Most people don't know—I certainly didn't—that at a campaign appearance, all the people in the first four rows of spectators would be campaign operatives—aides, secretaries, whoever was available—to act as a safety buffer between the candidate and the crowd. The candidate was warned never to go deeper than four rows of the crowd.

One of our tasks was, before an appearance, to collect as many as possible of the names, dates of birth, and social security numbers of the people in the crowd at an appearance. With that information in hand, the Secret Service could find out just about everything about a person. They especially wanted to know if he had ever made an attempt on the life of the president, or even talked to anyone about it.

We saw repeated showings of the film of the assassination attempt on Governor George Wallace of Alabama, who had, in a previous election, ignored the Secret Service instructions and plunged deep into a campaign audience to shake hands with people, shortly coming face-to-face with the man who shot him, putting him in a wheelchair for the rest of his life. This made a big impression on all of us.

At the end of the training, I got a call to go see Rufus Youngblood, who would have an assignment for me. Rufus told me that I would be the campaign advance man in Plains, Georgia. "Why," I asked, "would Governor Carter need an advance man in his own hometown?"

Rufus explained that the candidate returned to Plains once, sometimes twice a week. And on those occasions, I would meet the two jet aircraft at the Albany, Georgia, airport—Peanut One, containing the candidate and his senior staff, and Peanut Two, carrying the traveling press. I would have a truck and a bus at my disposal, the first for baggage and the second for the press, and I would see that there were a couple of cases of cold beer in the back of the bus, and that everyone would be transported to the defrocked Holiday Inn, now a Best Western, where they had all paid for their regular rooms for the duration of the campaign. One bedroom was assigned to me.

On my first day in Plains I drove my car down from Manchester and parked in front of campaign headquarters, which was in the old railway station. The only person there was Lillian Carter. The candidate's mother. She greeted me warmly and insisted on driving around town with me and introducing me to everyone she saw. She took me to the governor's house, a modest brick ranch, and out to the lake house, then to Peterson Field.

During the candidate's stay in Plains, usually a day or two, I would assist the senior staff in doing whatever they did, including driving the governor's visitors from Peterson Field, the private little grass strip where non-jet airplanes could land, to the governor's house or to his secluded lake cabin.

After I saw Peanuts One and Two off from Albany, a light airplane would take me back to either Manchester or Atlanta. I think they chose me for the job because I was more mature and dressed better than most of the other advance people.

This turned out to be the best advance job in the campaign.

I quickly got to know all of the traveling press and many of the senior staff. Everyone lunched at Plains's only restaurant every day, and I shared tables with people like Jody Powell, Hamilton Jordan, and Richard Holbrooke.

One Sunday morning at breakfast, Jody took me aside and told me that Dr. Schlesinger would be arriving in an hour or so, and I was to meet his light airplane at Peterson Field and transport him to the governor's church, where he would be conducting his regular Sunday school class.

One of the press people saw Jody talking to me and came over when he had gone. "What's going on?" he asked.

"Not much. Arthur Schlesinger is arriving, and I'm to take him to the church to sit in on his Sunday school class."

The reporter went immediately to a pay phone and made a call.

I was waiting when the Cessna 172 pulled up to the hangar at

Peterson Field and watched not Arthur, but Dr. James Schlesinger alight from the airplane. Oops!

I got him into my car and described what we were going to do. He declined to visit the Sunday school class, and it struck me, a little late, that he was Jewish. Regroup.

This was before the time when everyone had a cell phone. There was a Secret Service agent who knew me, standing at the airport gate; I got out of the car and told him that Dr. James Schlesinger had arrived and had declined to go to Sunday school. I asked him to call whatever agent was on Jody Powell, explain the situation, and ask him what he wanted done with Dr. Schlesinger. He did so, and the word came back, "Take him to the house."

There were few houses in Plains, and I knew which one he meant. I got back into the car. "The governor will meet you at his home after Sunday school," I said to Schlesinger. He nodded. He seemed to prefer speaking as little as possible.

I delivered him to the governor's house, took him inside, and asked if he would like some refreshment. He shook his head. I handed him the *New York Times* and got out.

At lunch I saw the reporter who had asked for information. "All of Baltimore thinks Arthur Schlesinger is here," he said.

I don't know what James Schlesinger and the governor talked about at their meeting, but, after the inauguration, Dr. Schlesinger became the next secretary of defense.

ONE EVENING, A GROUP OF us sat around the pool at the motel, as David Broder, the columnist for the *Washington Post*, chatted with members of the staff, particularly one younger member whose name I have, mercifully, forgotten. Broder had asked if there were any problems he was having to deal with.

"The advance people," the guy said. "I've worked on several

campaigns, and this is the worst advance operation I've ever seen. These people are terrible."

I was looking for a way to interrupt him before he could do any further damage, when Broder turned to me and asked my name. "And what do you do on the campaign, Stuart?" he asked.

"I'm an advance man," I replied.

The group erupted in laughter, and I hoped that had changed the subject.

"Except him," the staffer said, pointing at me, having turned a bright shade of red. I had a chat with him later.

ONCE IN A WHILE, THE governor got himself into a little hot water, as on the occasion when he told a reporter that, while rowing near his lake house, his boat had been attacked in the water by a rabbit. Hilarity reigned for days in the papers.

On another occasion he had honestly, but unwisely, told a reporter that he had occasionally lusted in his heart for women, perhaps before he married Rosalynn.

One of the reporters promptly wrote a little ditty called "Lust in My Heart," which was sung lustily on the press bus from time to time, after the beer had been passed.

Billy Carter was the family character, and he did not like the press hanging around his filling station while he and his cronies drank beer and played checkers. When Billy's wife gave birth to a son, he had been scheduled to pitch for the staff side of a softball game against the press team, and he showed up late. A female reporter for a radio network was there to greet him when he got out of the car, a live microphone in hand. "How much did the baby weigh, Billy?" she asked.

Billy leaned into the microphone. "Eight pounds, four ounces, with his dick and balls," he roared.

"I've been sandbagged before," the reporter said to me, as Billy strode to the mound. "But never like that."

THE GOVERNOR'S SCHEDULE WAS PUBLIC knowledge, and when he was in Plains, crowds would gather. Once I was approached by a handsome, well-dressed man of about sixty, who told me that he owned a large car dealership in a neighboring state. He had something to deliver to the governor, and it was vital that he see him as soon as possible. He had a sixty-five-page telegram containing important information. Alarm bells were going off in my head.

I asked for his name, date of birth, and social security number, and he freely gave them to me. I went in search of the Secret Service agent in charge of the governor's detail. He looked at the name. "We know him well," he said. "He's a CO2." That term referred to those people in an audience who might be a little off in the head. "He's harmless, but don't let him anywhere near the governor, or he'll bore him to death."

When the governor came out of the building to get into his waiting car, I made sure to keep myself between him and the CO2.

As the campaign wore on and I mastered my job, I discovered that, once I had settled everyone into Plains, I had some time on my hands. I went to see Tom Peterson, owner of the airport, and inquired about taking flying lessons. Next thing I knew, I was rolling down the grass strip at the controls of Tom's Cessna 172, while Tom told me what to do next.

After that, I didn't drive to Plains. I called Tom, he sent the airplane for me, and I flew it back with the instructor. Before the campaign was over I had amassed seventeen hours, mostly cross-country, and the bug had bitten.

On the last day of the campaign, I drove up to Atlanta, to the Omni, where the party would be held to celebrate our victory, we hoped. Our hopes were well-founded, as it turned out, and we had a great time. When the party was over, I was told to round up the staff people and get them aboard buses for the airport, where Peanut One was waiting to take everybody to Albany and then Plains.

I found a seat at a secretary's desk in the rear of the airplane, while others were standing in the aisles with their drinks in hand. Jody Powell, I remember, was sitting on top of a Xerox machine, clinging for dear life. I forget how I recovered my car.

And that ended my contributions to the election of Jimmy Carter. During the following four years, I gathered some new views about who should follow him in office. We'll get to that in due course.

I found myself with too little to do, except for the novel, and that could always be put off. Instead, I talked my editor into my doing another yachting book and a travel book, all in the same summer.

The yachting book would be about the Round Britain Race, a two-hander the course of which took the fleet all the way around the British Isles.

Unfortunately, the weather did not cooperate. Calm followed calm, and there was zero excitement. After a conversation with my editor, we agreed to abandon that book and concentrate on *A Romantic's Guide to the Country Inns of Britain and Ireland*. I ended up driving around the British Isles and visiting more than a hundred inns and restaurants.

The research was fun, even if I did gain fifteen pounds.

50

At the end of the summer, my research all done, I drove the Porsche to Southampton, where I had booked passage for both the car and myself aboard the *QE2* for the passage to New York. I had paid the cheapest fare, but a friend, Marvin Green, knew the chairman of Cunard, who arranged for me to have the best unsold cabin, which turned out to be in first class, comfortably large and well-appointed.

We sailed on time, stopped at Cherbourg, across the Channel, to pick up more passengers, then headed west, down the Channel and out into the North Atlantic Ocean. I toured the ship to get my bearings and stopped into the hairdressers for a haircut and to get my nails whittled. I noticed, from my perch in the barber's chair, that there were whitecaps showing on the sea. By the measure of the Beaufort Wind Scale, a means of judging the wind strength by the appearance of the sea, this meant twenty knots of wind. Nothing for the *QE2*.

That night, resting comfortably in my bed, I woke and felt an odd sensation. I was lying on my back, and it was as if there was a large hand on my chest, pressing me into the mattress, pausing, then allowing me to rise again. I got out of bed, went to the big porthole, pulled back the curtain, and was greeted by the sight of water, passing horizontally by. Odd, I thought. Then the water fell away and I tried to get a good look at the sea, which was sending a large wave up, momentarily obscuring the view from my porthole. I pulled the curtain shut and went back to bed.

The following morning, I rang for my cabin attendant, a helpful chap called Austin. He staggered into my cabin and asked if I'd like breakfast. I ordered scramble eggs, sausages, an English muffin, orange juice, and coffee. And a *New York Times*.

Austin memorized my breakfast order, then said, "I regret that the *New York Times* is on strike."

I remembered that he was right, not that it mattered much in the circumstances, so he brought me the ship's newspaper, which was faxed in from somewhere.

Breakfast done and the newspaper read, I went into my large bathroom for a shave and shower—an experience that turned out to be something akin to being a bean in a rattle. Fortunately, there were a number of handgrips scattered about the bathroom, so all went well, as long as I did everything with one hand.

I resumed my tour of the ship and soon found myself with a book, seated in a comfortable chair in one of the ship's bars, occasionally glancing out of the big window at the sea, which was not improving. Consulting the Beaufort Wind Scale in my head, I reckoned we were experiencing fifty knots of wind, a "strong gale" as Admiral Beaufort liked to put it. There was no safety belt in my seat, but I managed to continue reading, as long as I held on to one arm of my chair.

AT DINNERTIME, I TURNED UP in the dining room to find about half the tables empty. I joined a table and someone explained to me that the ship's doctor had a cure for seasickness. He went to a patient's cabin, gave them an injection of something, and they passed out for about twelve hours. When they woke, they were cured, supposedly.

Fortunately, I did not suffer from seasickness.

I guessed that the ship was rolling about ten to fifteen degrees, which turned the waiters into a sort of corps de ballet as they passed among the tables, their trays balanced on the fingertips of one hand, while they grabbed at passing chairs for support.

I looked forward, where something had caught my eye. A particularly big wave had temporarily increased our roll rate, and I saw a woman whose chair was tilting dangerously backward. Surely, she would right herself, I thought.

She did not. She continued to tip until the back of her chair met the carpeted floor, then she slid downhill until her head came to rest against a large stove in the center of the dining room, making a noise that sounded like the man in a J. Arthur Rank film striking the gong. People rushed to her side, and she was taken away on a stretcher. Word was passed later that she was not injured and resting comfortably in her cabin.

AFTER DINNER I WAS HAVING a cognac in the bar, and I fell into conversation with a young ship's officer named Derek, who was the assistant navigator. He invited me to lunch the following day in the officers' mess, and I accepted with alacrity.

Turned out that the officers' mess was one of only two places where one could sit and look forward, over the ship's bows—the other being the bridge, which was directly over our heads.

The view was magnificent, and a little terrifying. We were headed directly into the seas, and the ship was sailing into the troughs, then taking waves that crashed over the bows.

"How high is the bow above the water, in calm seas?" I asked Derek.

"Fifty feet," he replied calmly.

"Does that mean that we are taking fifty-foot waves?"

"Yes," he said. "I'm afraid we're going to have to bear away soon, if we're to avoid capsizing."

As he spoke, the ship began to turn slowly to port, and the waves were now striking at a less distressing angle. The captain came on the blower and addressed the passengers, telling us that we had turned off the wind and slowed to nine knots, less than half our normal cruising speed.

"Good," said Derek.

The captain also said that the rolling was not so bad, less than ten degrees. There was an inclinometer on a wall of the officers' mess. I had seen it a few minutes before, showing twenty degrees.

LATER, USING A MAP OF the ship, I went down to the garage where the passengers' cars were stowed, and the Porsche was managing well. I had had visions of it being tossed around the hold. Just beyond that hold was the ship's indoor swimming pool, and I took a look at it through a porthole. The surface of the pool was doing an excellent imitation of the sea outside, with its waves crashing to and fro.

WE SAILED INTO NEW YORK Harbor two days late. Less than an hour after docking and clearing customs and immigration, the Porsche was disgorged from the ship's bowels and sat waiting on the dock, unscratched. A porter loaded my luggage, the car started instantly, and I drove away, seeking a tunnel under the Hudson.

I headed south from there and by sunset was somewhere in Virginia. A couple of nights later, I was at home in Manchester, Georgia.

Nothing had changed. I sat in my grandfather's office and peeked out onto the sales floor now and then. The bookkeeper next door was doing her work, and so was everyone else. They didn't need me. Still, I had a book to occupy my time, before the novel.

51

Fortunately, I had work to do that would prevent boredom. During my travels, I had set up a file for each of the inns I thought worthy of my book, containing a photo and all the information I needed on each inn.

I engaged an illustrator of my acquaintance, Jennifer Miller Broadus, to make a pen-and-ink drawing of a photograph of each inn, which would give the little volume a consistent graphic look. Then, cranking up to my ad writer speed, I whipped up a few pages of what I hoped was inviting prose about each, listed the addresses and phone numbers. I found I could do about three inns a day.

I called the book *A Romantic's Guide to the Country Inns of Britain and Ireland.*

A few weeks later, I had a guidebook, which would be published by W. W. Norton, in America, and by an associate firm of theirs in London.

SOMEWHERE ALONG IN HERE, FRED arrived from Ireland, having begun his trip at Shannon Airport, where they regularly shipped racing greyhounds to the States, then to JFK airport, where he was fed and emptied by the ASPCA, and on to Hartsfield-Jackson Atlanta International Airport.

I drove up from Manchester and entered the customs building as instructed. I could hear distant yips, and I walked over to a door containing a small window and looked in to see Fred lying in a cage, looking around, as if to say, "Okay, now what?"

I got him all legal, and then, after about two minutes of going out of his mind when he saw me, took him outside to where there was real grass for him to inspect, and then home.

Dot, who had expressed concern about having a largish dog in the house, fell in love instantly, as I had hoped she might, and Fred returned her affection in full.

BACK ON THE GUIDEBOOK-PUBLISHING TRAIL, we hit a very large snag. The British libel laws, which I had feared when publishing my yachting memoir, fell on us from a great height. All it took was for the owner of an inn in Cornwall to have his solicitor write a letter to my British publisher, threatening to sue to stop publication, because of my comments about their food. I hope the statute of limitations has run out over the decades since. This is what I said about them:

Where this otherwise well-run hotel stumbles and falls is on its food. At dinner, my fish course had the consistency of minced terrycloth, and the duckling was underfed and overcooked. It is the only place I have ever stayed where the principal source of conversation among the guests over after-dinner coffee was how terrible the food was. This is inexcusable in a place of quality. I can only suggest that you ask for a room rate which does not include lunch and dinner, then dine at one of the restaurants down the street.

The owner took umbrage at this. Can you imagine? Actually, other reviewers had said as much, and worse. I spoke with Johnny Apple, the London correspondent of the *New York Times* who often wrote about food and wine, and he held much the same opinion and offered to testify for me in court, if necessary.

It would not be necessary, because my British publisher folded like a fan and pulped 4,500 copies. They explained that, in order to defend against a lawsuit, I would have to find all the guests who had dined there the same evening I did and have them testify.

The book was published in the United States and did pretty well, but these days, you would have to seek out a very good used bookstore to find a copy, or attend a great many garage sales.

THAT OUT OF THE WAY, I was confronted, once again, with the necessity, if I wished to become a bestselling novelist, of actually writing one, and I was only a hundred pages into it. I think there is no more daunting task for a would-be author than finishing it.

I traveled to New York in search of an agent. My editor and publisher, Eric Swenson, suggested several names, and I spoke to all of them, but only one, Peter Shephard, of Harold Ober Associates, would accept a new client whose credentials consisted of only a yachting memoir and a hundred pages of a novel. I signed with his agency.

Harold Ober Associates was an old-line firm representing many famous authors, among them F. Scott Fitzgerald, Ernest Hemingway (I think), and Agatha Christie, whose monumental backlist was said to keep the agency afloat. Please note that most of their authors were, like the aforementioned three, dead.

Peter Shephard was a kind, deliberate, and amusing man who seemed to think my novel had promise. He also thought that my novel *Chiefs*, being, essentially, three novellas sharing a common plot thread, might sell, but that beyond hardcover, not so well. He thought I might expect a modest paperback sale, but not a sale of movie or TV rights. At my insistence, he sent my hundred completed pages and a synopsis around to a number of publishers, none of whom found it acceptable. I still have a letter somewhere from Michael Korda, the editor-in-chief of Simon & Schuster, in which he explained that he didn't like the characters and didn't like the plot. In fact, he cordially despised the whole effort.

Never mind. I had to produce pages. Peter had a summer home in St. James, New York, on the north shore of Long Island, and he very kindly offered me the place. He and his family came out on weekends, but I would find the peace and quiet I needed to work. At home, Dot kept saying, "Stuart, why don't you get a *job?*" It is the refrain of writers' mothers everywhere.

So, Fred and I made the long drive from Manchester to Long Island and settled in. I liked the peace and quiet and began producing. Fred liked the woodlands around the house. Once I couldn't find him, and I followed the sound of children's voices at play to a school, where Fred was joining in the fun. After that, if he disappeared, I went looking for children.

By the end of my time there I had another hundred pages done. On the way south I stopped in New York and had lunch with Eric Swenson, who was getting his yacht ready for the Bermuda Race, which he sailed every year. I made a proposal: "Why don't you take *Toscana* across the Atlantic and do the Cowes Week Regatta and the Fastnet Race? I'll sail her over, and you can sail her back." Eric was immediately interested, and I left New York with another new adventure bouncing around inside my skull.

52

I arrived in London, en route to Cowes, on the Isle of Wight, and stopped overnight at the Royal Ocean Racing Club, something I had joined while living in Ireland. It provided a bed, a bath, and a bar, so it met my needs.

On the way in from the airport a violent thunderstorm arose, with huge raindrops hammering on the roof of the cab, its driver trying vainly to clear the windshield and muttering, over and over, "Jesus! Jesus!" I believe it was a prayer, not an oath.

When I finally arrived in Cowes I left my luggage at the place Eric Swenson had rented for his crew and went in search of his yacht. *Toscana*, when I found her, had rigging damage, a hole in the hull from a collision with a larger yacht the day before, and her pulpit was twisted like a pretzel. I found Eric who was worried and, uncharacteristically, angry. He put me in charge of the pulpit, which is a contrivance of stainless-steel tubing at the front of the boat, where a crewman changing sails can hang on for dear life. So, here I was, in a port I didn't know, looking for replacement or repair of something custom-made in a Finnish boatyard, at least a thousand miles away. No one in Cowes had one on the shelf.

To my astonishment it took me only half an hour to find a grimy workshop, where its no less grimy owner took one look at it and said, "I can fix that." Before the day was out I was able to return a serviceable pulpit to Eric aboard the yacht. He ignored the bill for sixty pounds and handed the pulpit to someone to rebolt to the bow. It fit perfectly, and a good thing, too. We were about thirty-six hours from the starting gun.

That evening before the start of the race a few of us had dinner at the Royal Yacht Squadron, England's oldest and most venerated yacht club, whose titular admiral was Prince Philip, Duke of Edinburgh. Eric and I and John Rousmaniere, a writer of nonfiction with a specialty in yachting, were members of the New York Yacht Club, which gave us visiting rights. We were joined by a member of the Squadron and a most remarkable man, Captain John Coote, Royal Navy retired, who Eric had invited to be our navigator on the Fastnet Race.

Johnny Coote was an Australian-born former captain of a Royal Navy submarine, who had been destined for the admiralty but, instead, had been lured away by his sailing friend Max Aitken, the son and heir of Lord Beaverbrook, the Canadian-born press baron and wartime colleague of Winston Churchill, serving as Churchill's head of aircraft production, in the runup to the Battle of Britain.

Johnny was appointed Max Aitken's number two and effectively ran several newspapers. A smart, garrulous companion and a superb yachtsman, he would find us the Fastnet Rock, off the coast of southern Ireland and bring us home to Plymouth, in Devon, where the Fastnet Race, the culmination of the five-race program of the Admiral's Cup, held every other year, would finish.

Much whisky, wine, and port were consumed, and a fine dinner enjoyed that evening, but we were all aboard *Toscana* the following morning in time to drop our mooring and make our way to the start, an imaginary line from the Castle, home of the Squadron, to a point on the south coast of England, a couple of miles away.

The start of any yacht race is organized chaos to any non-sailing spectator, but it is sailed according to rigid—and rigidly enforced—rules and the object is for a yacht to cross the line ahead of and to windward of all the other yachts at the sound of the starting gun. That would be the case from any dinghy race to the giants of ocean racing, the maxi-yachts, were it a dozen or fifty. On this day, August 11, 1979, a fleet of three hundred and three yachts crossed the line, the start marked by the roar of a cannon from the Squadron's array of highly polished brass artillery pieces.

It was a historic day and, unknown to its participants, was about to become even more so.

53

We started fairly well—that is, no collisions or other disasters struck—and we were soon beating down the English Channel in a fairly fresh breeze. The crew was strong. Those aboard were Eric Swenson, owner and skipper; Captain John Coote, navigator; John Rousmaniere, writer (and our historian, as it turned out); a female cook; and four of Eric's regular crew back home, two of them female, were sailmakers and, for us, sail trimmers in the race. Then there was I, of whom Rousmaniere later said, "Even our least experienced ocean racer had done a single-handed transatlantic race."

We sailed all day and with each change of watch there was less wind to take us along. At dawn the following morning, we had left Land's End behind and were now becalmed on the edge of the Irish Sea. As the sun came up we could see dozens of yachts rocking slowly in a light swell, their sails flapping, all, like us, hoping for wind.

Johnny Coote told us that, in the old days in conditions like these, sailors would drive a knife into the mast. This was supposed to make wind, but we had an aluminum mast. Then, gradually, as the morning drifted by, the swell increased and a breeze came up. Quickly, too, and we were scrambling to get the sail plan right and get out of there. The wind continued to increase, and we worked to shorten sail, and by afternoon it was blowing thirty to forty knots, and the horizon ahead was dark.

We had not had a forecast that predicted this, and now had only one that included what we were experiencing.

By dark, we were carrying only a storm jib and a reefed staysail, and it was really blowing. All we could do was point as far upwind as we could get and hang on. Then, in a very short time, the wind changed directions and the seas became confused and wild. The Fastnet light eventually hove into view, and so, in lightning flashes, did the coast of Ireland. Shortly, we would be in position to tack for the light. Then we looked up to windward and saw a small yacht, perhaps thirty-five feet, chugging along on her engine, with a storm jib set to hold her steady. She would be exactly in our path if we tacked.

We waited, impatiently, for her to overtake us, slowing as much as we could, then I looked up and saw the coast of Ireland dead ahead, looking as if it were about to fall on us.

Johnny Coote took one look at it and said, "I should tack *now*, if I were you." And that's what we did, sailing below our course to avoid the smaller yacht.

At about four in the morning we were abeam of the Fastnet light and beginning to bear away toward England. The light, on its rocky little island, made for a stunning sight in that weather. Then we bore away and began to sail fast, leaving the Fastnet behind us.

My watch went below to dry out, get some soup and some sleep. Johnny Coote switched on the radio to get the Irish weather forecast, and as it came alive we heard the words of a newscaster saying ". . . two dead in the Fastnet race." Then the radio became garbled, off and on, but we picked up what we could. What we could pick up sounded awful. We couldn't figure out why people were dying. Everybody aboard had experienced weather like this at one time or another, and we were alive. As it turned out, the large number of smaller yachts in the race, slower than our boat, were having a hard time fighting their way to windward, back where we had come from.

Yachts were being dismasted or knocked down or rolled over in the steep waves. A yacht was found adrift, her crew and life raft gone, God knew where.

I remembered what an old salt of a yachtsman said to me in the bar of the Royal Ocean Racing Club, a couple of years before.

"If you're in a bad way and don't know whether to abandon ship and take to the life raft, do this. Set the raft in the cockpit, inflate it, and get into it. If the yacht sinks, you will still be afloat; if it doesn't, you'll still have a boat to sail when the worst is over." It would have been good advice for many in that race.

As daylight came up we were sailing fast on a broad reach, and on course. And the seas, though large, had become more predictable. We passed yachts with no masts, with jury rigs set, doing the best they could. We passed *Morning Cloud*, the yacht belonging to Ted Heath, the former prime minister. She seemed to have been abandoned. We passed *Big Apple*, an Irish entrant with friends of mine aboard. Actually, they were no longer aboard. My friend Harold Cudmore told me later that, after considering the laws of salvage, they abandoned ship, but left a note stuck to the main hatch, saying "Gone for lunch; back soon." Apparently, an abandoned yacht was not subject to salvage if there was evidence that the crew intended to return to her.

Apple's rudder had broken, and when offered a helicopter ride, the crew, which included her designer and my friend Ron Holland, decided to accept and come back later for her. Her owner, Hugh Coveny, when he got back to land, chartered a fishing boat, found her, and towed her into port for repairs.

There were a number of boats, mostly those designed by Ron Holland, whose rudders broke, and eventually, the trouble was traced to faulty materials manufactured by DuPont.

As we got further down the course, the wind dropped, though we still had a thirty-foot sea behind us. We heard on the radio that Ted Turner had won the race in *American Eagle*, his maxi-rater. Being large and fast, she had been in position to take the best advantage of the high winds. A friend of mine, Spud Spedding, had been her navigator, and I asked him if rumors were true that, at times, they had been making twenty-six knots downwind. "It was *twenty-nine* knots," he replied.

We also learned that nineteen people had died in the race, fifteen competitors and four "observers," who had sailed out into the Irish Sea in a trimaran to watch the racing. Before we got to Plymouth, John Rousmaniere had already made a deal with Eric to publish a book about the race. He had interviewed all of us, and as soon as we set foot on land, he was roaming the marina, looking for officials and more competitors for their accounts. The resulting book would be called *Fastnet Force Ten*, and I believe it is still available.

When we finally made Plymouth, the town was jammed with members of the international press. I had promised to phone in a report to the *Atlanta Journal-Constitution* sports department, and I waited two hours in line for a pay phone to make the call.

When I returned to Atlanta, someone had saved a clipping of my report. The headline read:

NINETEEN DEAD IN FASTNET RACE.
TED TURNER SAFE.

54

I had thought that I would get the crew for the return trip together and set sail after a few days, but there were repairs to be made, and the boatyards were jammed with yachts needing their attention. It looked like some weeks before we could depart. *Toscana* found a place in line at a good yard in Falmouth, a few miles west of Plymouth. I went home to Atlanta and wrote an account of the race for the international edition of *Life* magazine.

I also got some pages of the novel written. My agent had had an offer from W. W. Norton: an advance of $7,500. It was smaller than I would have liked, and Norton had not published a novel for some years, not even having a fiction list in their catalog, but the offer provided me with something I had not anticipated: a publisher was willing to pay actual money for my work. I signed and accepted a third of the advance. This turned out to be a remarkable stimulus.

FINALLY, THE CALL CAME THAT *Toscana* was ready to sail. I returned to England and Falmouth, where Eric had already chosen a crew.

The best of them was a young man named Dale, who was highly experienced and, just as important, could repair almost anything on a boat. He turned out to be cheerful and efficient, even in a blow. His girlfriend came along as cook. We had two others, as well, one of them a son, I think, of one of Johnny Coote's friends. His name was Mark, and he was Australian, and this was to become a problem. Johnny was going to join us in the Canary Islands as "guest navigator." This made three aboard: besides me, Dale wanted to navigate, too. I told him that was fine, if he brought his own charts, instead of marking up mine, and that if we disagreed on something, my opinion, as captain, would carry the day. He agreed, and that went pretty well. Of course, I ceded that role to Johnny, once he was aboard.

We finally departed Falmouth on the first day of autumn, in the most glorious weather, with the wind putting us on a close reach, the fastest point of sailing without a spinnaker. We sailed comfortably and fast for three days. I should mention that, in those days, three days was about as much of a weather forecast as one could get, so we were chagrined when, after the third day, everything went to hell, with forty knots of wind on the nose, gusting sixty at times. When it was unchanged the next day, we turned to an expensive piece of equipment called a Weatherfax that Eric had bought for the transatlantic. Once we figured it out, it would call a phone number somewhere and download a weather map for the day, much the sort of thing you see daily in the *New York Times* and other newspapers.

When we finally got a printout, we were stunned: we were in a depression that covered the entire eastern half of the North Atlantic Ocean, and there was nowhere to go. Our choices were: return to England; sail to France, crossing the Bay of Biscay, a notoriously difficult stretch of water between us and the French coast that got increasingly shallow on approach, making for violent seas in bad weather; or bash on to our first destination,

Horta, in the Azores. I made the decision to bash on to Horta. It would normally have been a ten-day sail from England, and we already had four in the bank. Instead, it was another ten days from our position, all of it straight into the wind and at the same forty to sixty knots. All we could do was to sit tight, sail the yacht, reef or shorten sail as necessary, and sleep in wet clothes. On our last day out, the weather suddenly cleared, and we sailed under sunny skies, close-reaching again.

THERE ARE FEW MORE SATISFYING experiences than looking ahead and shouting "Land, ho!" after a hard passage, and on that day the peak of Mount Pico, across a channel from Horta, showed above the horizon and got higher as we approached. We set about making the boat livable again and viewable for visitors, too. It was a mess after our ten-day slog.

Horta is the most welcoming port for yachtsmen that I know, and every new arrival is received with shouts and waves from the others moored along the stone quay.

Peter's Sports Bar was in full swing, as usual, as yachties stopped by to get their mail and hoist a few, as well. We got a new diode for a failing battery and worked our way through a long squawk list. Our spirits were further lifted by the arrival of another Swan 47, this one brand-new and being delivered from the factory by a crew of Swedish blondes, most of them female and beautiful. Our crews mingled happily, and we learned that their route was the same as ours: from Horta to Madiera, then the Canaries, then south to the trade winds and across the Atlantic. We would race our boats, we decided.

SOON, WE WERE OFF AGAIN, and the Swedish yacht took an immediate lead. Finally, it occurred that our bottom was populated by barnacles and other sea life, whereas theirs was clean. They were about a knot faster.

We did catch up to them once, when they were becalmed. We drifted next to them for a few hours and had a swim. It is daunting to be swimming when the bottom is a couple of thousand feet below us, and we were careful not to let the wind come up and sail our boats away without us.

I had read an article in a yachting publication about a crew of ten, who left their large yacht for a swim, and when they were ready to leave, they could not get back aboard. No one had thought to leave a line in the water for that purpose. They were later found, all floating face-down, by another yacht.

The wind came up, and we sailed on for Madiera.

55

We sailed into the beautiful harbor at Funchal, on Madiera, where my friend Judy Tabb, from Atlanta, met us by previous arrangement, the plan being for her to finish the crossing with us.

We moved into a good hotel, had a hot bath and a good sleep, and dined on restaurant food, all of which was good for the soul.

Judy was having problems, though. She had left a ten-year-old daughter with friends in Atlanta, and the child was very unhappy about that. She seemed to think that her mother would die at sea, and no amount of reassurance was sufficient to calm her fears. As a result, after a number of shouting, screaming phone calls, Judy flew back to Atlanta while we continued to the Canary Islands.

As we approached the Canaries I learned for the first time from our Australian crew, Mark, that some sort of diplomatic impasse had developed between his country and Spain, which owned the Canaries, and that Spain, as a result, had banned all travelers from Australia. I wondered why this had not been mentioned to me sooner, and I couldn't get a sensible answer out of Mark, even when I explained to him that when we cleared customs inbound, and he couldn't present an acceptable passport, that he could well be arrested and jailed until the diplomatic seas had calmed. He shrugged that off.

Then I explained that if he were found aboard the yacht the authorities would be within their rights to impound the boat and jail us all for smuggling in an illegal immigrant. He shrugged that off, too.

Finally, I told him that as soon as we moored he was to disappear from the yacht until we were ready to sail again. I didn't want to see him in the bars ashore. He agreed to that, then did not keep his word. As soon as the customs boat had left us, he appeared on board again. I confined him to the yacht and in daylight hours, below decks, and pointed out that we had to have the bottom cleaned and a repair made to the mast, so it could be a few days.

It was all so much hot air to him. I would have been happy to turn him in as a stowaway, but I knew him well enough by then to know he would rat us out. So, I was stuck with him until we reached Antigua, our final destination.

CAPTAIN JOHN COOTE MET US in the Canaries, and we sailed down to Puerto Rico, our last stop before our crossing. We had lunch at a local restaurant, while Johnny gave us our routing; since there was little wind, we would motor due south, until we picked up the trade winds, which blow a steady breeze around the planet, from east to west. Then we would turn west, put up a lot of sail, and continue for seventeen hundred miles, until we reached our final destination in Antigua, in the Caribbean. We would abandon the yacht there, and Eric and some friends would take her and sail in Antigua Week, an annual regatta, then home to Connecticut. Johnny would be our navigator and, by right of his vast experience, de facto skipper.

We did exactly that: the trades winds appeared where they

were supposed to, and we were off for two weeks of fast, down-wind sailing, with hot meals not being spilled, and sleeping in dry clothes.

Soon, our cook announced that she would be teaching herself to play the flute in her spare time. If you have ever lived in a house where a child was being taught an instrument you will know what the experience is like. When the student is also the teacher, it is worse: endless scales, rough versions of simple tunes, many mistakes, which require starting over, never any improvement. I thought often of pretending to stumble and kicking the instrument overboard, but I never did.

We had fair weather, except for one lengthy squall that took us by surprise and required sail changes. I think it was the only time we got wet, and the flute went silent until it was over.

Antigua got nearer and, in our minds, bigger as we approached. Two weeks after finding the trades, we made our landfall in the middle of the night, and Johnny decided we should not enter a strange harbor at night, so we simply sailed up and down outside English Harbour until daylight came, then entered the harbor and berthed at a prearranged marina.

Everyone got packed up. Then the boat was thoroughly cleaned and we scattered ashore for errands and sightseeing. English Harbour is a charming village, with an atmospheric inn, where I would berth for the night, before catching my plane to Miami, thence to Atlanta.

Before I left the yacht, I had one more duty. I waited for a quiet moment, then I took Mark aside and explained that I was going ashore for a while, and when I returned, I wanted him gone from the yacht. Suddenly, he wanted to make friends. I told him, and I meant it, that if I returned to the yacht and found him there, I would throw him bodily overboard. And I meant it.

I think I finally got through to him, because when I returned, he was gone, and I never saw him again.

I had a good dinner with Johnny at the inn, got a night's sleep, and caught my plane the following morning. That night I slept in my own bed.

IT WAS THE AUTUMN OF '78, and I had a phone call from my half sister, Sharon Lee. I had met her only twice: once as an infant on my visit to California, when I was twelve. And then she came to see me in New York when she was sixteen.

Now she had a ten-year-old son—she hadn't married his father—and she wanted to come to Atlanta to get her son out of the culture in their neighborhood and to study for a nursing degree. I encouraged her to come.

I had started looking for a house, and I found one that would suit me and had room for an apartment for Sharon and Robbie on the lower floor. I had never owned a house before, and Judy guided me through the process. Because of my time on duty with the ANG, I was eligible for a VA mortgage, which meant no down payment and a maximum of one hundred thousand dollars.

I found a little contemporary house in a ravine in northwest Atlanta, on the edge of Buckhead, and bought it for ninety-five thousand dollars, then spent the other five thousand on building a bath and kitchen and two bedrooms downstairs.

We moved in at Christmastime 1979.

At the suggestion of my friends Nick Taylor and Barbara Nevins, I hired a firm called Moon Brothers. They were not named Moon and were not brothers: they were architect/builders/craftsmen, and they designed and built a dressing room for me in a former closet and turned a spare room into my first study, with a high wall of bookcases and a ladder on wheels, a computer station, and an Eames lounge chair where I could sit and read. The house had a living room, dining area, and kitchen, and upstairs, a master bedroom with a large bathroom and Jacuzzi and a guest room and bath.

Sharon and Robbie were comfortable in their apartment, and we got Robbie into a good private school nearby, within walking distance. I got my first and only experience in being a surrogate father. Robbie and Fred bonded instantly, and Fred went to school with Robbie every day.

One day I looked out the window and saw Robbie walking home, and Fred was carrying his baseball glove.

"He likes carrying things," Robbie explained.

Fred liked to roam the neighborhood and visit kitchens, and he was welcome everywhere. At Christmastime our mailbox filled with gifts for him, from bones to a Frisbee. Then Fred ran afoul of the law.

He was taking a nap in the sun one day on a neighbor's front lawn, when the dogcatcher arrived. "Excuse me, lady," he said to my neighbor, "is this your dog?"

"No," she said, "but he is here at my invitation."

"Sorry, lady, I gotta run him in."

Pretty soon, he was a three-time loser. Each bust involved a drive all the way across Greater Atlanta to the pound. Something had to be done.

So, I did what writers do: I wrote an op-ed piece for the *Atlanta Journal-Constitution* about my dog and his legal problems. This got more mail, they told me, than any other op-ed piece on any subject. It also started an op-ed debate with the head of the county council, which ended in a draw.

After that, Fred didn't get arrested anymore.

56

I had been thinking about the novel on the crossing, and I thought I saw a way forward. Since I had spent an entire year of high school learning to type, I could do it rapidly. What's more, I could think on the typewriter. I adopted what would become my method for working: I sat down and wrote, improvising the plot as I went, and at the end of about five pages I had a chapter.

The following day, I read what I had written the day before, made small changes, then wrote another chapter.

I had started my writing life on an office machine, in class, then, in college, I bought one of the first Smith-Corona electric portables, then later, a newer model that included a self-correcting feature. Finally, I bought my first computer, something called a PolyMorphic, which means "many-shaped" in Greek, the manual said. It had a small hard drive and three 5¼-inch floppies, for copying and backing up and had cost the earth: five thousand dollars. The daisy-wheel printer had cost nearly as much.

As I got near the end, Eric told me he would come to Atlanta and pick up the manuscript, so I had a hard deadline facing me now. I wrote faster. One day, I wrote thirty-five pages, a record for me. Then, on my last day, I wrote sixty-seven pages, and in spite of the speed, I thought they were some of the best writing in the book.

The novel now resided on my hard disk and on a stack of ten floppy disks. It took an entire day to print the thing on computer paper that made a carbon copy, so I had two stacks of manuscript.

Eric arrived, sat down, and read it in twenty-four hours. When he was done he had a few small suggestions, most of which I took. One of them was, I remember, my use of real people under their own names as characters, like Franklin D. Roosevelt. I held firm on that argument. He also wasn't entirely happy with some of the cinematic techniques I had used, such as cutting back and forth between scenes. I softened that a bit but clung to it.

Eric took the manuscript and flew back to New York. A couple of days later, I got a phone call from Starr Lawrence, an editor at Norton. "Good read," he said, and that was the extent of his praise. "You need an opening scene for the paperback market that gets it started faster. It's a little slow in the beginning."

I told him about a scene I had thought of. "I like it," I said, "but I don't know how to work it into the timeline."

"Forget the timeline," he said. "Just write it, stick it up front, then start the novel."

It was the best, not to say the only, advice I got for the book. I sent him the new chapter, labeled "Prologue," and he was happy.

My agent, Peter Shephard, was not happy. He was not critical, exactly, but he didn't sound enthusiastic. He repeated his earlier prediction: "I think it will fetch a modest paperback sale, but no movie or TV rights."

I mentioned an Irwin Shaw novel, *Rich Man, Poor Man*, that had been made into a multipart television film, the first miniseries.

"No," he said.

I hung up depressed. If my agent was not enthusiastic, what

would everyone else think? I pondered this for several days and didn't feel better. Then something good happened: I read an excerpt in the *New Yorker* from a book called *The Blockbuster Complex*, by Thomas Whiteside, about recent changes in the publishing industry, and the excerpt included a longish interview with a man named Morton L. Janklow, an attorney and literary agent of whom I had never heard. I was rapt. Janklow's opinions about publishing were what I had already come to believe.

I called the only person I knew in New York publishing, outside my publisher and agent, my old and good friend from New York and London, Susan Heath, who was now literary editor of the *Saturday Review*. I asked her if she knew an agent called Morton L. Janklow.

"Sure," she said, "I know him well. I think he's the best agent in New York."

"I've written a novel. Will you introduce me to him?" Susan was properly cautious.

"Send me the manuscript," she said.

I FedExed her the manuscript.

A couple of days later she called. "I think it's terrific," she said. That was one of the words I had wanted most to hear. "I'll send it to him," she said.

A few days after that, Morton L. Janklow was on the phone. "I've read some of it, but I'm very busy right now, so I gave it to one of my partners to read. He is rapt. I'd like to represent you."

I managed not to yell "YES!" and made a date to meet with him in New York. I asked Judy Tabb (she of the missed transatlantic crossing) to come with me. Judy didn't know anything about publishing, but she was very smart, my lawyer, and I wanted her opinion about all this.

A couple of days later we sat down with Mort Janklow and his principal associate, Anne Sibbald, a British transplant. I asked Mort every question I could think of, and Judy had a few, too. And he answered, as Mort always does, with machine-gun rapidity. I told him that I had sold the book to Norton.

"How much did you get?" he asked.

"Seventy-five hundred dollars."

"I'd have gotten you a hundred thousand," he said.

I told him I also had an agent.

"I know him," Mort said but didn't offer an opinion.

"I'll have to speak to him," I said.

WHEN I GOT HOME, I called Peter Shephard with a heavy heart. I had met him at a time when I desperately needed encouragement, and he had encouraged me. He had been very kind to me, lending me his summer house when I needed solitude to work. I explained the situation to him as plainly and simply as I could, then told him I wanted out of my contract with Harold Ober Associates. As a settlement, I offered him ten thousand dollars that I didn't have and didn't know where to find.

"I'll speak to my people and get back to you," he said.

A half hour later, Peter called back. "I've spoken to everybody here, and we've agreed to let you go. But we don't want your money."

I thanked him profusely and hung up, overwhelmed with relief. Now I was represented by the best literary agent in New York or anywhere else.

And I didn't owe anybody ten thousand dollars.

57

$\mathbf{M}$ort Janklow called. "How much do you want for the paperback rights?" he asked.

"It's the first time I've ever been asked that question," I said. "I have no idea."

"How does a hundred thousand dollars sound?"

I remembered my friend Pat Conroy told me that, when his agent asked him that question, he replied, "It sounds fine, but I don't think I can raise that kind of money."

"That sounds fine," I replied to Mort.

"Your contract with Norton specifies that they handle the reprint rights," he said. "You'll have to get their permission for me to do it for them."

I called Eric Swenson and told him what Mort had said. "That sounds just fine to me," he replied. "Tell him to go ahead."

I called Mort back and told him the news.

"Good. I know just the guy at Bantam who's looking for a good first novel. I'll get back to you." He hung up.

Mort called back the next day and said, "They love the book.

They offered two hundred thousand dollars for the reprint rights, but I got them up to two hundred fifty thousand dollars."

I was nearly speechless. "I can live with that," I said.

He laughed.

"Do you think we can get a miniseries out of this?"

"I've already sent it to Bill Haber at CAA. If anybody can do it, he can. On the East Coast, I know every publisher and editor, but not on the West Coast. CAA handles everything out there for us, and we split the commissions."

I hung up and started to find out what CAA was. It was Creative Arts Agency, the hottest talent agency in Los Angeles, famous for packaging their clients' work and casting it from their talent list. I waited.

A couple of weeks went by, then Mort called. (I was learning that Mort called when there was good news; more pedestrian information was passed along by his associate, Anne Sibbald.) "We've got an offer from Highgate Pictures for one hundred twenty thousand dollars for a six-hour miniseries for CBS TV. It's a good deal. I think you should take it."

"I'll take it," I replied.

FINALLY, *CHIEFS* WAS PUBLISHED BY W. W. Norton in the spring of 1981. I got a call from Eric, who said that they had had word from sources at the *New York Times* that the book was going to get a major review in the *New York Times Book Review*. They had no way of knowing whether it was favorable, but, he said, "They don't normally give first novels a major review just to pan them."

I was thrilled, of course, and I looked forward to the publishing date. The pub date came and went, and there was no review of any kind of *Chiefs* in the *Times*. Eric did some digging and reported back that the *Book Review* had lost some ad pages recently and had cut back the number of reviews. The one of *Chiefs* was one of them. We never learned who wrote the review, or if it was favorable. It was forty years ago, and I'd still like to know.

In the meantime, I had taken up flying. I had access to a Cessna 182 retractable through Judy's law firm, and after I got my license and instrument rating, I bought the airplane from the firm.

As soon as I was able, I moved up to a Beech Bonanza B-36 Turbo. It had more range and onboard oxygen for long, high flights.

IN EARLY 1983, I WAS at a party at someone's house who told me he was putting together a list of ten people to buy a château in the Loire Valley of France. The cost would be divided equally, and each owner would have his own bedroom. I was picking up another Porsche, a 944, at the factory and said I'd like to go and see the château.

I did so, and it was gorgeous. It was owned and had been renovated by an engineer—and was in immaculate condition. The rooms were beautifully decorated, and it was being sold furnished.

I drove on to England, thrilled at the prospect of being able to say, aloud, "I have a château in France."

While in England I drove down to the Isle of Wight to visit some friends from my London days, Dick and Maud Hedger, who lived weekends in a Jacobean mansion on a working farm. Dick had sold his advertising agency and had always had dreams of farming.

I told them about the château, and they reacted doubtfully. "There's no sailing in the Loire Valley," Dick said. "Why don't you let us find you something here?"

I said that sounded good and to call me if they found something special.

A COUPLE OF WEEKS LATER, I got a call from Dick Hedger. "We've found the house," he said. "It's on the waterfront, inside the main marina. It has three bedrooms, living room, dining, and kitchen and a large dock with a long pontoon, shared with the next door neighbor." The asking price was about the same as a share in the French château. I looked at my watch: "I'll be there the day after tomorrow," I said. If it worked, I could be in the house by the summer of '83.

THE HEDGERS DROVE ME INTO Cowes and showed me the house. It was on an extension of the High Street, at 15 Birmingham Road. On the ground floor were the master suite and a nice study with a fireplace; second floor was living room, dining room, kitchen, and a powder room; and the third floor had two bedrooms, a bath, and a little balcony overlooking the harbor. The view of Cowes Harbour from the living room was spectacular.

BY THE END OF THE day, we had a deal. A firm of builders was recommended to me, a man and his three sons. He gave me a good price for stripping the house back to its bones and putting in a whole new interior. I had the payment for the miniseries of *Chiefs* coming, so with a mortgage, I could swing it.

I called my solicitor from my London days and asked him to close the deal and arrange a mortgage. "I know the property well," he said. "The owner is my father-in-law."

I stuck around long enough to get some plans drawn for the redo, pick out some paints, etc., then I flew back to Atlanta for the winter, asking that the whole thing be done by my return in the summer.

———

SUDDENLY, IT OCCURRED TO ME that, having bought two houses, one of them abroad, I had not started a second novel, nor did I have an idea for one. I got to work on *Run Before the Wind*, which would be based on my experiences in the transatlantic race and my relationship with Mike and Lizzie McMullen.

THAT WINTER I ASSEMBLED A list of things I wanted to buy in the States and ship to Cowes. They included a large washer and dryer, an American refrigerator, dishwasher, and ice machine for the little bar in the living room. I also bought sheets, towels, and a lot of other things I knew where to find in the United States, but not in England. As the move-in date approached I called a moving company and arranged to ship everything there as household goods. I saved enough on lower American prices to pay for the shipping.

58

$\mathbb{A}$ long writers' strike in L.A. had delayed the start of production of the *Chiefs* miniseries until 1983, and now I got a lesson in how Hollywood casting gets done. Jeff Bridges had expressed a willingness to play Will Lee, the starring role, but it took so long to persuade the network that he was famous enough, that they lost him. I had my own ideas about casting, which I expressed freely, and they seemed to be considering them, but all choices had to be approved by the network, the producers, and the director.

I suggested Hal Holbrook for the banker, Hugh Holmes; Danny Glover, whom I had seen in *Master Harold and the Boys*, on Broadway, for Marshal Peters; and Cary Guffey, the young lad who had played the child who was kidnapped by aliens in *Close Encounters of the Third Kind*, for Will Lee as a boy. Also, Brad Davis, for the second of the three chiefs of police. The last three got the roles, but Charlton Heston was cast as Holmes. I thought that an interesting choice. I later sent him the tapes of my interview with Mr. Jim Peters, the model for Holmes, so that he could work on his accent, and I loaned him my gold pocket watch and chain for his costume.

I asked for a role as an FBI agent in part three, because it was the smallest role I would take and, I figured, the largest they would give me. I was told I'd have to come to New York and read for the part. Under protest, I flew up and read and was cast on the first try.

The other thing I wanted was for the Delano scenes to be shot in Manchester, the real site of what had happened. Instead, they were leaning toward Chester, South Carolina, which I had never heard of. My slogan was "Let's keep the Man in Manchester," but it didn't work. Chester had a more picturesque downtown and photographed better.

I WAS VISITING FRIENDS IN Hilton Head, and three of us squeezed into a Jaguar roadster and drove up to Chester, where production was in full swing. I met the director, Jerry London, and the producer, Martin Manulis, and, of course, Heston, who was a thoughtful and unassuming man, who liked to be called Chuck, saying that the only person ever to call him Charlton was his mother. He didn't have to be unassuming, since he was the biggest star on the project and was being paid a million dollars more than any actor had ever been paid for a television part, I was told. This was in 1983.

I WENT BACK TO CHESTER later to shoot my scene, and it worked out that I would be on my way to England to move into the Cowes House shortly after that. I had been seeing a ballet dancer in Atlanta and invited her to meet me in London.

On arrival in Chester, I watched a scene being filmed between Billy Dee Williams, who played the Black lead, Tucker Watts, and John Goodman, who played a police officer called Tub and who was, at the time, the skinniest I had ever seen him.

My big scene was with Billy Dee Williams, whose sobriquet was "The Black Clark Gable," a compliment to both of them, I think. I was playing the Agent in Charge of the Atlanta FBI field office, to whom the Black chief of police in Delano came for help in getting a federal search warrant. To my astonishment, Billy Dee was having trouble speaking his lines without stumbling, which required many retakes. I thought, This acting thing isn't so hard. After all, I was letter perfect, and the big movie star couldn't get out a line without screwing up.

Later, when I saw the episode on a big screen in New York, Billy Dee looked wonderful, and I looked like an idiot. I thought, Well, maybe there is something to this acting thing, after all.

I FINISHED MY SCENE, THEN got a cab to Charlotte, North Carolina, and a plane to New York. I had accepted an invitation from someone I saw occasionally in New York, Amanda Haynes, to spend the weekend at the Southampton home of her friends, Jack and Hillary Geary. We walked into their living room to find the premiere interior designer in America, Mark Hampton, spreading fabric over the sofas, which gave me an idea of the standard she was accustomed to.

I walked out to the pool later and discovered the actress Valerie Perrine disporting herself in a bikini. We chatted for a while, and she told me that she painted seriously, sitting in her California garden, naked, and wearing a pistol belt as she worked. I guess she didn't want to be disturbed.

We dined at the home of the head of one of the big New York auction houses, who later went to prison for some misdeeds there, and another evening at the restaurant of Jerry Della Femina, whom I had known while I was still a New York adman. Jerry seemed to be enjoying himself.

————

FIRST OF THE WEEK, I got on a plane for London where Lorenne, the ballerina, awaited me at the Connaught. I wondered what sort of room service bills she had been running up.

We went to the Harrods annual one-day sale, and I picked up some fireplace tools and a large TV for the Cowes bedroom. The Connaught rented a station wagon for me, which turned out to be a Mercedes. The TV wouldn't fit inside, so we had to strap it to the roof. The next day we set out for Cowes and made it without getting arrested for the TV.

We walked into the house, where all my goods from Atlanta had been delivered, but not to the proper rooms. The house had been completely stripped, but nothing at all had been installed or painted.

I rousted out the builders and told them I wanted a working bedroom and bath on the top floor by the cocktail hour. Then, while they installed plumbing and other stuff, Lorenne and I unpacked various boxes.

By six o'clock, we had a place to sleep and bathe, a sofa from which to enjoy the view of the harbor, and drinks with ice from the machine. (I like ice and tend to have multiple machines in a house, since one of them is always broken.) We went out to dinner, work to resume the following day.

By the following evening, the place looked as if someone lived there. All the furnishings had been distributed and the packing materials disposed of, and the master suite and its new bath were operational. It was almost like home.

Another month, and the place was painted, the bedrooms carpeted or wallpapered, and the new kitchen had been installed. It was as finished as it was going to get, until I bought more stuff.

My paneled study had been finished and my computer and printer installed there, so I had no excuse not to work.

59

As word got around, my friends who sailed started strolling in from the marina for a drink, and sometimes an overnight stay. I installed two berths and a shower in the basement, which opened onto the dock and could sometimes house a crew.

My friend Derek Aslet turned up one day for a drink with a friend named Roger Taylor. Since my tastes run to jazz and classical, it had to be explained to me that Roger was the lead guitarist for Queen, and what that was.

I VISITED THE ISLAND'S ANTIQUE shops, filling in the gaps in the house, like a dining table and chairs. One day I sailed in the Channel Race, to France and back, with a friend. I got back in time to attend a marine auction at the town hall in Cowes. I was powerfully thirsty and hit the punch bowl a little too hard. I saw an antique whalebone cane I liked, and a picture, and bid for both. When I picked them up, I discovered that I had bid for the wrong cane and a different picture. Never consume alcohol when you're thirsty, and if you do, never bid at auctions.

I had a drink one evening with my next-door neighbors John and Caroline Powers. Also, there was a cousin of one of them, who worked for Jaguar. My friend in Atlanta Judy Tabb had said she wanted one, but I couldn't find a new one at a dealer's; it had to be ordered way ahead of time. The cousin said they sometimes had a cancellation on an American-ordered car, and he'd ask around.

A week or so later, I got a call. Jaguar had had a cancellation: it was black with tan leather. I could pick it up at the factory whenever I liked.

The next day I took a train to London and another to Coventry, where Jags were made, then had a tour of the place. It was contained in a huge, galvanized steel shed, except for the upholstery shop, which was better housed.

I drove the car back to Cowes, taking my time and enjoying the ride, and when I got back to Atlanta and the car arrived, I reluctantly turned it over to Judy. I would have to marry her to get it back.

THERE WAS A VERY LARGE hiccup in my relationship with her, though. It was over, and she had moved in with another man. I cursed myself for not committing sooner, and had to wait for a year or so, until she tired of him, and I could reclaim the Jaguar, sort of.

The car had been built at the end of a period when Jags had been built with faults, and it developed a habit of sometimes refusing to start. The dealer would send over a mechanic, and when he turned the key, the car would start immediately. It took months before it was discovered that a small part in the electrical system needed replacing. The marriage was like that, too: fine at first, then not so much. As we approached our fifth year together, I remember telling her that we should have a silver wedding anniversary party because it *seemed* like twenty-five years. That didn't go down so well.

I believe that no one can ever understand what goes on in someone else's marriage, so I won't try to explain it. It was just over, except for the trial.

Judy wouldn't file for divorce, so finally, I had to. I had never been a party to a trial before, and I have but one memory of the daylong event. Judy, as my attorney, had always impressed upon me the importance of telling the truth on a loan application or a financial statement, as it was a crime not to.

To my surprise, when I was on the stand, her attorney produced a financial statement that I had signed for a loan some years before, listing an unspecified asset of fifty thousand dollars. I wracked my brain to remember what it was for but couldn't. Finally, I said, "I'm sorry, I can't remember that. I can only assume it was an act of optimism." The courtroom erupted in laughter. Everyone, including the judge and Judy's attorney, was laughing, but not Judy. The divorce was granted, and the settlement was a lot less than what I had already offered.

It was my first marriage, and I have always held that I married too young. I was only forty-seven.

Chiefs was nominated for the Edgar Allen Poe Award in 1982, and at the gala I met Steven Bochco and his wife, Barbara Bosson. Steven was up for an Edgar, too, for *Hill Street Blues*, and we both won—I for best first novel—and the Bochcos offered me a lift in their limo to the after-event party for the winners. We spent most of the evening talking to each other, and they asked me to call them for dinner when I was next in L.A. They also mentioned that they had a house in Santa Fe.

Judy and I visited Santa Fe late in the marriage, with my good friends Mark and Winanne Sutherland. The Bochcos were the only people I knew there, and I called Steven for hotel and restaurant suggestions. Steven insisted that we stay at their house, which went unused for most of the year, and I accepted. Judy, a keen amateur photographer, rented a car and drove north to Abiquiú, near Georgia O'Keeffe's home, where she spent the whole time alone, photographing the landscape O'Keeffe had painted.

The Bochco house was marvelous, with mountaintop views and beautiful interior design. The three of us saw the town and even looked at some houses. I was sensing the end of the marriage, and when we finally separated, I packed up my car and shipped it to Santa Fe, then packed up my Beech Bonanza B-36 Turbo and flew it out there. I rented a small house off Canyon Road and began thinking about building a house.

In the meantime, I had a call from Mort Janklow, in New York. "I have another client in Santa Fe," he said. "I thought you might like to meet him."

"Love to."

His client was John Erlichman, of Watergate fame. This ought to be interesting, I thought.

It was even more interesting than I had thought. We met for lunch, along with his wife, Christy, and I found him to be charming and amusing. I suppose I had been expecting a younger Nixon.

Christy was a real estate agent, and when she heard I wanted to build, she took me out to see a twenty-five-acre plot off Tano Road. I looked at a plat and made an offer for half of it, which was accepted. The divorce wasn't final, then, but Judy graciously signed a quitclaim deed so that I could finance the project.

I HAD BEEN IN SANTA Fe for about six months when I met a young woman, Chris Connor (like the singer, but not) in the bookstore where she worked. We chatted amiably, and I thought about asking her out, but the age difference seemed too great.

A few days later, our carts collided at the grocery store,

and we resumed our conversation and agreed to spend Sunday together.

I flew her up to Monument Valley for some sightseeing, then we flew across the Grand Canyon and stopped for lunch and refueling. That night we dined at Santa Café, a restaurant the Bochcos had recommended. I was uncomfortable, being out with someone so much younger—twenty-two years younger. I felt that people were staring at us and talking about the geezer with the babe, and I decided I wouldn't call her again.

After a few days, she called me and invited me to dinner at her house. On that occasion, I began to get over the age problem, and we began seeing a lot of each other. Then she moved in with me. Soon my first year's lease was up, and we had to move to another house—larger, where we could start collecting furniture for the new house, when it was finished.

I found us a Labrador puppy in the paper, and Chris, who had been hesitant, fell in love with him before we got home. The second Fred had stayed with Judy, who had given him to me to replace Fred One, who had gone to his final reward, so this was my third Fred.

Labs are smart dogs. When he was still a tiny puppy Chris would take Fred in her arms when she went outside for the newspaper, then let him hold it in his mouth while they came inside and delivered it to me, in bed. Soon, Fred was going out for it alone, and Chris would carry him upstairs to me. As soon as he could manage the stairs, he made the whole trip every day.

Barbara Bosson had recommended a builder, Sharon Woods, who had gained some fame by coauthoring a popular book, *Santa Fe Style*, and by building a house on *This Old House*.

We had lunch to talk about it, and she asked if I had any ideas for the house. I produced a sheet off a legal pad on which I had drawn a childish floor plan, and in a matter of minutes, she had turned it into something that included everything I wanted. I hired her on the spot, and she gave her sketch to her in-house architect, who produced final plans.

We started the house in the spring of '92, and Sharon did something very smart: she assigned a full-time supervisor named C.J. who worked in a trailer on the site, and who kept the flow of subcontractors and materials moving. About two weeks after we started, Sharon produced a spreadsheet that listed every sub and the days they would work. It called for a move-in date of November 21.

As it turned out, we moved in on November 21, after a seven-month build, and the only thing left to do was to install the bookcases and cabinets built for my study, which took another week.

It was a six-thousand-square-foot house in a cruciform shape, a central hallway that went all the way through to a back terrace, and a wing that went to the kitchen and dining room, and another that went to the bedrooms. The master suite was a bedroom, sitting room with a kitchenette, two baths and two dressing rooms, and a study for Chris. There were two guest bedrooms. The main house consisted of my study and the living room, which had a bar concealed in what appeared to be a cabinet, and a kitchen and dining room. The central hallway hid two closets and a powder room.

The terrace at the rear of the house had stunning views of the Jemez Mountains, where Los Alamos is, and we had a pool, a pool house, and a tennis court. We also had a two-car garage and room out back for a guesthouse, already plumbed and wired, if I ever had enough money again to build it.

60

We had the summer ahead of us, and the house was well in hand, so, after a lot of preparations and a new engine for the Bonanza, we set off for Cowes, Isle of Wight. Aboard was everything from a long list of equipment required of single-engine aircraft departing Canadian territory to fly across the Atlantic, to include a pup tent, an axe, many pounds of food, mostly trail mix, sleeping bags, a life raft, an emergency radio for use on the raft, a high-frequency radio for long-distance transmissions, and so on. We flew to Bangor, Maine, where a two-hundred-gallon ferry fuel tank was installed, while we waited at the home of our friends Pegram and Ann Harrison on the island of Islesboro for a few days.

That accomplished, we flew to New Brunswick, Canada, to the city of Moncton, where we would be questioned on our qualifications and experience and where everything on the aircraft would have to be unloaded, inspected, then reloaded. The next morning, having satisfied the Canadians, we flew to Gander, Newfoundland, where we stayed the night and had dinner and, finally, filled our giant ferry tank. I had to do the pumping because the ground crew wouldn't touch it. It was raining steadily.

When I had finished I deplaned, and when I stepped off the foot rest behind the wing, the Bonanza sat on her ass, with her prop high in the air. And I had done the weight and balance calculations so carefully! However, at this point, the front seats hadn't been filled yet. I put a large suitcase under the tail to hold it up, and when we were in our seats, signaled to the ground crew to remove it and put it in the rear luggage compartment. The airplane behaved as she should.

I started the engine and ran through all the checklists carefully. I checked the stormscope to ascertain that we were facing only rain, not thunderstorms, then I called the tower on the high frequency radio, who confirmed that it was working. It was the last time it would do so.

I was cleared for takeoff, and I taxied onto the huge runway. Normally, the Bonanza took off without flaps, but I put fifteen degrees in to give us some extra lift. I ran the engine up to full power and took my feet off the brakes. We began to roll down the 12,000-foot runway. To my surprise, the airplane flew itself off the ground after a couple of thousand feet, and we were climbing. At 3,000 feet of altitude, we broke out of the clouds and were above the rain, with unlimited visibility.

My plan was to climb to 11,000 feet, the highest altitude that we could use with oxygen, then, when we were four hours from Shannon, climb to flight level 250 (25,000 feet), hoping for a tailwind, and to breathe oxygen. The airplane would not climb above 6,000 feet. Figuring that the reason was our heavy fuel load, I flew along for another hour or two, then I noticed a yellow light on the instrument panel. It was a warning that our flaps were still down. I slapped my forehead, retracted them, and climbed to 11,000 feet, and the airplane flew faster, as it should. I hoped that we had not burned too much fuel down low.

We were happy at the higher altitude until we flew into a cloud and started to pick up ice on the wings. This was not good. I called Gander on the HF radio and asked for lower. I got no response. Finally, I started a descent, looking for the bottom of the clouds. I found it at 6,000 feet, and the warmer air melted away the ice.

We got out the manual for the HF, which turned out to have been translated literally from the Japanese. Nothing we tried had worked. Finally, I called, "Any aircraft," on the VHF radio and got an immediate response from an airliner. I asked them to call Gander and explain my actions and situation.

The pilot came back, "They're annoyed that you didn't request an altitude change, but I made them understand your situation. Continue at your present altitude and call them when you can."

We did so, along the route, speaking to a couple more airliners, the corporate jet of Rolls-Royce, and a crop duster, who was ferrying in the opposite direction, his chemical tanks filled with fuel. I hoped he had a good book to read.

EVENTUALLY, THE CLOUDS LIFTED, AND we were able to climb back to 11,000, then finally, with Shannon four hours away, to FL 250, where we put on masks and breathed oxygen. Also, after flying over so much water, it was time to pass some. We had aboard a box of RestStops, originally created for hospital patients. You peed into a plastic cup, conveniently shaped for the female anatomy, then sealed it and discarded it upon landing. This worked fine for me; I had already used it a couple of times—but not for Chris, in spite of the fact that she had tested it at the kitchen table before departure. She just could not find a position in her seat that would allow the proper flow. After many tries, she settled back into her seat. "Let me know when we're at Shannon," she said.

WE WERE USING A VERY early version of the Global Positioning System, a unit designed for aircraft. There would, eventually, be something like twenty-four satellites working, but at the moment, there were fewer than half that number up, so there were gaps in our reception, while the unit employed dead reckoning to instruct the autopilot. The longest interval without GPS was twenty minutes, and we remained on course, so we were doing well. We knew our position and our ETA.

Finally, we had used our four-hour oxygen supply, and it was time to descend to an air-breathing altitude. We began to pick up airliners getting radio landing instructions for Shannon, and at the proper distance made contact with the tower, which instructed us to fly the instrument landing system for runway 36, then had nothing else to say. They had us on radar.

We landed safely, after ten hours and one minute of flying, thereby setting a record for a woman not using a toilet. Chris leapt out of the airplane to look for the ladies'. Unfortunately, the tower had directed us to a spot on the ramp a long way from the terminal, there to wait for the arrival of customs. Chris was not waiting. She was seeking relief when the customs car drove up.

We spent the night at a small hotel and pub near the airport and made phone calls to let our nearest and dearest know that we had found Europe. The following morning, we departed for England and stopped at Southampton Airport, a few miles from the Isle of Wight, to clear customs and immigration. An hour later, we landed on a grass airstrip near Sandown, on the Isle of Wight. A taxi ride, and we were home in Cowes.

The good news was that the house was perfect, as it should have been after ten years. Everything was installed and working, including paint, carpets, wallpaper, and what passed for satellite TV in those days—six channels, I think, one of them for movies.

The bad news was threefold: 1. There were no people of Chris's age for her to meet; 2. There was no shopping, unless you wanted to buy something to wear while sailing; and 3. Chris didn't sail.

I HAD CONTINUED TO USE the Squadron as my other club, and after a couple of years, my friend Giles Chichester called to ask if I would like to be proposed for membership. I would, I replied.

The process was informal, not conforming strictly to the rules in the handbook. Giles went to the commodore, then Sir John Nicholson, and asked what he thought about his proposing Stuart Woods for membership.

Sir John chewed on his pipe for a moment, then said, "Tell him to stop coming around so much." End of conversation.

Giles explained things, I stayed away from the Squadron for a year, then I was elected as a foreign member. Some years later, that category was changed to, simply, member, so I could vote in elections. The Squadron publishes a list in its annual handbook of members, arranged by length of membership. Prince Philip is member number one, of something over two thousand, having been elected in 1948. Enough members have died off that I am member number ninety-four. Since, at this writing, Prince Philip has passed away at the age of ninety-nine, I suppose I am member number ninety-three.

In August, with my friends Harold and Laurel Cudmore, who lived in Cowes, we flew to the south of France. The ferry tank had been uninstalled when we arrived on the island, and we returned two rear seats to service for the trip.

Harold is a high-level yachtsman who had sailed in the Olympics and had skippered a British America's Cup entry, and who now hired out to ambitious yacht owners who wanted to win races. "My job," Harold likes to say, "is to stand in the stern, look around and say, 'Tack now.'"

We landed at Cannes, rented a car, drove to Saint-Tropez, and spent much of a week watching the regatta and doing the things one did in Saint-Tropez, including getting naked, sort of, on Pineapple Beach.

The flight back was uneventful, which is the way you want it.

We were in Cowes for four months, and as time passed it became clear that I was going to have to choose between Cowes and Chris. I capitulated, put the house on the market, and sold it very quickly. We sold it furnished and packed and shipped the things we wanted to keep back to Santa Fe.

Now we had to get back across the Atlantic, and that meant re-installing the ferry tank. I put fifty gallons of extra fuel into it and we flew to Lisbon for a couple of nights, refueled, then headed west to Santa Maria, in the Azores, where we spent the night, got a good forecast from the weather station there, and took off the following morning for St. George, Newfoundland, a nonstop trip. It was slower going, but the distance was less than before, and we flew it in the same ten hours. Chris had devised a method of getting to her knees on her seat, facing aft, and her plumbing worked, a great relief to both of us.

We spent a night or two in St. George, then put some fuel in the ferry tank and flew, nonstop to Bangor, Maine, where U.S. Customs treated us as if we had arrived from another planet, putting us in a fenced-off area and taking two hours to clear us. After that, we had the ferry fuel tank removed and stored at the shop that had built and installed it. As far as I know, it is still there.

After an R&R stop in New York, we headed to Santa Fe and our new house. It was right on schedule, and we started planning our move.

While the house was finishing, Chris and I decided to get married, and she trotted out the calendar to pin me down. I chose May 1, because we were planning a mostly outdoor event, and we would be past winter by then.

We had a guest list of a hundred and twenty, which included people from coast to coast and from as far away as England and Ireland, and as the day approached we had rented tables set up around the pool and on the rear terrace. We went to bed on April 30, satisfied that everything had been done that could be done before the next day.

On the morning of May 1, we woke early and threw back the curtains to reveal a bright, sunny day—and six inches of snow, covering everything, including the tables and chairs out back. And there was the five miles of dirt road from my house to the main highway to consider.

The first thing to do was not to panic, and we managed that. People kept calling, asking if the wedding was still on. I replied yes, but indoors.

That afternoon, the caterer's truck skidded of Tano Road into a ditch and they and the truck were rescued by wedding guests. Chris's cousins from L.A. had driven to Santa Fe. They took one look at Tano Road, turned around and drove back to L.A. They didn't even call, and they were the only no-shows.

We had managed to get the parking area plowed, and the car valets hid vehicles everywhere. The jazz group showed up on time, and people began to arrive. Where would we be seating a hundred and twenty people? *Everywhere.* They spilled all over the house, even into the bedrooms, but we got them fed.

Fellow novelist Doug Preston had written a toast and borrowed Steven Bochco's glass of wine for the purpose. He whipped out several typed pages and began to read. About two pages in, Steven said to Doug, "I want my wine back," and the laughter shut it down.

It was a riotously fun evening, and finally, people began to drift out, still faced with the mud on Tano Road that had turned to ice. Everybody made it.

61

After moving in, we had to face the fact that we no longer had a second home. I had spent a few days in Key West, Florida, once, and had been charmed by it. There were a lot of writers living there, too, though they seemed to last only a few years before realizing how much they were drinking and then moving to drier climes.

We found a delightful little cottage at 3 Higgs Lane, off Elizabeth Street. We moved in, renovated inside and out, added a small swimming pool, and enjoyed ourselves. Our first couple of winters we had a house sitter, an actor named Rex Linn; we met while he was working on *Wyatt Earp*, the Kevin Costner film being shot at a movie village near Santa Fe. Then we found a woman who lived in Key West and was on the same schedule we were, so we just swapped houses for the season.

Back in Santa Fe, we lost Chris's father, Jim Connor, a former White House staffer under Gerald Ford. Jim was two years younger than I, but he developed a brain tumor, which was successfully removed. A couple of years later it recurred, and he died following surgery. He had become my best friend, and it was a great loss.

Jim's death cut a bond between Chris and Santa Fe, and she started talking about wanting to live in a green and pleasant place. She read an article in *W Magazine* about a village called Washington, Connecticut, in Litchfield County, and I agreed to have a look at it. I had some friends, William and Susan Kinsolving, who lived in a neighboring village, Bridgewater, so we stayed with them, and they introduced us to Carolyn Klemm, a local real estate agent.

Carolyn showed us a bunch of places, and I liked one very much. It was a shingle-style "cottage" called The Rocks, built in 1869 on a little over five acres, and I was besotted. Unfortunately, the owners wanted a lot more than we could afford. "Give it some time," Carolyn said, so we flew down to Key West. A few weeks later, out of the blue, I got a call from Carolyn. "The owners are getting a divorce," she said, "and they have to sell in order to divide the assets. I can get it for you at your price."

I was thunderstruck, but not so much so as to stop me from giving her the go-ahead. A phone call or two later, it was ours.

We packed up the Santa Fe House into two moving vans, sold the house quickly, and headed for Washington, Connecticut. We arrived in time for the closing, and so did one of our two moving vans, so we had to stay in Carolyn Klemm's guest room for a week, until the second van caught up with us.

The Rocks had been built by an architect called Ehrick Rossiter, who had designed twenty-seven other houses and public buildings in the village over the years. The Rocks was designed to be his own home, and he lived there until his death.

The rooms were large and many. The house was eight thousand square feet, and the cottage had another three thousand square feet and three apartments. We installed our Santa Fe housekeeper, Marlene Mullings, and her daughter, Carmen, a fourteen-year-old, there, and they were very comfortable.

There was a large swimming pool and a half dozen gardens

that Chris couldn't wait to get started on. We also had a tennis court, and I had a regular Saturday game with Dr. Paul Marks, my next-door neighbor in another Rossiter house.

My secretary from Santa Fe, Karen Copeland, and her husband, Bob, came east to help us get settled in. They stayed for nearly a year, then Karen hired me someone new, trained her, and went home to Santa Fe. Bob was an art dealer and spent his time visiting country auctions and shipping his buys west.

We had eight bedrooms, one of them with its own sitting room, and a study for each of us. Chris was working on her own novel when she wasn't gardening. For her birthday, I gave her a golf cart with a truck bed bolted onto the back, to carry her tools and fertilizer from garden to garden.

Washington was ninety miles from New York, convenient for us to go down for a night or two and some theater, but inconvenient for commuters, which was perfect. Most of our neighbors were arts-oriented couples who came up from the city for weekends, many of them celebrities. Everybody gave dinner parties, especially Carolyn Klemm, who during our first month there, introduced us to half the county at dinners.

I had moved up from the Bonanza to a Piper Malibu Mirage, which was pressurized and much faster, and we flew back to Key West when winter threatened, then back to Washington in the spring. It was ideal.

It got hot in the summer in Washington, though, and I have never liked heat, so we flew up to Maine and had a look around Islesboro for a cottage near our friends Pegram and Ann Harrison. Everything had eighteen rooms and no insulation, and I didn't want to get caught up in a million-dollar renovation. Then Chris read about the hiking trails on nearby Mount Desert (pronounced "Dessert") Island, so we had a look around there.

After four days of seeing everything, we had found nothing. Then our agent asked, "Would you consider building?"

We had had such a great building with Sharon Woods, in Santa Fe, that I immediately said, "Sure!"

He took us to two acres on Broad Cove, off Somes Sound, where the owners had built a guesthouse, but never got around to the main house.

Suddenly, I thought of the beach house we had designed for Vero Beach. It was to be a shingle-style house, and it suddenly occurred to me that it might fit on this property. I called Carol, and they came up the next day, brought our plans and measured the lot. "It fits just a foot inside the set-backs," Carol said. We flipped the plan to get the kitchen near the guesthouse, and it worked.

We spent the summer in the guesthouse, planning. Then during the winter, we had it gutted and replaced virtually everything.

In the meantime, Chris had decided she didn't like Key West anymore, so a new house hunt ensued. We ended up buying a golf cottage at a development called Orchid Island, in Vero Beach. We also bought some beachfront property in preparation for building. In the end, the builder who had given us an estimate on building tripled his price, so I sold the land but kept the plans our architect friends Carol Nelson and Harry de Polo had designed for the property.

When we got back to Maine in the summer, it was done, and it was time to start on the big house.

What we had bitten off was more than we had expected to chew.

62

In the meantime, Chris had said to me one day, "I can't get enough help to work all our gardens, and I'm exhausted. I think we should sell The Rocks and buy a pied-à-terre in New York. The Maine house is building, and we don't need two country houses."

It made sense, and we put it on the market. We sold the house to the Broadway and film producer Scott Rudin and his partner, John Barlow, and set about shopping for a smaller place in New York. We found it, but it was a co-op, and we had to go through the building's approval process, which included a background investigation and a meeting with the co-op board. We also had to give them a list of personal references.

Since I had not lived in New York since 1969, we had few local ones, and the broker said, "How about well-known people?"

Chris said she knew Dick Cheney, and she wrote to him.

This surprised me, but it turned out that as a sixteen-year-old, she had spent an election season living in a trailer with Dick and Lynne Cheney and taking care of their kids while Dick ran for Wyoming's only seat in Congress.

Cheney's secretary said he was in the Mediterranean on somebody's yacht, but she'd fax him our letter. The following day we got a fulsome reference from Mr. Cheney. When we met the co-op board, they all looked like Republicans, so I think his letter put us over the top.

One other thing: "You have a dog?"

"Yes, a yellow Lab named Fred."

"Does he bark?"

"Fred only barks at deer," I replied. "So unless you have a deer problem in the building, he'll be fine."

We were in.

Chris gave a lot of our furniture to her brother, a farmer in Vermont. We warehoused most of the rest, but managed to get the pied-à-terre furnished.

BACK TO MAINE. THE THING was, there was a building boom and a labor shortage. Our builders, the brothers Bill and Butch Haynes, would not advertise for help, saying that people they recruited that way couldn't pass the drug test, and they would only hire people they knew. This was admirable, unless the house they were building was yours.

A full crew was twelve people; we never had more than eight. The two brothers framed the house without other hands to help. The upshot was that the whole project, which was planned to take a year, a year and a half, took two and a half years. And because of our annual schedule, we were not present when the finish work was done on the big house.

By that time, Chris and I had been married for nine years, and there were signs of strain. Then one day she came to me and said, "I think the marriage is over, and we should get a divorce."

I tried not to look relieved and just said, "Okay."

WHEN TIME FINALLY CAME TO move into the Maine house, Chris wanted some things from it, so she took our housekeeper, Marlene, along, and they were there to receive our furniture. A week later I arrived and was ready to inspect the house. (I had bought back Chris's share of our real estate.) I grabbed a pad to take notes on what still remained to be done and toured the house with Chris. It was perfect. When I finished my tour, I had not a single note. The pots and china were in the kitchen, my clothes were in my dressing room, the pictures were hung, and all the books were in their bookcases. I couldn't believe it.

I SPENT THAT FIRST SUMMER there, with guests for company, and was very happy. I ordered a Hinckley 38 Convertible boat from them; they were fifteen minutes up the road, so I got to see it building. I put in a floating dock to receive her. She would be called *Indian Summer.*

THE MAINE HOUSE HAD TWO guest rooms, plus three bedrooms and two baths in the guesthouse, not to mention a two-car garage. There was a living room with a dining area, a large kitchen with a sitting room off that, a library/study for me and my books, and a master suite upstairs with two baths and dressing rooms, plus a kitchenette/laundry room. There was also a main-level screened porch and an upstairs deck off the master suite. Today, twenty years later, even with extensive improvements to the landscaping, it looks substantially the same.

THAT FALL, FREE FROM MARRIAGE, I sold the golf cottage in Vero Beach and moved back to Key West. Lynn Kaufelt, the wife of the writer David Kaufelt and the selling agent of my last house, found me a lovely place at 1011 South Street, one with a two-story living room and just enough space for a bachelor who liked having guests.

Finally, I was settled into my main and legal residence, Key West, with a summer house in Maine and a pied-à-terre for visits to New York.

MY WORK PLANS HAD CHANGED. I had been with Putnam publishers for some years, when my publisher, Ivan Held, had lunch with me. He seemed a little nervous, and I wondered if I was about to get fired or have the number of my publications reduced. I was writing two books a year now.

Finally, he spoke. "Stuart, would you consider writing three books a year?"

"Yes," I said without hesitation.

He looked surprised and relieved. What he didn't know was that I was working only two or three days a week, so I could increase that to five days a week and easily get another novel done. He also didn't know that I wrote a chapter—about five pages—at a sitting, so I could complete a novel in sixty working days. This was not rushing for me. I could write almost as fast as I could think, so the day after writing a chapter I would read it, make small corrections, and go on to the next chapter. I had a gift for holding the book in my head, so I didn't even reread the manuscript when I was done, I just sent it to my editor. I was, and have always been, lightly edited.

———

MY NET INCOME WAS INCREASING, so I did the logical thing: I bought another airplane, trading my Malibu Mirage for the same model, but with a jet engine installed, driving a propeller. This was a faster and more reliable airplane: a jet engine has only a dozen or so moving parts, whereas a piston engine has hundreds.

SOCIALLY, I SEEMED TO BE a serial monogamist, and my relationships seemed to last about a year.

I suppose that a man who ends up marrying four times is doomed to screw up badly at least once. I did, and with a woman I had known, if not well, for twenty years. Let's call her Betty.

But first, I have to tell you about Elaine's.

63

Elaine Kaufman was a woman from Queens who had spent most of her adult life in the restaurant business, working her way up the ladder from waitress to manager.

In fact, Elaine and I had spent a lot of evenings in the same room, without ever meeting. Back in the early sixties I started singing at the Surf Maid, a bar on Bleecker Street with a grand piano and a wonderful accompanist named Kenny Watts. There were a dozen or so regulars, ranging from talented amateurs (me) to failed professionals, a few of whom were terrific.

Elaine was the manager, but she spent her evenings behind the cash register, so we didn't meet. The owners, Harry and Grace, mingled with the customers, while Elaine made everything work. Eventually, she and a boyfriend got a lease on a building around the corner and opened their own place. After a few years they split up, and Elaine bought a building on Second Avenue between Eighty-Eighth and Eighty-Ninth Streets, fixed it up, and named it after herself.

One night, a bunch of writers came into the place, had dinner and a lot of drinks, and discovered that Elaine would give them charge accounts. Word spread.

Elaine, God bless her, loved writers. Oh, she liked actors and directors and, sometimes, producers, but writers were her favorites. The writers brought all those other people in, and before she knew it, she was running a saloon that was a temple for the arts. (She liked painters and sculptors, too.)

She opened in 1982, but although I had heard about the place, I wasn't living in New York, and I figured it was the kind of place where you had to know somebody to get a table.

I was living in Atlanta and single at the time, and I got a subscription to the Metropolitan Opera on alternate Friday nights. I would fly to New York on Thursday, have dinner with friends, go to the opera on Friday, have dinner with friends on Saturday and fly home on Sunday.

Then, one Thursday, my friends Dick and Shirley Clurman invited me to join them at a book party they were throwing for the son of their friends Bill and Pat Buckley. Christopher Buckley's first book, *Steaming to Bamboola*, was being published, and the party was held at Mortimer's, a hangout for the Upper East Side glitterati, and I went along and shook hands with a lot of people, among them an editor from Bantam, Esther Margolis, who had had a hand in the paperback publication of *Chiefs*, and Bill Buckley's long-time secretary, Frances Bronson.

The party began to wane around nine o'clock, so I went into the bar and asked for a dinner table. There was a wait for a table, and while I was doing that Esther and Frances came out of the party room and said, "If you're alone, would you like to come to Elaine's for dinner with us?"

I certainly would, and we had a rousing good time there. They introduced me to Elaine, who sat down and grilled me for a few minutes and apparently decided I was okay.

I went to the opera the following night, and back to Elaine's on Saturday evening. Elaine welcomed me warmly and sat me down at a table with a stranger. "I want you to meet another writer from the South," she said. "This is Winston Groom."

I sat down, and eventually our table filled with writers, and I had the time of my life.

Winston and I remained friends until his recent death at his home in Fairhope, Alabama.

I didn't see Winston as often as I would have liked, because he had an overwhelming fear of flying, the result of having been in two aircraft crashes when he was serving in the Seventh Cavalry in Vietnam.

On one occasion I learned that Winston and I were both appearing at a booksellers' convention in Amarillo, Texas, and I offered to fly him back to Santa Fe for a visit. It was a short flight, I told him, and not scary.

When I arrived at the convention, I stopped by his publisher's booth and asked where to find him. They replied that he had already left the convention. I completed my appearance and flew home to Santa Fe. I aimed for my house and waggled my wings in greeting, and as I did, I saw a white stretch limousine driving out Tano Road.

I landed and drove home, to find Winston waiting for me there. His publisher had given him the limo for a day, so he had commandeered it for the four-hour drive to Santa Fe. He spent a couple of days with us, then we drove him down to the depot in Lamy and put him on a train for Los Angeles.

There are dozens of friendships and events in my life that can be traced back to a dinner at Elaine's. When, during my divorce, I decided to move to Santa Fe, I ran into a friend at Elaine's, Ed Zuckerman, a show-runner on a TV series. "Oh," he said, when he heard the news, "if you're going to Santa Fe, you should look up another writer, Doug Preston, who lives there."

I called Doug shortly after my arrival, then met him and his then girlfriend, Christine, for lunch at a local restaurant. They were later married, and we are still friends. They live a couple of hours from me in Maine, in the summer, and they are the only friends I have who are willing to swim in the paralyzingly cold water off my dock.

I met my next wife at Elaine's, too, twenty years before we became maritally entangled. I remember what the director John Huston said in response to a question about how he would change his life if he had it to relive. "I would spend my money after I got it, rather than before, and I wouldn't marry my third wife." That is very close to my own view. I think we lasted about five months, most of it spent apart, before I filed for divorce. The less said about that, the better.

After Elaine and Elaine's were gone, there was a long period when, reflexively, I would nearly grab a cab before it hit me. I think it must be like the sensation experienced by an amputee, who can still feel the missing limb.

I would very much like to believe that there is now an Elaine's in the sky, filled with old friends, where a Knob Creek on the rocks awaits my arrival, and Elaine and I will sit down together once again for her osso buco.

64

Elaine liked people who ate, not just drank. On one occasion I and a half dozen other guys showed up in tuxedos after a dinner at our mutual club. It was late, and all we wanted was an after-dinner drink.

Elaine immediately spotted what was going on and was on us like a guard dog. "You goddammned rich guys come in here in your tuxedos and take up a table for eight, and all you order is a drink?"

We quickly ordered dessert and another drink.

A. E. Hotchner (known as Hotch) wrote the book on Elaine, literally. It's called *Everybody Comes to Elaine's*, and I recommend it to you. Hotch asked me and several other writers to contribute to it, and I did so with pleasure.

A couple of Elaine stories. At her well-attended memorial service, the police commissioner Bill Bratton, a regular at the restaurant, told of the day Rudolph Giuliani fired him (for the second time, I think). Giuliani came into his office on his last day and gave him the Key to the City. (Go figure.) Bill and his wife, Rikki

Klieman, had dinner at Elaine's later, and she spotted the box on the table. "What's that?" she asked.

"That's the Key to the City," Bill replied. "Giuliani gave it to me this afternoon."

Elaine opened the box and regarded the Key. "I'll bet the son-ofabitch has already changed the locks," she said.

ANOTHER: ELAINE HAD EXPERIMENTED FOR a short time with opening for lunch, but not many people came. During that period, the director Mike Nichols brought Jack Nicholson for lunch. The three of them were eating, and Nicholson looked around the room. "You're a little short of customers, aren't you?"

Elaine gave him her best withering gaze and asked, "You ever been to one of your movies in the afternoon?"

ELAINE PREFERRED MEN TO WOMEN, but she liked a few women, and usually, the ones I brought to dinner. Once I came in with somebody who didn't pass the test, whatever it was, and I immediately found myself dining in that area of the restaurant called "Siberia," far from the action. Thereafter, I chose my guests more carefully.

George Steinbrenner was a dear friend of Elaine's, and one evening, to my surprise, he asked to be introduced to me. "I'm a big fan," he said.

Not long afterward, Elaine invited me to go to a Yankees game with her. There were just the two of us, and her limo was met at the curb by a team official who escorted us up to Steinbrenner's private box, which was the size of an apartment, with a bar, dining facilities, and an outdoor reserved section of seats. There was hardly anyone there, but when I went outside to watch the game, there was only one other person in the reserved seats: Yogi Berra.

In September of 2019 I pitched for the Yankees—that is to say, I was invited to throw out the first ball. I had not thrown a baseball for about seventy years, and I had to try to learn all over again in my driveway. In Yankee Stadium, when I wound up and let go, I'm relieved to say that the ball bounced only once. Afterward, the catcher said to me, "You did well. You'd be surprised how many people don't even get it to the plate."

On that occasion, the Yankees threw in a private suite and dinner for thirty. I think Gay Talese had the best time of anybody. My friends were kind about my pitching performance: hardly anyone mentioned it.

I attended all sorts of events at Elaine's, book parties, birthday fests, weddings, but I think the best night of all was also the saddest. Elaine died in December of 2010. The restaurant struggled on under her manager, Diane, for a few more months, but in truth, there was no Elaine's without Elaine. However, the last night was a riot. The waiters packed in as many new tables as possible and put larger tops on the others. You had to walk on people to get to the restrooms. *Everybody* was there, and it was covered by all the newspapers, magazines, and TV news shows.

Elaine would have loved every minute of it.

65

For a few years I saw the widow of another writer, an airline captain, and a documentary film producer, for a year or so each. The widow, Suzanne, moved to Texas; the airline captain, another Suzanne, didn't want to give up her job for a more extended relationship. The third wife was a pothole in the road to happiness.

The producer, Sandy, and I had a grand time, traveling a lot. We actually circled the globe together, flying from New York to Hong Kong, where we both indulged ourselves in tailor-made clothing, then taking a cruise ship to Dubai, for twenty-eight days, stopping at eleven ports, then flying back to New York on the exquisite Emirates Air. Sandy didn't want to get off the airplane in New York. During that voyage she edited a film on her computer, and I wrote half a novel.

The relationship ended as I was preparing for a dinner party at home; she didn't give any reason, and I didn't ask for one. My view was that if a woman no longer wanted to spend her days and nights with me, I would not argue with her judgment. She stayed for dinner, and the evening was a good one.

NOT LONG AFTER THAT I was back in Key West, having dinner with my good friends Karl and Stephanie Walters, when I learned, to my surprise, that Stephanie had a sister, called Sissie Cooper. Three of them, in fact, but only one was a free woman. Figuring that a sister of Stephanie's couldn't be all bad, I asked her to arrange a blind date; she did, and the sister didn't show. We rescheduled, and she turned up, and the evening went swimmingly.

The following day I got a phone call. "This is Jeanmarie; I wanted to thank you for last night," a female voice said. I drew a blank. "You don't remember me? Stephanie had us to dinner."

"But your name is Sissie Cooper," I protested. "It was when I was a girl," she said. We got over that patch and arranged another dinner, then another and another. After a few weeks of this I invited her to move in with me. She hesitated. "You'll get half the dog," I offered, pointing at Fred. She accepted.

After a year's whirlwind romance, I made an honest woman of her—over the Christmas holiday when her three grown children were visiting.

We had a small wedding at home in Key West. Since, in Florida, any notary public can perform a marriage ceremony, I asked my lawyer, Jack Spottswood, to officiate.

There was a story about Jack. His secretary decided to marry a man Jack thought not good enough for her. He performed the ceremony, then filed away the marriage certificate. When things didn't work out, as Jack had feared, she came to him and asked him to get her a divorce. He reached into a desk drawer, pulled out the certificate, and tore it to pieces. "Congratulations," Jack said, "you're divorced." He had never filed it with the county.

When Jeanmarie heard this story, she went down to the county clerk's office, to be sure Jack had filed our certificate.

———

JEANMARIE IS, AMONG OTHER THINGS, intrepid.

After we had been married for a year or two, I asked her if she'd like to learn to fly. "Yes," she replied. She had never flown anything before.

Twenty months later she qualified as a single pilot of my jet airplane, a Citation M2, and we began swapping seats on every other flight. When she was flying, I would sit in a rear seat and read while wearing a headset that allowed communications with the cockpit. Now and then she would ask something like: "I'm headed for the wrong runway. What do I do?"

"Handle it," I would reply, and she always did. I stopped flying entirely when, on every flight, I got a free flying lesson— just as, whenever I'm at the wheel of the car, I get a free driving lesson.

As I write this, we've lasted for nine years, one living in sin, which was fun, and eight married to each other. Soon, I'll have a new record as a husband.

66

We enjoyed having the New York apartment for visits to the city, and I was always careful to characterize it as the pied-à-terre. Then I gave an interview to the *Wall Street Journal*. The writer was a stringer, not a staffer, and before we began, I explained to her the nature and use of the apartment and asked her to be sure that, when she wrote her article, not to characterize it as a residence or home. She made a note and continued. When I read the piece, I was appalled at her handling of the subject.

Some time passed before I got a call from my accountant saying that the New York State tax authorities were questioning my real estate presence in the city. We gave them a full explanation and, eventually, every piece of paper relating to the apartment.

Finally, after a couple of years of wrangling, we had a face-to-face meeting, during which they asked me all the questions they had previously put in writing. I answered them all truthfully.

I should explain that my life is scattered all over the place. I have my legal residence in Key West and vacation houses in Santa Fe and Maine. Recently we bought a vacation house in Connecticut, where I lived in the nineties, and put the Santa Fe place on the market. God willing, that will have sold by the time you read this.

My secretary lives and works in Santa Fe; my principal bankers are in North Palm Beach, Florida; I have doctors, dentists, and chiropractors in Maine and Florida and an attorney in Florida; I have a dermatologist and an accountant in New York City. I established legal residence in Florida in 1993 and have a notarized document to prove it. I have not been a resident of New York State since December 31, 1969. The next day I moved to London. I owned a vacation house on the Isle of Wight in England for ten years, and rented one in Ireland for nearly four years.

After putting all of that in a blender and straining the result, New York State determined that I was a New York resident. Go figure. After three years of arguing, I was getting ready to sue them, when my attorney suggested that it would be much cheaper to buy them off. I paid them some extortion money, sold my apartment—excuse me—pied-à-terre, and fled the city. I don't believe I've spent more than three successive nights there since; in case you work for New York State.

After getting that off my chest, I'm exhausted, so I won't bring it up again. I have bought my last house.

I have also owned a long line of airplanes: for the curious, a Cessna 182 RG, a Beech Bonanza B36-TC, a Piper Malibu Mirage, a Jet Prop (a Mirage reequipped with a jet engine, turning a propeller), a Citation Mustang, and a Citation M2, the last two proper jets. I flew them all on my book tours, sometimes to as many as twenty-four cities. When COVID stopped the book tours, I sold the last airplane. It had been a business expense; now it was just an expense, and a considerable one. From here on in, we will charter while in this country. I've done the arithmetic; it will be cheaper.

67

This is how I live: I wake at seven, have breakfast in bed. Fred, who can open any door in the house, inside or out, greets the paper deliveryman and brings me the *New York Times*. I read that and do the crossword until eleven a.m., when I rise and go to work. I work for one hour, seven days a week. In each session I write a chapter, 1,000–1,200 words, about five pages. In six weeks of work, I write a novel. I write four novels a year.

I have lunch, then I read all afternoon or watch old movies on a big-screen television set. I love old movies. What more could anyone ask from life?

I have been able to earn an excellent living by writing. This is fortunate because writing is the only thing I know how to do. If I couldn't write, I would be working down at the car wash, and my life would be very different. My grandfather, Henry Washington Denham, a merchant, taught me to always buy the best things I could afford, because quality lasts longer. Over the years, the best things I can afford have become, mostly, the best things there are, so I live well. Wealth? A poor man would consider me rich; a rich man would not. Extravagant? Yes, but in the broader sense of the word.

My wife, Jeanmarie, takes very good care of me, and I hardly ask anything of her, because she anticipates my every need. I love her dearly, more than my three previous wives put together. She is seventeen years younger than I, so I expect her to outlive me.

We have an annual schedule: we spend the winters at home in Key West. There is much to be said for wintering in a warm place. We summer on Mount Desert Island in Maine, in a house I built twenty years ago. There is much to be said for summering in a cool place. We spend the spring and autumn in Litchfield County, Connecticut, where both those seasons are lovely—flowers in the spring, riotous colors in autumn.

We have often spent a month abroad in the autumn, taking apartments in London, Paris, and Rome. We start by picking up a new car in Germany, then driving everywhere and shipping the car home. Two years ago, we booked passage on the *Queen Mary II*, from Southampton, England, to New York. We are still trying; almost certainly we'll sail in 2022.

I've written eighty-five novels—seventy of them *New York Times* bestsellers—and two nonfiction books, this one will make three. I have a shot at making it to a hundred books; we'll see.

As I write this, I'm eighty-three years old, born January 9, 1938. I'm healthy, and I still have my wits about me; it just sometimes takes a little longer to remember things.

I thank my readers for making me possible. I wish you all an extravagant life.

AUTHOR'S NOTE

I am happy to hear from readers, but you should know that if you write to me in care of my publisher, three to six months will pass before I receive your letter, and when it finally arrives it will be one among many, and I will not be able to reply.

However, if you have access to the Internet, you may visit my website at www.stuartwoods.com, where there is a button for sending me e-mail. So far, I have been able to reply to all my e-mail, and I will continue to try to do so.

If you send me an e-mail and do not receive a reply, it is probably because you are among an alarming number of people who have entered their e-mail address incorrectly in their mail software. I have many of my replies returned as undeliverable.

Remember: e-mail, reply; snail mail, no reply.

When you e-mail, please do not send attachments, as I never open these. They can take twenty minutes to download, and they often contain viruses.

Please do not place me on your mailing lists for funny stories, prayers, political causes, charitable fundraising, petitions, or sentimental claptrap. I get enough of that from people I already know. Generally speaking, when I get e-mail addressed to a large number of people, I immediately delete it without reading it.

Please do not send me your ideas for a book, as I have a policy of writing only what I myself invent. If you send me story ideas, I will immediately delete them without reading them. If you have a good idea for a book, write it yourself, but I will not be able to advise you on how to get it published. Buy a copy of *Writer's Market* at any bookstore; that will tell you how.

Anyone with a request concerning events or appearances may e-mail it to me or send it to: Putnam Publicity Department, Penguin Random House LLC, 1745 Broadway, New York, NY 10019.

Those ambitious folk who wish to buy film, dramatic, or television rights to my books should contact Matthew Snyder, Creative Artists Agency, 2000 Avenue of the Stars, Los Angeles, CA 90067.

Those who wish to make offers for rights of a literary nature should contact Anne Sibbald, Janklow & Nesbit, 285 Madison Avenue, 21st Floor, New York, NY 10017. (Note: This is not an invitation for you to send her your manuscript or to solicit her to be your agent.)

If you want to know if I will be signing books in your city, please visit my website, www.stuartwoods.com, where the tour schedule will be published a month or so in advance. If you wish me to do a book signing in your locality, ask your favorite bookseller to contact his Penguin representative or the Putnam publicity department with the request.

If you find typographical or editorial errors in my book and feel an irresistible urge to tell someone, please write to Gabriella Mongelli at Penguin's address above. Do not e-mail your discoveries to me, as I will already have learned about them from others.

A list of my published works appears in the front of this book and on my website. All the novels are still in print in paperback and can be found at or ordered from any bookstore. If you wish to obtain hardcover copies of earlier novels or of the two non-fiction books, a good used-book store or one of the online book-stores can help you find them. Otherwise, you will have to go to a great many garage sales.

INTERIOR PHOTO CREDITS